# Enhanced Cooperation Revisited

Johannes Graf von Luckner

# Enhanced Cooperation Revisited

## The European Union's Differentiated Integration Tool Between Past Experiences and Future Challenges

Springer VS

Johannes Graf von Luckner
Erfurt, Germany

This book was written as a doctoral thesis at the University of Erfurt (Faculty of Economics, Law and Social Sciences).

ISBN 978-3-658-51062-6 ISBN 978-3-658-51063-3 (eBook)
https://doi.org/10.1007/978-3-658-51063-3



This Springer VS imprint is published by the registered company Springer Fachmedien Wiesbaden GmbH, part of Springer Nature.
The registered company address is: Abraham-Lincoln-Str. 46, 65189 Wiesbaden, Germany

# Preface

Enhanced cooperation (Art. 20 TEU, Art. 326 ff. TFEU) is a mechanism in European law, with the help of which groups of European Union Member States may pass EU law without all Member States participating. More precisely, if the Member States in the Council cannot agree on a measure, a group of at least nine of them may establish an enhanced cooperation in which they adopt the desired measure only among themselves. The results of an enhanced cooperation, which may be authorised as a last resort by the Council, become fully-fledged EU law, with the sole exception that they do not apply to all Member States.

The enhanced cooperation mechanism is the subject of this dissertation.

The main thesis of the dissertation is that the legal framework on enhanced cooperation allows an innovative reading, permitting a new typology of uses of the enhanced cooperation mechanism.

The primary question I set out to answer is, in essence, which potential still lies in the enhanced cooperation mechanism. Almost 25 years after first being inserted in the Treaties, and after first lying dormant for over elven years, enhanced cooperation has successfully been used in practice, though only in the very limited number of five cases, without much public attention and arguably not in the most crucial fields of EU law making. Thus, it has neither proven to be the threat to European unity that some feared nor the silver bullet that some hoped it would be. In the light of this, my thesis sets out to answer what role the mechanism might still have to play in future, especially with a view to the numerous crises that the EU has been facing recently. In particular, I set out to analyse whether there still are plausible interpretations of the Treaty framework on enhanced cooperation that allow for a use of enhanced cooperation that has not been proposed or conceived yet. My dissertation takes the position that there are indeed interpretations that are plausible, yet innovative and that consequently, enhanced cooperation could play a bigger role in overcoming the EU's challenges if applied accordingly.

The perspective on European integration taken in doing so is one strongly influenced by the idea of subsidiarity, which according to Art. 5.3 TEU is applicable to all enhanced cooperation projects.[1] EU integration is not and should not be an end in and of itself. However, where the objectives of any proposed action cannot be sufficiently achieved by the Member States at central, regional or local level, but can rather be better achieved at Union level, it is desirable that the Member States have the possibility to pursue such action—even if the group that considers it to be desirable or preferable on the Union level is smaller than the Union as a whole. Institutionally, the perspective of this thesis is one focussing mostly on the Member States as relevant actors. This is by no means due to a minor importance of the other institutions, especially of the European Parliament, in the EU decision making process but because by design of the enhanced cooperation mechanism, the Member States are the main driving factors for the establishment of an enhanced cooperation. For the European Parliament, the main change when a project is enacted through enhanced cooperation is that is has to give its consent to the establishment of the enhanced cooperation in addition to participating in the legislative process depending on the respective legal base.

To describe the course of the present work in more detail, the dissertation aims to situate the enhanced cooperation mechanism in the overall framework of EU law. In particular, I aim to explore the possibilities still laying in enhanced cooperation in its present form—not least by analysing its past—and what a future form of enhanced cooperation could look like.

Looking into experiences made with the enhanced cooperation mechanism, the thesis sets out to gain insights in the legal framework of the mechanism, its functioning, limitations and possibilities, always looking for insights that promise an innovative use of enhanced cooperation. Experience from over ten years of enhanced cooperation projects provide a set of insights and findings that enable a new, more detailed understanding of the mechanism than what was possible closer to the introduction of enhanced cooperation to the Treaties, which is when most research on the mechanism was conducted. Equipped with this knowledge, it is the aim of the thesis to examine the possibilities and potentials lying in the present

[1] According to Art. 20.1 TEU, enhanced cooperation may be established "within the framework of the Union's non-exclusive competences". Art. 5.3 TEU lays down the principle of subsidiarity for "areas which do not fall within its exclusive competence".

enhanced cooperation framework. Some of these potentials are rather hidden, others are in plain sight. This understanding of the legal framework on enhanced cooperation will aim to understand how it can provide the EU with opportunities in living up to its objectives. Where the analysis comes to the conclusion that, especially in particularly difficult situations, enhanced cooperation in its present form does not offer many possibilities, it will propose a targeted Treaty change making the use of enhanced cooperation more appealing in future.

As regards the analysis of the current Treaty framework, I will move along the questions of *what* enhanced cooperation is, *where* it may be applied in terms of policy fields, *when,* that is under which circumstances, it may be resorted to and *how* it must be legally designed.

In a first step, introduce the enhanced cooperation mechanism to give an overview of *what* it is, how it works and how it fits into the overall theme of European integration (Chap. 1). To set the scene, I will describe how EU action is often caught between the diverging poles of the principle of unity in the EU and the interest of vanguard groups of Member States to proceed faster in integration (Sect. 1.1). I will show that enhanced cooperation is one possibility to address this conundrum, briefly explain the enhanced cooperation mechanism in very general terms and how it is perceived in literature (Sect. 1.2), and investigate what image of differentiated integration enhanced cooperation follows in this situation, i.e. how it is placed in the general debate on differentiation in the EU (Sect. 1.3). More abstractly, and again pursuing a better general understanding of the mechanism, I will set out to position the enhanced cooperation mechanism between the conflicting poles of supranationality and intergovernmentalism (1.4).

In a second step (Chap. 2), I will examine the scope of application of enhanced cooperation—i.e. the question of '*where*', in which policy fields, can it come into action. The Treaty text offers little guidance in this respect. For that reason, the approach in this chapter will be an inter-disciplinary one. Legal interpretation of the EU competence framework will be paired with insights from social sciences which provide predictions in which fields enhanced cooperation may be expected and in which it is unlikely to occur. Putting these two aspects together results in a 'field map' of the factual (as opposed to the purely legal) scope of application in practice. This allows a somewhat thorough understanding of where enhanced cooperation has a chance of occurring in the future and where it is very unlikely from the outset.

The question of where, in which fields enhanced cooperation may occur is only one part of the equation on its prospective uses; another one is the question of *when,* i.e. under which circumstances enhanced cooperation may be resorted to. The legal requirement of using enhanced cooperation only as a "last resort" is often considered to be the highest hurdle and the most relevant obstacle for its use. The chapter on this ultima ratio principle (Chap. 3) aims to aims to provide a much closer look at when, exactly, Member States can resort to enhanced cooperation than what has been provided by previous research. It will explore how serious an obstacle the criterion is and what action must be pursued prior to resorting to enhanced cooperation. Crucially, it will be argued that there is a possibility to opt for a 'fast-track enhanced cooperation' if need be, for example in crisis situations.

A third central question regarding the use of enhanced cooperation is that of *how* it is used, i.e. how an enhanced cooperation project must designed. The arguably most crucial requirement regulating these questions of the use enhanced cooperation is the need for it to be open to all non-participating Member States. This notion has a high value within the enhanced cooperation legal framework, as it defines the mechanism's nature as one that is profoundly favouring integration by the EU as a whole. Yet, the right for non-participants to join an enhanced cooperation is not an absolute one—in fact, it is subject to a number of limitations. The legal process of joining an enhanced cooperation is not the same throughout the trajectory of an enhanced cooperation project, nor are the benefits that Member States can draw from joining at a specific point of this trajectory, affecting the legal position of the Member States outside the enhanced cooperation. The interplay of these factors will be explored in Chap. 4. A central—and novel—argument of this chapter will be that there is a so far unexplored possibility of including notions of conditionality in enhanced cooperation projects—Member States can, under very specific circumstances, make the participation in an ongoing enhanced cooperation subject to the fulfilment of conditions, which the participants can arguably use to influence their peers (thus turning the 'condition' into a 'conditionality'). This opportunity might open an array of new possibilities for Member States in the most conflict-ridden areas of EU policymaking, if recognised by the Member States and institutions.

Having explored what enhanced cooperation is, where it might be used and what kinds of unconventional and innovative usage it might still offer, I will look further into the future (Chap. 5). In doing so, I will look at policy fields where, so far, enhanced cooperation cannot be expected to be applied despite relevant and on-going controversies over policy measures. In such disputed policy fields, the reason for Member States not to resort to enhanced cooperation can often be found in the incentive structures at work, as is explained previously in Chap. 2. If Member States want to encourage the use of enhanced cooperation in such fields, a change of these incentive structures is necessary. Therefore, the thesis will propose a targeted Treaty amendment which would introduce a so-called "incentivised enhanced cooperation" or "incentivised cooperation". This mechanism could change the incentive structures of some of the most disputed policy areas and therefore motivate interested Member States to join forces and pass differentiated EU law, rather than not acting at all or only in a non-binding voluntary manner, as is currently the case.

In conclusion, the findings of this thesis in their entirety aim to present the enhanced cooperation mechanism in a new light—or illuminate it from a new angle. It will be shown that enhanced cooperation still bears a lot of unused potential and could be used in innovative ways (fast track, conditionality,…) to resolve particularly difficult political situations. In addition, with targeted Treaty changes, this potential could be vastly extended and cover areas that under the current Treaty framework are unlikely to ever see an enhanced cooperation. Taking both together promises an enhanced cooperation mechanism that has a lot to offer to European integration for years to come.

This books takes into account developments until the end of 2024. For this reason, in particular the sixth enhanced cooperation on the establishment of a loan for Ukraine could not be analysed and into account anymore. However, it can be observed that in several aspects, the sixth enhanced cooperation aligns well with several assumptions made in this book, be it the last resort character confirmed by a European Council statement, the speedy adoption that was made possible by all actors together, or generally the use of enhanced cooperation in the field of funding and in a field governed by qualified majority voting in the Council. This being said, a detailed analysis will have to be left to future research.

The views expressed in this book are my own and in no way reflect the views of the Council of the European Union or the European Council.

Johannes Graf von Luckner

# Acknowledgements

This book has been written as a doctoral thesis at the University of Erfurt between 2019 and 2024, and was made possible by generous support from the regional budget of *Thuringia*, which I am very grateful for.

However, the journey of writing a thesis starts way before the first day as a PhD researcher. At Frankfurt's *Johann Wolfgang Goethe-University*, *Prof. Dr. Astrid Wallrabenstein* entrusted me with a position in her team when I had barely arrived in university, allowing me to look behind the scenes of the fascinating world of academia and the way it mingles with real-life issues. At the same time, *Prof. Dr. Stefan Kadelbach* showed me what I had until then been missing in law: a field that combines the bindingness and tools for enforcement typical for national law with the fascination of legal instruments bridging cultural differences and national borders – in short, European Union law. It never ceased to fascinate me, and I do not believe it ever will. I am very thankful to both for shaping me and my legal thinking for years to come. What should not go unnoticed, moreover, is that it takes more than professors to make it through university. Three persons sticking out among the many wonderful friends I made during this time, sticking out for countless hours sitting next to each other trying to climb the mountain of legal education together, are *Dominik Schmidt*, *Paul Lorenz* and *Christopher Scheid*. Thank you! And thank you also to *Università degli Studi Roma Tre* for an unbelievably unbureaucratic way to come and study abroad – with or without the Erasmus programme.

A logical next step after a law degree and a burning desire to dive deeper into the world of European law was to go closest to the beating heart of EU legal academia: the *European University Institute*. Thank you to the team, the bubble and in particular to *Prof. Deirdre Curtin* for supervising my work, which has eventually become a part of this thesis. Among the countless extraordinary people I met in Florence, *Louisa Bayerlein* and *Sophia M. Hunger* cannot go unnamed. Thank you!

Fully understanding European law is impossible without having breathed Brussels air for some time: Thank you to *Jesca Beneder* and *Isabelle Perignon* for an insightful time at the European Commission's DG Justice.

And finally, the University of Erfurt. *Prof. Dr. Hermann-Josef Blanke* barely knew me when we rolled out the red carpet for me at the university and in his team. He enabled me to make invaluable experiences in the process of editing his one-of-a-kind "Treaty on the Functioning of the European Union—A Commentary", a truly *European* EU law commentary with authors from every Member State and beyond. Even more importantly, *Prof. Dr. Blanke* supervised my research until he tragically passed away just months before I defended my thesis. For this reason, I am grateful not only to *Prof. Dr. Blanke* but very much also to *Prof. Dr. Michael Riegner* who took over the supervision, allowing me to conclude and defend my thesis, and to *Prof. Dr. Jelena von Achenbach* for her work as second reviewer. Thank you, finally, to the improbable Duo that I spent most time with on the sidelines of writing this dissertation: *Judith Riemer* and *Rüdiger Morbach.*

Last but not least, it goes without saying that none of this would have been possible without the eternal support from the most important persons in my life:

Naomi

Annelie

Valentina

This book is gratefully and joyfully dedicated to you.

# Contents

# Abbreviations

| | |
|---|---|
| AFSJ | Area of Freedom, Security and Justice |
| AG | Advocate General |
| CCCTB | Common Consolidated Corporate Tax Base |
| CCTB | Common Corporate Tax Base |
| CFSP | Common Foreign and Security Policy |
| CJEU | Court of Justice of the European Union |
| ECT | Treaty Establishing the European Community |
| EEA | European Economic Area |
| EFTA | European Free Trade Association |
| EMU | Economic and Monetary Union |
| EP | European Parliament |
| EPPO | European Public Prosecutor's Office |
| ESA | European Space Agency |
| EU | European Union |
| FTT | Financial Transaction Tax |
| ILO | International Labour Organisation |
| IMF | International Monetary Fund |
| OECD | Organisation for Economic Co- operation and Development |
| OJ | Official Journal of the European Union |
| Pesco | Permanent Structured Cooperation |
| QMV | Qualified majority voting |
| TEU | Treaty on European Union |

| | |
|---|---|
| TFEU | Treaty on the Functioning of the European Union |
| UK | United Kingdom of Great Britain and Northern Ireland |
| UN | United Nations |
| VAT | Value Added Tax |
| WTO | World Trade Organisation |

# Enhanced Cooperation 1

## 1.1 The European Union Between Unity and Blockade

For as long as the European Union has existed, it has been in subject to disputes concerning the speed of its development, between integration and blockade, evolution and the status quo. In fact, as a Union consisting of individual Member States, it can be deemed a certainty that this will not change as long as the EU exists: Differing opinions within any group, or union, is a matter of course,[1] it is obvious, natural, and, from a long-term perspective, probably even a necessity for success and standing the tests of time. Yet, from a less macroscopic point of view, disputes can, depending on the capacities of single elements with diverging interests to claim these, become stumbling blocks or even cause logjams within the evolution of a group. It is precisely this phenomenon that has kept scholars and politicians wondering how to deal with fundamental opposition from within the EU, whether it regards single policy projects or matters of importance for the project of European integration as a whole.

The history of reactions to this phenomenon is long and diverse. Interestingly, from the beginning, the European Treaties anticipated this and foresaw single elements of majority voting among the Member States in the Council (see Art. 28 (5) Treaty establishing the European Coal and Steal Community, ECSC-Treaty), which is one way of consolidating the desires of a majority with those of a minority—the majority prevails. Yet, unanimous voting among Member States was predominant in the early phases of EU and was even made a practical necessity in decision-making by the Luxembourg Accords in 1965, in which Member

[1] Cantore, C. (2011), 'We're One, but We're Not the Same: Enhanced Cooperation and the Tension between Unity and Asymmetry in the EU', *Perspectives on Federalism*, No. 3, E-1—E-21.



J. Graf von Luckner, *Enhanced Cooperation Revisited*,
https://doi.org/10.1007/978-3-658-51063-3_1

States promised to seek unanimity even where decisions could legally be taken by majority voting.[2] Subsequently, qualified majority voting was continuously extended, reaching its preliminary peak in the Lisbon Treaty agreed in 2007. Yet, even under the current Treaty framework, the Council remains bound to unanimity decision-making in a vast number of instances and policy areas—meaning every time that any single Member State can stop progress, demand changes in its own interest and change the course of the development of a Union policy or even the EU trajectory as whole.

In the light of this, Member States and leaders have for a long time been looking for ways to proceed with EU projects despite the resistance of single Member States. The notion of "differentiated integration"[3] in the sense of EU integration steps taken not by all Member States at the same time (or at all) is to a large degree based on this challenge. This resulted in a multitude of different approaches to reconcile the different interests of Member States within the EU. Member States were granted derogations from single Treaty or secondary law provisions,[4] or even opt-outs which allowed them to refrain from participating in entire policy areas, such as the Area of Freedom, Security and Justice or the participation in the Euro as a common currency.[5] While these latter instruments were often regarded as a means to cater the particular interests of states such as especially (though not only) the UK, they were to the same extend a means allowing the other Member States to proceed with integration steps that would otherwise have been impossible due to the lack of unanimity.

---

[2] van den Bogaert, S. (2008), 'Qualified Majority Voting in the Council: First Reflections on the New Rules', *MJ*, Vol. 15, No. 1, pp. 97–108.

[3] See i.a. Leruth, Benjamin; Gänzle, Stefan; Trondal, Jarle, eds. (2022), *The Routledge handbook of differentiation in the European Union*, Routledge International Handbooks, New York, Routledge Taylor & Francis Group; Blockmans, Steven, ed. (2014), *Differentiated integration in the EU: From the inside looking out*, Bruxelles, CEPS. On the conceptual and semantic difficulties around this notion, see Stubb, A. C.-G. (1996), 'A Categorization of Differentiated Integration', *JCMS: Journal of Common Market Studies*, Vol. 34, No. 2, pp. 283–295.

[4] See e.g. Article 17 Council Directive 93/104/EC of 23 November 1993 concerning certain aspects of the organisation of working time (as amended by Directive 2000/34 of 22 June 2000).

[5] See e.g. Protocol (No 15) on Certain Provisions Relating to the United Kingdom of Great Britain and Northern Ireland; Protocol (No 19) on the Schengen Acquis Integrated into the Framework of the European Union; Protocol (No 22) on the Position of Denmark. On recent developments, see Graf von Luckner, J. (2021), 'A Brexit last call: The strange practice of pre-Brexit opt-ins', *Maastricht Journal of European and Comparative Law*, Vol. 28, No. 4, pp. 556–572.

The rift between unity, blockade and progress of groups smaller than the EU in its entirety is difficult to approach not least because the so-called *principle of unity* is hard to get hold of. Rather than being an explicit or implicit legal principle, it is a political dogma, an underlying assumption of EU law and policy. Bar in EU foreign relations, where it may be understood as unity in international representation (Art. 26.2 (2) TEU),[6] the principle of unity is hardly spelled out or even mentioned in the Treaties. Rather, the principle of unity in the EU lies in the spirit of the Treaties, visible in its very name, European *Union*, or the overarching aim of creating an *ever-closer union* (Art. 1 (2) TEU), present in the Treaties since the Treaty of Rome in 1957. Some rare exception to this, in which the principle of unity gets some minor legal specification, are the Preamble of the TFEU, mentioning the anxiousness of the Member States to "strengthen the unity of their economies",[7] and Art. 256.2 (2), Art. 256.3 (2, 3) TFEU, which lay down measures within the relationship General Court and Court of Justice when one of the two considers the unity of Union law[8] to be at risk, but beyond this, the principle of unity is not made explicit in the Treaties. Needless to say, all of these existing allusions to unity and union imply the togetherness of *all* the Member States, the Union as a whole.

A closer look at the legal content of the principle of unity reveals that it can be derived first and foremost from the principle of primacy of EU law. Already in its famous judgement in Costa./.E.N.E.L., the CJEU stated that "the executive force of Community law cannot vary from one state to another […] without jeopardising the attainment of the objectives of the Treaty."[9] This development can be traced until the current CJEU case law: Accordingly, "by virtue of the principle of the primacy of EU law, a Member State's reliance on rules of national law, even

---

[6] Pasquale, P. de (2013), 'Art. 26 TEU' in: Blanke, H.-J., Mangiameli, S. (eds.), *The Treaty on European Union (TEU): A commentary,* Berlin, Springer; see also e.g. CJEU, C-246/07 (Commission v Sweden), ECLI:EU:C:2010:203.

[7] In this, that is the economic regard, the principle of unity can also be traced in single secondary law instruments, e.g. Art. 1 Regulation (EU) No 1024/2013: "'This Regulation confers on the ECB specific tasks concerning policies relating to the prudential supervision of credit institutions […] with full regard and duty of care for the unity and integrity of the internal market […].

[8] Cf. Bogdandy, A. von (2010), 'Founding Principles of EU Law', *Revus*, No. 12, pp. 35–56.

[9] CJEU, Case 6/64 (Costa v E.N.E.L.), ECLI:EU:C:1964:66; on this see also Thym, D. (2009), The Evolution of Supranational Differentiation, WHI-Paper Similarly CJEU, Case 11/70 (Internationale Handelsgesellschaft), ECLI:EU:C:1970:114, at para. 3.

of a constitutional order, cannot be allowed to undermine the unity and effectiveness of EU law."[10] While these judgments concern unregulated deviations from uniform EU law and consequently do not apply directly, at least in this rigidity, to regulated forms of differentiation such as the one this thesis is about—enhanced cooperation –, they depict both the background and the fundamental value of the principle of unity in the EU.[11]

It is with this principle of fundamental value that all forms of internal differentiation, by their very nature, conflict with.[12] Pursuing the fulfilment of the principle of unity always comes at a cost. Especially where unanimity in the Council is required for decision-making, it goes hand in hand with the Union moving only as fast as its slowest component member. At the same time, it gives single Member States the possibility to attach a price tag to their willingness for further integration. In a Union of currently 27 Member States, this creates significant room for conflicts. The alternative in the current legal framework with its numerous instances of unanimity requirements is to *deviate* from the principle of unity and let groups of Member States proceed and integrate further in single policy areas whilst others stay at the integration level reached jointly. Opening a way towards such deviations from the principle of unity, as well as every single case of application of such a possibility, is an instance of weighing up integration policy interests. Consequently, it must be handled with care in light of the conflicting interests between unity, blockade and progress. The immanent challenge is an "accommodation of political diversity within the European legal order without contradicting its [...] underlying quest for unity."[13] Achieving this "allows respect for national democratic majorities without this majority, as a European minority, preventing the realisation of the European majority preference."[14] This

[10] CJEU, C-430/21 (RS (Effet des arrêts d'une cour constitutionnelle)), ECLI:EU:C:2022:99, at para 51. The same wording can be found in CJEU, C-409/06 (Winner Wetten), EU:C:2010:503, para. 61; on this Lenaerts, K. (2020), 'No Member State is More Equal than Others'.

[11] For a general critique of the dogma of unity of the EU legal system, Paggi, E. (2017), *Acquis, integrazione differenziata, unità dell'ordinamento dell'unione: verso nuovi modelli di integrazione in Europa?: Spunti di una riflessione teorica a valle dell'introduzione del c.d. pacchetto sul brevetto europeo con effetto unitario.*, Padua.

[12] Cantore, C. (2011), 'We're One, but We're Not the Same: Enhanced Cooperation and the Tension between Unity and Asymmetry in the EU', *Perspectives on Federalism*, No. 3, E-1—E-21.

[13] Thym, D. (2009), The Evolution of Supranational Differentiation, WHI-Paper.

[14] Thym, D. (2009), The Evolution of Supranational Differentiation, WHI-Paper, with reference to Bogdandy, A. von (2003), 'Europäische Prinzipienlehre' in: Bogdandy, A. von

is the background against which the legal framework on differentiated integration, such as the enhanced cooperation mechanism, must be regarded, and which must be kept in mind in the process of interpreting it.

## 1.2 Enhanced Cooperation—a Mechanism for Differentiated Integration

### 1.2.1 A Brief History

It was against the background of this inherent dichotomy of unity and blockade that a sound, Treaty-based mechanism to diverge from the principle of unity in single cases was devised. Although certain forms of differentiation were part of the European integration since its very beginning,[15] it was in the 1970s that politicians started sharing visions of a possibility for certain Member States to integrate faster or more profoundly than others. German chancellor *Willy Brandt* laid out the possibility of economically stronger states taking up a temporary pioneering role in 1974 and similar thoughts were prominently put forward by Belgian Prime Minister *Leo Tindemans* in 1975[16].[17] However, the discussion only really took off some twenty years later, when a contribution by French Prime Minister Édouard Balladur[18] and a paper by German politicians *Wolfang Schäuble* and *Karl Lamers*[19] brought the idea back on the political agenda. Finally, French President *Jaques Chirac* and his German colleague Chancellor *Helmut Kohl,* in a joint letter to the Intergovernmental Conference leading up the Treaty of Amsterdam, turned the discussion towards introducing a secondary law-level possibility to introduce differentiated integration steps. According to their idea, in situations in which some Member States struggle to keep up the pace of integration

---

(ed.), *Europäisches Verfassungsrecht: Theoretische und dogmatische Grundzüge,* Berlin, New York, Springer, pp. 149–203.

[15] Lansdaal, A. (2002), 'Differentiation or Enhanced Cooperation: Formalizing Flexibility' in: Schrauwen, A. (ed.), *Flexibility in Constitutions: Forms of Closer Cooperation in Federal and Non-Federal Settings,* Groningen, European Law Publishing, pp. 47–57; Blanke, H.-J. (2013), 'Art. 20 TEU' in: Blanke, H.-J., Mangiameli, S. (eds.), *The Treaty on European Union (TEU): A commentary,* Berlin, Springer, pp. 787–830.

[16] Tindemans, L., European Union, Bulletin of the European Communities.

[17] Blanke, H.-J. (2013), 'Art. 20 TEU' in: Blanke, H.-J., Mangiameli, S. (eds.), *The Treaty on European Union (TEU): A commentary,* Berlin, Springer, pp. 787–830.

[18] Balladur, É. (1994), 'L'Union à trois cercles', *Le Figaro,* 31 August 1994.

[19] Schäuble, W., Lamers, K. (1994), 'Überlegungen zur europäischen Politik'.

that others desire, a general clause should enable interested states to establish "closer cooperation among themselves within the single institutional framework of the Union".[20] Upon these interventions, and through Italian and Dutch concept texts,[21] the concept of "closer cooperation" was finally enshrined in the Treaty of Amsterdam (ex-Art. 40, 43 ff. TEU, Art. 11 EC). Closer cooperation could, accordingly, be resorted to by a majority of Member States in the areas of the first and third pillars. Closer cooperation was to be authorised by the Council, acting by qualified majority on a proposal from the Commission and after consulting the Parliament. Every Member State had the possibility of blocking the cooperation by referring it to the European Council, which required unanimity to let the cooperation go ahead, which of course constituted a major hurdle to its application.[22] In consequence, the closer cooperation clause in the Treaty of Amsterdam was never used in practice. Rather, in light of the upcoming 2004 enlargement round, which was going to bring the number of EU Member States up from 15 to 25, and following interventions of German foreign minister *Joschka Fischer*[23] *and French President Jacques Chirac*[24] the clause was revised and reintroduced in the Treaty of Nice as "enhanced cooperation". Other than this and other editorial changes, the minimum number of participants was brought down to eight, the European Council no longer needed a unanimous vote to let enhanced cooperation continue, and the European Parliament's consent was required in some cases to authorise enhanced cooperation.[25] Finally, in the process leading up the current

---

[20] European Parliament, 'White Paper on the 1996 Intergovernmental Conference: Volume II'; see also Böttner, R. (2021), *The Constitutional Framework for Enhanced Cooperation in EU law*, Nijhoff studies in European Union law, Leiden The Netherlands, Koninklijke Brill NV.

[21] Lansdaal, A. (2002), 'Differentiation or Enhanced Cooperation: Formalizing Flexibility' in: Schrauwen, A. (ed.), *Flexibility in Constitutions: Forms of Closer Cooperation in Federal and Non-Federal Settings,* Groningen, European Law Publishing, pp. 47–57.

[22] Martenczuk, B. (2013), 'Enhanced Cooperation: The Practice of Ad Hoc Differentiation in the EU since the Lisbon Treaty', *StudDipl*, pp. 83–100.

[23] Joschka Fischer (2000).

[24] Chirac, J. (2000), *Notre Europe: Discours Prononce par Monsieur Jacques Chirac, President de la Republique Francaise, devant le Bundestag Allemand*, Berlin.

[25] Martenczuk, B. (2013), 'Enhanced Cooperation: The Practice of Ad Hoc Differentiation in the EU since the Lisbon Treaty', *StudDipl*, pp. 83–100; Blanke, H.-J. (2013), 'Art. 20 TEU' in: Blanke, H.-J., Mangiameli, S. (eds.), *The Treaty on European Union (TEU): A commentary,* Berlin, Springer, pp. 787–830 Furthermore, the last criterion was relaxed, as is argued in Chap. 3. For a detailed account of the process leading to this result, see Böttner, R. (2021), *The Constitutional Framework for Enhanced Cooperation in EU law*, Nijhoff studies in European Union law, Leiden The Netherlands, Koninklijke Brill NV.

Treaty of Lisbon, the necessary number of participants was raised to 9, reflecting the further growth of the EU. The European Parliament's consent is now needed in all cases of enhanced cooperation (bar in the area of CFSP). The general possibility for a single Member State to bring an enhanced cooperation before the European Council was abolished altogether, together with further clarifications and changes in other procedural details.[26]

### 1.2.2 Enhanced Cooperation under the Treaty of Lisbon and its Practical Application

According to the current Treaty framework, enhanced cooperation is laid down as an instrument of EU law in Article 20 TEU, Article 326 ff. TFEU. In situations in which Member States do not manage to find a compromise on a political project such as a new legal act, it allows smaller groups of Member States to pass the act among themselves, without affecting the opposing states.

Enhanced cooperation is the most general and multi-purpose possibility to introduce differentiation, meaning that a group of Member States adopts and implements an EU legal act that not all Member States participate in to the *acquis communautaire*. Furthermore, it is the easiest way to adopt such differentiation within EU law, as no Treaty changes are necessary, nor do all Member States have to agree to it.

In the case of enhanced cooperation, at least nine Member States must come together (Article 20.2 TEU). It may only be adopted as a last resort when a solution involving all Member States cannot be found in the Council. Depending on the legal base, this could theoretically mean both, unanimity or a qualified majority which cannot be found. However, in practice all cases of enhanced cooperation so far concerned cases of unanimous decision-making in the Council.

---

[26] Martenczuk, B. (2013), 'Enhanced Cooperation: The Practice of Ad Hoc Differentiation in the EU since the Lisbon Treaty', *StudDipl*, pp. 83–100; Blanke, H.-J. (2013), 'Art. 20 TEU' in: Blanke, H.-J., Mangiameli, S. (eds.), *The Treaty on European Union (TEU): A commentary,* Berlin, Springer, pp. 787–830; Blanke, H.-J., Böttner, R. (2019), '§ 13 Binnenmarkt, Rechtsangleichung, Grundfreiheiten' in: Niedobitek, M. (ed.), *Europarecht: Grundlagen und Politiken der Union,* Berlin, De Gruyter, pp. 887–1114 There are some exceptions to this general rule in Art. 82 ff. TFEU.

When Member States want to establish an enhanced cooperation, their request must first be endorsed by the Commission (Article 329.1 (1) TFEU). The Commission then submits a proposal to that effect to the Council, which must adopt it with qualified majority after obtaining the consent of the EP (Article 329.1 (2) TEU). This so-called authorisation decision effectively brings the enhanced cooperation among the participating Member States into being. Enhanced cooperation is governed by strict guidelines: not only must it be open to non-participants at any time (Article 328 TFEU), but it must also aim to further the objectives of the Union and protect its interests (Article 20.1 (2) TEU), must not undermine the internal market or economic, social and territorial cohesion (Article 328.2 TFEU) and respect the competences, rights and obligations of those Member States which do not participate in it (Article 327 TFEU). Deliberations on enhanced cooperation in the Council are open to all Member States, but only the participants take part in votes (Article 330 TFEU). Enhanced cooperation thus aims not to divide Member States, but to invite them to accept their differences and find ways to cooperate despite them. Non-participating Member States may join at any time (Article 20.1 (2) TEU, Article 328 TFEU). If a Member State wants to join an enhanced cooperation, it must incorporate and comply with all legislation passed in the enhanced cooperation framework and, if applicable, fulfil any condition of participation laid down in the authorising decision (Article 328 TFEU). The interested state notifies the Council and the Commission of its attention to join, and the latter verifies if the criteria are met and confirms its participation. This procedure may vary slightly depending on the status quo of the enhanced cooperation (see Chap. 4).

So far, five enhanced cooperation have been authorised: two in family law (regulating the divorce law of international couples and the law on their shared property), one on the introduction of unitary European patent, one on the introduction of a financial transaction tax, and finally one creating the EPPO, the European Public Prosecutor's Office.[27]

The first-ever enhanced cooperation was authorised in 2010 in the area of the law applicable to divorce and legal separation.[28] The project aims to is to facilitate

[27] For a detailed and up-to-date synthesis on all projects pursued by way of enhanced cooperation, see Böttner, R. (2021), *The Constitutional Framework for Enhanced Cooperation in EU law*, Nijhoff studies in European Union law, Leiden The Netherlands, Koninklijke Brill NV.

[28] Council Decision of 12 July 2010 authorising enhanced cooperation in the area of the law applicable to divorce and legal separation (2010/405/EU).

the resolution of cross-border family law disputes in the light of diverse national divorce law frameworks and jurisdictional rules within the EU. While the instrument was supported by a majority of states, the need to pass the instrument by unanimity in the Council led to a blockade given the fundamental disagreement by Member States such as Sweden and Malta.[29] Eventually, it was concluded that unanimity could not be reached and a group of 14 Member States was authorised to proceed using enhanced cooperation. Eventually, the participating Member States passed a regulation on law and legal separation among themselves.[30] Given that it was the first implementation of enhanced cooperation, the process was met with significant scholarly interest.[31]

The second enhanced cooperation concerned the protection of patents in Europe. Since the 1960s, the EU had tried to introduce a single, European patent, protecting inventions throughout the EU. A proposal for a regulation was presented by the Commission in 2000, but failed to find the necessary unanimity in the Council, as did another attempt some ten years later. As a result, enhanced cooperation was pursued by initially ten and finally 25 Member States.[32] A mixed

---

[29] Both were worried about the possibility of having to apply divorce law from other Member States in their own courts, though from opposing positions: at the time, divorce was not possible in Malta, whereas Sweden had a particularly liberal divorce law; Kuipers, J.-J. (2012), 'The Law Applicable to Divorce as Test Ground for Enhanced Cooperation', *ELJ*, Vol. 18, pp. 201–229.

[30] Council Regulation (EU) No 1259/2010 of 20 December 2010 implementing enhanced cooperation in the area of the law applicable to divorce and legal separation.

[31] Kuipers, J.-J. (2012), 'The Law Applicable to Divorce as Test Ground for Enhanced Cooperation', *ELJ*, Vol. 18, pp. 201–229; Boele-Woelki, K. (2008), 'To Be, Or Not to Be: Enhanced Cooperation in International Divorce Law within the European Union', *Victoria U. Wellington L. Rev.*, Vol. 39, p. 779; Peers, S. (2017), 'Enhanced Cooperation: the Cinderella of differentiated integration' in: Witte, B. de, Ott, A., Vos, E. (eds.), *Between Flexibility and Disintegration: The Trajectory of Differentiation in EU Law,* Edward Elgar Publishing Limited, pp. 76–91; Zeitzmann, S. (2011), 'Das Verfahren der Verstärkten Zusammenarbeit und dessen erstmalige Anwendung: Ein Ehescheidungs- und Trennungsrecht für Europa', *ZEuS*, pp. 87–113.

[32] Council Decision of 10 March 2011 authorising enhanced cooperation in the area of the creation of unitary patent protection (2011/167/EU).

group of scholars from EU and patent law accompanied the process.[33] Implementing legislation was passed eventually,[34] but a complicated design depending on an accompanying international law agreement introducing a unified patent court, as well as legal challenges of the project before the CJEU[35] and the *Bundesverfassungsgericht*[36] held up the project for a long time.[37] This notwithstanding, both the unitary patent and the unified patent court have in the meantime come into existence, bringing the enhanced cooperation into full effect.

The third enhanced cooperation concerned a Financial Transaction Tax (FTT). In the wake of the financial crises and the enormous sums of taxpayers' resources

---

[33] See e.g. Almeida, J., Costa, G. O. e. (2018), 'From the Unitary Patent Package to a Federal EU Patent Law', *Perspectives on Federalism*, Vol. 10, No. 1, pp. 126–146; Jaeger, T. (2017), 'The End to a Never-Ending Story? The Unitary Patent Regime' in: Giegerich, T., Schmitt, D. C., Zeitzmann, S. (eds.), *Flexibility in the EU and beyond: How much differentiation can European integration bear?,* Oxford, Hart Publishing, pp. 269–281; Lamping, M. (2011), 'Enhanced Cooperation—A Proper Approach to Market Integration in the Field of Unitary Patent Protection?', *IIC*, No. 42, p. 879; Lamping, M. (2013), 'Enhanced Cooperation in the Area of Unitary Patent Protection—Testing the Boundaries of the Rule of Law', *Maastricht J. Eur. Comp. L.*, pp. 589–600; Peers, S. (2011), 'The Constitutional Implications of the EU Patent', *European Constitutional Law Review*, Vol. 7, No. 2, pp. 229–266; Ullrich, H. (2013), 'Enhanced cooperation in the area of unitary patent protection and European integration', *ERA Forum*, pp. 589–610; Zeitzmann, S. (2013), 'Patentrecht: Ermächtigung zur Verstärkten Zusammenarbeit', *EuZW*, pp. 475–480.

[34] Council Regulation (EU) No 1257/2012 of the European Parliament and of the Council of 17 December 2012 implementing enhanced cooperation in the area of the creation of unitary patent protection and Council Regulation (EU) No 1260/2012 of 17 December 2012 implementing enhanced cooperation in the area of the creation of unitary patent protection with regard to the applicable translation arrangements.

[35] Cases C-274/09, 295/09 (*Spain and Italy v Council*) ECLI:EU:C:2013:240; see also Fabbrini, F. (2013), 'Enhanced Cooperation under Scrutiny: Revisiting the Law and Practice of Multi-Speed Integration in Light of the First Involvement of the EU Judiciary', *LIEI*, pp. 197–224; Jaeger, T. (2013), 'Einheitspatent—Zulässigkeit der Verstärkten Zusammenarbeit ohne Spanien und Italien', *NJW*, pp. 1998–2001 Pistoia, E. (2014), 'Enhanced Cooperation as a tool to…enhance integration?: Spain and Italy v. Council', *CMLRev*, pp. 247–260.

[36] Bundesverfassungsgericht, 13 February 2020, 2 BvR 739/17, https://www.bundesverfassungsgericht.de/SharedDocs/Entscheidungen/EN/2020/02/rs20200213_2bvr073917en.html (last access 14 July 2023).

[37] Graf von Luckner, J. (2022), 'The End of Satellite Treaty Law as We Know It? The German Federal Constitutional Court, European Integration by International Law and Treaties "Supplementing or Being Otherwise Closely Tied to the EU"', *German Law Journal*, Vol. 23, No. 2, pp. 157–172; Graf von Luckner, J. (2021), 'Stay home, stay healthy: Das „Ergänzungs- oder besondere Näheverhältnis zum Unionsrecht" in der BVerfG-Rechtsprechung und die europäische Integration durch Völkerrecht', *Europarecht*, No. 2, pp. 209–224.

that had been used to stabilise the financial system, the EU aimed at establishing a new tax to make the financial system participate in repaying the accumulated debt. The idea was to tax all or at least a large part of financial transactions with a very small levy, which in sum was imagined to result in major public revenue. As the Council was very divided on the matter, a relatively small group of eleven Member States was eventually authorised to proceed using enhanced cooperation.[38] The United Kingdom's opposition to the measure was so fierce that it brought a case against the authorisation of enhanced cooperation before the CJEU. The case was, however, dismissed because it attacked effects that were only due to be exist once implementing law was passed.[39] Despite intense debates over the following years, the participating Member States never passed legislation implementing a Financial Transaction Tax, which leads to the enhanced cooperation being in a dormant status.[40] Despite or even because the lack of implementation, academic literature actively accompanied the process.[41]

The fourth enhanced cooperation again concerned family law. A regulation on matrimonial property was supposed to complete the EU framework of judicial cooperation in the area of family law. However, largely due to a dispute around the question of including same-sex partnerships, Member States did not manage together and find a uniform solution including unanimity in the Council.[42] Consequently, the legislative proposals, which at that point of time had already been subject to substantive negotiations were, brought forward by way of enhanced

---

[38] Council Decision of 22 January 2013 authorising enhanced cooperation in the area of financial transaction tax (2013/52/EU).

[39] CJEU, C- 209/ 13 (United Kingdom v. Council), ECLI:EU:C:2014:283.

[40] In the most recent developments surrounding the Financial Transaction Tax, such as a Roadmap towards new own resources no mention is made of the existing enhanced cooperation; see Interinstitutional Cooperation on a Roadmap Towards the Introduction of new Own Resources, O.J. LI 433/28 (2020).

[41] Cadet, F., Vascega, M. (2013), 'Fewer Woods for Robin Hood: Financial Transaction Tax under Enhanced Cooperation', *EuZW*, pp. 574–579; Fabbrini, F. (2014), 'Taxing and Spending in the Eurozone: Legal and Political Challenges Related to the Adoption of the Financial Transaction Tax', *ELRev*, Vol. 39, No. 2, Taxing and spending in the Eurozone: legal and political challenges related to the adoption of the financial transaction tax; Nerudová, D., Dvořáková, V. (2014), *Financial Transaction Tax: Can it be Sufficient Resource of EU Budget when Introduced through Enhanced Cooperation?*; Heber, C. (2021), *Enhanced Cooperation and European Tax Law*, Oxford University Press.

[42] Böttner, R. (2021), *The Constitutional Framework for Enhanced Cooperation in EU law*, Nijhoff studies in European Union law, Leiden The Netherlands, Koninklijke Brill NV.

cooperation.[43] Within a month of the authorising decision, the implementing legislation was passed.[44] In a sign of what could be interpreted as getting used to enhanced cooperation being applied, scholarly attention was largely limited to contributions from the field of family law.[45]

Finally, the fifth enhanced cooperation started in 2017, when the European Public Prosecutor's Office was established. In doing so, the Member States made use of a special form of enhanced cooperation, named 'facilitated enhanced cooperation' in this thesis. In a few legal bases in the Area of Freedom, Security and Justice (AFSJ), which formerly belonged to the so-called Third Pillar under the Treaties of Maastricht, Amsterdam and Nice,[46] the enhanced cooperation procedure is modified in in that Member States can refer controversial proposals to the European Council. If the presidents and heads of states in the European Council fail to find a compromise among all Member States, nine states may notify the institutions of their wish to establish an enhanced cooperation, which is then automatically deemed to be authorised. Hence, without the usual need for an authorising decision, taken by a qualified majority in the Council, Member States can proceed using enhanced cooperation. As such, the hurdle to launch enhanced cooperation is lowered substantially. Beside the facilitated enhanced cooperation, groups of Member States can still, however, opt for the regular enhanced cooperation procedure in the AFSJ. In the case of the European Public Prosecutor's

---

[43] Council Decision (EU) 2016/954 of 9 June 2016 authorising enhanced cooperation in the area of jurisdiction, applicable law and the recognition and enforcement of decisions on the property regimes of international couples, covering both matters of matrimonial property regimes and the property consequences of registered partnerships.

[44] Council Regulations (EU) 2016/1103 and 2016/1104 of 24 June 2016 implementing enhanced cooperation in the area of jurisdiction, applicable law and the recognition and enforcement of decisions in matters of matrimonial property regimes and of registered partnerships.

[45] See e.g. Gray, J., Quinzá Redondo, P. (2013), 'Stress-Testing the EU Proposal on Matrimonial Property Regimes: Co-operation between EU private international law instruments on family matters and succession', *Familie & Recht*; Valentová, L. (2016), 'Property Regimes of Spouses and Partners in New EU Regulations—Jurisdiction, Prorogation and Choice of Law', *ICLR*, Vol. 16, No. 2, pp. 221–240; Viarengo, Ilaria; Franzina, Pietro, eds. (2020), *The EU Regulations on the Property Regimes of International Couples: A Commentary*, [S.l.], Edward Elgar.

[46] Articles 82.3, 83.3, 86.1, 87.3 TFEU.; van Cleynenbreugel, P., Devroe, W. (2017), 'The Financial Transaction Tax Project' in: Witte, B. de, Ott, A., Vos, E. (eds.), *Between Flexibility and Disintegration: The Trajectory of Differentiation in EU Law,* Edward Elgar Publishing Limited, pp. 282–303; Wernsmann, R., Zirkl, C. (2014), 'Die Regelungskompetenz der EU für eine Finanztransaktionssteuer', *Europäische Zeitschrift für Wirtschaftsrecht*, No. 05, pp. 167–171.

Office (EPPO), following years of fruitless negotiations, Member States resorted to enhanced cooperation and made the EPPO, competent for prosecuting certain crimes to the detriment of the EU, operational in 22 Member States by 2021. Needless to say, the introduction of a new supranational authority was met with great academic interest, some of it focussing specifically on the fact that it was introduced by way of enhanced cooperation or specificities of its differentiated application.[47]

### 1.2.3 Enhanced Cooperation in Academia

In what can only be a very rough, selective, and by definition incomprehensive overview, the following sets out to characterize some trends in the academic literature on enhanced cooperation over the past decades and position this thesis within them.

In the early days of research on differentiated integration, scholars focused largely on differentiation per se.[48] However, once the then-called closer cooperation had been enshrined in the European Treaties by the Treaty of Amsterdam, enhanced cooperation became a prominent part[49] or even the main subject of

[47] Di Francesco Maesa, C. (2006), 'Repercussions of the Establishment of the EPPO via Enhanced Cooperation: EPPO's Added Value and the Possibility to Extend its Competence', *eucrim—The European Criminal Law Associations' Forum*; Cach, C. (2014), 'Die Verstärkte Zusammenarbeit und ihre Bedeutung für die Errichtung der Europäischen Staatsanwaltschaft', *EuR Europarecht*, Vol. 49, No. 6, pp. 716–729; Franssen, N. (2018), 'The future judicial cooperation between the EPPO and non-participating Member States', *New Journal of European Criminal Law*, Vol. 9, No. 3, pp. 291–299; Pawelec, S. (2015), 'Implications of Enhanced Cooperation for the EPPO Model and Its Functioning' in: Erkelens, L. H., Meij, A. W. H., Pawlik, M. (eds.), *The European public prosecutor's office: An extended arm or a two-headed dragon? / L.H. Erkelens, A.W.H. Meij, M. Pawlik, editors,* Hague, Asser Press, pp. 209–227; Giuffrida, F. (2023), 'The relations between the European Public Prosecutor's Office and the Member States that do not participate in the enhanced cooperation', *New Journal of European Criminal Law*, Vol. 14, No. 1, pp. 80–99.

[48] See e.g. Grabitz, E., Iliopoulos, C. (1984), 'Typologie der Differenzierungen und Ausnahmen im Gemeinschaftsrecht' in: Grabitz, E., Franzmeyer, F. (eds.), *Abgestufte Integration: Eine Alternative zum herkömmlichen Integrationskonzept?,* Kehl am Rhein, Engel, pp. 31–46; Curtin, D. (1993), 'The Constitutional Structure of the Union: A Europe of Bits and Pieces', *CMLRev*, Vol. 30, pp. 17–69; Stubb, A. C.-G. (1996), 'A Categorization of Differentiated Integration', *JCMS: Journal of Common Market Studies*, Vol. 34, No. 2, pp. 283–295, who in a seminal piece sought to categorize types of differentiated integration discussed at the time and thus sought to overcome what he perceived as a "severe case of semantic indigestion".

[49] See e.g. Thym, D. (2004), *Ungleichzeitigkeit und europäisches Verfassungsrecht*, Schriftenreihe europäisches Verfassungsrecht, Baden-Baden, Nomos; Gaja, G. (1998), 'How

research.[50] In this period, several studies on enhanced cooperation or its predecessors were conducted, which, in lack of practical application of the enhanced cooperation mechanism, by default lacked insights derived from the functioning of enhanced cooperation in practice. Studies were conducted both in an overarching manner looking at enhanced cooperation at large[51] or focusing on single aspects and legal questions, such as enhanced cooperation and CSDP,[52] or the relationship between enhanced cooperation law and the *acquis communautaire*.[53]

---

Flexible Is Flexibility Under the Amsterdam Treaty?', *Common Market Law Review*, Vol. 35, No. 4, pp. 855–870.

[50] See e.g. Constantinesco, V. (1994), 'Les clauses de "coopération renforcée". Le protocole sur l'application des principes de subsidiarité et de proportionnalité', *Revue trimestrielle de droit europeen*, Vol. 33, No. 4, pp. 751–767; Mangas Martín, A. (1998), 'Las cooperaciones reforzadas en el Tratado de Ámsterdam', *Comunidad Europea Aranzadi*, No. 10, pp. 27–38; Ehlermann, C. D. (1998), 'Differentiation, Flexibility, Closer Co-operation: The New Provisions of the Amsterdam Treaty', *European Law Journal*, Vol. 4, No. 3, pp. 246–270; Philippart, E., Edwards, G. (1999), 'The Provisions on Closer Co-operation in the Treaty of Amsterdam: The Politics of Flexibility in the European Union', *JCMS: Journal of Common Market Studies*, Vol. 37, No. 1, pp. 87–108; Weatherill, S. (1999), "If I'd Wanted You to Understand I Would have Explained it Better': What is the Purpose of the Provisions on Closer Co-operation Introduced by the Treaty of Amsterdam?' in: O'Keeffe, D., Twomey, P. M. (eds.), *Legal issues of the Amsterdam Treaty*, Oxford, Portland, Or., Hart Pub, pp. 21–40; Buttlar, C. von (2001), 'Rechtsprobleme der "verstärkten Zusammenarbeit" nach dem Vertrag von Nizza', *ZEuS*, pp. 649–688; Philippart, E. (2003), *A new mechanism of enhanced co-operation for the enlarged European Union*, Notre Europe.

[51] See e.g. Derpa, U. (2003), *Die verstärkte Zusammenarbeit im Recht der Europäischen Union: Dogmatik, Interpretation und Praxis eines alternativen Integrationskonzeptes*, Schriften zum öffentlichen, europäischen und internationalen Recht, Stuttgart u.a., Boorberg; Cannone, A. (2005), *Le cooperazioni rafforzate: Contributo allo studio dell'integrazione differenziata*, Pubblicazioni della Facoltà giuridica dell'Università di Bari, Bari, Cacucci; Linke, G. (2006), *Das Instrument der verstärkten Zusammenarbeit im Vertrag von Nizza: Möglichkeiten eines Europas der differenzierten Integration*, Interdisziplinäre Europa Studien, Frankfurt am Main, Lang; Bribosia, H. (2007), *Les coopérations renforcées: quel modèle d'intégration différenciée pour l'Union européenne?: analyse comparative du mécanisme général de la coopération renforcée, du projet de coopération structurée permanente en matière de défense, et de la pratique d'autres coopérations renforcées "prédéterminées" en matière sociale, au sein de l'Espace de liberté, sécurité et justice, et dans l'Union économique et monétaire.*

[52] Cremona, M. (2009), 'Enhanced Cooperation and the Common Foreign and Security and Defence Policies of the EU', *EUI Working Papers*, No. 21.

[53] Zeitzmann, S. (2015), 'Zuviel gewollt, zu wenig geregelt? Das komplizierte Verhältnis der Verstärkten Zusammenarbeit zum aquis communautaire' in: Stratenschulte, E. D. (ed.), *Der Anfang vom Ende?: Formen differenzierter Integration und ihre Konsequenzen*, Nomos, pp. 103–134.

Moreover, in light of the fact that for a long time, the enhanced cooperation mechanism did not see any practical application, it was attempted to find innovative readings of the legal framework in earlier Treaty versions in order to invite Member States to make use of the mechanism despite procedural doubts.[54]

After the enhanced cooperation mechanism was finally put to use for the first time in 2010, a new trend of contributions materialized, analysing the specific enhanced cooperation attempts with more or less emphasis on the fact that the individual measure did not comprise all Member States as participants and the effects thereof.[55] Yet, a relevant trend in research focused specifically the single practical examples as material to better understand the enhanced cooperation mechanism as such.[56]

Equipped the benefit of experience, scholars once again started turning their attention towards enhanced the cooperation at large, and published articles on the overarching experiences gained from several instances of enhanced cooperation.[57] Recently, this culminated in two major studies being published. One covers

---

[54] Kochenov, D., Amtenbrink, F. (2009), 'Towards a More Flexible Approach to Enhanced Cooperation' in: Ott, A. (ed.), *Fifty years of European integration: Foundations and perspectives,* The Hague, Asser Press, pp. 181–199.

[55] For contributions on all five instances of enhanced cooperation in action, see above Sect. 1.2.2.

[56] See e.g. Peers, S. (2010), 'Divorce, European Style: The First Authorization of Enhanced Cooperation', *Eur. Const. L. Rev*, pp. 339–358; Lamping, M. (2011), 'Enhanced Cooperation—A Proper Approach to Market Integration in the Field of Unitary Patent Protection?', *IIC*, No. 42, p. 879; Kuipers, J.-J. (2012), 'The Law Applicable to Divorce as Test Ground for Enhanced Cooperation', *ELJ*, Vol. 18, pp. 201–229; Fabbrini, F. (2013), 'Enhanced Cooperation under Scrutiny: Revisiting the Law and Practice of Multi-Speed Integration in Light of the First Involvement of the EU Judiciary', *LIEI*, pp. 197–224; Pistoia, E. (2014), 'Enhanced Cooperation as a tool to…enhance integration?: Spain and Italy v. Council', *CMLRev*, pp. 247–260; Paggi, E. (2017), *Acquis, integrazione differenziata, unità dell'ordinamento dell'unione: verso nuovi modelli di integrazione in Europa?: Spunti di una riflessione teorica a valle dell'introduzione del c.d. pacchetto sul brevetto europeo con effetto unitario.*, Padua.

[57] See e.g. Cantore, C. (2011), 'We're One, but We're Not the Same: Enhanced Cooperation and the Tension between Unity and Asymmetry in the EU', *Perspectives on Federalism,* No. 3, E-1—E-21; Martenczuk, B. (2013), 'Enhanced Cooperation: The Practice of Ad Hoc Differentiation in the EU since the Lisbon Treaty', *StudDipl*, pp. 83–100; Feraci, O. (2013), 'L'attuazione della cooperazione rafforzata nell' Unione Europea: un primo bilancio critico', *Riv. dir. internaz.*, pp. 955–964 Böttner, R. (2016), 'Eine Idee lernt laufen—zur Praxis der Verstärkten Zusammenarbeit nach Lissabon', *ZEuS*, Vol. 19, No. 4, pp. 501–550; Peers, S. (2017), 'Enhanced Cooperation: the Cinderella of differentiated integration' in: Witte, B. de, Ott, A., Vos, E. (eds.), *Between Flexibility and Disintegration: The Trajectory of Differentiation in EU Law,* Edward Elgar Publishing Limited, pp. 76–91.

the specific implications of tax law on enhance cooperation and vice versa,[58] analysing the legal framework on enhanced cooperation primarily with a view to whether it might be used in the arena of tax law. The second study is a comprehensive analysis of the "Constitutional Framework for Enhanced Cooperation in EU Law",[59] which by broadly updating the knowledge on the enhanced cooperation legal framework can be regarded as kind of handbook on enhanced cooperation law.

Within this substantive body of research, this thesis sets out to interpret key aspects of the Treaty framework with a view to the question what their contribution to the current challenges in the EU may be. It does so with the benefit of the experience of over ten years of enhanced cooperation in practice. It is an addition to the recent, extensive studies in that it does not aim to cover the enhanced cooperation mechanism and legal questions it raises in an extensive manner, but it focusses on single aspects of the enhanced cooperation mechanism in a very detailed manner and at least partly with the help of so-far unused research methods and sources. Rather than analysing every legal aspect of the legal framework on enhanced cooperation, it focuses on two decisive procedural hurdles—the principles of openness and last resort—and the material legal question of the scope of application, in order to find interpretations of the Treaty framework that are plausible in light of the black letter law as well as practical experiences, and that offer avenues for innovative uses of enhanced cooperation.

## 1.3 Fifty Shades of Integration—Which Image of Integration does Enhanced Cooperation Follow?

### 1.3.1 Imagery on Differentiated Integration and Enhanced Cooperation

The question of how to *imagine* differentiated integration has been dividing academics since the beginning of scholarship on differentiation. *Core Europe, Europe à la carte, Variable Geometries, Abgestufte Integration, Europe of Concentric Circles, Multi-Speed Europe*—the list of metaphors and images to describe

[58] Heber, C. (2021), *Enhanced Cooperation and European Tax Law*, Oxford University Press, see also Böttner, R. (2022), 'Book review: Enhanced Cooperation and European Tax Law by Caroline Heber', *CMLRev*, Vol. 59, Issue 4, pp. 1255–1257.

[59] Böttner, R. (2021), *The Constitutional Framework for Enhanced Cooperation in EU law*, Nijhoff studies in European Union law, Leiden The Netherlands, Koninklijke Brill NV.

non-uniform EU action is long and diverse. They usually describe differentiated integration at large, i.e. all forms of it, including not only enhanced cooperation but also the EMU with its current 20 members, the *Area of Freedom, Security and Justice* (AFSJ) with its opt-outs, international satellite treaties accompanying EU law, or even integration measures going beyond EU membership such as EFTA or the European Council. Whereas in the beginning of the debate, there were actual misunderstandings based on the terminology and images which were not well defined or researched,[60] the concepts largely seem to be well understood nowadays. Yet, conflicts still arise, simply because the users of different terminology interpret differentiated integration in different ways, causing what has fittingly been labelled a "semantic indigestion"[61] or even a "Babylonian linguistic chaos and conceptional labyrinth"[62] around differentiated integration. Within this labyrinth, it is a level of its own to ask which image of integration enhanced cooperation specifically follows or which concept it falls into. Yet, for the understanding of this thesis, it seems useful to establish a common ground as to how to imagine the situation brought about by enhanced cooperation. It is therefore the main purpose of the following remarks to find and present an image grasping the realities of enhanced cooperation to serve as an imaginative foundation for the rest of this thesis.

In terms of enhanced cooperation specifically, there has been little to no specific debate as to what image this specific mechanism adheres to among the various visualisations of differentiation. What is it then? Is enhanced cooperation a matter of picking and choosing, paving the way for a Europa à la carte? Is it just an example of some Member States going ahead, a multi-speed Europe, or one of different concentric circles revolving around a hard core of common EU policies? In order to answer this, a number of concepts describing differentiated integration will be described and tested for their ability to represent enhanced cooperation.

Numerous publications have given comprehensive overviews over different integration concepts;[63] it is not the aim of this chapter to reproduce the efforts

[60] Stubb, A. C.-G. (1996), 'A Categorization of Differentiated Integration', *JCMS: Journal of Common Market Studies*, Vol. 34, No. 2, pp. 283–295.

[61] Stubb, A. C.-G. (1996), 'A Categorization of Differentiated Integration', *JCMS: Journal of Common Market Studies*, Vol. 34, No. 2, pp. 283–295.

[62] Blanke, H.-J. (2013), 'Art. 20 TEU' in: Blanke, H.-J., Mangiameli, S. (eds.), *The Treaty on European Union (TEU): A commentary*, Berlin, Springer, pp. 787–830.

[63] Thym, D. (2004), *Ungleichzeitigkeit und europäisches Verfassungsrecht*, Schriftenreihe europäisches Verfassungsrecht, Baden-Baden, Nomos; slightly more condensed in English: Thym, D. (2009), The Evolution of Supranational Differentiation, WHI-Paper; seminal

made in this extensive research, which is why the concepts will be presented more briefly. Moreover, given the almost endless list of concepts, this cannot possibly be a thorough presentation of all concepts presented in the past, but is necessarily selective. The selection will be based either on particularly popular concepts (multi-speed Europe, core Europe, Europa *à la carte*), or ones that are particularly insightful for enhanced cooperation, though possibly less prominent (concentric/eccentric circles). As this chapter sets out to find an image to base the rest of the thesis on, certain prominent models such as that of 'variable geometries' will intentionally be left out of the scope of the analysis. 'Variable geometries' describes first and foremost the existence of different Member States with different integration statuses as such, rather than characterising a specific idea of *how* the differentiated result plays out. It therefore makes sense that it is a notion that actively evades the possibility of being visualised, in fact its comparative vagueness describes precisely what it sets out to depict. Similarly, the notion of *Abgestufte Integration* was invented as a collective term for instances of "incomplete" integration.[64] Both, consequently, have no added value for the specific purpose set out in this subchapter—this is not, however, meant to underrate the relevance of the concepts in other contexts.

## 1.3.2 Models for Enhanced Cooperation

### 1.3.2.1 Core Europe

A most prominent fear and critique of enhanced cooperation is that it may lead to a *core Europe*, featuring a 'hard core' of most integrated EU Member States and a 'periphery' of—expectedly less wealthy—states that cannot make it to the centre. Historically, the idea was much less negatively connotated: Especially French

---

overview Stubb, A. C.-G. (1996), 'A Categorization of Differentiated Integration', *JCMS: Journal of Common Market Studies*, Vol. 34, No. 2, pp. 283–295; brief, yet very concise overview Blanke, H.-J. (2013), 'Art. 20 TEU' in: Blanke, H.-J., Mangiameli, S. (eds.), *The Treaty on European Union (TEU): A commentary,* Berlin, Springer, pp. 787–830.

[64] Thym, D. (2004), *Ungleichzeitigkeit und europäisches Verfassungsrecht*, Schriftenreihe europäisches Verfassungsrecht, Baden-Baden, Nomos with reference to Grabitz, E., Iliopoulos, C. (1984), 'Typologie der Differenzierungen und Ausnahmen im Gemeinschaftsrecht' in: Grabitz, E., Franzmeyer, F. (eds.), *Abgestufte Integration: Eine Alternative zum herkömmlichen Integrationskonzept?,* Kehl am Rhein, Engel, pp. 31–46 Do note, however, that *Abgestufte Integration* is sometimes used interchangeably with "multi-speed Europe" (see e.g. Karakas, C. (2005), 'Für eine Abgestufte Integration: Zur Debatte um den EU-Beitritt der Türkei', *HFSK Standpunkte*, No. 4, pp. 1–16.) In this regard, the relevant idea is discussed below.

and German politicians and academics repeatedly brought up the topic from a perspective within perceived core. Famous contributions such as the *Schäuble-Lamers-Paper* proposed a core Europe of "integration oriented and cooperative countries" (imagined to consist of France, Germany and the Benelux states) in order to "oppose the centrifugal forces in the ever-growing Union with a strong centre".[65] Although claiming that the hard core was to be characterized by an inherent openness towards willing periphery states, it did not fail to mention that this was the case "in principle" and "as soon as they have solved certain current problems and as far as they are willing to engage in the sense described".[66] Until today, reservations such as this may have been nurturing worries by states not considered part of potential 'hard core'. Similar proposals to the initial *Core Europe* concept were brought forward by actors such as *Jacques Delors*[67] or *Joschka Fischer*[68].

The core Europe concept is based on the idea of a dichotomy of EU Member States, distinguishing all states willing to integrate deeply and swiftly in one, and more doubtful state in a second group. There should not be a possibility to pick and choose, but a single decision for one of the two groups.[69] Confronted with the realities of enhanced cooperation, this is where we can clearly see a massive divergence from the idea of a core Europe, no matter whether connotated positively or negatively. As a matter of fact, each Member State participates in at least one enhanced cooperation[70] and the group of states participating in all enhanced cooperation projects consists of eight highly diverse Member States,[71]

---

65 Schäuble, W., Lamers, K. (1994), 'Überlegungen zur europäischen Politik'.

66 Schäuble, W., Lamers, K. (1994), 'Überlegungen zur europäischen Politik'.

67 "Jacques Delors critique la stratégie d'élargissement de l'Union", in: Le Monde, 19 January 2000, p. 2; see also Busse, C. (2000), 'Braucht Europa einen harten Kern?', *A PuZ*, B47 B42, available at https://www.bpb.de/apuz/25338/braucht-europa-einen-kern?p=all (last access 07 January 2022).

68 J. Fischer, Vom Staatenverbund zur Föderation—Gedanken über die Finalität der europäischen Integration. "Humboldt-Rede", 12. Mai 2000, available at https://www.europa.clio-online.de/quelle/id/q63-28290 (last access 19 January 2022).

69 Thym, D. (2004), *Ungleichzeitigkeit und europäisches Verfassungsrecht*, Schriftenreihe europäisches Verfassungsrecht, Baden-Baden, Nomos.

70 Zeitzmann, S. (2017), 'A Rather Strange Animal, this "Enhanced Cooperation":—May it Serve as King of the Europen Zoonion? or: Is Enhanced Cooperation Anywhere Near a Constitutional Principle?' in: Giegerich, T., Schmitt, D. C., Zeitzmann, S. (eds.), *Flexibility in the EU and beyond: How much differentiation can European integration bear?*, Oxford, Hart Publishing, pp. 87–105 Although Zeitzmann's analysis comes from a time before the start of the EPPO enhanced cooperation, the numbers stay the same.

71 Austria, Belgium, France, Germany, Greece, Italy, Portugal, Slovenia.

which can hardly be described as a solid, exclusive and unified core, nor does it mirror the imagined initial core-Europe states or the expectance that a core would be made up of wealthy, western-European members. This is also due to a legal reality of enhanced cooperation: The openness of enhanced cooperation (Art. 20(1) TEU, Art. 328 TFEU)[72] has been maintained to the fullest extend in all projects. Even the possibility of introducing conditions on the participation as foreseen in Art. 328(1), 331 TFEU[73] has not been made use of, extending the practiced openness of the existing enhanced cooperation projects even beyond what would be a legal necessity. In sum, one can agree with *Bruno De Witte*, who pointed out that: "If one takes together these procedural constraints, it is clear that a self-appointed vanguard cannot engage in a broad cross-policy cooperation project whilst ignoring the other member states. The enhanced cooperation mechanism was, from the start in the 1990s, conceived as antithetical to the core Europe idea, and it remains so today."[74] The idea of a core Europe is not one that is apt to describe the realities as caused or enabled by the enhanced cooperation mechanism.

#### 1.3.2.2 Multi-Speed Europe

The concept of a *multi-speed Europe* is one of the more self-explanatory concepts in the arena of differentiated integration imagery. The idea is that all EU Member States share the same aim in terms of integration, but do not necessarily approach it at the same speed, meaning that states can integrate fully in a given policy area, whereas others may still be approaching it at paces of their liking. This results in a state of temporary differentiation until the last state catches up.

At first sight, the notion of a multi-speed Europe may seem closer to the realities of enhanced cooperation than the dichotomy of core versus periphery. As the overall idea of multiple speeds can entail also the possibility of different speeds adopted by one state in different policy areas, it seems a better fit to capture the diverse and not necessarily coherent membership in the different enhanced cooperations. Furthermore, enhanced cooperation is characterised by a legal framework that favours the idea of approaching a policy aim at different speeds in that its principled openness allows outsiders to join at any time (see Chapter 4).

---

[72] See Chap. 4.

[73] Which could, if desired politically, even include a conditionality compontent: See Chap. 4.2.3.

[74] Witte, B. de (2019), *The Law as Tool and Constraint of Differentiated Integration*, EUI Working Papers RSCAS.

Undisputedly, the multi-speed concept is put to use in the area of the EMU: All Member States, safe those with opt-outs, have an obligation to join the Eurozone. When this happens, however, is subject to the fulfilment of convergence criteria and thus does not happen at the same time, but gradually.[75] As the name of the concept of a multispeed Europe unveils unequivocally, it assumes and builds upon the idea that all Member States share a vision on the necessity and design of certain projects or integration steps and merely disagree on when to achieve them.[76] Yet, in practice, projects like the two enhanced cooperations on family law build on profound societal differences. It is hard to see any kind of movement among the non-participants that would justify speaking of actual multi-'speed' integration,[77] with a group of pioneers just waiting for the other Member States to catch up—in fact, the non-participants often have no intention of catching up, and therefore the notion of 'speed' is misleading.[78] In the case of the unitary patent, profound disagreements on the policy design (the patent's

---

[75] See also Thym, D. (2004), *Ungleichzeitigkeit und europäisches Verfassungsrecht*, Schriftenreihe europäisches Verfassungsrecht, Baden-Baden, Nomos. Note, however, that Sweden has been undermining this logic by formally not fulfilling criteria that economically it would.

[76] Thym, D. (2004), *Ungleichzeitigkeit und europäisches Verfassungsrecht*, Schriftenreihe europäisches Verfassungsrecht, Baden-Baden, Nomos.

[77] Trüten, D. (2015), *Die Entwicklungen des Internationalen Privatrechts in der Europäischen Union: Auf dem Weg zu einem europäischen IPR-Gesetz*, Europäisches Privatrecht (Bern, Switzerland), Bern, Baden-Baden, Stämpfli Verlag; Nomos, p. 631.

[78] See also Witte, B. de (2017), 'The future of variable geometry in a post-Brexit European Union', *Maastricht Journal of European and Comparative Law*, Vol. 24, No. 2, pp. 153–157, p. 156; Paggi, E. (2017), *Acquis, integrazione differenziata, unità dell'ordinamento dell'unione: verso nuovi modelli di integrazione in Europa?: Spunti di una riflessione teorica a valle dell'introduzione del c.d. pacchetto sul brevetto europeo con effetto unitario.*, Padua; *Paggi* points out that this lack of *speeds* in the philosophy of enhanced cooperation has also been endorsed by the CJEU in C-274/11, C-295/11. See also the fitting description of *De Witte*, which, however, goes beyond enhanced cooperation and describes differentiated integration at large: "The old and still often used expression of 'multi-speed integration is not a very appropriate term to describe this reality, since many of the existing cases of flexibility are marked by the fact that the Member States can no longer be said to pursue common goals at a different pace. Rather, they tend to have different views of the appropriate degree and scope of integration, and these different views are considered by the others to be both legitimate and durable. So, when the Rome Declaration mentions 'different paces' and 'moving in the same direction', this sounds like wishful thinking appropriate for a solemn occasion such as the 60th anniversary of the Rome Treaties, but not as a realistic description[…]." Witte, B. de (2018), 'An undivided Union? Differentiated integration in post-Brexit times', *Common Market Law Review*, Vol. 55, No. 2, pp. 227–249.

working languages) led to using enhanced cooperation. While Italy has overcome its doubts in the meantime, Spain stays out of the project, which counters the idea of a previous agreement in substance. The same goes for the *European Public Prosecutor's Office* (EPPO), on which Members States disagreed profoundly. While future governments in the non-participating Member States may change course, an initial agreement on the need for the project was clearly not in place. It is therefore fair to say that "[a]lthough legally enhanced cooperation had been designed as an intermediate step on the way to uniform integration, with strict requirements regarding admissibility, it will probably *permanently* shape the Union politically."[79] In this sense the design of enhanced cooperation as an intermediate step towards an integration measure eventually including all Member States clashes with political realities.

A multi-speed Europe is therefore not fitting to describe—at least—the *realities* enhanced cooperation brought about.[80]

#### 1.3.2.3 Europe à la Carte

The gastronomic metaphor of *Europa à la carte* invokes a visit to a restaurant, where one is given a menu and may pick and choose at will. The idea is to build upon the existing EU *acquis* on a voluntary case-by-case basis, depending on the interest of individual Member States.[81] As such, the concept is contrary to the community method, which, through QMV decision-making in the ordinary legislative procedure, allows to create unity even against the will of single Member States. An *à la carte* logic has most clearly been applied in the case of the opt-outs the UK secured for itself in terms of the EMU and the AFSJ,[82] which, in consequence, were extended to other Member States such as Denmark and Ireland. In addition, the numerous international Treaties accompanying the EU integration outside the EU law framework function, by their very nature, on a pick and choose basis; however, one reason for moving them outside the EU legal

---

[79] Blanke, H.-J. (2013), 'Art. 20 TEU' in: Blanke, H.-J., Mangiameli, S. (eds.), *The Treaty on European Union (TEU): A commentary,* Berlin, Springer, pp. 787–830 (emphasis added).

[80] Malíř, J. (2019), 'Enhanced Cooperation in the EU: Its Evolution and Position of the Czech Republic', *Studia Europejskie*, No. 1, pp. 89–112.

[81] Stubb, A. C.-G. (1996), 'A Categorization of Differentiated Integration', *JCMS: Journal of Common Market Studies*, Vol. 34, No. 2, pp. 283–295; Thym, D. (2004), *Ungleichzeitigkeit und europäisches Verfassungsrecht*, Schriftenreihe europäisches Verfassungsrecht, Baden-Baden, Nomos.

[82] Thym, D. (2009), The Evolution of Supranational Differentiation, WHI-Paper; see also Graf von Luckner, J. (2021), 'A Brexit last call: The strange practice of pre-Brexit opt-ins', *Maastricht Journal of European and Comparative Law*, Vol. 28, No. 4, pp. 556–572.

order may precisely be because Member States object the measures within the EU framework;[83] to remain in the gastronomic metaphor: in order to get what they want, in this case, the Member States have change restaurants. A treaty-based *à la carte* approach to European integration is, in a most extensive form, in place in the Council of Europe. In this international organisation, the single integration instruments—called conventions—are entirely voluntary to participate in (with the exception of the European Convention on Human Rights).[84]

The *à la carte* image invokes total liberty of the participants. Even if one takes the existing acquis and most importantly the internal market law out of the equation, as it is unlikely that a future integration model could put EU law in its entirety in question, an *à la carte* model can be imagined for future integration steps. The idea of the integration concept is that Member States alone decide whether or not to participate in given measures when they are being discussed and decided and thus shape their own integration status at will. This is where the image clashes with enhanced cooperation: The only hard power non-participants have in the evolution of a project that eventually becomes an enhanced cooperation is to initially vote against it in the Council; however, at most (that is, in the case of unanimous decision-making), this blocks the project for the EU as a whole and does not mean a decision on the state's individual participation. What happens then is not in the uninterested state's hands. The decision of whether a project is carried out despite the veto by way of enhanced cooperation is entirely in the hands of the interested Member States.[85] *Becerril* pointed out that a "*Europe à la carte* [...] allow[s] self-exclusion"—enhanced cooperation, if anything, allows self-inclusion. In fact, it will be shown further on[86] that from an individual Member State's isolated perspective, an ideal outcome may even be that a project is carried out, while itself stays outside of it.[87] However, the Member

[83] See the example of the so-called Fiscal Compact, Graf von Luckner, J. (2018), 'How to Bring It Home—The EU's Options for Incorporating the Fiscal Compact into EU Law', *European Law Blog*.

[84] Witte, B. de (2019), *The Law as Tool and Constraint of Differentiated Integration*, EUI Working Papers RSCAS.

[85] Provided they form a qualified majority.

[86] See Chap. 2 on incentive structures in the evolution of enhanced cooperation projects.

[87] A particularly insightful example for this is the participation of Poland in the Unified Patent Court; a controversial economic consultancy came to the conclusion that it would be more advantageous for Poland not to participate, as Poland would then avoid implementation costs, but Polish innovations could still be protected in the participating countries: *Deloitte*, Analysis of prospective economic effects related to the implementation of the system of

States interested in not participating in a project has no influence on whether the project will see the light of day after its veto. Moreover, the enhanced cooperation mechanism has been used too sparingly and to dispersedly within the area of EU competences to allow a Member State to thoroughly shape its membership status in an *à la carte* sense. The enhanced cooperation mechanism thus differs significantly from the *à la carte* logic.[88] As such Europe *à la carte* is not an appropriate way to describe the enhanced cooperation mechanism.

#### 1.3.2.4 Europe of Concentric Circles

The notion of a 'Europe of Concentric Circles' does not split up the Member States in two categories, a hard core and a periphery, but imagines Europe to be built of an indefinite number of circles, one lying within the other. These circles are 'concentric', meaning that they all share the same centre. Each circle is thus further away from the centre than its predecessor. This is what defines the idea of European 'concentric circles': A number of Member States, which are most advanced in EU integration, make up the inner circle. They are all on the same integration level. From there, every following circle groups Member States that are less integrated, but again share the same level of integration.[89] The outermost circle or circles are made up of non-EU Member States who are associated with the Union, such as the EFTA states.[90] The former French Prime

unitary patent protection in Poland (2012), http://www.uil-sipo.si/uploads/media/UPP-Analiza-PL.pdf. As the Unified Patent Court Agreement is an international treaty, which allows picking-and-choosing, Poland could freely apply this tactic without fearing disadvantages from its behaviour. For a critical assessment of this approach, see Fiolka, J. (2015), 'Patent Enforcement in Poland' in: Heath, C., Stauder, D. (eds.), *Patent enforcement worldwide: Writings in honour of Dieter Stauder,* Oxford, Hart Publishing.

[88] Diverging opinion: Jaeger, T. (2015), 'Nach l ' Europe à la carte nun la loi européenne à la carte? Zur Erlaubnis der Umgehung der Unionsmethode nach dem Urteil in Rs. C-146/13 u.a', *EuR Europarecht*, Vol. 50, No. 4, pp. 461–476.

[89] Walker, N. (1998), 'Sovreignty and Differentiation', *ELJ*, Vol. 4, pp. 355–388; Avbelj, M. (2013), 'Differentiated Integration—Farewell to the EU-27?', *GLJ*, Vol. 14, No. 1, pp. 191–212. For an impressive contextualisation of the term "concentric circles", including it being a reference to Dante Alighieri's *Divine Comedy,* see Savat-Gündüz, M. (2013), *Variable Geometrie: Subsidiarität und differenzierte Integration im Mehrebenensystem der Europäischen Union*, Europäische Hochschulschriften. Reihe II, Rechtswissenschaft, Frankfurt am Main, PL Academic Research.

[90] On the outer circles, see Lavenex, S. (2011), 'Concentric circles of flexible 'EUropean' integration: A typology of EU external governance relations', *Comparative European Politics*, Vol. 9, 4–5, pp. 372–393.

Minister Édouard Balladur is often associated with this concept.[91] An example for three circles could be the EMU states without any AFSJ opt-outs as inner circle, a second circle including Member States fully participating in the AFSJ but not in the EMU, and a third one containing Member States not fully participating in both the EMU and the AFSJ. However, this example already shows the concept's problem: What about a Member States like Ireland, that is part of the EMU but has certain AFSJ opt-outs? Is it more or less integrated than a state like Sweden without AFSJ-optouts, but which has not introduced the Euro as a currency? This shows that the idea of concentric circles fails to capture the complexities of differentiated integration in the EU.[92] It is based on an idea of hierarchy between instances of EU integration that does not exist.

For a point of view focussing on enhanced cooperation, one could create a numbers-based image of enhanced cooperation-based integration by way of concentric circles. Numbers-based in this context would mean that the number of enhanced cooperation projects a state participates in would equal the status of its integration (i.e. belonging to an 'inner circle'), which is questionable. Moreover, such an approach would, due to the difficulties described, not be able to enter into contact with the rest of the EU *acquis* and its manifold instances of differentiation. A model of concentric circles would, therefore, be able to describe enhanced cooperation participation, though the notion of hierarchy that it invokes is questionable. Beyond enhanced cooperation, concentric circles are hardly able to represent differentiated integration in the EU.

#### 1.3.2.5 Various Alternatives

The examples above tried to show that different models discussed to describe enhanced cooperation are not able to capture the situation of differentiated EU integration as enhanced cooperation as brought about by enhanced cooperation. However different authors did present further ideas—without necessarily turning them into major theories—that might be closer to the image this chapter is set out to look for.

In the following, I will gather these elements in order to try and incorporate them into a single image.

---

[91] Koenig, N. (2015), A Differentiated View of Differentiated Integration, Policy Brief, Berlin, Jacques Delors Institute.

[92] For similar critique, see Della Cananea, G. (2019), 'Differentiated Integration in Europe After Brexit: An Institutional Analysis' in: Pernice, I., Guerra Martins, A. M. (eds.), *Brexit and the Future of EU Politics: A Constitutional Law Perspective,* Baden-Baden, Nomos Verlagsgesellschaft mbH & Co. KG, pp. 45–89, calling the image of concentric circles a "misleading simple idea".

*Somek*, for example, described "the emergence of different, not even concentric, overlapping circles of Member States".[93] In doing so, he acknowledges the weakness of the model of *concentric circles*, namely its underlying idea of a hierarchy of integration steps. Removing the concentricity of the integration circles enables the model to display various differentiated integration steps without having to decide on which is closer to the centre than others. The approach is based on policy, not on participants. A similar path is described by the idea of *Lansdaal*, who mentions "ex-centric" overlapping circles.[94] This is a clear distinction from the *concentric* circles idea. Whereas 'concentric' means sharing a centre (con 'together' + centrum 'centre'),[95] "ex-centric" (ex 'out of' + centrum 'centre'), which is a variant of the more frequently used "eccentric", means "not placed centrally or not having its axis or other part placed centrally".[96] The idea of *ex-centric/eccentric circles* is therefore a more concise description of the overlapping circles as depicted by *Somek*.

*Schmidt*, on a similar note, speaks of a "*soft-core* Europe made up of the multiple clusters of member-states that overlap in their participation in the EU's many policy communities."[97] These clusters, in her image, work on the basis of a single set of institutions, thus staying fairly close to the image of concentric/overlapping circles.

To add yet another similar (but very imaginative) approach, *Gerards* and *Wessels* speak of a "'spaghetti bowl' of overlapping groupings".[98]

---

[93] Somek, A. (2002), 'On Supranationality', *EIoP*, Vol. 5, No. 3, pp. 1–15.

[94] Lansdaal, A. (2002), 'Differentiation or Enhanced Cooperation: Formalizing Flexibility' in: Schrauwen, A. (ed.), *Flexibility in Constitutions: Forms of Closer Cooperation in Federal and Non-Federal Settings,* Groningen, European Law Publishing, pp. 47–57; the idea is appropriated to former French Prime Minister Balladur. See also former President of Slovenia Borut Pahor, http://www.up-rs.si/up-rs/uprs-eng.nsf/pages/634DD98EE4E68474C1257C360048DC08?OpenDocument (last access 26 January 2022).

[95] "Concentric", Lexico.com dictionary, https://www.lexico.com/definition/concentric (last access 20 January 2022).

[96] „Eccentric", Lexico.com dictionary, https://www.lexico.com/definition/eccentric (last access 20 January 2022).

[97] Schmidt, V. A. (2019), 'The future of differentiated integration: a 'soft-core,' multi-clustered Europe of overlapping policy communities', *Comparative European Politics*, Vol. 17, No. 2, pp. 294–315 Note also p. Thinking of the future of the EU in this way is best adapted to the already high level of EU differentiation: "Thinking of the future of the EU in this way is best adapted to the already high level of EU differentiation."

[98] Wessels, W., Gerards, C. (2018), *The implementation of enhanced cooperation in the EU: Study*, [Brussels], European Parliament.

However, all of these models suffer from a problem of their own, which is best illustrated by showing attempts to visualise the differentiation in the EU (Fig. 1.1):

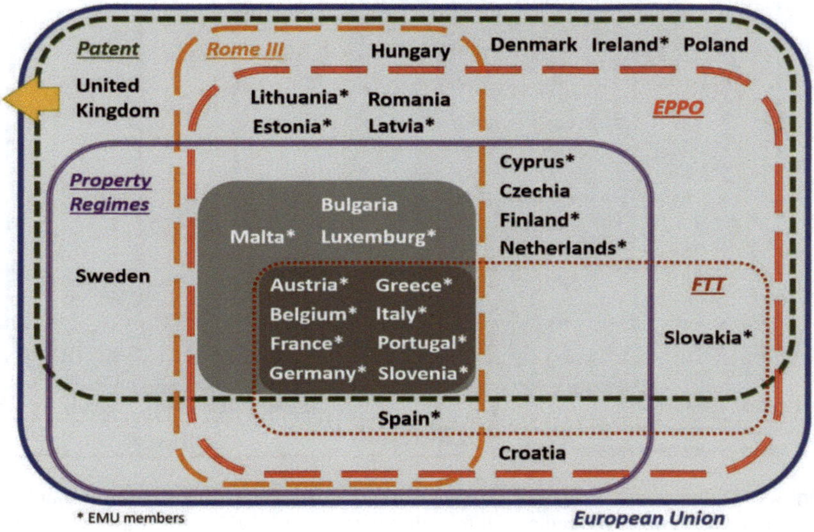


**Fig. 1.1** Europe United in Diversity. "'Spaghetti Bowl' of Enhanced Cooperation" (Wessels, Gerards 2018 at p. 26)

This image by *Wessels* and *Gerards* depicts merely the existing enhanced cooperations. The image (which does not exactly depict circles, but the concept stays the same) unveils that complexity of an image adequately representing a mere five (or six, if one counts the asterisk added to display EMU members) instances of differentiation is immense. In fact, already at this point, the added value in terms of informing an audience of the state of integration of the EU as a whole, as well as of single Member States, is marginal. This effect is even stronger when regarding an image that sets out to more thoroughly represent differentiation in the EU. The following image, designed by *Kreilinger*, adds Schengen, the TSCG ('Fiscal Compact'), the Euro Plus Pact and the EEA to the picture. While these are still by far not all instances of differentiation in the EU, the complexity of the image is telling (Fig. 1.2).

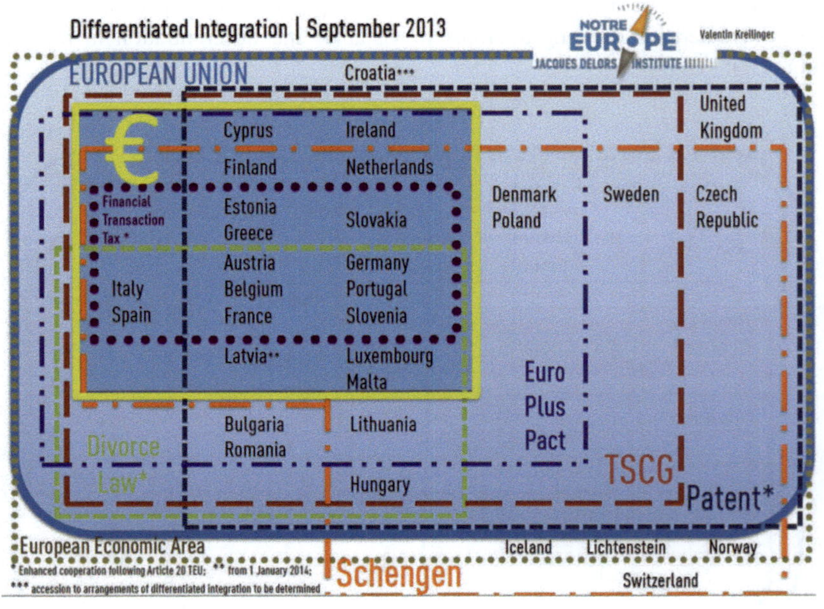


**Fig. 1.2** Differentiated Integration (September 2013). Kreilinger, https://institutdelors.eu/content/uploads/2025/04/vkreilingerdifferentiatedintegration9-2013-3.pdf (last access 02 May 2026)

In addition, the impressive attempt of *Tekin*, pushing the concept of circles to its boundaries, should not go unnoticed. It does not, however, display differentiation based on enhanced cooperation; especially the inner circle in her graph would in that case have to be subdivided further, leaving only eight states in the centre (Fig. 1.3).

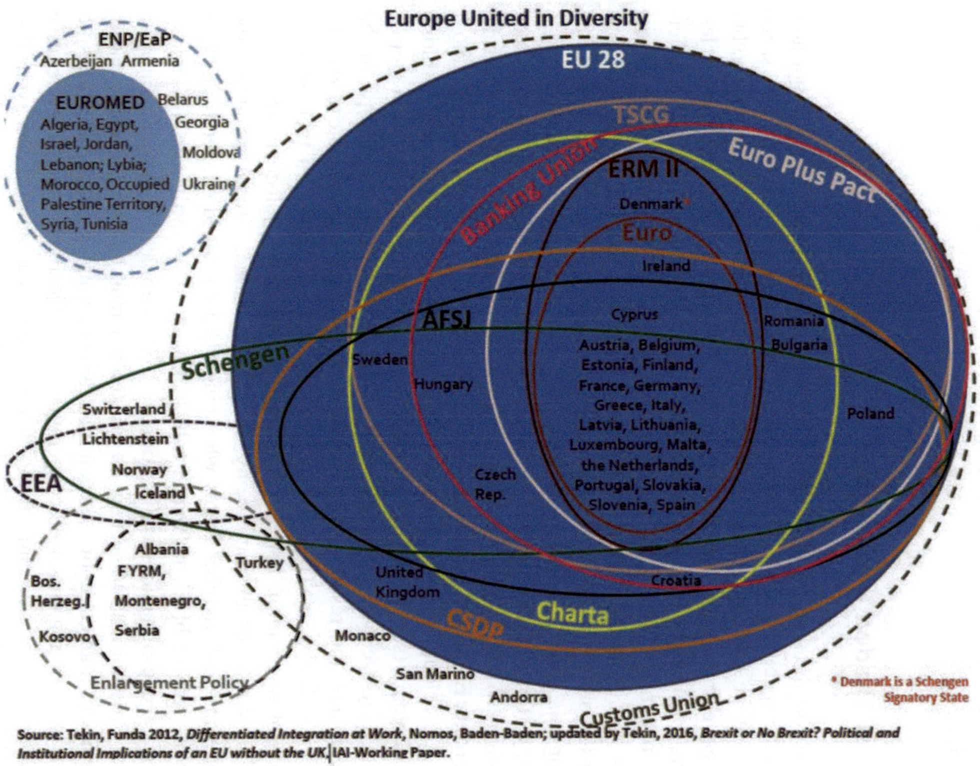


**Fig. 1.3** Europe United in Diversity. Tekin, http://archiv.iep-berlin.de/wp-content/uploads/2017/03/Funda-Tekin-Differentiated-Integration-Online-Paper2017.pdf?it=wp-content/uploads/2017/03/Funda-Tekin-Differentiated-Integration-Online-Paper2017.pdf at p. 5

The eccentric/overlapping circles, soft-core,'spaghetti bowl' models have in common that they are excellent tools to visualize the membership of many individual differentiated polices. However, regarding European (differentiated) integration at large, they basically allow only one, albeit very true, conclusion: It is complicated.

### 1.3.3 A Shaded Integration?

To summarise the findings made above, the models presented are either not able to grasp the specific realities of enhanced cooperation (core Europe, multi-speed Europe, Europe *à la carte*, concentric circles) or may grasp them effectively, but tend to get extremely complicated when doing so (eccentric/overlapping circles, soft-core,'spaghetti bowl'). Therefore, if aiming to introduce an image of differentiated integration shaped by enhanced cooperation to work with in this thesis, it seems that another descriptive dimension needs to enter the arena of models in order to combine clarity and effectiveness. To achieve this clarification, in the following this dimension shall be colour, and more precisely *shades*.

Thus, differentiated cooperation, especially that brought about by enhanced cooperation, will tentatively be described as a 'shaded integration'. For the sake of this image, European integration steps are imagined to be comparable to colour screens, i.e. coloured foils like the ones used to visualise how light and filtration result in colours (see visualisation below, Fig. 1.4). If every integration step is represented by a colour screen stacked on top of each other on a graph of the Member States, the result is that the more integration steps a state does, the "darker" it will appear. Thus, each Member State will appear in their individual shade of integration, it is clear which Member States joined more, or less integration steps. For the time being, this will be done without weighting the different steps—all Member States who joined two enhanced cooperations wear the same 'shade of blue', no matter which projects they participate in. This is, of course, a questionable simplification, as for example the introduction of a European Prosecutor's Office may be greater repercussions on the participation Member States than common rules on international couples' property regimes, to name but two existing enhanced cooperation. Yet, objectively naming the relative integrative impact of a certain enhanced cooperation is a complex endeavour that would go beyond the purpose of the present reflections. While the model would allow factoring in such comparative differences without contradictions, in light of the fact that all enhanced cooperation so far have been enacted in single, limited policy areas, it does not seem totally incorrect to initially give each enhanced cooperation the same value.[99]

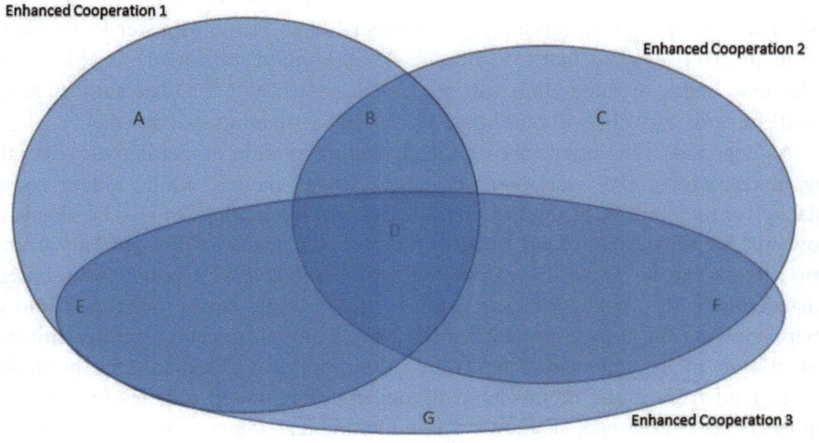


**Fig 1.4** Three overlapping blue circles represent three groups labeled Enhanced Cooperation 1, Enhanced Cooperation 2, and Enhanced Cooperation 3. Light and filtration

> Shaded integration:
> Member States A, B, C, D, E, F, and G in enhanced cooperations 1, 2, and 3.
> The group consisting of A, C, and G numerically shares the same level of overall integration (visualised by the same shade of blue), albeit through participation in different enhanced cooperations. The same goes for group B, E, F. Member State D is the most integrated state.

As the image does not imply ongoing dynamics, it is more precise than the idea of a multi-speed integration and more neutral (that is, less hierarchical) than the notions of a core Europe or a Europe of concentric circles. In the image above,

---

[99] Extending the image to further instances of differentiation, such as EMU or AFSJ participation, would, however, make a quantification of the integrative impact compulsory, as a mere numerical logic would deprive the image of any explanatory value in this context.

the approach resembles that of the overlapping/eccentric circle models, while adding the benefit that the shared number of integrative steps taken by, e.g. states E, F, and B are the same.

This is not the first time differentiated integration is imagined as being 'shaded': European Commissioner and former Italian Prime Minister Paolo Gentiloni in 2017 stressed that "we need a flexible union, reformed, united where different shades of integration can coexist successfully."[100] Other authors have used the term as well, without, however, further explaining its content.[101]

As depicted in the image above, the shaded integration model is policy-based, again resembling the overlapping/eccentric circles models while adding some clarity for the purpose of interpreting it. However, the model can also be changed towards Member State-based imagery. In fact, the result of the shaded eccentric circles can be *taken over* from the policy-oriented to a purely state-based visualization. In other words, the result of the shading can be integrated into a map, showing the degree to which a Member State participates in differentiated integration in its colour shading. While this approach eliminates the possibility to read from it the membership in single differentiated policies (e.g. single enhanced cooperations), it allows a non-hierarchical impression of the state of enhanced cooperation-based integration of all Member States (within the limits laid out above, as the integrative impact of the single enhanced cooperations are not weighted). The following map shows the participation in enhanced cooperations, ranging from Member States who participate in one to those who participate in all five instances of enhanced cooperation (Fig. 1.5):

[100] Pop, V. (2017), 'Once Scorned, 'Multispeed Europe' Is Back', *WSJ*, 1 March 2017.

[101] Koenig, N. (2015), A Differentiated View of Differentiated Integration, Policy Brief, Berlin, Jacques Delors Institute; Vimont, P. (2018), *Flexibility is not the miracle solution*, available at: encompass-europe.com/comment/flexibility-is-not-the-miracle-solution; see also, in a different context, Röttger-Wirtz, S., Eliantonio, M. (2019), 'From Integration to Exclusion: EU Composite Administration and Gaps in Judicial Accountability in the Authorisation of Pharmaceuticals', *European Journal of Risk Regulation*, Vol. 10, No. 2, pp. 393–411.

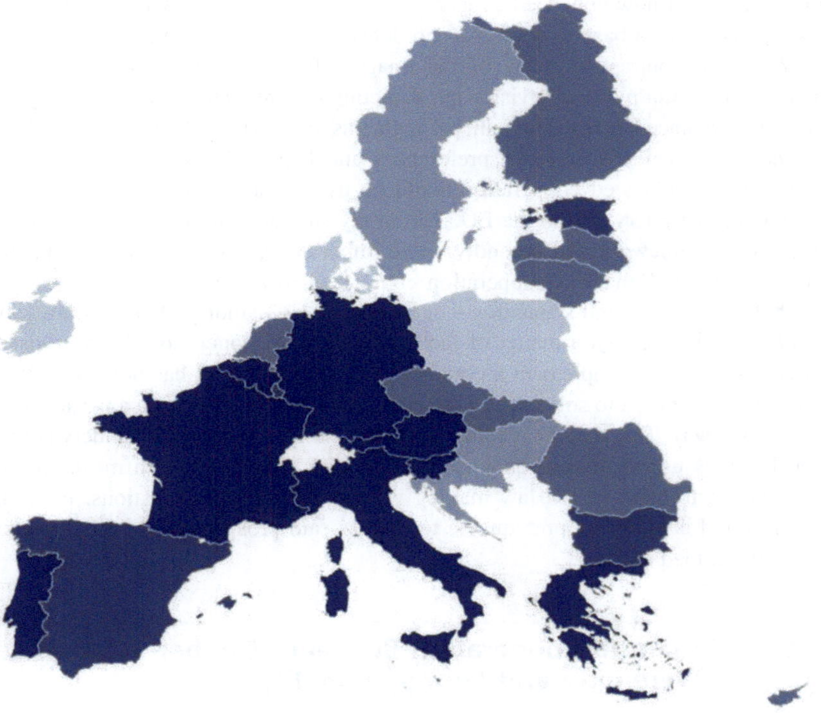

**Fig. 1.5** Participation in Enhanced Cooperations

It is a matter of fact that European integration, is not always uniform but often results in a multitude of *shades of blue*, brought about by instruments like enhanced cooperation, Treaty clauses allowing diverging Member State behaviour or even by the degree to which Member States implement EU law. Yet, as *Thym* declared, "Political concepts about European integration at multiple speeds have rarely been translated into specific Treaty provisions."[102] For this reason the concept above does not try to envision a new type of European integration, or lay out how EU integration ideally ought to be. Rather, it tries to make the current status of differentiation as brought about by enhanced cooperation visible and comprehensible. This a politically more neutral view on of differentiation in the

[102] Thym, D. (2009), The Evolution of Supranational Differentiation, WHI-Paper.

EU shall depict how enhanced cooperation is treated in this thesis—and it might also be useful as a base to open-minded debates on European integration.

While, in contrast to many of the images above, not formulating political demands or being politically visionary, depicting differentiated integration at general and enhanced cooperation in particular as it *is* rather than as it *could* or *should* be, depending on one's preferences and fears, allows us to draw some conclusions. Enhanced cooperation could be used in a way that creates a hard core and a periphery within the EU. Yet, firstly such a scenario is not embedded in its legal framework and secondly, more importantly, it is not what is happening in practice. Enhanced cooperation could lead to a multi-speed EU, yet we see both movement and stagnation—or be and let be—among Member States. A *shaded* EU is a reality, a matter of fact and enhanced cooperation has been used as an instrument to implement a certain degree of *shading*. It has not been functioning as a panacea to solve the EU's crises, nor has it been used in a particularly oppressive way. This may be a conclusion that some might consider underwhelming, but it is useful to treat enhanced cooperation as what it is, a means to an end, and instrument of EU law making with prospects and limitations. Bearing this in mind is a helpful prerequisite to discuss said prospects and limitations in an open-minded fashion.

## 1.4 Enhanced Cooperation Between Member State Sovereignty and Supranationality

Enhanced cooperation is situated in a special position in European law. Acts passed in an enhanced cooperation are EU law with all of its effects and as such supranational. Yet, they reserve a special role for Member States and in giving them a free choice to participate or not, they empower the single states in a way that is unusual for EU law. In fact, one could argue the possibility to independently decide upon participation or not is contrary to the usual logic of EU integration, the so-called community method,[103] and thus contrary to supranationalism. This illustrates that integration via enhanced cooperation has an element strongly focussed on the single states' governments, i.e. an intergovernmental element. One could, therefore, gain the impression that in fact, enhanced cooperation is both, supranational and intergovernmental at the same time—a paradox.

[103] For general thoughts on currenBlanke, H.-J., Pilz, S. (2020), 'Europa 2019 bis 2024—Wohin trägt uns der Stier?: Sieben Thesen zu den Herausforderungen der Europäischen Union', *EuR*, pp. 270–300t challenges around the community method and supranationalism vs. intergovernmentalism, see.

So where exactly is enhanced cooperation situated on the scale between intergovernmentalism and supranationality? Is it an "exit" for Member States to flee from the EU's "unitarisation and juridification", as has been claimed in literature?[104] Or is it really a means of "supranational differentiation", as has equally been argued in academia?[105]

In the following, I will delineate both the supranational and intergovernmental elements of enhanced cooperation in order to draw a final picture of the mechanism and its position between the two poles.

### 1.4.1 Supranationality and Intergovernmentalism

There has been a vivid debate among predominantly European scholars as to what supranationality is. However, this multi-faceted debate was not so much on elements that define or make up supranational policymaking or that have supranational effects, but on supranationality' s finality and its relation to the nation state, as well as to democracy.[106] Regarding those former elements, there is more unity in academia. A very general statement is the idea of *Ipsen*, according to whom supranationality can be defined as constitutional enforceability of Union authority against national authority.[107] Developing this further, a common approach

[104] Schroeder, W. (2003), 'Verfassungsrechtliche Beziehungen zwischen Europäischer Union und Europäischen Gemeinschaften' in: Bogdandy, A. von (ed.), *Europäisches Verfassungsrecht: Theoretische und dogmatische Grundzüge,* Berlin, New York, Springer, pp. 373–414, p. 413 f.; see also Hein, J. von (2017), 'EU Competence to Legislate in the Area of Private International Law and Law Reforms at the EU Level' in: Beaumont, P., Danov, M., Trimmings, K., Yüksel, B. (eds.), *Cross-Border Litigation in Europe,* Bloomsbury Publishing.

[105] Thym, D. (2009), The Evolution of Supranational Differentiation, WHI-Paper; see also Paggi, E. (2017), *Acquis, integrazione differenziata, unità dell'ordinamento dell'unione: verso nuovi modelli di integrazione in Europa?: Spunti di una riflessione teorica a valle dell'introduzione del c.d. pacchetto sul brevetto europeo con effetto unitario.*, Padua, para. 209, Fn. 511 on the concept of supranational differentiation: "La cooperazione rafforzata in quest'ottica ne costituisce codificazione e paradigma."

[106] See i.a. Somek, A. (2002), 'On Supranationality', *EIoP*, Vol. 5, No. 3, pp. 1–15; Joerges, C. (2002), "Deliberative Supranationalism'-Two Defences', *European Law Journal*, Vol. 8, No. 1, pp. 133–151; Bogdandy, A. von (1999), 'Die Europäische Union als supranationale Föderation', *integration*, Vol. 22, No. 2, pp. 95–112.

[107] Ipsen, H. P. (1972), *Europaisches Gemeinschaftsrecht*, Tubingen, J.C.B. Mohr; in a subsequent publication, *Ipsen* further elaborated on his concept, naming the question of sovereignty of Member States, the recognition of public Community [today: Union] interests, independence of the institutions, autonomy and effectiveness of Community [Union]

when trying to define why the EU legal framework differs from other spheres in a way that can be regarded as 'supranational' is the enumeration of elements which together make a legal order—and specifically the EU legal order—supranational.[108] The different lists largely overlap or name related aspects, which is why it is possible to combine their content to a list of EU supranationality features. Hence, as a synthesis, elements characterising the EU legal order as supranational that are relevant for enhanced cooperation can be divided in three categories:

- Supranational law-making:
    - Monopoly of initiative is carried by the independent Commission, the task of which is to "promote the general interest of the Union" (Art. 17 (1) TEU)
    - Majority-voting in the Council
    - Obligatory involvement of the European Parliament, the members of which are "representatives of the Union's citizens" (Art. 14 (2) TEU) irrespective of their own nationality and where they were elected
- Supranational law:
    - Direct effect of primary and secondary EU law vis-à-vis individuals
    - Primacy of primary and secondary EU law over national law (constitutional and ordinary)

law, and the primacy and national enforcement of Community [Union] law as elements of supranationality, Ipsen, H. P. (1973), 'Über Supranationalität' in: Ehmke, H., Scheuner, U. (eds.), *Festschrift für Ulrich Scheuner zum 70. Geburtstag,* Berlin, Duncker & Humblot, pp. 211–225.

[108] See the lists in Blanke, H.-J. (2013), 'Art. 1 TEU' in: Blanke, H.-J., Mangiameli, S. (eds.), *The Treaty on European Union (TEU): A commentary,* Berlin, Springer, para. 30 (emphasis added); Bogdandy, A. von (1999), 'Die Europäische Union als supranationale Föderation', *integration*, Vol. 22, No. 2, pp. 95–112; Müller-Graff, P.-C. (2011), '60 Jahre Grundgesetz aus der Sicht des Europarechts' in: Häberle, P., Mahrenholz, E. G. (eds.), *60 Jahre deutsches Grundgesetz: Beiträge aus dem Jahrbuch des öffentlichen Rechts der Jahre 2009–2011,* Tübingen, Mohr Siebeck, pp. 174–201, p. 176 ff. For another illustrative set of (partly different) criteria, see Schermers, Henry G.; Blokker, Niels, eds. (2011), *International institutional law: Unity within diversity*, Leiden, Boston, Brill Nijhoff. For critique on definitions including too many elements, factually limiting supranationality to the EU from the start, see Niedobitek, M. (2019), '§ 1 Vertragliche Grundlagen, rechtliche Gestalt, Institutionen der Union' in: Niedobitek, M. (ed.), *Europarecht: Grundlagen und Politiken der Union,* Berlin, De Gruyter, pp. 3–204.

  - The duty for Member States to ensure the implementation of EU law by taking any appropriate measure (Art. 4 (3) TEU)
  - Legal mechanisms on EU level to enforce implementation (esp. infringement procedure, Art. 258 ff. TFEU

- Supranational judicial system:

  - Obligatory jurisdiction of the CJEU
  - Monopoly of interpretation of the CJEU
  - Unified judicial system with CJEU and Member States' courts, ensured by preliminary reference procedure (Art. 267 TFEU)

In addition, the role of Member States' sovereignty plays an important role when speaking about supranationality: "[w]ith few exceptions,...the criteria for the loss of sovereignty coincide with those which much of the literature regards as the elements of supranationalism."[109] Hence, wherever Member States' sovereignty is preserved or secured, e.g. by unanimity requirements, one can assume that the respective policy area is less supranational than others.

An additional helpful distinction of the elements of supranationality has been proposed by *Weiler*, who differentiates *decisional* and *normative supranationalism.* Normative supranationalism describes the relationship between (in our case) Union policies and competing national measures. A high degree of normative supranationalism is a hierarchy in which the Union policy takes precedent over the national one. Decisional supranationalism concerns the decision-making processes that depart from the traditionally intergovernmental mode of requiring consent by all members. Decisional supranationalism can be reached by decision-making bodies independent from the Member States or by decision-making by/with Member States which departs from the system of unanimity.[110]

---

[109] Hay, P. (1966), *Federalism and supranational organizations; patterns for new legal structures*, University of Illinois Press, p. 69 as quoted by Leal-Arcas, R. (2007), 'Theories of Supranationalism in the EU', p. 97; see also Falkner, G. (1994), *Supranationalität trotz Einstimmigkeit?: Entscheidungsmuster der EU am Beispiel Sozialpolitik*, Europäische Schriften des Instituts für Europäische Politik, Bonn, Europa Union Verlag, p. 72 ff., for a broader discussion of this matter.

[110] Weiler, J. H. H. (1981), 'The Community System: the Dual Character of Supranationalism', *Yearbook of European Law*, Vol. 1, No. 1, pp. 267–306.

Multi-national cooperation that does not have such supranational elements and effects is considered intergovernmental for the purpose of this analysis.[111] However, the different elements show that a system or a policy can have certain, but not all the elements of one or the other. In fact, decision-making in many international organisations features, for example, significant elements of decisional supranationalism, such as the UN General Assembly, the WTO, IMF, or ILO, which all include majority-voting in their statutes (although even then, decisions are made between the governments of the involved stated, which is not a sign of decisional supranationalism).[112] However, their degree of normative supranationalism is low if at all existent—one could argue that so-called Chapter VII-measures of the UN Security Council, which features no *decisional* supranationalism in its unanimous decision-making, have a degree of *normative* supranationalism e.g. when determining sanctions—although they rely on states to enforce them and have few means to ensure this. They certainly cannot, therefore, be described as supranational overall.[113] In sum, both supranationalism and intergovernmentalism are not absolute, but relative concepts. Policies can be more or less supranational or intergovernmental, while still possessing some aspects of the other.[114]

## 1.4.2 Enhanced Cooperation—Caught in the Middle?

In order to position the enhanced cooperation between the poles of intergovernmentalism and supranationality, I will first analyse the most crucial moment in terms of decision-making in the evolution of an enhanced cooperation—its authorisation procedure. Secondly, I will analyse the effects enhanced cooperation has *internally* on its participants and *externally* on non-participating Member

---

[111] For more details on the concept, see e.g. Schermers, Henry G.; Blokker, Niels, eds. (2011), *International institutional law: Unity within diversity*, Leiden, Boston, Brill Nijhoff, para. 59.

[112] See Tijmes-Lhl, J. (2009), 'Consensus and majority voting in the WTO', *World Trade Review*, Vol. 8, No. 3, pp. 417–437; Osieke, E. (1984), 'Majority Voting Systems in the International Labour Organisation and the International Monetary Fund', *ICLQ*, Vol. 33, No. 2, pp. 381–408; Weiler, J. H. H. (1981), 'The Community System: the Dual Character of Supranationalism', *Yearbook of European Law*, Vol. 1, No. 1, pp. 267–306.

[113] Weiler, J. H. H. (1981), 'The Community System: the Dual Character of Supranationalism', *Yearbook of European Law*, Vol. 1, No. 1, pp. 267–306.

[114] Schermers, Henry G.; Blokker, Niels, eds. (2011), *International institutional law: Unity within diversity*, Leiden, Boston, Brill Nijhoff.

States in terms of their sovereignty and on the supranationality of the outcome. Finally, I will take into account the particularities of special forms of enhanced cooperation.

#### 1.4.2.1 Authorisation Procedure

A first element to look at when trying to position the enhanced cooperation mechanism between supranationality and intergovernmentalism is how an enhanced cooperation is established.

As a first precondition before launching an enhanced cooperation, it must be established that the envisioned objective "cannot be attained within a reasonable period by the Union as a whole" (Art. 20 (2) TFEU). This itself needs to be confirmed by the Council, giving its members full influence in the process, though the decision is taken by qualified majority.[115] It is only then that Member States may move to enhanced cooperation "as a last resort". To establish that this is the case, it usually (while not necessarily) takes a failed legislative procedure.[116] In the words of the CJEU, it is "quite clearly" not possible that "all fruitless negotiations could lead to one or more instances of enhanced cooperation, to the detriment of the search for a compromise enabling the adoption of legislation for the Union as a whole".[117] Therefore, it can hardly be argued that Member States critical of a project can merely be bypassed when establishing enhanced cooperation.[118]

Secondly, a minimum of nine Member States need to address the European Commission with "a request [...] specifying the scope and objectives of the enhanced cooperation proposed" (Art. 329 (1) TFEU). Thus, in a procedure that is exceptional in EU law, it is not the Commission which does the first step in a procedure, but the Member States, which gain a sort of a "*right to initiative—initiative*"[119]. While this somewhat weakens the position of the Commission in the process of establishing an enhanced cooperation, and strengthens that of the Member States, it underlines the Commission's role as a "neutral guardian

[115] See e.g. Council Decision 2010/405/EU, para. 4, or Council Decision 2013/52/EU, para. 5.

[116] For more details, see Chap. 3 on the last resort principle.

[117] CJEU, C-274/09, 295/09 (Spain and Italy v Council), ECLI:EU:C:2013:240, para. 49.

[118] Arguing in this direction, see e.g. Lamping, M. (2013), 'Enhanced Cooperation in the Area of Unitary Patent Protection—Testing the Boundaries of the Rule of Law', *Maastricht J. Eur. Comp. L.*, pp. 589–600.

[119] Zeitzmann, S. (2011), 'Das Verfahren der Verstärkten Zusammenarbeit und dessen erstmalige Anwendung: Ein Ehescheidungs- und Trennungsrecht für Europa', *ZEuS*, pp. 87–113, p. 95.

of community interests", leaving the divisive first step in the procedure to the Member States.[120] Only after the first step from Member States' side does the Commission get to decide whether to submit a proposal for a decision authorising enhanced cooperation. Its only obligation in this respect is to inform the requesting states of its reasons in case of not doing so (Art. 329 (1) TFEU). Hence, while not being able to do the first step towards an enhanced cooperation, the supranational Commission has an irreplaceable role early in the authorisation process.

If the Commission does submit such a proposal, enhanced cooperation requires the consent of the European Parliament. Having obtained this, the Council can adopt an authorising decision by qualified majority. These hurdles, again, ensure that community interests are duly taken into account when authorising an enhanced cooperation. At the same time, the qualified majority in the Council makes sure that every Member State has a significant, but not solely decisive role in the process.

In sum, the authorisation procedure of enhanced cooperation in many ways resembles the community method when adopting EU legislation. A strong involvement of supranational actors ensures that community interest are duly protected when an enhanced cooperation is launched. Despite the fact that the first step towards an enhanced cooperation needs to be done by Member States, the authorisation procedure is characterised by strong supranational elements. The main, yet significant, counterargument to a classification of the mechanism as supranational is the fact that Member States have total freedom in launching the enhanced cooperation procedure, an in deciding whether they want to participate in the enhanced cooperation by being part of the group requesting it, or whether they opt to remain outside the cooperation.

#### 1.4.2.2 Internal Effects

Another crucial element to look at is the effect an enhanced cooperation has on its participants. When an enhanced cooperation is formed or proposed, it gives Member States a fully sovereign possibility and right to choose whether or not to participate. However, once a Member States has opted to join the enhanced cooperation, thus becoming a *participant*, its freedom to act as pleased diminishes significantly. In fact, it has been argued that from communicating the wish

[120] Thym, D. (2009), The Evolution of Supranational Differentiation, WHI-Paper, p. 19.

to participate and its granting by way of authorisation of the enhanced cooperation[121], a Member State is obliged to participate in it and cannot withdraw anymore[122] or only by way of a change of the authorising decision by the Council.[123] Thus, the authorisation of an enhanced cooperation would constitute an act exercising a competence by the EU for the participating Member States, and thus a renunciation of the possibility for those Member States to exercise that competence which cannot be reversed unilaterally.[124] However, the Council secretariat as responsible actor does not share this view,[125] nor does the Commission,[126] both of which concur that withdrawing before the adoption of implementing acts is possible. In fact, Estonia on 10 March 2016 successfully withdrew from the enhanced cooperation on the FTT after its authorisation but before implementing law was passed.[127] Estonia's withdrawal was let passed unchallenged by participants and institutions. With this precedent, it seems that with the authorising decision adopted, but no implementing law passed, Member States are not prevented from withdrawing.[128] Thus, in practice an enhanced cooperation does not have supranational effects before implementing law is passed.

---

[121] Or the confirmation of the participation if the enhanced cooperation is already in progress, (Art. 329 (1) or 331 (1) TFEU).

[122] See e.g. House of Commons, European Scrutiny Committee, 39th Report: Withdrawal from enhanced cooperation: the Committee's evidence session with Baroness Wilcox, https://publications.parliament.uk/pa/cm201012/cmselect/cmeuleg/1341/134102.htm (last access 06/05/2020), para. 25 ff.

[123] Editorial Comments (2011), 'Enhanced cooperation: A Union à taille réduite or à porte tournante?', *CMLRev*, pp. 317–327, p. 323 ff.; Martenczuk, B. (2013), 'Enhanced Cooperation: The Practice of Ad Hoc Differentiation in the EU since the Lisbon Treaty', *StudDipl*, pp. 83–100.

[124] Except by withdrawing from the EU, see Art. 50 TEU.

[125] Council of the European Union, doc. no 6524/11, at http://register.consilium.europa.eu/doc/srv?l=EN&f=ST%206524%202011%20INIT (last access 06/05/2020), para 15; see also Letter to the Chairman from Angel Boixareu, Acting Director General, Directorate-General C, Council of the European Union, 16 November 2011, at https://publications.parliament.uk/pa/cm201012/cmselect/cmeuleg/1822/182205.htm (last access 06/05/2020).

[126] Council document 6520/11 ADD 1 of 11 Feburary 2011, at https://data.consilium.europa.eu/doc/document/ST-6520-2011-INIT/en/pdf (last access 07/05/2020).

[127] See notification of withdrawal by Estonia, http://data.consilium.europa.eu/doc/document/ST-7808-2016-INIT/en/pdf (last access 06/05/2020), and http://data.consilium.europa.eu/doc/document/ST-9602-2016-INIT/en/pdf, para. 4 (last access 06/05/2020).

[128] This may be different if a withdrawal would cause the number of participants to drop under the minimum number of nine required to form an enhanced cooperation (Art. 20 (2) TEU).

This effect is ultimately turned to the opposite once the participating Member States pass implementing law within the enhanced cooperation. Enhanced cooperation legal acts are passed by the usual procedures foreseen for the respective policy areas. This includes the monopoly of initiative by the European Commission and regularly an involvement of the European Parliament. Despite the fact that in lack of transnational lists, MEPs are elected in their respective Member States, the EP always acts as a whole. It is not internally differentiated in the sense that it would represent only members from participating Member States.[129] The EP, therefore, retains its full authority as a supranational representation of Union citizens. Furthermore, enhanced cooperation, so far, has only been used in fields governed by unanimity in the Council. The fact that enhanced cooperation enables interested Member States to pass EU law in such areas against the opposition of one or several Council Members moves the decision-making away from the intergovernmental method, in which a single veto stops a legislative process altogether and closer to the Community method—limited, of course, by the fact that the opposing Member States are not bound by the outcome. As such, the enhanced cooperation mechanism allows for *more* decisional supranationality, but limited normative supranationality. Regarding the latter, enhanced cooperation acts are part of the EU's *acquis*. On the participants, they are binding just like any other EU legal act.[130] As such, enhanced cooperation is a vehicle to lift a matter of—thus far—Member State action out of the national states' hands to the level of supranational Union action for the states involved. From this point on, enhanced cooperation legal acts are endowed with all character traits of supranational acts, such as uniform direct effect, primacy of application, a duty to ensure fulfilment of arising obligation by taking all appropriate domestic means (Art. 4 (3) TEU),

[129] On this, see Curtin, D., Fasone, C. (2017), 'Differentiated representation: is a flexible European Parliament desirable?' in: Witte, B. de, Ott, A., Vos, E. (eds.), *Between Flexibility and Disintegration: The Trajectory of Differentiation in EU Law,* Edward Elgar Publishing Limited, pp. 118–145; Paggi, E. (2017), *Acquis, integrazione differenziata, unità dell'ordinamento dell'unione: verso nuovi modelli di integrazione in Europa?: Spunti di una riflessione teorica a valle dell'introduzione del c.d. pacchetto sul brevetto europeo con effetto unitario.*, Padua, para. 306; Thym, D. (2004), *Ungleichzeitigkeit und europäisches Verfassungsrecht*, Schriftenreihe europäisches Verfassungsrecht, Baden-Baden, Nomos, p. 365 ff.; an astonishing proposal in this regard is made by the EP itself, which proposed by the EP itself, which proposes parliamentary scrutiny by sub-committes made up "primarily" of MEPs elected in the participating Member States: European Parliament resolution of 12 February 2019 on the implementation of the Treaty provisions concerning enhanced cooperation (2018/2112(INI), para. 26.

[130] Blanke, H.-J. (2013), 'Art. 20 TEU' in: Blanke, H.-J., Mangiameli, S. (eds.), *The Treaty on European Union (TEU): A commentary,* Berlin, Springer, pp. 787–830.

and an obligatory jurisdiction of the CJEU with the monopoly of interpretation. The application of enhanced cooperation law, like that of any other type of EU law, is monitored by the European Commission, which can bring infringement proceedings to the CJEU if need be.

In addition, Member States have the opportunity to opt for even further-going (decisional) supranational effects within an enhanced cooperation: Again, enhanced cooperation is thought to be—and so far has only been—used in fields governed by unanimous decision-making in the Council, though not excluded in fields governed by QMV.[131] Within enhanced cooperation, Member State have the possibility to switch from unanimous decision-making in the Council to a regular legislative procedure and QMV decision-making instead (the so-called *passarelle clause*, Art. 333 TFEU). Outside enhanced cooperation, this is only possible in a limited number of fields,[132] and with higher formal hurdles.[133] This enables enhanced cooperation Member States to further supranationalise enhanced cooperation policies.

Although all previous enhanced cooperations occurred in fields requiring unanimity in the Council, such cooperations in fields governed by QMV are legally possible—in fact, enhanced cooperation is admissible from groups as small as nine Member States.[134] Logically, this would take a situation in which less Member States than required for a qualified majority would pursue a project through enhanced cooperation. However, the authorisation of such an enhanced cooperation would still require a qualified majority in the Council (Art. 329 (1) subpara. 2 TFEU and Art. 16 (3) TEU). Hence, the interested states would require a 'helper-state', i.e. a state that would be willing to lend its vote to the group without wanting to participate (for more details on this concept, see Sect. 2.2.1 on QMV enhanced cooperation). This hypothesis puts the statement that enhanced cooperation entails decisional supranationality in question: not only would interested Member States not be able to pass the law they are interested in at least among themselves, but they would even have to convince at least one other state to grant them its aid in pursuing the project. The

---

[131] See Sect. 2.2.1 (→ scope of enhanced cooperation, QMV enhanced cooperations).

[132] Böttner, R. (2017), 'Brückenklauseln im europäischen Verfassungsrecht', *EuR*, Vol. 52, No. 3, pp. 381–400.

[133] Thym, D. (2009), The Evolution of Supranational Differentiation, WHI-Paper, p. 24; Zeitzmann, S. (2015), 'Zuviel gewollt, zu wenig geregelt? Das komplizierte Verhältnis der Verstärkten Zusammenarbeit zum aquis communautaire' in: Stratenschulte, E. D. (ed.), *Der Anfang vom Ende?: Formen differenzierter Integration und ihre Konsequenzen,* Nomos, pp. 103–134 p. 121 ff.

[134] See Sect. 2.2.1 (→ scope of enhanced cooperation, QMV enhanced cooperations).

same goes for enhanced cooperations in areas with unanimous decision-making for groups smaller than the QMV threshold requires.[135] In both cases, intergovernmental negotiations seem inevitable to reach the desired effect. This effect in only mitigated by the paradox that once authorised, a QMV enhanced cooperation would automatically use QMV decision-making also internally when passing implementing law, which then marks a high level of decisional supranationality.

In conclusion, it is important to point out that "supranationality does not strive for unity".[136] Despite the fact that not all Member States are involved, and while in a way the position of Member States' governments before enhanced cooperation has been enacted is even strengthened, once this has occurred, enhanced cooperation has full supranational effects on its participants that can even go beyond what is possible in regular EU decision making. In sum, enhanced cooperation is characterised by strong decisional supranationality and existent—but only internal—normative supranationality.

#### 1.4.2.3 External Effects

A look at external effects unveils a different pattern. In fact, when a policy field is governed by an enhanced cooperation, it is lifted to the European level only for the participating Member States. For non-participants, the policy area stays within the competence of the national authorities. For them, first of all, enhanced cooperation therefore has the opposite of a supranational effect. As they are free to choose whether or not to participate, and can change their opinion and join the enhanced cooperation almost unilaterally whenever they want (Art. 20 (1) TEU, Art. 331 TFEU). Moreover, they are privileged in that they have the possibility to observe developments and even participate in discussions regarding ongoing enhanced cooperations in the Council (without, of course, being able to vote), Art. 330 TFEU. Thus, non-participating Member States, in a way, are even in a particularly sovereign position, which points towards an intergovernmental nature of enhanced cooperation.

However, this observation excludes several aspects. Firstly, it must be noted that the reason why large parts of the European integration occur is because the European states individually lack the possibility to regulate phenomena that go beyond their borders, and the possibility to influence the behaviour of other

[135] This case actually occurred when the enhanced cooperation on a financial transaction tax was authorised.

[136] Somek, A. (2002), 'On Supranationality', *EIoP*, Vol. 5, No. 3, pp. 1–15, with further reference to Weiler, J. H. H. (2000), 'Federalism and Constitutionalism: Europe's Sonderweg'.

states.[137] Secondly, it has been widely observed that the effects of EU law often go beyond its borders ("extra-territorial effects").[138] This has also been observed with respect to effects of enhanced cooperation-law on non-participating Member States.[139] This further limits the sovereignty of non-participants. Finally, and maybe most importantly, non-participation in an enhanced cooperation does not mean that the respective state disagrees with a policy measure. The outsiders' opposition may just regard the way the measure is supposed to be implemented, rather than the measure itself.[140] In this case, an enhanced cooperation in a given field deprives them of their means to meaningfully change the proposal in their interest.[141] Thus, with regard to the mere decision of participation in an enhanced cooperation, the mechanism gives the outsiders a strong sovereign position, while when viewing the sovereignty of Member States at large, the picture is more nuanced.

At the same time, not participating in an enhanced cooperation, and thus avoiding the supranational effect of EU law in a specific field of law, does not in any way move the respective Member State away from the supranational order of the EU in general. *Weiler* described the EU as having an "all-or-nothing-effect" as a fundamental element of the EU's supranationality. According to this, a state is either completely *in* and has to apply EU law due to supremacy, direct effect and the system of judicial review, or has to withdraw from the EU—selective application or disapplication is not possible.[142] While this remains true for the

[137] Weiler, J. H. H. (1981), 'The Community System: the Dual Character of Supranationalism', *Yearbook of European Law*, Vol. 1, No. 1, pp. 267–306, p. 304.

[138] [34] Scott, J. (2014), 'Extraterritoriality and Territorial Extension in EU Law', *American Journal of Comparative Law*, Vol. 62, No. 1, pp. 87–125; for a wider view on the topic, see Cremona, M., Scott, J. (2019), *EU law beyond EU borders: The extraterritorial reach of EU law / edited by Marise Cremona and Joanne Scott*, The collected courses of the Academy of European Law, Oxford, Oxford University Press.

[139] Especially regarding the enhanced cooperation on a Financial Transaction Tax, should it ever see the enactment of implementing law: see arguments of UK in case C-209/13 (*United Kingdom v Council*), ECLI:EU:C:2014:283, para. 18 ff.

[140] As was the case in the enhanced cooperation on a unitary patent, which Spain and Italy only opposed because of language regime foreseen by the majority of Member States, and were otherwise positive about.

[141] A practice that the CJEU did not object to, see C-274/09, 295/09 (*Spain and Italy v Council*) ECLI:EU:C:2013:240.

[142] Weiler, J. H. H. (1981), 'The Community System: the Dual Character of Supranationalism', *Yearbook of European Law*, Vol. 1, No. 1, pp. 267–306, p. 297. According to Weiler, this is nothing less than a "replacement of the virtually voluntary character of state obedience which characterises the classical international order with a binding judicial process."

vast majority of legal fields, the completely free Member State decision to join an enhanced cooperation or not—as opposed to differentiated policy areas with predetermined membership, such as Eurozone or Schengen law—is a notable exception from this all-or-nothing-effect.[143] If one were to regard the all-or-nothing-effect as a substantive trade of a supranational legal order, the existence of enhanced cooperation could put the supranational nature of the entire EU legal order in question. However, the fact that the right to choose only occurs in fields not determined by the outsiders, but on the contrary only in fields where *other* Member States decided to move ahead in integration, as well as the fact that non-participation in an enhanced cooperation leaves other EU law obligations entirely untouched, counters this hypothesis. Notwithstanding this, the position outsiders find themselves is enough to say that enhanced cooperation cannot be regarded as an entirely supranational mechanism.

#### 1.4.2.4 Special Cases

Enhanced cooperation can be used in a large number of fields in the Union's non-exclusive competences. For a number of fields, however, there are special rules for the implementation of enhanced cooperation, which may shed a different light on the level of supranationality of the mechanism.

On the one hand, these are special rules regarding enhanced cooperations in the AFSJ, which were previously introduces as 'facilitated enhanced cooperation clauses'. In fields such as the establishment of a European Public Prosecutor's Office (Art. 86 TFEU), legislation in procedural or substantive criminal law (Art. 82, 83 TFEU), or police cooperation (Art. 87 TFEU), enhanced cooperations can be passed using a facilitated authorisation mechanism.

On the other hand, according to Art. 329 (2) TFEU, enhanced cooperations can be passed in the field of CFSP. Most importantly, authorisation to proceed in these fields is granted by the Council acting unanimously, as *opposed to QMV in regular enhanced cooperation.*

##### 1.4.2.4.1 AFSJ Enhanced Cooperations

In general, the AFSJ, although having been unionised by the Lisbon Treaty, "still bears the indelible mark of its historically intergovernmental nature and

[143] On this, see also Paggi, E. (2017), *Acquis, integrazione differenziata, unità dell'ordinamento dell'unione: verso nuovi modelli di integrazione in Europa?: Spunti di una riflessione teorica a valle dell'introduzione del c.d. pacchetto sul brevetto europeo con effetto unitario.*, Padua.

its highly sensitive nature in terms of national sovereignty".[144] Therefore, first of fall, decision-making in the Council still tends to be unanimous, giving the Member States a strong say on policy measures.

Against this background, it is AFSJ and more precisely the judicial cooperation on criminal matters where Treaty-drafters referred to enhanced cooperation in the most experimental manner throughout the Treaties to calibrate the equilibrium between intergovernmental and supranational elements.

On the one hand, even where QMV decision-making is used for a change, so-called 'emergency brakes' where introduced to the Treaties (Art. 82 (3), 83 (3) TFEU): where Member States fundamentally disagree with a policy measure that could be passed by QMV, they may suspend the legislative procedure and refer the matter to the European Council. The procedure only goes on if the European Council finds a solution that all Member States agree to. As such, the community method and consequently supranational decision-making is significantly weakened by the emergency breaks. As a counter-measure in favour of Member States interested in policy measures, the adoption of enhanced cooperation is significantly facilitated in these cases.[145] If the European Council does not reach a conclusion within four months after an emergency break has been invoked, a group of at least nine Member States may notify the Council, Commission and Parliament of their intention to launch enhanced cooperation. The authorisation to proceed, which usually would require the multi-step procedure set out above, shall then be deemed to be granted.[146] Notably, given the fact that decision-making under both legal bases concerned would regularly be governed by QMV, this also applies within an enhanced cooperation, with no more emergency brakes applicable. In sum, enhanced cooperation serves a counter-balance partially preserving the possibility of supranational decision making for interested Member States where emergency brakes are inserted in the Treaties in the AFSJ.

On the other hand, the contrary happens in the cases of Art. 86, 87 TFEU. Both of these legal bases are governed by unanimous decision-making in the Council, following what one would expect in AFSJ. However, here, too, Treaty-drafters used enhanced cooperation to add a pinch of supranationality as a counter-balance. In this case, in absence of unanimity, a group of at least nine

---

[144] Weyembergh, A. (2018), 'Enhanced cooperation in criminal matters: past, present and future' in: Kert, R., Lehner, A. (eds.), *Vielfalt des Strafrechts im internationalen Kontext: Festschrift für Frank Höpfel zum 65. Geburtstag,* Wien, Graz, NWV, pp. 605–624, p. 606.

[145] Weyembergh, A. (2018), 'Enhanced cooperation in criminal matters: past, present and future' in: Kert, R., Lehner, A. (eds.), *Vielfalt des Strafrechts im internationalen Kontext: Festschrift für Frank Höpfel zum 65. Geburtstag,* Wien, Graz, NWV, pp. 605–624, p. 609.

[146] Art. 82 (3), 83 (3), 86 (1) subpara. 3, 87 (3) TFEU.

Member States may refer a the European Council. In case of disagreement, at least nine Member States may notify the Council, Commission and Parliament and enhanced cooperation shall, again be deemed to be authorised without further procedural steps ('brake and accelerator clause'). Here, enhanced cooperation give interested chance to forge ahead, again acting as a counter balance against the intergovernmental nature of the policy area concerned.

What is interesting about these facilitated enhanced cooperation measures is that they are—as explained above—explicitly meant to be a counterweight to measures strengthening the intergovernmental aspects of AFSJ (i.e. to emergency brakes or unanimity requirements). Yet, in skipping the usual authorisation procedure and consequently the involvement of the supranational actors Commission and EP, they leave out important actors ensuring the safeguarding of Union interests and abandon the supranational decision-making with QMV, affecting decisional supranationality. In enabling EU law to come into effect without having been endorsed in any way by a majority of Member States, it also strengthens the sovereignty of interested Member States, especially in case of smaller subgroups resorting to the facilitated authorisation procedure[147]. Nevertheless, the outcome of such cooperations continues to be internally normative supranational EU law.

In consequence, while the facilitated enhanced cooperation mechanism is designed to counterbalance the intergovernmental elements of the emergency break in some and unanimity in other AFSJ legal bases, it does so by weakening supranational elements in decision-making. The outcome is nevertheless a supranational legal act. As such, AFSJ enhanced cooperation facilitates the access to law with normative supranational effects, but weakens the decisional supranationality of the process leading to it.

#### 1.4.2.4.2 CFSP Enhanced Cooperation

Enhanced cooperations in the field of CFSP depart from the regular enhanced cooperation mechanism in a very different way than AFSJ enhanced cooperations do. In fact, the term 'facilitated' enhanced cooperation, as used for the AFSJ particularities, would in no way be appropriate for the CFSP area.

The Common Foreign and Security Policy traditionally has been and still is by far the most intergovernmental area of EU politics. This is exemplified by the

---

[147] It is important to note that in practice, such small group action has not occurred so far. The only enhanced cooperation passed in the facilitated authorisation procedure as of today was the enhanced cooperation on a European Prosecutor's Office, which initially had 16 participants, which would have constituted a qualified majority at the time; Notification letters EPPO, Council, Doc. No. 8027/17.

facts that Art. 24 (1) TEU prohibits the adoption of legal acts in the CFSP area, limiting the EU's capabilities to non-legislative action such as joint programmes, and Art. 275 TFEU withholds the field from the jurisdiction of the CJEU. Nevertheless, Art. 329 (2) TFEU explicitly mentions the possibility and sets out a procedure to establish enhanced cooperations in the CFSP area.[148]

According to Art. 329 (2) TFEU, a request for a CFSP enhanced cooperation is not addressed to the Commission but directly to the Council. Consequently, a Commission proposal for the authorisation decision is not necessary.[149] The authorisation decision must be taken unanimously in the Council—a requirement that completely changes the mechanism and turns its purpose from being a "veto-buster"[150] or at least a way for interested Member States to proceed despite the resistance of other states to a procedure depending on the goodwill of *all* Member States, even if some do not want to participate in a project themselves. As such, its functioning may overlap with the possibility of constructive abstentions as offered by Art. 31 (1) TEU. Prior to the authorisation of a CFSP enhanced cooperation, the request must be forwarded to the High Representative on Foreign Affairs for an opinion on its compatibility with the Union's overall foreign and security policy, as well as to the Commission for an opinion on the compatibility with other EU policies. Both opinions are non-binding. The Parliament merely needs to be informed.

To join a CFSP enhanced cooperation, interested Member States must be admitted by a unanimous Council decision of the participating Member States (Art. 331 (1) TFEU). The principle of openness (Art. 328 (1) TFEU) that usually characterises enhanced cooperation formally applies to CFSP enhanced cooperation as well as to a regular one, however its enforceability is limited, as the participating Member States and not the neutral Commission decide on the participation. While this limits sovereignty of non-participants, which could be an indication of supranationality, it gives a fully sovereign decision to each of the participating Member States' governments on whether the applying state may join the enhanced cooperation, while supranational actors guarding Union interests are once again excluded. The *passarelle*-clause that allows passing from unanimous to QMV voting in the Council in enhanced cooperation set-ups is not

[148] See Cremona, M. (2009), 'Enhanced Cooperation and the Common Foreign and Security and Defence Policies of the EU', *EUI Working Papers*, No. 21; and below, Sect. 2.3.2.3.1).

[149] On the effect of this on supranationality, Thym, D. (2004), *Ungleichzeitigkeit und europäisches Verfassungsrecht*, Schriftenreihe europäisches Verfassungsrecht, Baden-Baden, Nomos.

[150] Thym, D. (2005), 'United in Diversity: The Integration of Enhanced Cooperation into the European Constitutional Order', *GLJ*, pp. 1731–1747.

totally exempted from applying to CFSP enhanced cooperation, but is limited to decision without military and defence implications (Art. 333 (3) TFEU).

Summarising, the CFSP enhanced cooperation largely differs from the regular mechanism, mirroring the intergovernmental nature of CFSP. The involvement of supranational actors is reduced to providing (Commission, High Representative) and receiving information (Commission, Parliament). The CJEU is totally excluded. In line with the rest of the EU framework on CFSP, the supranational community method does not apply and the area is governed intergovernmentally. While this hinders swift Union action on foreign affairs, it can be argued that this lack in supranationalism ensures that where external Union action is adopted, all Member States subscribe to it, or they are at least not openly against it. Anything else would impair the policy's effectiveness towards external entities much more than internal differentiation does.[151]

#### 1.4.2.5 Enhanced Cooperation as a Case of 'Supranational Differentiation'?

If one were to define the term 'supranational differentiation' in the EU on an empty drawing board, one would most effectively refer back to the criteria defining supranationalism as laid out above, and probably start looking at the normative supranationalism. According to this, for differentiated EU law to be supranational, it would have to have primacy over national law, direct effect, would oblige Member States to implement it and feature obligatory CJEU jurisdiction. With the exception of the non-participants, who naturally do not have to implement enhanced cooperation law, all these boxes are ticked by the enhanced cooperation legal framework. Regarding decisional supranationalism, one would have to conclude that supranational differentiation would have to be proposed by the Commission and enacted on the EU level with a majority decision in the Council and the Parliament. The authorisation of an enhanced cooperation decision is indeed passed by the EP and the Council, which uses qualified majority voting. However, the decision is proposed by Member States and not the Commission. More importantly, however, while the authorisation is decided by qualified majority in the Council, the effects of this decision leave non-participants untouched on the basis of their own individual choice. One could argue that an 'ideal' supranational differentiation mechanism ('ideal' is not, in any way, meant in the sense of 'desirable' in this context, but as thoroughly fulfilling the criteria of supranationality) could address the EU as a whole and could determine *on the supranational level* who participates and who does not, as opposed

151 Thym, D. (2009), The Evolution of Supranational Differentiation, WHI-Paper.

to that decision being taken on the national (i.e.: governmental) level. Such a mechanism would probably determine the participants and non-participants on the basis of certain objective criteria.

In reality, a number of scholars have been writing about the existence of *supranational differentiation* within the EU legal order, and have concluded that enhanced cooperation is part of it. In doing so, they have chosen a less far-reaching definition of supranational differentiation based on the idea that it features normatively supranational EU law with a limited geographic scope of EU law and a corresponding suspension of the voting rights of the non-participating Member States in the Council.[152] From the perspective depicted above, one could conclude that the term 'supranational' differentiation is misleading in this context, as the decision on participation or not is taken on an individual, governmental level.[153] However, the authors focus on the numerous other supranational effects of enhanced cooperation, which still go far beyond the degree of supranationality of other legal orders beyond the nation-state and thus conclude that it is, in fact, a supranational differentiation mechanism because it is "deliberately designed on the basis of the supranational integration method"[154], which is still "compatible with the cherished principles of legal supranationalism"[155]. It is for these reasons, they argue, that enhanced cooperation, which from this point of view could even be named "enhanced integration"[156] or "intensified or reinforced integration"[157], "do[es] not contradict the Community method; [its]

[152] Thym, D. (2009), The Evolution of Supranational Differentiation, WHI-Paper; Becerill, B. (2009), 'The regulation of enhanced cooperation and its reform in Lisbon: Towards a model of differentiation that is closer to the community method' in: Beneyto Pérez, J. M., Baquero Cruz, J. (eds.), *Unity and flexibility in the future of the European Union: The challenge of enhanced cooperation,* Madrid, CEU Ediciones, pp. 9–20; Böttner, R. (2021), *The Constitutional Framework for Enhanced Cooperation in EU law*, Nijhoff studies in European Union law, Leiden The Netherlands, Koninklijke Brill NV.

[153] Similarly Paggi, E. (2017), *Acquis, integrazione differenziata, unità dell'ordinamento dell'unione: verso nuovi modelli di integrazione in Europa?: Spunti di una riflessione teorica a valle dell'introduzione del c.d. pacchetto sul brevetto europeo con effetto unitario.*, Padua.

[154] Thym, D. (2009), The Evolution of Supranational Differentiation, WHI-Paper.

[155] Thym, D. (2018), 'Legal Solution vs Discursive Othering: The (Dis)Integrative Effects of Supranational Differentiation', *SSRN Electronic Journal.*

[156] Böttner, R. (2021), *The Constitutional Framework for Enhanced Cooperation in EU law,* Nijhoff studies in European Union law, Leiden The Netherlands, Koninklijke Brill NV.

[157] Own translation: „Integracíon intensificada o reforzada", Mangas Martín, A. (1998), 'Las cooperaciones reforzadas en el Tratado de Ámsterdam', *Comunidad Europea Aranzadi,* No. 10, pp. 27–38.

strength is the accommodation of national political diversity with supranational integration through law".[158]

#### 1.4.2.6 Conclusion on Enhanced Cooperation's Position Between Supranationality and Intergovernmentalism

When evaluating the degree of supranationality of the enhanced cooperation mechanism—at least in its regular form –, much depends on the perspective.

Internally, enhanced cooperation has strong supranational features. It is characterised by full involvement of supranational Union institutions, including an obligatory jurisdiction of the CJEU. Enhanced cooperation legal acts have the primacy and direct effect of all EU law vis-à-vis the participating Member States. If the policy area in question is not already governed by majority voting, enhanced cooperation makes it easier to switch to that procedure. One could also conclude that enhanced cooperation always causes *internal* supranationalisation. On the other hand, non-participants are not primarily affected, let alone bound against their will, by enhanced cooperation law and they retain a completely sovereign decision on whether or not to participate in an enhanced cooperation project. Nevertheless, their sovereignty may still be touched more by an enhanced cooperation than by international law that they do not participate in. The special nature of EU law, even if passed within an enhanced cooperation, leaves a mark also on non-participants. In sum, therefore, it seems largely justified to regard the regular enhanced cooperation as an example of "supranational differentiation",[159] although it can never have the same degree of supranationality as uniformly applicable Union law.[160]

[158] Thym, D. (2009), The Evolution of Supranational Differentiation, WHI-Paper.

[159] Thym, D. (2009), The Evolution of Supranational Differentiation, WHI-Paper; Becerill, B. (2009), 'The regulation of enhanced cooperation and its reform in Lisbon: Towards a model of differentiation that is closer to the community method' in: Beneyto Pérez, J. M., Baquero Cruz, J. (eds.), *Unity and flexibility in the future of the European Union: The challenge of enhanced cooperation,* Madrid, CEU Ediciones, pp. 9–20; Böttner, R. (2021), *The Constitutional Framework for Enhanced Cooperation in EU law*, Nijhoff studies in European Union law, Leiden The Netherlands, Koninklijke Brill NV.

[160] Paggi, E. (2017), *Acquis, integrazione differenziata, unità dell'ordinamento dell'unione: verso nuovi modelli di integrazione in Europa?: Spunti di una riflessione teorica a valle dell'introduzione del c.d. pacchetto sul brevetto europeo con effetto unitario.*, Padua, para. 389, "una forma di differenziazione partecipativa che ambisce ad essere il più possibile vicina al metodo comunitario, in cui tuttavia resta evidente una certa tensione tra le due componenti".

When regarding the special form of enhanced cooperation, facilitated enhanced cooperation in the AFSJ and CFSP enhanced cooperation, the mechanism loses some of its supranational features. In AFSJ, this is the cost for facilitating the access to supranational law. In CFSP, in which even enhanced cooperation is governed by unanimity, it rather tends to be a mechanism for rebalancing Member States' interests in an area strongly characterised by intergovernmental decision-making.

As a final note on practical experiences with the enhanced cooperation mechanism, it is interesting to note that the contrast between supranationality and intergovernmentalism of enhanced cooperation reappeared within the implementation of one of the enhanced cooperation projects, namely the European Public Prosecutor's Office (EPPO). In fact, the rift between the Council and the Parliament in terms of casting the head of the new EPPO—established by 22 Member States via enhanced cooperation—in many ways resembles the rift between intergovernmentalists and supranationalists. The—supranational—Parliament favoured one candidate, the Council—representative body of the EU Member States' governments and therefore by definition an intergovernmental body—favoured another. The Parliament's pick was a strong public prosecutor, a fighter with an uncompromising attitude who was not supported by its own government, and who would most likely fight corruption and fraud wherever she saw it, without much concern for national—or any other—sensitivities. In other words, one could say the Parliament chose a supranational type of candidate. The Council's candidate on the other hand is a true diplomat, multilingual, well-connected in all European capitals, a power broker who would ensure a smooth start of the new office, making sure the EPPO would be respected by national courts, have allies and get support wherever it tries to prosecute a case. This could have, however, in the eyes of critics possibly required some looking-the-other-way.

On 17 December 2019, the European Parliament's favourite Laura Kövesi was confirmed as the first European Public Prosecutor.

# 2 The Real Scope of Application of Enhanced Cooperation—Between Legal Constraints and Incentive Structures

A fundamental question regarding enhanced cooperation, defining the mechanism and the possibilities it has to offer to EU politics, is when it can be put to use. In what follows, I aim zoom in on what little Treaty text that there is on the scope of application of enhanced cooperation, taking into account also the surrounding Treaty provisions that significantly shape how the black-letter law is lived in practice, as well as political considerations and incentive structures that factually exclude enhanced cooperation in many areas. All of this is done with the aim of understanding *where* the use of enhanced cooperation is legally and practically imaginable—and thus, in which areas decision makers can realistically consider enhanced cooperation when trying to overcome challenges at hand.

## 2.1 Legal Framework

Enhanced cooperation's scope of application is set out at the very beginning of the norms regulating the mechanism, namely in Art. 20.1 TEU:

> *Member States which wish to establish enhanced cooperation between themselves within the framework of the Union's non-exclusive competences may [...] exercise those competences by applying the relevant provisions of the Treaties [...].*

Moreover, it is repeated in Art. 329 (1) TFEU:

> *Member States which wish to establish enhanced cooperation between themselves in one of the areas covered by the Treaties, with the exception of fields of exclusive competence and the common foreign and security policy, shall address a request to the Commission, specifying the scope and objectives of the enhanced cooperation proposed.*


J. Graf von Luckner, *Enhanced Cooperation Revisited*,
https://doi.org/10.1007/978-3-658-51063-3_2

The latter norm gives the expression that the common foreign and security policy (CFSP) is excluded from the scope of application of enhanced cooperation. However, Art. 329 (2) TFEU clarifies that CFSP enhanced cooperations just follow a different authorisation procedure.

This leaves us with a partitioning of EU competences in exclusive and shared competences which is all the Treaties explicitly say on where enhanced cooperation can be put to use. This rough division in fields of exclusive competence that enhanced cooperation is banned from and fields of shared competence where it is admissible opens a vast field of potential applicability of the differentiation mechanism. However, this black-letter law answer is, in reality, only a timid first step in assessing the question. Enhanced cooperation is limited further by several factors that lie both in additional legal criteria in Art. 20 TEU, Art. 326–334 TFEU, which formally regulate other matters but strongly influence the mechanism's scope.

To approach the legal framework of the scope of application of enhanced cooperation, as a first step, I will look into the history of the general norm outlining it, tracing back earlier versions (1). As the scope of application of enhanced cooperation is pre-defined by the EU's competence typology, it will then be crucial to explore it from an enhanced cooperation point of view (2). This will include an analysis of the CJEU's case-law regarding the scope of application of enhanced cooperation. Finally, I will explore the other material legal boundaries of the enhanced cooperation in order to duly take them into account when assessing the factual scope of application of enhanced cooperation (3).

### 2.1.1 History

The Treaty of Amsterdam was the first treaty mentioning a structurally embedded form of differentiated integration under the name of "closer cooperation".[1] Regarding its scope of application, it stated:

[1] This applies for the English language version. Other, e.g. the Italian and German versions already changed the name of the mechanism to what in English later became "enhanced cooperation" ("verstärkte Zusammenarbeit" and "cooperazione rafforzata" rather than the earlier terms "engere Zusammenarbeit" and "cooperazione più stretta").

Art. 11 (1)(a) ECT (Amsterdam):

> *Member States which intend to establish closer cooperation between themselves may be authorised [...] provided that the cooperation proposed: (a) does not concern areas which fall within the exclusive competence of the Community; [...] (d) remains within the limits of the powers conferred upon the Community by this Treaty;*

The Treaty of Nice, succeeding the Amsterdam Treaty, introduced the current term "enhanced cooperation", but left the scope of application largely unchanged. However, in the TEU (Nice), parallel to Art. 11 ECT, a reference to the non-exclusive competences was added in Art. 43:

Art. 43 TEU (Nice)

> *Member States which intend to establish enhanced cooperation between themselves may make use of the institutions, procedures and mechanisms laid down by this Treaty and by the Treaty establishing the European Community provided that the proposed cooperation:*
>
> *[...]*
>
> *(d) remains within the limits of the powers of the Union or of the Community and does not concern the areas which fall within the exclusive competence of the Community;*

Hence, both predecessors to nowadays' Lisbon Treaty already outlined the scope of application of enhanced cooperation in a similar way to their successor, limiting the mechanism to the EU's non-exclusive competences. However, the major difference was that the competence system prior to the Lisbon Treaty was largely defined by CJEU case law and therefore unwritten.[2] The explicit, written categorisation of certain competences as exclusive as opposed to other non-exclusive competences was only effectively introduced by the Lisbon Treaty.[3]

The draft Constitutional Treaty, which never entered into force, was identical to the Lisbon version in terms of both, categorisation of competences and its statement regarding the scope of application of enhanced cooperation.

---

[2] Garben, S., Govaere, I. (2017), 'The Division of Competences between the EU and the Member States: Reflections on the Past, the Present and the Future' in: Garben, S., Govaere, I. (eds.), *The Division of Competences between the EU and the Member States: Reflections on the Past, the Present and the Future,* Hart Publishing;

[3] Streinz, R. (2018), 'Art. 2 AEUV' in: Streinz, R. (ed.), *EUV/AEUV: Vertrag über die Europäische Union, Vertrag über die Arbeitsweise der Europäischen Union, Charta der Grundrechte der Europäischen Union,* München, C. H.Beck.

## 2.1.2 Non-Exclusive Union Competences

There are three main types of competences outlined in the Treaties: Exclusive competences (Art. 2 (1), 3 TFEU), shared competences (Art. 2 (2), 4 TFEU), and complementary competences[4] ("competence [...] to support, coordinate or supplement", Art. 2 (5), 6 TFEU). Parallel competences as outlined by Art. 4 (3, 4) TFEU and the coordinating competence in economic, employment, and social area (Art. 5 TFEU) can be regarded sub-cases of the category of shared competences.[5] In addition, there is a separate competence type for the CFSP (Art. 2 (4) TFEU), which is governed mostly on an intergovernmental level and therefore situated closest to the competence sphere of the Member States.

Besides, there are, of course, the exclusive Member States' competences. They are explicitly mentioned for national security in Art. 4 (2) TEU, but the underlying assumption of the competence system is that each policy field which is not attributed by the Treaties to the Union is subject to exclusive competence of the Member States, following the principle of conferral (Art. 5.2 TEU).

Hence, an enhanced cooperation is possible where a competence is conferred upon the EU and falls within the categories of shared (with all its subcategories) or complementary competences. In addition, Member States have the possibility to launch a special enhanced cooperation following Art. 329 TFEU, in the area of CFSP.

---

[4] Schütze, R. (2015), 'EU Competences: Existence and Exercise' in: Chalmers, D., Arnull, A. (eds.), *The Oxford Handbook of European Union Law,* Oxford University Press, pp. 75–103.

[5] Arg. e. Art. 4 (1) TFEU: "The Union shall share competence with the Member States where the Treaties confer on it a competence which does not relate to the areas referred to in Articles 3 and 6."; Garben, S., Govaere, I. (2017), 'The Division of Competences between the EU and the Member States: Reflections on the Past, the Present and the Future' in: Garben, S., Govaere, I. (eds.), *The Division of Competences between the EU and the Member States: Reflections on the Past, the Present and the Future,* Hart Publishing; Craig, P. (2004), 'Competence: Clarity, conferral, containment and consideration', *ELRev*, Vol. 29, No. 3, pp. 323–344, speaks of "particular instances of shared powers". Others, however, regard them as competence categories of their own, see Blanke, H.-J. (2021), 'Art. 1 TFEU' in: Blanke, H.-J., Mangiameli, S. (eds.), *Treaty on the Functioning of the European Union—A Commentary*; Streinz, R. (2018), 'Art. 4 AEUV' in: Streinz, R. (ed.), *EUV/AEUV: Vertrag über die Europäische Union, Vertrag über die Arbeitsweise der Europäischen Union, Charta der Grundrechte der Europäischen Union,* München, C. H.Beck, Art. 4 para. 12 considers it to be an "aliud" besides the "actually shared competences"; Obwexer, W. (2015), 'Art. 4 AEUV' in: Groeben, H. v. d., Schwarze, J., Hatje, A. (eds.), *Europäisches Unionsrecht,* Baden-Baden, Nomos considers them to be in a "hybrid position", which makes them "shared parallel competences".

Exclusive and non-exclusive competences of the EU are divided by a line that has traditionally been volatile. This is why the current categorisation has partly been described as "problematic":[6] Prior to the Lisbon Treaty, neither the exclusive, nor the non-exclusive competences were explicitly enumerated. The earlier competence demarcation stemmed largely from necessity in light of the principles of primacy and *effet utile*, was categorised only in the academic literature and partly outlined by the CJEU.[7] As EU legislation in a given policy field developed further, it was possible that this field 'switched' from being a shared competence to a field where there was no more space for national regulation, i.e. an exclusive competence. Since the Lisbon Treaty set out to delineate both areas, this is not the case anymore. Nowadays, when determining whether an area is part of the EU's exclusive competences, Art. 3 TFEU largely sets the scene. This does not answer the theoretical question of what would happen if a competence that is not enumerated in this norm grew into a competence that factually excluded any Member State law by way of CJEU legislation, and therefore developed into a *de facto* exclusive competence. However, the clear wording of the Art. 2, 3, 4 TFEU leaves no doubt that such a 'switch' is not foreseen under the ambit of the Lisbon Treaty. The result, a clearer demarcation line between shared and exclusive competences at the price of less flexibility in the development of EU primary law, was indeed actively pursued when drafting the (failed) Constitutional Treaty and subsequently the Lisbon Treaty.[8] Moreover, Art. 2 (2)(3$^{rd}$ sentence) TFEU expressly foresees the possibility that the EU can cease to exercise a shared competence, reopening it for Member State action. This is a further indication that a shared competence stays within the category of shared competences, even if the EU has acted exhaustively within this field.[9]

---

[6] Garben, S., Govaere, I. (2017), 'The Division of Competences between the EU and the Member States: Reflections on the Past, the Present and the Future' in: Garben, S., Govaere, I. (eds.), *The Division of Competences between the EU and the Member States: Reflections on the Past, the Present and the Future,* Hart Publishing.

[7] Streinz, R. (2018), 'Art. 2 AEUV' in: Streinz, R. (ed.), *EUV/AEUV: Vertrag über die Europäische Union, Vertrag über die Arbeitsweise der Europäischen Union, Charta der Grundrechte der Europäischen Union,* München, C. H.Beck; Art. 3 para 2.

[8] See e.g. Craig, P. (2004), 'Competence: Clarity, conferral, containment and consideration', *ELRev*, Vol. 29, No. 3, pp. 323–344.

[9] Calliess, C. (2016), 'Art. 2 TFEU' in: Calliess, C., Ruffert, M. (eds.), *EUV/AEUV: Das Verfassungsrecht der Europäischen Union mit Europäischer Grundrechtecharta: Kommentar,* München, C. H. Beck.

### 2.1.3 Defining the Exception to Understand the Rule: Exclusive EU-Competences

Art. 2.1 TFEU and Art. 3 TFEU lay down the framework of the EU's exclusive competences. They are designed to be the exception to the rule: Wherever a Union competence is not explicitly conferred on the EU exclusively, the competence shall be shared (Art. 4.1 TFEU).

Art. 3 TFEU outlines the areas in which the EU has exclusive competences. These are the customs union, the competition rules necessary for the functioning of the internal market, the monetary policy for the Eurozone, the common commercial policy, and the conservation of marine biological resources within the common fisheries policy. Moreover, the EU has exclusive competence for the conclusion of international agreements in case its conclusion is provided for in a secondary EU legal act, it is necessary to exercise an internal EU competence, or insofar as the agreement may affect EU rules.

It is important to add that Art. 3 TFEU only broadly defines the areas of exclusive EU competences, and consequently the inapplicability of enhanced cooperation. The precise scope of these areas depends, according to Art. 2.6 TFEU, on the treaty provisions relating to those areas. In practice, this means that prior to any EU action, it must be verified that there is a legal base in the TFEU that covers the intended measure. If so, it must be determined by way of interpretation of Art. 3 TFEU whether this subject is part of the EU's exclusive, or its shared or complementary competences. If the latter is the case, the project can, if necessary majority cannot be attained within the Council, be pursued via enhanced cooperation. However, drawing the line between different competence types is an inherently controversial and difficult task, as will be demonstrated below.

### 2.1.4 Scope of Application in the CJEU Case-Law

The issue of competence demarcation has rightfully been described as "the most explosive of federal battlegrounds"[10] and as "*the* key question of a federal European order"[11]. Where competences are divided between two different levels, vital

---

[10] Garben, S., Govaere, I. (2017), 'The Division of Competences between the EU and the Member States: Reflections on the Past, the Present and the Future' in: Garben, S., Govaere, I. (eds.), *The Division of Competences between the EU and the Member States: Reflections on the Past, the Present and the Future,* Hart Publishing.

[11] Blanke 2004, p. 230.

interests of both are touched by definition when deciding whether a policy field is assigned to one or the other.

In the case of disputes regarding EU competences and the division between shared and exclusive competence fields, the positions that can be expected from both are rather clear: When in doubt, the Union level will tend to argue that a field is a matter of an exclusive competence, whereas the Member States will tend to consider subjects to fall under the shared competences.[12] Interestingly, this is not what happens in controversies on enhanced cooperation: When trying to prevent an enhanced cooperation, a coherent position from Member States is to argue that the field in question falls within the *exclusive* competences, whereas the EU, having invested political capital in advancing the enhanced cooperation project, might argue that it is a matter of *shared* competences. This is what happened in the only case in which the question of the scope of application of enhanced cooperation was discussed before the CJEU, namely the case on the Unitary patent,[13] which will be analysed in the following.

#### 2.1.4.1 Background of the Unitary Patent Case

In *Spain/Italy v Council*[14], Spain and Italy tried to stop an enhanced cooperation that the Council had authorised with the aim of creating a unitary patent. After it had been discussed for decades, Member States could not reach the unanimity required for establishing the patent's language regime. As a result, Spain and Italy refused to grant their approval for the project in the Council, and the remaining Member States proceeded using enhanced cooperation.

To stop the project, in their joint action for annulment, Spain and Italy argued, among other things, that the power to create a unitary patent (Art. 118 TFEU) fell within the EU's exclusive competences, and could therefore not be pursued through enhanced cooperation. It is worth noting, however, that the political question which languages should govern the patent and *not* the legal question of competence typology gave rise to the enhanced cooperation. This makes the question of competences a subsequent legal skirmish rather than the main battle.

---

[12] As a recent example, see e.g. CJEU C-626/15, C-659/16 (*Commission v Council*), ECLI:EU:C:2018:925.

[13] CJEU C-274/11, 295/11 (*Spain/Italy v Council*), ECLI:EU:C:2013:240; predicting the outlined paradox: Schauer, M. (2000), *Schengen—Maastricht—Amsterdam: Auf dem Weg zu einer flexiblen Union*, Juristische Schriftenreihe, Wien, Verl. Österreich.

[14] CJEU C-274/11, 295/11 (*Spain/Italy v Council*), ECLI:EU:C:2013:240.

### 2.1.4.2 Argument of the Parties

Both Italy and Spain argued that the Council lacked competence to authorise the enhanced cooperation because the establishment of the unitary patent was an exclusive Union competence. Specifically, they argued that a patent grants a monopoly for its holder and consequently *restricts competition.* Therefore, they claimed, Art. 118 TFEU and thus the unitary patent falls within the exclusive competence to create the "competition rules necessary for the functioning of the internal market" (Art. 3(1)(b) TFEU).[15] Moreover, they argued that the creation of a unitary patent could logically only be an exclusive competence since otherwise, there could be different European patents coexisting.[16]

In addition, Italy argued that the list of exclusive competences in Art. 3 TFEU only outlines a non-binding classification of the EU's sphere of competences. Therefore, Art. 118 TFEU regarding the unitary patent could be considered an exclusive competence even if it does not fall within one of the categories explicitly mentioned in Art. 3 TFEU.[17]

The Council and several parties intervening in its support (Commission, Member States) argued mostly from a systematic point of view. Title VII of the TFEU, which contains both the norms on competition and on the internal market, is divided clearly into "Rules on Competition" (Chap. 1), "Tax Provisions" (Chap. 2), and the "Approximation of Laws" (Chap. 3), which contains the rules on the internal market. Given that Art. 118 TFEU on the unitary patent is included in Chap. 3 and not Chap. 1, and given also that Art. 2.6 TFEU stresses that the provisions of the Treaties relating to each area determine the scope of the competences, it cannot be alleged that Art. 118 TFEU is part of the rules on competition.[18]

Moreover, regarding the argument that a unitary patent could logically only be an exclusive competence, the Commission and Poland pointed out that this argument confuses the nature of the competence conferred and the instrument envisaged for the exercise of that competence. The content of a competence conferred depends on the act of conferral by the Member States, not on the

---

[15] CJEU C-274/11, 295/11 (*Spain/Italy v Council*), ECLI:EU:C:2013:240, para. 1; Opinion of AG *Bot* in C-274/11, C-295/22 (*Spain/Italy v. Council*), ECLI:EU:C:2012:782, para. 34.

[16] Opinion of AG *Bot* in C-274/11, C-295/22 (*Spain/Italy v. Council*), ECLI:EU:C:2012:782, para. 35.

[17] CJEU C-274/11, 295/11 (*Spain/Italy v Council*), ECLI:EU:C:2013:240, para. 14.

[18] CJEU C-274/11, 295/11 (*Spain/Italy v Council*), ECLI:EU:C:2013:240, para. 15; Opinion of AG *Bot* in C-274/11, C-295/22 (*Spain/Italy v. Council*), ECLI:EU:C:2012:782, para. 36 ff.

instrument available.[19] This was underlined by AG *Bot*'s opinion, in which he argued that the principle of subsidiarity ensures that Union action in the field of shared competences is only taken where the Member States cannot or not sufficiently take action. As such, "[t]he fact that the objectives pursued cannot be achieved by the Member States does not [...] mean that the Union has exclusive competence."[20]

#### 2.1.4.3 Findings of the Court

The CJEU largely followed the Council and its supporting parties in their reasoning. The Court starts its findings by stating that "it is of importance to declare straight away" that the competence to create a unitary patent (including the controversial language arrangements) is conferred in the context of the internal market, as stated by Art. 118 TFEU.[21] Moreover, the Court admitted that there is a connection between a unitary patent and competition rules. However, Art. 26 TFEU on the internal market indicates that the rules on the internal market do not only entail the harmonisation competences in Art. 114, 115 TFEU, but also related "relevant rules" (see wording of Art. 26.2 TFEU).[22] Art. 118 TFEU on the unitary patent must not, therefore, be disregarded as a rule on the internal market. In addition, the Court explicitly follows the systematic interpretation of the Council and several Member States according to which the fact that Art. 118 TFEU is not situated within the chapter on competition rules indicates that it does not belong to the latter group of exclusive competences. The argument according to which the competence to create a unitary patent must be exclusive because otherwise, there could be more than one European patent with unitary effect in Europe in parallel, is not even mentioned by the CJEU, which can be interpreted as silent agreement with the counter-arguments of AG *Bot*.

Summarising, the Court states that:

> *To regard Article 118 TFEU as forming part of that area would therefore be contrary to Article 2(6) TFEU and the result would be to extend unduly the scope of Article 3(1)(b) TFEU.*[23]

---

[19] Opinion of AG *Bot* in C-274/11, C-295/22 (*Spain/Italy v. Council*), ECLI:EU:C:2012:782, para. 39.

[20] Opinion of AG *Bot* in C-274/11, C-295/22 (*Spain/Italy v. Council*), ECLI:EU:C:2012:782, para. 62; see also 48 ff.

[21] CJEU C-274/11, 295/11 (*Spain/Italy v Council*), ECLI:EU:C:2013:240, para. 17 f.

[22] CJEU C-274/11, 295/11 (*Spain/Italy v Council*), ECLI:EU:C:2013:240, para. 20 ff.

[23] CJEU C-274/11, 295/11 (*Spain/Italy v Council*), ECLI:EU:C:2013:240, para. 24, emphasis added.

It is noteworthy that it is the first time that the Court uses the strongly worded formula "the result would be to extend unduly the scope of [the EU's exclusive competences]" in its extensive competence case law.[24] Given the contentious nature of competence demarcation disputes, this can also be interpreted as a signal towards the Member States regarding the CJEU's intended future interpretation of the competence framework.

In the literature, the judgement was harshly criticised from the direction of intellectual property lawyers.[25] Their main point of criticism was that Art. 118 TFEU was introduced into the Treaties to supplement Art. 114 TFEU, acting as a counter-part. While Art. 114 TFEU, undisputedly a shared competence, allows for the approximation of (national) intellectual property laws but not the creation of genuine Union rights, Art. 118 TFEU leaves the national rights aside and allows to create a purely European property title, which is interpreted to mean that it should be a matter of exclusive competence despite its location in the TFEU.

However, as can be followed from the CJEU judgment, the relationship to Art. 114 TFEU may be a decisive argument only from an intellectual property law point of view. From the point of view of EU competence law, and especially the essential principle of conferral, it has to be taken into account that decisions for an exclusive competence in case of doubt have to be taken extremely cautiously, especially since the Lisbon Treaty explicitly set out to *contain* EU competences.[26] Most importantly, however, one has to stress the importance of Art. 4.1 TFEU, which states clearly that the default scenario is always that a competence is shared, whereas exclusive competences must be designated clearly in Art. 3 TFEU. In the light of this, an specific relationship to another provision is not enough to justify a classification of Art. 118 TFEU as an exclusive competence. Accordingly, the judgment, or at least its part on competences, was praised

---

[24] As a contrast, see e.g. CJEU C-626/15, C-659/16 (*Commission v Council*), ECLI:EU:C:2018:925.

[25] Lamping, M. (2013), 'Enhanced Cooperation in the Area of Unitary Patent Protection—Testing the Boundaries of the Rule of Law', *Maastricht J. Eur. Comp. L.*, pp. 589–600, 595: "Indeed, a functional allocation of competences requires a little bit more than a glance into the Treaty's table of contents."; Jaeger, T. (2013), 'Einheitspatent—Zulässigkeit der Verstärkten Zusammenarbeit ohne Spanien und Italien', *NJW*, pp. 1998–2001, 1999: "Der schwächste Teil der Urteilsbegründung".

[26] Craig, P. (2004), 'Competence: Clarity, conferral, containment and consideration', *ELRev*, Vol. 29, No. 3, pp. 323–344.

by authors from other disciplines with stronger focus on general EU law and EU Treaty law.[27]

### 2.1.5 Material Legal Boundaries for Enhanced Cooperation

Where a policy field falls under the EU's non-exclusive competences and enhanced cooperation is admissible in principle, the Treaties entail another set of material legal boundaries for enhanced cooperation spread out over Art. 20 TEU, Art. 326–334 TFEU. Other than the procedural principles of last resort[28] and openness[29], the material legal principles do not limit specific enhanced cooperations based on the situation in which they are considered or their specific design. On the contrary, these legal principles are in a position to permanently exclude projects from the scope of enhanced cooperation. The principles are in particular:

1. The aim to further the objectives of the Union, protect its interests and reinforce its integration process (Art. 20.1 (2) TEU)
2. The duty to comply with the Treaties and Union law (Art. 328.1 TFEU)
3. The obligation not to undermine the internal market or economic, social and territorial cohesion. Enhanced cooperation shall not constitute a barrier to or discrimination in trade between Member States, nor shall it distort competition between them (Art. 328.2 TFEU)
4. The duty to ensure consistency of activities undertaken in the context of enhanced cooperation and the consistency of such activities with the policies of the Union (Art. 334 TFEU)

#### 2.1.5.1 Furthering the Objectives of the Union, Protecting its Interests and Reinforcing its Integration Process

The fundamental principle that enhanced cooperation projects must aim to further the objectives of the Union (Art. 20.1 (2) TEU) is one of the first and most important principles to set out the philosophy of the mechanism. It clearly relates to Art. 3 TEU, which defines the aims of the Union. At the same time,

---

[27] Zeitzmann, S. (2013), 'Patentrecht: Ermächtigung zur Verstärkten Zusammenarbeit', *EuZW*, pp. 475–480, Pistoia, E. (2014), 'Enhanced Cooperation as a tool to…enhance integration?: Spain and Italy v. Council', *CMLRev*, pp. 247–260.

[28] Chapter 3.

[29] Chapter 4.

the obligation to further the aims of the Union unveils a structural difficulty of enhanced cooperation: the inherent tension between unity and differentiation.[30] As a starting point, the question whether the objectives of the cooperation further the objectives of the Union can be tested based on the assumption that the law adopted becomes part of the *acquis* eventually, meaning that all Member States joined, which is what enhanced cooperation aims at.[31] Beyond this question of whether a policy generally serves the integration process, the obligation to further the objectives of the Union can substantially be interpreted as an obligation to non-regression; while enhanced cooperation can by definition never reach further integration in the same way as uniform action with all Member States would,[32] enhanced cooperation must not undermine the integration that has been achieved and raise the chances for achieving the objectives and aims of the Union as defined in Art. 3 TEU.[33] In this context, it is important to remember that in the areas of shared competence that enhanced cooperation can be applied in, the Member States are free to act until the Union does. Thus, from the outset, any Union policy may reduce fragmentation among the states, even if cooperation among all states would do so even more.[34]

#### 2.1.5.2 Duty to Comply with the Treaties and Union Law (Art. 328.1 TFEU)

The first and second aims are closely related: Complying with the Treaties and the existing *acquis* as demanded by Art. 328.1 TFEU is, after all, a *conditio sine qua non*, a necessary condition for furthering the objectives of the Union. To some extent, one could argue that it is an obligation that should be clear from the outset—of course any project within the Union must comply with EU law. The legal added value of Art. 328.1 TFEU can be seen in it being a special derogation

---

30 See Sect. 1.1.

31 Böttner, R. (2021), *The Constitutional Framework for Enhanced Cooperation in EU law*, Nijhoff studies in European Union law, Leiden The Netherlands, Koninklijke Brill NV.

32 And this fact has been accepted by the Court, C-274/11 and C-295/11, *Spain and Italy v Council*, ECLI:EU:C:2013:240, para 68, 75.

33 Cede, P. (2019), 'Art. 20 EUV' in: Jaeger, T., Stöger, K. (eds.), *Kommentar zu EUV und AEUV: 85.—220. Lieferung. Kommentar in Faszikeln in Fortführung des Kommentars zu EU- und EG-Vertrag*, Wien, MANZ Verlag Wien; Martenczuk, B. (2013), 'Enhanced Cooperation: The Practice of Ad Hoc Differentiation in the EU since the Lisbon Treaty', *StudDipl*, pp. 83–100.

34 Martenczuk, B. (2013), 'Enhanced Cooperation: The Practice of Ad Hoc Differentiation in the EU since the Lisbon Treaty', *StudDipl*, pp. 83–100.

from the lex posterior principle[35] and at the same time making clear that new enhanced cooperation law cannot fall behind the existing *acquis* in integration. Enhanced cooperation law must therefore strictly and exclusively be added 'on top' of what is already in existence.[36]

#### 2.1.5.3 Internal Market, Cohesion, Non-Discrimination in Trade (Art. 328.2 TFEU)

The regulatory principles of adherence to internal market, cohesion, competition and non-discriminating trade are largely similar to the obligation to comply with Union law, and arguably exist already as a matter of general EU law.[37]

The duties not to undermine the internal market and not to constitute a barrier to or discrimination in trade between Member States overlap and can be read together.[38] As the evolution of the formula's wording shows, it was originally a direct refence to the CJEU's *Dassonville* judgment, which was subsequently lost in translation rather than willingly changed.[39] Thus, rather than largely excluding internal market law from the scope of enhanced cooperation, as some argue,[40] the formula demands any enhanced cooperation to strictly respect the fundamental freedoms.[41] It primarily prohibits arbitrary and protectionist measures by way of enhanced cooperation, but does not exclude measures that affect the internal

---

[35] Fischer-Lescano, A., Kommer, S. (2011), 'EU in der Finanzkrise: Zur Leistungsfähigkeit des Verfahrens der verstärkten Zusammenarbeit für eine Intensivierung der Wirtschafts- und Sozialpolitik', *KJ*, 412–433, p. 421. Kellerbauer, M. (2019), 'Art. 326 TFEU' in: Kellerbauer, M., Klamert, M., Tomkin, J., Bogensberger, W., Bouquet, A., Erlbacher, F. (eds.), *The EU treaties and the Charter of Fundamental Rights: A commentary,* Oxford, Oxford University Press.

[36] Brackhane, B. (2008), *Differenzierte Integration im Recht der Europäischen Union*, Ius Europaeum, Baden-Baden, Nomos.

[37] Ruffert, M. (2016), 'Art. 326 AEUV' in: Calliess, C., Ruffert, M. (eds.), *EUV/AEUV: Das Verfassungsrecht der Europäischen Union mit Europäischer Grundrechtecharta: Kommentar,* München, C. H. Beck.

[38] Fischer-Lescano, A., Kommer, S. (2011), 'EU in der Finanzkrise: Zur Leistungsfähigkeit des Verfahrens der verstärkten Zusammenarbeit für eine Intensivierung der Wirtschafts- und Sozialpolitik', *KJ*, 412–433 f.

[39] Thym, D. (2018), 'Supranational Differentiation and Enhanced Cooperation' in: Schütze, R., Tridimas, T. (eds.), *Oxford principles of European Union law,* Oxford, Oxford University Press, pp. 849–883.

[40] Gerards, C., Wessels, W. (2019), Enhancing 'Enhanced Cooperation': constraints and opportunities of an inflexible flexibility clause, CEPOB, Bruges.

[41] Thym, D. (2018), 'Supranational Differentiation and Enhanced Cooperation' in: Schütze, R., Tridimas, T. (eds.), *Oxford principles of European Union law,* Oxford, Oxford University Press, pp. 849–883; Fischer-Lescano, A., Kommer, S. (2011), 'EU in der Finanzkrise: Zur

market in a limited way due to its limited geographical scope,[42] as was also confirmed by the Court in its case-law on the unitary patent.[43] Similarly, cohesion is not undermined by the mere fact that individual measures are taken to strengthen it on a part of the EU territory made up of the participating Member States.[44] However, Art. 326 (2) TFEU does require particular sensitivity when action in the fields defined by Art. 174–178 TFEU on cohesion is considered.[45]

#### 2.1.5.4 The Duty to Ensure Consistency (Art. 334 TFEU)

According to Art. 334 TFEU, participants have to ensure the consistency of activities undertaken in the context of enhanced cooperation and the consistency of such activities with the policies of the Union. Consistency in this context means that individual legal acts may not contradict one another.[46] It aims to coordinate policy measures on all levels in order to ensure their conceptual coherence and to avoid contradictory action orientated towards common goals.[47] In its second variant, the duty to ensure consistency of any enhanced cooperation with the policies of the Union, the principle is closely related to the obligation to further the aims and objectives of the Union. However, it is more operative, since it is aimed at the organisation of an ongoing enhanced cooperation. The first variant, to ensure consistency within the enhanced cooperation, seems obvious at first sight, hardly restricting the mechanism and of little added value. Yet, at least in the context of

---

Leistungsfähigkeit des Verfahrens der verstärkten Zusammenarbeit für eine Intensivierung der Wirtschafts- und Sozialpolitik', *KJ*, 412–433, p. 421 f.

[42] Brackhane, B. (2008), *Differenzierte Integration im Recht der Europäischen Union*, Ius Europaeum, Baden-Baden, Nomos; Kellerbauer, M. (2019), 'Art. 326 TFEU' in: Kellerbauer, M., Klamert, M., Tomkin, J., Bogensberger, W., Bouquet, A., Erlbacher, F. (eds.), *The EU treaties and the Charter of Fundamental Rights: A commentary*, Oxford, Oxford University Press.

[43] Cases C- 274/ 11, C- 295/ 11, *Spain and Italy v Council*, EU:C:2013:240, paras 75, 68.

[44] Becker, U. (2015), 'Art. 326 AEUV' in: Groeben, H. v. d., Schwarze, J., Hatje, A. (eds.), *Europäisches Unionsrecht,* Baden-Baden, Nomos.

[45] Fischer-Lescano, A., Kommer, S. (2011), 'EU in der Finanzkrise: Zur Leistungsfähigkeit des Verfahrens der verstärkten Zusammenarbeit für eine Intensivierung der Wirtschafts- und Sozialpolitik', *KJ*, 412–433, arguing even that enhanced cooperation is excluded in the field of cohesion policy.

[46] Siems, K. (1999), *Das Kohärenzgebot in der Europäischen Union und seine Justitiabilität*, Nomos-Universitätsschriften, Baden-Baden; see also Böttner, R. (2021), *The Constitutional Framework for Enhanced Cooperation in EU law*, Nijhoff studies in European Union law, Leiden The Netherlands, Koninklijke Brill NV.

[47] Blanke, H.-J. (2018), 'Art. 334 AEUV' in: Grabitz, E., Hilf, M., Nettesheim, M. (eds.), *Das Recht der Europäischen Union,* München, Beck.

the enhance cooperation-related *Schengen* acquis, the CJEU stressed the importance of coherence within a cooperation. In fact, the Court stated that the required internal coherence[48] of the cooperation may be a counter-weight to the need to take into account the interests of non-participants.[49] Thus, rather than restricting it, the need to ensure internal coherence grants enhanced cooperation projects a certain degree of liberty in their design, as it bears similar importance as the requirement to respect non-participants.

## 2.2 Theoretical Framework

Having outlined the legal boundaries of enhanced cooperation in terms of its scope of application, in the remainder of this chapter, I set out to critically assess the remaining policy fields in terms of their abstract suitability for enhanced cooperation. My aim is to draw a realistic picture of which fields *could* see a or several enhanced cooperation attempts in the near or distant future.[50] I explicitly do not want to make specific *predictions* on which policy areas will or will not be subject to an enhanced cooperation, as such outcomes underly institutional and political formulas that go beyond what can reasonably be predicted (as witnessed by past attempts of such predictions, see below). Rather, my aim is to map the field of non-exclusive Union competences in terms of their suitability for, and consequently also their likelihood to see enhanced cooperation. Note that the term likelihood is not, as in a prediction, meant in an abstract, but in a relative sense—i.e. how likely one field is to see an enhanced cooperation in comparison to another.

In order to do this, I will draw on the experiences made in the past (the five ongoing enhanced cooperations, as well as fields where the mechanism was seriously contemplated but not put in action) and the legal criteria prescribed for

[48] The terminology of "coherence" required by the Court and "consistency" prescribed by Art. 336 TFEU only seemingly draws a border between two different concepts; in fact, other languages, such as French in which CJEU cases are deliberated, speak of "coherence" (cohérence) in Art. 336 TFEU.

[49] Case C-482/08, UK v. Council (VIS), ECLI:EU:C:2010:631, para. 48 f.; on this, see Weyembergh, A. (2018), 'Enhanced cooperation in criminal matters: past, present and future' in: Kert, R., Lehner, A. (eds.), *Vielfalt des Strafrechts im internationalen Kontext: Festschrift für Frank Höpfel zum 65. Geburtstag,* Wien, Graz, NWV, pp. 605–624.

[50] It has to be noted that all following considerations assume an unchanged applicability of the Lisbon Treaty, as a major constitutional reform seems unrealistic at this point of European integration.

enhanced cooperation by the Treaties. I will take up the element of whether a field is governed by unanimous of qualified majority voting in the Council and explain why it influences the likelihood of enhanced cooperation. Finally, I will use elements from the two theories existing on enhanced cooperation in political science which set out to explain when enhanced cooperation occurs. This is not so much to create a new theory, but to borrow and use criteria developed in the past for the mapping exercise outlined above.

### 2.2.1 Unanimous vs QMV Council Voting

While being a clearly law-based aspect, the question of whether a policy area to be considered for enhanced cooperation is governed by unanimous or qualified majority voting in the Council does not legally shape the scope of enhanced cooperation, as it does not exclude or prohibit anything. Yet, it significantly changes the likelihood of Member States resorting to enhanced cooperation, as will be shown in the following.

An important question when trying to outline the factual—as opposed to the purely legal—scope of application of enhanced cooperation regards the voting procedures in the Council in the single policy areas. So far, all enhanced cooperations took place in fields governed by unanimous Council decision making. The application of enhanced cooperation in fields that are governed by qualified majority voting (QMV) is not legally banned; however, it was not considered in practice yet.[51] The reason for this is a practical one: according to Art. 329.1 TFEU and Art. 16.3 TEU, the decision to authorise an enhanced cooperation is taken by a qualified majority in the Council. Hence, if the group of Member States interested in a measure is great enough to reach a qualified majority to authorise an enhanced cooperation, then those states could have decided the measure as a legal act applicable to all Member States in the first place, even against the votes of some disagreeing countries. If, in such a scenario, the interested Member States wanted to respect the dissenting states and legislate in an enhanced cooperation setting despite their majority, it could not be said that "it has [been] established that the objectives of such cooperation cannot be attained [...] by the Union as a whole". Since the majority could outvote the minority, the objective could in fact be attained by the Union as a whole and,

[51] Peers, S. (2010), 'Divorce, European Style: The First Authorization of Enhanced Cooperation', *Eur. Const. L. Rev*, pp. 339–358.

therefore, enhanced cooperation would not be a *last resort*, rendering it illegal under Art. 20 (2) TEU.

Hence, the only scenario in which an enhanced cooperation in a field governed by QMV would be feasible is a case in which a group too small to form a QMV majority agreed on a measure, and at least one of the dissenting Member States voted yes on the authorisation decision to start enhanced cooperation while not joining the project itself ('helper-state'). Such an approach of 'agreeing to disagree' and actively letting willing states go ahead is easy to imagine from a legal point of view, but would require substantial changes in the consensus-oriented mentality of the Council. However, it would not be entirely without precedent, as the following example shows. When the enhanced cooperation on a FTT was passed, the envisioned legal act was to be based on Art. 113 TFEU, a legal basis requiring unanimity. It was therefore not a case of QMV enhanced cooperation. However, the planned enhanced cooperation only had eleven participants when authorised, i.e. way less than needed for a qualified majority. In this situation, six non-participating Member States decided to support the project despite not being willing to participate, acting as a kind of 'helper-states'.[52]

It needs to be added that if a "helper-state" in this scenario was to join the enhanced cooperation at a later moment in time, it would be an easy target for anyone to call the whole procedure a hand trick to circumvent the last resort criterion. The authorisation decision could be annulled by the CJEU (Art. 263 TFEU), as could be any implementing legal acts. Therefore, timing would be crucial—the more time passes between the authorisation and joining, the less problematic the procedure would look from the angle of the last resort criterion.

---

[52] Note that at the time of adoption (2013), the transitional rules on voting foreseen in Protocol (No 36) on Transitional Provisions applied. As a consequence, according to its Art. 3 (3), a qualified majority required a simple majority of Member States uniting 255 weighted votes. Member States' votes were weighted with a factor of 4 to 29 depending on their size. The eleven enhanced cooperation participants were neither a majority of Member States (the EU consisted of 27 Member States prior to the accession of Croatia), nor did they reach 255 votes (175 votes). However, the non-participants Sweden, Denmark, Poland, Romania, Bulgaria and Hungary "respect[ed] that a financial transaction tax is a question of high political priority for several Member States and therefore support[ed] the authorisation" (see statement annexed to the minutes of the 3215th meeting of the Council of the European Union (Economic and Financial Affairs), doc. no. 5740/1). With their support, the decision was passed with exactly 255 votes. On possible reasons for supporting the FTT from the outside, see Kroll, D. A., Leuffen, D. (2015), 'Enhanced cooperation in practice. An analysis of differentiated integration in EU secondary law', *Journal of European Public Policy*, Vol. 22, No. 3, pp. 353–373.

As a side note, what needs to be kept in mind concerning QMV enhanced cooperation is that of course Member States which wanted a project and therefore joined a QMV enhanced cooperation could be outvoted—again by QMV—when it comes to its implementation in secondary law within the enhanced cooperation.[53] Hence, a Member State could voluntarily join a project only to find that it is implemented in a way the state deems unacceptable. It is easy to imagine that Member States would join QMV enhanced cooperations more reluctantly than the ones governed by unanimity. In this context, the undecided question of whether and until when a Member State can withdraw from an ongoing enhanced cooperation would become highly relevant.[54]

To sum up, a QMV enhanced cooperation would be legally possible. Because of the different implications of QMV described above, QMV enhanced cooperations would likely be particularly dynamic when it comes to legislation and Member States joining or withdrawing. The legal framework is in place, and the circumstances and developments in politics will show if they will eventually be used accordingly. Since, however, as of today QMV enhanced cooperations have not been a matter of major discussion, let alone of political planning, the question whether a field is governed by QMV or unanimity continues to be an important indicator on how likely enhanced cooperation is factually, with a strong assumption that QMV enhanced cooperations will not occur for the time being.

[53] In the case of a QMV enhanced cooperation, the qualified majority must be calculated differently since there are by definition less Member States in an enhanced cooperation than in the regular Council setting. Therefore, Art. 238 (3)(a) TFEU adapts the majority rules in that the majority must comprise at least 55% of the participating Member States comprising at least 65% of the population of these states. Minimum numbers, as foreseen for the regular QMV in Art. 16 (3) TEU, are dropped. The most relevant difference is that a blocking minority must comprise Council members representing more than 35% of the population of the participating Member States plus one State. Failing this, the qualified majority is deemed attained.

[54] On this controversial question, see e.g. Editorial Comments (2011), 'Enhanced cooperation: A Union à taille réduite or à porte tournante?', *CMLRev*, pp. 317–327; H-J Blanke, 'Art. 20 TEU' in Hermann-Josef Blanke and Stelio Mangiameli (eds), *The Treaty on European Union (TEU): A commentary* (Berlin, Springer, 2013) para. 51; Thym, D. (2004), *Ungleichzeitigkeit und europäisches Verfassungsrecht*, Schriftenreihe europäisches Verfassungsrecht, Baden-Baden, Nomos.

### 2.2.2 Theoretical Approaches

Having reached the boundaries of what a purely legal analysis of the enhanced cooperation framework can tell us on when enhanced cooperation might occur, when trying to paint a broader picture, it is inevitable to draw on the findings of other disciplines. Political sciences, and particularly political economy, offer models and methods specifically designed to provide answers such as those needed here. Such methods will now be introduced in order to accompany the legal findings made above. There is plenty of literature in the field of political science looking into when differentiation happens, i.e. when Member States decide not to move with the rest of the Union or when Member States decide to move on without single states, which stay behind.[55] However, there are merely two studies looking more specifically at enhanced cooperation. One relatively recent study was conducted by *Kroll* and *Leuffen* in 2015, and an older one by *Kölliker* around 2001, both analysing the motivations for the usage of enhanced cooperation.[56] *Kroll*'s and *Leuffen*'s approach to explain when enhanced cooperation occurs focusses on externalities, i.e. the costs (political and economic) that *non*-participating Member States have to bear for staying out of the respective integration step. *Kölliker* focusses more on the internal perspective, using the criteria of excludability and rivalry in consumption of a public good.

#### 2.2.2.1 Externalities

*Kroll* and *Leuffen,* building on rationalist institutionalism, focus on the impact of *externalities*[57] on the occurrence of enhanced cooperation, i.e. the effects that the enhanced cooperation would have on potential non-participants. According to their study, *neutral external effects* of a project that Member States have fundamentally different opinions on make enhanced cooperation most likely, mirroring a spirit of live and let live among Member States. Arguably, the two enhanced cooperations in family law (divorce/legal separation and international couples' property law) can be seen as a proof of this theory. If, however, a project is set to

[55] See Leruth, B., Gänzle, S., Trondal, J. (2019), 'Exploring Differentiated Disintegration in a Post-Brexit European Union', *JCMS: Journal of Common Market Studies*, Vol. 57, No. 5, pp. 1013–1030, for a "state of the art review of existing literature on differentiation".

[56] Kroll, D. A., Leuffen, D. (2015), 'Enhanced cooperation in practice. An analysis of differentiated integration in EU secondary law', *Journal of European Public Policy*, Vol. 22, No. 3, pp. 353–373.

[57] For a distinct analysis of externalities in the constitutional choices of a federal system, see Posner, R. A. (2007), *Economic analysis of law*, New York, NY, Wolters Kluwer Law & Business: Aspen Publishers.

have *negative external effects*, outsiders will try to prevent the project altogether. If that is not possible—which enhanced cooperation is precisely made for—outsiders will rather join a project than stay outside and face the costs, preventing enhanced cooperation from occurring. The European Arrest Warrant might be an example for this case: during the negotiations, Member States such as Italy vetoed the adoption of the founding act. Only when the other Member States started considering enhanced cooperation as a way forward, Italy gave in and participated. *Positive external effects* equally make it less likely that enhanced cooperation is resorted to. In this scenario, however, it is the participants who favour not to use enhanced cooperation, as they would have to bear the costs of the project whereas outsiders would get free benefits from it ("free-riding"). In this case, according to *Kroll* and *Leuffen*'s theory, states will only resort to enhanced cooperation if their own benefits outweigh the costs of the freeriding outsiders.

While this theory contains a lot of important insights, overall, it seems agreeable only so far as it is acknowledged that it focusses only one arm of the multi-dimensional arena of costs and benefits. However, the focus when trying to understand why Member States resort to enhanced cooperation should not be lying exclusively or predominantly on the outsiders, but to a large extent also on the insiders. *Kroll* and *Leuffen* argue that it is harder to establish enhanced cooperation when externalities are negative. However, besides CJEU litigation, which may cost time, but so far never stopped an enhanced cooperation nor explicitly halted implementation, the behaviour of outsiders cannot legally slow enhanced cooperation in a significant way if interested Member States are determined to go ahead. In fact, the very purpose of enhanced cooperation is for Member States to be able to proceed without taking note of objections from what the authors call "laggards". Moreover, whether the negative externalities for the outsider(s) are great enough to make them want to join the project rather than staying behind, again, depends on many other factors than just an abstract negative nature of the consequence—as does the decision whether the interested states actually opt for enhanced cooperation in the consensus-oriented Council. What seems to be more decisive is the internal perspective of the would-be participants of a potential enhanced cooperation: reference is made to this when the authors speak of positive externalities, which create the risk of 'free-riding'. Here, the idea is that enhanced cooperation only takes place if the benefits of the enhanced cooperation outweigh the costs created by free-riders. This seems to be an essential factor. If the costs caused by the existence of *non*-participation is neutral or even positive[58] *for participants*, enhanced cooperation can be resorted to by interested Member States. If, however, non-participation causes additional costs for participants because it allows free-riding, Member States are less likely to use enhanced cooperation (e.g. if there was to be an enhanced cooperation on a system of resettlement of refugees within the EU, participating Member States would have to bear the costs of the system while unwilling states would profit from the solution to the political dispute surrounding resettlement and save on the costs caused by accommodation, integration etc.).[59] Moreover, additional costs of differentiation can go beyond free-riding: in some cases, states could even be *harmed* by the non-participation of others. If there was an enhanced cooperation on the reduction of environmental emissions, the participating Member States would bear costs for keeping the air (or water, soil, etc.) clean. Non-participating neighbours would be able to free-ride in two ways: they could profit from the cleaner air which, naturally, cannot be stopped at the border and they could attract investments by way of less regulation. However, beyond this free-riding effect, the neighbouring (participating) countries would also be *harmed* by the pollution produced, which again passes borders, and lowers the air quality in the participating state. This exemplifies why enhanced cooperation in such scenarios becomes very unlikely.

Yet a different category of costs that needs to be distinguished are costs that occur simply because of a lower number of participants and a lower benefit of the project (in cases where more participants mean more benefit for all). While not being externalities at all, it is hard to imagine that such costs do not influence the decision of interested Member States on whether or not to apply enhanced cooperation.

#### 2.2.2.2 Public Goods Theory

All of these considerations show that the *Kröll/Leuffen* approach is insightful and explains a lot of political activity in the area of enhanced cooperation, but also leaves certain aspects of the decision-making mechanisms uncovered. This

[58] See e.g. the different scenarios for a Common Consolidated Corporate Tax Base in Bettendorf, L., van der Horst, A., Mooij, R. A. D., Vrijburg, H., 'Corporate Tax Consolidation and Enhanced Cooperation in the European Union', *Fiscal Studies*, Vol. 31, No. 4, pp. 453–479. This would, however, count the same as being neutral: given the principle of openness of enhanced cooperations, Member States could always join, reversing any positive effect of their non-participation.

[59] Outsiders could neither be forced to shoulder other costs, such as additional investments in Frontex or "return sponsorship" as proposed by the Commission. Enhanced cooperation can exclusively have legal results for participants. If outsiders are supposed to act in different fields instead, they would have to be part of the legal framework. On this topic, see below Sect. 2.3.1.10.1 and Chap. 5.

is where a second, older study on when enhanced cooperation (rather than differentiation in more general terms) occurs comes into play. *Kölliker* assessed 'closer cooperation', as enhanced cooperation was called at the time of publication of the study, in the light of public goods theory.[60] According to this approach, states' policy decisions regarding differentiated integration (and specifically enhanced/closer cooperation) depends largely on the character of the respective policy area. It is characterised by two sets of factors, namely the *excludability* of the good 'produced' by a policy and its *rivalry in consumption.*

The *excludability* measures whether non-participants can be excluded from the benefits of a specific good—a similar approach to focussing on externalities. To give examples, excludability is high for a highway bridge (non-participants can be forbidden to use it), but low for a radio broadcast, as the waves cannot easily be stopped from single recipients in its range. Accordingly, the *excludability* also measures the potential for free-riding by non-participants, i.e. the possibility to benefit from a good without participating in the sharing of its costs.

*Rivalry in consumption* describes the effect that additional users of a good have on the good's benefits. Consumption can be *rival, neutral* or *complementary. Rival consumption* means that additional consumers lead to a decrease of the benefit; figuratively speaking, the benefit has to be shared. A classic example of this is a drink: an additional user (drinker) leads to lower benefit (less to drink) for the initial user. *Neutral consumption* means that the benefit of the good stays the same even if further users benefit from it, such as a user of a radio broadcast is not affected by additional listeners of said programme. Finally, *complementary consumption* leads to an increase of the benefits, as for example a language becomes more useful the more people speak it, or a technical standard becomes more useful the more producers apply it.[61]

*Kölliker* uses this framework to determine the *centripetal effect* of a policy if introduced in a differentiated matter. The stronger the *centripetal effect*, the more likely it is that an initial non-participant joins the ongoing cooperation. This, according to the author's theory can be used as an indicator to predict whether Member States are ready to start a project through enhanced cooperation. The *centripetal effect* is higher the higher the excludability (i.e. the harder it is for

60 Milner, F., Kölliker, A. (1999), How to Make Use of Closer Cooperation?, Working Paper; further developed in Kölliker, A. (2001), 'Bringing together or driving apart the union? Towards a theory of differentiated integration'.

61 Milner, F., Kölliker, A. (1999), How to Make Use of Closer Cooperation?, Working Paper; Kölliker, A. (2001), 'Bringing together or driving apart the union? Towards a theory of differentiated integration'.

non-participants to free-ride) and the lower rivalry in consumption (as especially complementary consumption makes cooperating attractive per se).

*Kölliker*'s approach was developed before the entry into force of the Treaty of Nice, let alone the Treaty of Lisbon. Therefore, while laying very relevant groundwork, in terms of enhanced cooperation, it lacks an assessment of the experience that was made in the meantime. Particularly, the main assumption is that EU Member States *per se* seek unity and therefore "centripetal effects" on non-participants, i.e. whether and to what extent further Member States successively join an ongoing enhanced cooperation, is the prime indicator of how successful the project is. The reality, however, has shown that while there are dynamics in Member States joining enhanced cooperations, the lines are not very volatile. Especially in the enhanced cooperations in family law, it is unlikely that there will be significant further movement any time soon, as they are built on fundamental differences between Member States' attitudes. Nevertheless, the family law enhanced cooperations were implemented efficiently without major frictions and their participants are satisfied with their functioning, which is why they could well be described as successful. As such, the *centripetal effect* as an overall success indicator for enhanced cooperations may not be the most helpful value as an outcome, but the formula used by *Kölliker* equally describes the likelihood of the occurrence of enhanced cooperation in a useful manner. Thus, the model *Kölliker* developed can add further criteria to assessing whether enhanced cooperation in a certain field is likely or not.

#### 2.2.2.3 Path Dependency

Another factor that may play a role, and that seems to be thus-far underrepresented in enhanced cooperation-specific research is *path dependency.*[62] Path dependency describes the tendency of processes to follow the 'path' of preceding processes. Past decisions on a given matter inform future decisions and make a development in the same direction more likely, thus predetermining future decision. The reasons for this process can be numerous and depend on the field in observation. For example, a past decision pursuing a certain goal can make the pursuit of a different road towards that goal less efficient.[63] Regarding European integration, the path dependency hypothesis predicts that integration, i.e.

[62] For a critical perspective on path dependency in legal studies: Volkmann, U. (2016), 'Pfadabhängigkeiten im Recht' in: Wagner, E. E., Ganglbauer, N. M. (eds.), *Pfadabhängigkeit hoheitlicher Ordnungsmodelle,* Baden-Baden, Nomos, pp. 27–45.

[63] Grosche, N., Wagner, E. E. (2016), 'Einführung in das Tagungsthema: Pfadabhängigkeit hoheitlicher Ordnungsmodelle' in: Wagner, E. E., Ganglbauer, N. M. (eds.), *Pfadabhängigkeit hoheitlicher Ordnungsmodelle,* Baden-Baden, Nomos, pp. 11–26.

the regulation of a policy field on the European level, leads to a need for further regulation on the same level. The more integration there is, the higher the costs of a revision of this system become. At the same time, the supranational institutions can be expected to use their power in favour of more europeanised rather than nationalised policies. In terms of differentiated integration, the path dependency hypothesis predicts that the effects of a differentiated policy affect the participants more than the non-participants, again creating a need for further integration, which as a result is likely to again be differentiated. Thus, according to the idea of path dependency, differentiation leads to more differentiation.[64]

In terms of enhanced cooperation, path dependency could lead to a higher likelihood to use the mechanism in any policy field in which it has already been used. It is a salient case in point that after the first successful enhanced cooperation took place in family law, and more precisely in the context of international couples (international couples' divorce and legal separation law), another enhanced cooperation was authorised six years later with regard to the property regimes of international couples, i.e. a closely related field. One will have to see whether similar path dependent enhanced cooperations will follow. For the time being, however, it seems to be a viable working assumption that path dependency effects do, in fact, occur when enhanced cooperation is being resorted to.

### 2.2.3 Conclusion: A Theoretical Framework

Having laid out the theoretical considerations above, the following aspects of a framework for a field mapping exercise of the EU's non-exclusive competences emerges:

First of all, an area being subject to *unanimity* in the Council makes enhanced cooperation significantly more likely. Whether there has already been an enhanced cooperation in a policy field further raises the likelihood of another one in the light of *path dependency.*

Moreover, if the public good that is supposed to be regulated by Member States is *complimentary in consumption* (more users lead to an increased benefit of a project) or at least *neutral* (more users leave the benefit unaffected), that makes cooperating even if not all Member States join more attractive, as does the

[64] Holzinger, K., Schimmelfennig, F. (2015), 'Eurokrise und differenzierte Integration', *Politische Vierteljahresschrift: PVS*, Vol. 56, No. 3, pp. 457–478; Schimmelfennig, F. (2015), 'Differentiated Integration Before and After the Crisis' in: Cramme, O., Hobolt, S. B. (eds.), *Democratic politics in a European Union under stress,* Oxford, Oxford University Press, pp. 120–134.

possibility to exclude non-participants from the benefits of a project (*excludability*), preventing free-riding. This is the case if a project has neutral or negative external effects. That being said, negative external effects (*externalities*) can make an enhanced cooperation less likely, as non-participants in this case will try to prevent an enhanced cooperation. Where they cannot do so, they are more likely to participate in a project they are unhappy with, effectively preventing enhanced cooperation.

Hence, in the following, the mapping exercise laid out above will assess the principal areas of non-exclusive Union competences, paying special attention to *externality structures*, the *excludability* and *jointness in consumption*, *path dependency* and whether decisions in the Council are taken unanimously or by QMV.

## 2.3 Field Mapping—the Factual Scope and Possible Applications of Enhanced Cooperation

The above findings make it possible to analyse any policy field to determine its suitability for enhanced cooperation. When thoroughly applied to the EU competence catalogue, the result is

an outline not only of the purely legal but of the *factual* scope of application of the enhanced cooperation mechanism. This allows a broad view at the so far underexplored question of "what makes an issue in principle eligible for [enhanced cooperation]".[65]

It has to be taken into account that as laid out before, the non-exclusive competences are numerous and not limited to a list of subjects. However, there is a list of 'principal areas' of EU competence in Art. 4 (2) TFEU, which lists eleven broad fields[66] that are typical shared EU competences. Therefore, these fields will serve as an orienting frame for the following analysis. Moreover, predictions made by academics in the past as to where enhanced cooperation may occur will

[65] Describing exactly this as "missing in literature": Kroll, D. A. (2022), 'Promise unfulfiled?: Managing differentiated integration in EU secondary law through enhanced cooperation' in: Leruth, B., Gänzle, S., Trondal, J. (eds.), *The Routledge handbook of differentiation in the European Union,* New York, Routledge Taylor & Francis Group, pp. 170–183.

[66] Internal market; social policy, for the aspects defined in the TFEU; economic, social and territorial cohesion; agriculture and fisheries, excluding the conservation of marine biological resources; environment; consumer protection; transport; trans-European networks; energy; area of freedom, security and justice; common safety concerns in public health matters, for the aspects defined in the TFEU.

be taken into account. Finally, and crucially, the experiences made with enhanced cooperation, i.e. areas it was used or areas where it was considered, but did not end up being used,[67] will play an important role informing the analysis. This latter category of "non-cases" is particularly insightful, since the enhanced cooperation mechanism's nature as a 'veto buster' leads to the situation in which the actual cases of application are only the "tip of the iceberg"[68] of situations in which enhanced cooperation had a role in a legislative procedure.

The chosen approach is to take a given 'principal area'—say, e.g. the Internal Market—and list the legal bases that the Treaties contain on this specific matter. These legal bases will then be examined against a cascade of factors. As a first sort of filter, it will—implicitly or explicitly—be checked whether any of the legal factors limiting enhanced cooperation as laid out above exclude the use of enhanced cooperation in the matter at hand. If this is not the case, the remaining legal bases will be tested—as a second filter—for whether or not the findings from political science predict that they are suitable for enhanced cooperation. As a result, it becomes possible to tell under which legal bases it is realistic to expect an enhanced cooperation from a legal and practical perspective.

For reasons of legibility, the method will only be applied in full detail for the first principal area, the internal market, in order to exemplify how the criteria developed above can be put to use in a given area. In the following principal areas, the underlying analysis will follow the same pattern, but the presentation will be more focussed on the most relevant legal bases and findings.

## 2.3.1 Principal Areas

### 2.3.1.1 Internal Market

The competence to establish an internal market has a long history of being the EU's most important single competence. It touches a vast number of different

[67] Kroll, D. A., Leuffen, D. (2015), 'Enhanced cooperation in practice. An analysis of differentiated integration in EU secondary law', *Journal of European Public Policy*, Vol. 22, No. 3, pp. 353–373; Heber, C. (2021), *Enhanced Cooperation and European Tax Law*, Oxford University Press; Böttner, R. (2023), 'The Instrument of Enhanced Cooperation: Pitfalls and Possibilities for Differentiated Integration'.

[68] Kroll, D. A. (2022), 'Promise unfulfiled?: Managing differentiated integration in EU secondary law through enhanced cooperation' in: Leruth, B., Gänzle, S., Trondal, J. (eds.), *The Routledge handbook of differentiation in the European Union,* New York, Routledge Taylor & Francis Group, pp. 170–183.

policy fields, affecting almost every area of the economic life.[69] It was used extensively, which according to critics at times even amounted to a "competence creep" of the EU, by which it allegedly gained competences that had not been conferred to it initially. Given this, it can surely be described as the most far-reaching Union competence.

The single market competences are generally characterised by an open and therefore ambiguous wording. The CJEU took a central role in interpreting them extensively, developing the EU internal market competences in a progressive manner.[70]

As Art. 26 (2) TFEU defines, "[t]he internal market shall comprise an area without internal frontiers in which the free movement of goods, persons, services and capital is ensured in accordance with the provisions of the Treaties." Thus, the core of the internal market is constituted by the four fundamental freedoms. However, these freedoms have direct effect, which is why they themselves do not empower the EU to legislate.[71] Hence, what the *principal area* actually refers to are the single legislative competences "with the aim of establishing or ensuring the functioning of the internal market" outlined in Art. 26 (1) TFEU and laid down in the following norms[72]:

- Art. 46, Art. 48 TFEU (acts implementing the free movement of workers)
- Art. 50, Art. 51 (2), Art. 52 (2), Art. 53 TFEU (freedom of establishment)
- Art. 56 (2), Art. 59, Art. 60 TFEU (free movement of services)

---

[69] See references in Blanke, H.-J., Böttner, R. (2019), '§ 13 Binnenmarkt, Rechtsangleichung, Grundfreiheiten' in: Niedobitek, M. (ed.), *Europarecht: Grundlagen und Politiken der Union,* Berlin, De Gruyter, pp. 887–1114; de Witte, B. de (2017), 'Exclusive Member State Competences—Is There Such a Thing?' in: Garben, S., Govaere, I. (eds.), *The Division of Competences between the EU and the Member States: Reflections on the Past, the Present and the Future,* Hart Publishing.

[70] Davies, G. (2017), 'The Competence to Create an Internal Market: Conceptual Poverty and Unbalanced Interests' in: Garben, S., Govaere, I. (eds.), *The Division of Competences between the EU and the Member States: Reflections on the Past, the Present and the Future,* Hart Publishing, p. 75 f.: "[The CJEU's] interpretations of competences have become much more important than the Treaty text itself."; See e.g. CJEU C-267/91, 268/91 (*Keck und Mithouard*), 1993, I-6097; CJEU C-120/78 (*Rewe-Zentral AG/"Cassis der Dijon")*, 1979, 649, CJEU C-376/98 (*Tobacco Advertising),* ECLI:EU:C:2000:544.

[71] Streinz, R. (2018), 'Art. 4 AEUV' in: Streinz, R. (ed.), *EUV/AEUV: Vertrag über die Europäische Union, Vertrag über die Arbeitsweise der Europäischen Union, Charta der Grundrechte der Europäischen Union,* München, C. H.Beck, para. 4.

[72] Obwexer, W. (2015), 'Art. 4 AEUV' in: Groeben, H. v. d., Schwarze, J., Hatje, A. (eds.), *Europäisches Unionsrecht,* Baden-Baden, Nomos, para. 12.

- Art. 64 (2,3), Art. 65 (4), Art. 66 TFEU (free movement of capital and payments)
- Art. 113 AEUV (harmonisation of indirect taxes)
- Art. 114—Art. 118 TFEU (approximation of laws, harmonisation).

As a general remark, it can be said that large parts of the single market, but especially the fundamental freedoms are like a 'holy grail' in the EU. Therefore, it is continuously repeated that the four freedoms are indivisible and unnegotiable (for an illustrative example, see the intense negotiations with the UK regarding Brexit and future arrangements, or with Switzerland regarding the mutual interconnections). Therefore, differentiation touching the implementation of the fundamental freedoms seems rather unlikely, as it would (the closer it gets to the core of free movement) come with very high, almost unsurmountable policy cost regarding the EU's overall image. Even more importantly, there is an inherent tension between enhanced cooperation and the internal market, as Art. 326 (2) TFEU explicitly states: "*Such cooperation shall not undermine the internal market or economic, social and territorial cohesion. It shall not constitute a barrier to or discrimination in trade between Member States, nor shall it distort competition between them.*" This formula clarifies that, particularly in the field of the internal market, enhanced cooperation cannot be applied at will, but needs to be closely aligned with the overall aim of a well-functioning market with equal market access and opportunities, and must respect the current internal market *acquis*. As soon as the threshold of damage or regression ("undermining") to the internal market is reached, the measure, no matter how useful for the participants, cannot be justified under this formula and would be illegal.

That being said, the Unitary Patent, which was established by an enhanced cooperation, is part of the single market competence (as confirmed by the CJEU, see above), as is the Financial Transaction Tax, which also saw an enhanced cooperation. Hence, enhanced cooperation is by no means excluded in the area of the single market. In fact, in its judgment on the Unitary Patent, the Court made clear that a *new* measure added to the internal market *acquis* does not undermine the internal market merely because it does not bring together the Union as a whole.[73]

For this reason, the following paragraphs will explore the likelihood of enhanced cooperation attempts in the single competence fields outlined above.

**Art. 46 TFEU** enables the EU to legislate in order to pass the "measures required to bring about freedom of movement for workers". It is therefore key

[73] CJEU C-274/11, 295/11 (*Spain/Italy v Council*), ECLI:EU:C:2013:240, para. 75.

for the implementation of the free movement of workers. As set out above, not only is it difficult to imagine differentiated legislation in this area, because it would harm the image of the indivisible four freedoms and also weaken the EU's negotiation position with external partners (Brexit, etc.). More importantly, any measure aiming to bring about the freedom of movement for workers but not for all workers would be most likely to be inadmissible under Art. 326 (2) TFEU. Hence, enhanced cooperation in this field is highly unlikely.

**Art. 48 TFEU** allows the EU to "adopt such measures in the field of social security as are necessary to provide freedom of movement for workers". The idea is to create law flanking the freedom of workers, mostly by coordinating the social security systems to make sure persons working in different Member States do not suffer any disadvantages from their mobility in terms of social security.[74] This shows that, as in the case of Art. 46 TFEU, due to the proximity of the legislative competence to the core of the free movement of workers, differentiated integration in this field could raise problematic implications under Art. 326 (2) TFEU. In addition, in the case of social benefits for non-nationals, there are already rather clear fault lines between older and newer Member States. Differentiated integration in this field could have the implication of wanting to leave the poorer states out of a more advanced social security coordination. Moreover, it should be noted that Art. 48 (2) TFEU contains a special mediation mechanism for the Council. In case of disagreement among the Member States, any Council member may suspend the legislation process and refer the matter to the European Council. The Heads of State and Government may then within four months dismiss the proposal, ask the Commission to submit a modified one, or refer the original proposal back to the Council for decision. This raises the hurdle for enhanced cooperation, as the entire process has to be concluded before enhanced cooperation can be resorted to as "last resort" (Art. 20 (2) TEU).

**Art. 50 TFEU** allows the EU to pass directives "in order to attain freedom of establishment as regards a particular activity". As such, its scope hardly allows for legalisation that does not touch the core of the fundamental freedom of establishment (Art. 49 TFEU). The same is true for legislation on the mutual recognition of diplomas, which is possible under **Art. 53 TFEU**. Hence, as laid out above for the fundamental freedoms in general, enhanced cooperation does not seem viable in these areas.

**Art. 51 (2) TFEU** allows the EU to name exceptions of the freedom of establishment for "certain activities". It has never been made use of, or seriously

[74] See e.g. Farahat, A. (2016), 'Solidarität und Inklusion', *DÖV*, pp. 45–55.

considered, although it has been in the Treaties since the Treaty of Maastricht.[75] This alone makes legislative activity in the foreseeable future seem unlikely, path dependency surely does not make its use seem likely. If however, there were to be a law establishing such an exception, it could be passed using QMV, making enhanced cooperation unlikely. Moreover, drafting an exception not applicable to all Member States while still abiding to the legal limits of non-discrimination and the need to adhere to all other EU law seems hardly feasible. In addition, if a Member State opposed such legislation, but found itself in a situation where the law was passed against its will, there would be no reason not to participate in it: No state would be forced to exclude other Member States' nationals from any activity in its territory, and therefore would not be affected internally (whereas any external affectedness, i.e. affectedness of the opposing state's nationals when abroad, would be beyond its competence). The same goes for the exceptions because of public policy, security and health, which can be coordinated by way of EU legislation under **Art. 52 (2) TFEU**.

**Art. 56 (2) TFEU** foresees the possibility to extend the provisions on the freedom to provide services to nationals of third countries. As this profoundly affects the core of the fundamental freedom, it is not conceivable that such an act could be passed only for a limited number of Member States. The same goes for **Art. 59 TFEU**, which regulates the liberalisation of specific services.

**Art. 60 TFEU** addresses the Member States individually, as well as the Commission, which is assigned the task to make recommendations to single Member States. Where only single Member States are meant to be addressed from the outset, a differentiation tool could not take effect.

**Art. 64 (2),(3) TFEU** allow to restrict the free movement of capital to or from third countries. The liberalisation of capital movements *erga omnes,* i.e. also towards third countries, is a centrepiece of the free movement of capital as laid down in Art. 63 TFEU. Hence, it is yet another norm too close to the core of a fundamental freedom to make enhanced cooperation seem possible. Moreover, as measures passed under it address third states, it is largely a foreign policy instrument. Differentiation would therefore come at high policy costs, as the EU would lose negotiation powers towards other countries. Finally, restricting investments to or from third states only for some Member States would allow the others to free-ride and attract said investments instead.

**Art. 65 (4) TFEU** gives yet another possibility to address single Member States' policies, and therefore per se does not concern uniform EU action.

---

[75] Art. 55 (2) ECT (Maastricht); see Tiedje, J. (2015), 'Art. 51 TFEU' in: Groeben, H. v. d., Schwarze, J., Hatje, A. (eds.), *Europäisches Unionsrecht,* Baden-Baden, Nomos, para. 26.

**Art. 66 TFEU** allows the Council to take protective measures against third countries if capital movements cause serious difficulties to the EMU. Although the aim of the measures is to protect the EMU, decisions are taken by all Member States via QMV.[76] Despite the fact that a conflict line between EMU and non-EMU Member States is imaginable (as seen previously in the Eurozone crisis when the TSCG or "Fiscal Compact" had to be passed via international treaty[77]), QMV makes enhanced cooperation seem less likely from the outset. On the other hand, Art. 66 TFEU could be one of the rare occasions in which there might be a logical reason—a danger to the EMU, but not to the non-EMU states—why a Member State is opposed to a measure, but is ready to authorise an enhanced cooperation in which it does not have to participate. Yet, Art. 66 TFEU is an emergency measure that has not even been used during the financial and sovereign debt crisis. Thus, its usage in the foreseeable future in general is not particularly likely. If there were to be a QMV enhanced cooperation, however, Art. 66 TFEU would be a fitting candidate.

**Art. 113 TFEU** enables the Council (the Parliament only needs to be consulted) to pass measures for the harmonisation of taxes, to be precise "legislation concerning turnover taxes, excise duties and other forms of indirect taxation to the extent that such harmonisation is necessary to ensure the establishment and the functioning of the internal market and to avoid distortion of competition".[78] Decisions must be taken unanimously. As regards the concept of path dependency, the enhanced cooperation on a Financial Transaction Tax was authorised on this legal basis. This would make another enhanced cooperation seem more likely. However, since the authorisation decision of the FTT in 2015,[79] no implementing law has been passed. Whether a 'stuck' enhanced cooperation can actually serve as an example in the sense of path dependency is up for debate. On the other hand, the FTT is not the only field in which enhanced cooperation is brought up regularly. Ideas on a Common Consolidated Corporate Tax Base (CCCTB)

---

[76] Bröhmer, J. (2016), 'Art. 66 AEUV' in: Calliess, C., Ruffert, M. (eds.), *EUV/AEUV: Das Verfassungsrecht der Europäischen Union mit Europäischer Grundrechtecharta: Kommentar*, München, C. H. Beck.

[77] Graf von Luckner, J. (2018), 'How to Bring It Home—The EU's Options for Incorporating the Fiscal Compact into EU Law', *European Law Blog*.

[78] On enhanced cooperation and taxes in general, see Heber, C. (2021), *Enhanced Cooperation and European Tax Law*, Oxford University Press.

[79] Council Decision (2013/52/EU) of 22 January 2013 authorising enhanced cooperation in the area of financial transaction tax, para. 2, 10.

based on enhanced cooperation are repeatedly being brought forward by academics and politicians.[80] However, the CCCTB would be collected directly from the (legal) persons carrying the economic burden of the tax. Therefore, unlike the FTT[81], the CCCTB would a direct tax and could consequently not be based on Art. 113 TFEU, but on Art. 115 TFEU (see below).[82] Nevertheless, further minimum tax standards in indirect taxes could in future be decided and implemented via enhanced cooperation.[83] *Cédelle* argues that the differences between Member States' revenue interests and redistribution policies are so great that "a smaller territorial scale of integration may simply offer a better alternative to the 'lowest common denominator' approach."[84]

One idea concerning new tax legislation under Art. 113 TFEU is a reform of the VAT system[85]. As of today, the VAT system is already harmonised to a significant degree.[86] Enhanced cooperation in this area could therefore collide with the VAT law already in place, which is forbidden by Art. 326 (1) TFEU. Enhanced cooperation in this area therefore seems unlikely. Another often-discussed indirect tax is the "carbon tax" or "CO2 tax", which would tax the emission of CO2, but be charged on e.g. the sale of fuels. Whether such a project would be conceivable as an enhanced cooperation depends significantly on the political context. If all Member States agreed on individually binding CO2 limits, but

---

[80] See Cédelle, A. (2015), Enhanced cooperation: A way forward for tax harmonisation in the EU?, Working Paper Series; Bettendorf, L., van der Horst, A., Mooij, R. A. D., Vrijburg, H., 'Corporate Tax Consolidation and Enhanced Cooperation in the European Union', *Fiscal Studies*, Vol. 31, No. 4, pp. 453–479; Kroll, D. A., Leuffen, D. (2015), 'Enhanced cooperation in practice. An analysis of differentiated integration in EU secondary law', *Journal of European Public Policy*, Vol. 22, No. 3, pp. 353–373, p. 353 f.; see also Commission Proposal for a Council Directive on a Common Consolidated Corporate Tax Base (CCCTB), COM/2011/0121 final. Doubtful: Heber, C. (2021), *Enhanced Cooperation and European Tax Law*, Oxford University Press.

[81] Meyer, F. C., Heidfeld, C. (2011), 'Europarechtliche Aspekte einer Finanztransaktionssteuer', *EuZW*, pp. 373–378, p. 374.

[82] Commission Proposal for a Council Directive on a Common Consolidated Corporate Tax Base (CCCTB), COM/2011/0121 final, p. 10.

[83] Fischer-Lescano, A., Kommer, S. (2011), 'EU in der Finanzkrise: Zur Leistungsfähigkeit des Verfahrens der verstärkten Zusammenarbeit für eine Intensivierung der Wirtschafts- und Sozialpolitik', *KJ*, 412–433, p. 424 f., 433.

[84] Cédelle, A. (2015), Enhanced cooperation: A way forward for tax harmonisation in the EU?, Working Paper Series.

[85] Communication from the Commission on an action plan on VAT, COM(2016) 148 final.

[86] Kamann, H.-G. (2018), 'Art. 113 AEUV' in: Streinz, R. (ed.), *EUV/AEUV: Vertrag über die Europäische Union, Vertrag über die Arbeitsweise der Europäischen Union, Charta der Grundrechte der Europäischen Union,* München, C. H.Beck, para 13 ff.

could not agree on the regulatory measure to reach these, a carbon tax could be introduced by a group of Member States, while others could reach the CO2 reduction with other instruments (or trust their existing instruments, such as Sweden, which has had a carbon tax already since 1991[87] and could be uninterested in changing it). If, however, the tax were proposed without, or instead of prior agreement on binding CO2 reduction, an enhanced cooperation would regulate a good with low excludability (every Member State would benefit from the participant's efforts in bringing down emissions) and thus positive externalities, almost inviting non-participants to free-ride on achievements of participants. Enhanced cooperation will in all likelihood not occur under such conditions. The very same effect occurred as early as 2005: In the context of a larger effort to lower CO2 emissions to fulfil the Kyoto Protocol, the Commission proposed a directive, based on Art. 93 EC (Nice) which is now Art. 113 TFEU, that was supposed to base, among other things, the taxation of passenger cars on their CO2 emissions per kilometre.[88] When Member States in the Council did not reach unanimity, the EP's rapporteur on the file noted that "should the Council fail to reach an agreement on the issue, the countries favouring the Commission's proposal in question should proceed with the enhanced co-operation procedure, according to Art. 43–45 of the Treaty. Especially within the environmental objectives of the proposal that would provide for a way forward and comply with most of the Member States' desire to make progress in the area."[89] However, rather than proceeding with enhanced cooperation, the proposal was dropped altogether.[90] This perfectly fits the expectation that Member States avoid enhanced cooperation in fields with positive externalities and low levels of excludability which would allow for free-riding, such as emission reduction.[91]

**Art. 114 TFEU** is the legal basis for most harmonisation measures in the internal market. It is therefore particularly important to the functioning of the market, hence frequently applied and central also symbolically. What was said above about legal bases at the core of the fundamental freedoms applies similarly to Art. 114 TFEU, which is the legislative core norm for the internal market

---

[87] https://www.government.se/government-policy/taxes-and-tariffs/swedens-carbon-tax/ (accessed 08/11/2019).

[88] European Commission, 'Proposal for a Council Directive on Passenger Car Related Taxes', COM(2005) 261 final.

[89] European Parliament, Report A6-0240/2006 on the proposal of a Council Directive on Passenger Car Related Taxes, Explanatory Statement (Rapporteur's Position).

[90] Heber, C. (2021), *Enhanced Cooperation and European Tax Law*, Oxford University Press.

[91] Böttner, R. (2023), 'The Instrument of Enhanced Cooperation: Pitfalls and Possibilities for Differentiated Integration'.

law: Enhanced cooperation in this area would have the ability to harm a core value of the functioning of the EU, the intactness of the internal market. On the other hand, it must be admitted that the areas harmonised by Art. 114 TFEU are not completely free of differentiation. Examples for this are Denmark's and Sweden's infamous exceptions to the internal market law, Sweden allowing for the oral-use tobacco 'Snus' to be sold in Sweden despite its general prohibition in the EU[92] and Denmark restricting the acquisition of second homes by citizens from other countries, including EU Member States.[93] Consequently, an academic proposal for the use of enhanced cooperation in the context of Art. 114 TFEU is the introduction of an optional Common European Sales Law[94] in a differentiated manner.[95] However, Art. 114 TFEU is governed by the ordinary legislative procedure, which makes enhanced cooperation less likely, as legislation can be passed also against the resistance of single states. Thus, it seems most likely that the Sales Law has so far not been adopted is mostly due to a lack of interest among the Member States. Beyond this example, the limitation set by Art. 329 (2) TFEU, which prohibits to undermine the internal market, limits any potential scope of application of enhanced cooperation within Article 114 TFEU drastically.[96]

In contrast, **Art. 115 TFEU** requires unanimous decision-making. It applies to the cases of internal market law-making that are excluded from the scope

[92] See Article 151 and Annex XV, X of the Act of Accession of Austria, Finland and Sweden.

[93] Protocol (no 32) on the Acquisition of Property in Denmark.

[94] European Commission, 'Proposal for a Regulation on a Common European Sales Law', COM(2011) 635 final.

[95] Proposals by Zeitzmann, S. (2011), 'Das Verfahren der Verstärkten Zusammenarbeit und dessen erstmalige Anwendung: Ein Ehescheidungs- und Trennungsrecht für Europa', *ZEuS*, pp. 87–113, 113; Böttner, R. (2021), *The Constitutional Framework for Enhanced Cooperation in EU law*, Nijhoff studies in European Union law, Leiden The Netherlands, Koninklijke Brill NV, Section 9.2.1., picked up also by the European Commission, 'White Paper on the Future of Europe', COM(2017)2025, p. 21. The fact that the Common European Sales Law would from the outset work as an optional, second legal framework beside the Member States' existing sales laws would facilitate the co-existence of Member States with and without that second framework. Nevertheless, there would undoubtedly be a certain practical fragmentation of the internal market, which might arguably still be within the limitations of Art. 329 TFEU prohibiting enhanced cooperation to undermine the single market. That being said, the Common European Sales Law has not been high on the political agenda for years and is therefore unlikely to see legislative activity in the foreseeable future.

[96] Diverging opinion, Amort, M. (2020), *Zur Ordnung des Verbraucherrechts. Mit europäischem Verbraucherschutz zu verfassungskonformer Typisierung* [currently unpublished manuscript], who claims—unfortunately wihtou any further explanation—that despite its optional character, a differentiated Common European Sales Law would create "an 'internal market within the internal markt'" [own translation].

of Art. 114 TFEU by its second paragraph: rights and interests of employees, the free movement of persons, and fiscal provisions.[97] The free movement of persons is, once again, a topic so close to the heart of the internal market that differentiation is hard to imagine under Art. 329 TFEU. Equally, different levels of employee's rights would have the potential of undermining the EU in the eyes of millions of employees and therefore is something that decision-makers in all likelihood will not take into consideration. However, Art. 115 TFEU could, as Art. 113 TFEU, be used in the field of taxes. As Art. 113 TFEU is a *lex specialis* dealing with indirect taxes, Art. 115 TFEU-based tax regulation would come into question only for direct taxation.[98] That being said, what was laid out above regarding taxes largely applies to Art. 115 TFEU as well. Especially, the much-debated Common Consolidated Corporate Tax Base (CCCTB) could be passed on this legal basis, including in an enhanced cooperation set up. The idea of basing the CCCBT on enhanced cooperation was even brought up by the European Commission as early as 2001[99] and CCCBT continues to be mentioned in the context of subjects for enhanced cooperations.[100] The Commission published a first proposal for a directive on a CCCTB in 2015, which was never adopted.[101]

---

[97] Obwexer, W. (2004), 'Gesetzgebung im Binnenmarkt—die Kompetenzverteilung im Verfassungsentwurf' in: Hatje, A., Terhechte, J. P. (eds.), *Das Binnenmarktziel in der europäischen Verfassung,* Baden-Baden, Nomos, p. 164 ff.

[98] Kamann, H.-G. (2018), 'Art. 113 AEUV' in: Streinz, R. (ed.), *EUV/AEUV: Vertrag über die Europäische Union, Vertrag über die Arbeitsweise der Europäischen Union, Charta der Grundrechte der Europäischen Union,* München, C. H.Beck, para. 5, 11 f.

[99] European Commission (2001), 'Towards an Internal Market without tax obstacles: A strategy for providing companies with a consolidated corporate tax base for their EU-wide activities', COM(2001) 582 final; see also European Commission (2004), 'A Common Consolidated Corporate Tax Base: Commission Non-Paper to informal Ecofin Council, 10 and 11 September 2004'.

[100] See Cédelle, A. (2015), Enhanced cooperation: A way forward for tax harmonisation in the EU?, Working Paper Series; Bettendorf, L., van der Horst, A., Mooij, R. A. D., Vrijburg, H., 'Corporate Tax Consolidation and Enhanced Cooperation in the European Union', *Fiscal Studies*, Vol. 31, No. 4, pp. 453–479; Kroll, D. A., Leuffen, D. (2015), 'Enhanced cooperation in practice. An analysis of differentiated integration in EU secondary law', *Journal of European Public Policy*, Vol. 22, No. 3, pp. 353–373, p. 353 f.; Cerioni, L. (2006), 'The Possible Introduction of Common Consolidated Base Taxation via Enhanced Cooperation: Some Open Issues', *European Taxation*, pp. 187–196; O'Brien, M. (2005), 'Company Taxation, State Aid and Fundamental Freedoms: is the Next Step Enhanced Cooperation?', *ELRev*, 209–233.

[101] European Commission, Proposal for a Council Directive on a Common Consolidated Corporate Tax Base (CCCTB), COM/2011/0121 final.

As mentioned above (Art. 113 TFEU) there is a precedent for an authorisation of an enhanced cooperation in the field of taxation (path dependency). Moreover, since the CCCTB has been debated for decades, including an unsuccessful Commission proposal, one could argue that the ground for a decision stating that unanimity cannot be attained within a reasonable period of time (last resort criterion, Art. 20 (1) TFEU) is largely prepared. However, the discussion on the CCCTB is a case that shows particularly well the importance of taking into account the costs (excludability and rivalry in consumption) and externalities of a project.

The main idea of a CCCTB is that Member States offer multinational companies a second tax code parallel to their national tax codes (at least as far as some aspects of the tax code are concerned). This second code, which is the same in all (participating) Member States allows companies to calculate their taxable income etc. using one single set of rules throughout all Member States, including subsidiaries they may have in other Member States and companies they control. Moreover, they can declare their taxes in one single Member State, namely the state where the parent company is located. That state conducts all tax calculations and then attributes the taxable profits to the states where they were effectively generated. This is done using a formula that takes into account the companies' (and subsidiaries') employees, capital, and sales per country. Each involved country than taxes its own share of the profits by its own corporate tax rates, which the concept does not aim to harmonise. The introduction of such a company tax system would follow several aims: It is intended to avoid over-taxation and double taxation for companies operating in the single market, thus strengthening the latter, while allowing for savings in compliance costs. At the same time, the system should allow "fair competition on tax rates" between the Member States. Moreover, it is foreseen that where companies use the additional system, they would have "fewer opportunities for tax planning by companies using transfer pricing or mismatches in Member State tax systems".[102]

This latter aspect shows why some Member States profiting from such "tax planning" are opposed to the proposed system. The system was first intended to be introduced as a purely optional system for companies, with a thorough common tax system in place upon the entry into force of the model.[103] Later, facing the deadlock in the Council, the Commission renewed its strategy, proposing a two-step approach: A first step, according to the proposal, could be a less refined

[102] European Commission Proposal for a Council Directive on a Common Consolidated Corporate Tax Base (CCCTB), COM/2011/0121 final, p. 4 ff.

[103] Ibid.

common tax system running parallel to the national systems (Common Corporate Tax Base, CCTB, sometimes referred to as "'simple' common tax base"[104]). However, addressing the increasing problem of aggressive tax planning by multinational corporations, the system should be mandatory for all companies with a turnover of 750 million Euros per year or more, and optional for all other groups.[105] As a second step, the system is supposed to be refined to the level foreseen in the first proposal (including cross-border tax consolidation within a group).[106]

The different proposals and ideas regarding a common (consolidated or not) corporate tax system show how much the system's design can affect its benefits for participants as well as its externalities. The first design proposed by the Commission foresaw a purely optional system for companies. As such, the externalities would have been rather small: Low corporate tax Member States like Ireland could have still offered companies tax rates so low that the savings in compliance costs generated by using the CCCTB would have been significant enough to convince them to use the CCCTB rather than paying a bigger share of its tax burden in e.g. Ireland. Thus, outsiders would have likely not invested too much political capital to block such an approach. However, this low excludability also affects the benefits that could be generated by way of the CCCTB, and in fact Member States refrained from using enhanced cooperation.[107]

The new system however, featuring a compulsory taxation for the biggest corporations (which would mean capturing almost two thirds of turnover generated by groups[108]) could lead to major shifts in the tax distribution between Member States, including between participants and non-participants (depending on the exact final design, especially on whether subsidiaries of parent companies based in non-participant Member States would still be complied to tax their profits where they were created, as currently foreseen see in Art. 2 (2) of the proposal). Such a design would mean a high degree of excludability and high

[104] European Commission (2004), 'A Common Consolidated Corporate Tax Base: Commission Non-Paper to informal Ecofin Council, 10 and 11 September 2004', p. 2.

[105] European Commission, Proposal for a Council Directive on a Common Corporate Tax Base, COM(2016) 685 final.

[106] European Commission, Proposal for a Council Directive on a Common Consolidated Corporate Tax Base (CCCTB), COM(2016) 683 final.

[107] For details on several issues arising from such a design, see Cerioni, L. (2006), 'The Possible Introduction of Common Consolidated Base Taxation via Enhanced Cooperation: Some Open Issues', *European Taxation*, pp. 187–196.

[108] European Commission, Proposal for a Council Directive on a Common Corporate Tax Base, COM(2016) 685 final, p. 8.

externalities[109], which could raise the appetite for enhanced cooperation among interested states, but also incentivise non-participants to join an enhanced cooperation if established or even help to solve a deadlock in the first place, making enhanced cooperation less likely. Currently, the CCTB and CCCTB are still being discussed and on the political agenda.[110] A new approach is now to adjust the idea of a CCCBT to make it fit the OECD's two-pillar approach to taxation of international corporations.[111] A move towards enhanced cooperation was unsuccessfully brought up repeatedly for as long as the idea of a CCCTB has been around. Nevertheless, it is still a valid possibility and one of the areas with the highest likelihood of eventual further moves towards differentiation. As a side note, it should be borne in mind that these explanations also apply to other, similar proposals regarding taxes within the EU, such as a proposed Digital Tax, should it not be passed on an OECD level.[112] It should also be added, finally, that the CJEU in its case law on the FTT indicated that it is ready to keep Member States on a long leash when it comes to externalities in non-participant Member States.[113]

*Excursus: Taxing Companies—Harmonisation of Tax Rates*

Taxes that can be collected from a company can generally be regarded as a common pool resource: The corporate taxes can be collected first and foremost by the country where the company's headquarters is located;

[109] Stressing this aspect: Cédelle, A. (2015), Enhanced cooperation: A way forward for tax harmonisation in the EU?, Working Paper Series, pp. 40, 42.

[110] Scholz, O. (2019), 'Germany will consider EU-wide bank deposit reinsurance', *Financial Times*, 11 June 2019; see also: Joint Position Paper of Germany and France on the CCTB-Proposal: https://www.bundesfinanzministerium.de/Content/DE/Standardartikel/Themen/Europa/2018-06-20-Meseberg-Anl2.pdf?__blob=publicationFile&v=1 (accessed 06/11/2019).

[111] The initiative is now being discussed under the title Business in Europe: Framework for Income Taxation (BEFIT), for which an impact assessment has been launched by the European Commission, see (https://ec.europa.eu/info/law/better-regulation/have-your-say/initiatives/13463-Business-in-Europe-Framework-for-Income-Taxation-BEFIT-_en (accessed 21/06/2023).

[112] https://www.politico.eu/article/margrethe-vestager-competition-digital-europe-tax-privacy-data-european-commision/ (accessed 06/11/2019).

[113] CJEU, case C-209/13 (UK v Council), ECLI:EU:C:2014:283.

there is only so much income that can be taxed (the tax base) and if several users (i.e. states) share the benefit (tax) generated by it, the income is lower than if one state manages to tax the tax base in its entirety. At the same time, the excludability from the benefits of a country (the taxes that can be collected) is low: a company is free to relocate its seat to any country it chooses, allowing for tax competition among states—including the potential of a race to the bottom. It is for this reason, and for the vast differences among Member States' corporate tax rates, that EU policy makers, prominently from France and Germany, repeatedly call for a harmonisation in tax rates.

However, under these preconditions, harmonising corporate taxes would only make it easier for outsiders to lower their taxes under the rate set by the insiders and attract companies. Hence, externalities would be positive while potentially harming the participants, even if they gained more taxes from the companies that did not relocate their seats. Hence, under such preconditions, differentiation would allow "freeriding of an egregious kind, to the great detriment of the socioeconomic health of other member states, and the politics of the EU as a whole" (V. Schmidt). However, as illustrated above, by binding the tax to be paid to the territory where the added value is created, e.g. by apportionment through a formula including labour, capital and sales, the overall, non-excludable resource (common pool resource) is divided into single, excludable pools for every Member State ("private goods"). Therefore, tax harmonisation, which was traditionally regarded as unfit for differentiation, could be turned into a field where differentiation is possible, if the proposal managed to effectively change the logic of taxation. The global tax reform package brokered by the OECD consequently follows a similar logic. It is no surprise, then, that when the implementation of that very OECD tax reform package faced resistance from Hungary, Member States were quick to propose that it could be passed without Hungary using—of course—enhanced cooperation, which once again proves that the mechanism could indeed be bound for further application in the field of taxation.

**Art. 116 (2) TFEU** enables the EU to pass directives against national provisions distorting the conditions of competition in the internal market after an unsuccessful consultation procedure according to Art. 116 (1) TFEU. Directives are passed by the ordinary legislative procedure, i.e. following QMV in the Council.

Because of the particular requirements as compared to Art. 114, 115 TFEU, no legislation was passed on this competence yet.[114] For its potentially far-reaching impact on the internal market as a whole and the fact that Art. 116 (2) TFEU does not require unanimity in the Council, a usage (if one ever occurs at all) through enhanced cooperation seems unlikely. On the contrary, it has been argued that Art. 116 TFEU could provide a measure to "sanction" enhanced cooperations infringing the prohibition to distort competition between Member States laid down in Art. 326 (2) TFEU.[115] The idea is that if an enhanced cooperation distorted the competition between Member States, the Commission could act according to Art. 116 TFEU and eventually, the EU could pass a directive defusing the enhanced cooperation. However, this idea is built on several unlikely preconditions: Firstly, an infringement of a legal condition of enhanced cooperation could more easily be removed by the CJEU. Secondly, the hypothetical scenario would only arise if the Commission first supported a project (Art. 329 TFEU) and then turned against it. Thirdly, to pass a directive according to Art. 116 (2) TFEU, there would be a need for a qualified majority in the Council—as for the prior authorisation of an enhanced cooperation. Thus, as the Commission, several Member States would have to turn diametrically against their own previous decisions for such a situation to arise.[116]

**Art. 117 TFEU**, again, is designed for bilateral work between the EU and single Member States, which is why differentiation cannot apply in this area.

**Art. 118 TFEU**, finally, enables the EU to create European intellectual property rights for the uniform protection of intellectual property in the internal market. It is used when the aim of the Union action is not to harmonise the existing national intellectual property rights (in which case the correct legal basis is Art. 114 TFEU, see e.g. the controversial Directive (EU) 2019/790 on copyright and related rights in the Digital Single Market), but to create new, genuinely European rights. While the creation of such rights is governed by QMV, language

[114] Schröder, M. (2018), 'Art. 116 AEUV' in: Streinz, R. (ed.), *EUV/AEUV: Vertrag über die Europäische Union, Vertrag über die Arbeitsweise der Europäischen Union, Charta der Grundrechte der Europäischen Union,* München, C. H.Beck, paras. 3 f.

[115] Schröder, M. (2018), 'Art. 116 AEUV' in: Streinz, R. (ed.), *EUV/AEUV: Vertrag über die Europäische Union, Vertrag über die Arbeitsweise der Europäischen Union, Charta der Grundrechte der Europäischen Union,* München, C. H.Beck, para. 5; Khan, D.-E., Eisenhut, D. (2015), 'Art. 116 TFEU' in: Geiger, R., Khan, D.-E., Kotzur, M. (eds.), *European Union Treaties: Treaty on European Union Treaty on the Functioning of the European Union,* Munich, Oxford, Beck, Hart, para 2.

[116] See also Korte, S. (2016), 'Art. 116 AEUV' in: Calliess, C., Ruffert, M. (eds.), *EUV/AEUV: Das Verfassungsrecht der Europäischen Union mit Europäischer Grundrechtecharta: Kommentar,* München, C. H. Beck.

arrangements can only be laid down unanimously (Art. 118 (2) TFEU). The latter is an indicator that enhanced cooperation could be sought in this area, and indeed, the Unitary Patent passed on this legal basis was the second act adopted via enhanced cooperation.[117] Although only the language regime required unanimity, the entire package was passed in one single regulation.[118] Following the logic of path dependence, another enhanced cooperation based on this competence seems likely. Yet, passing the Unitary Patent was a burdensome process with no less than three cases brought to the CJEU, plus national legislation further halting the process,[119] making it anything but an example of a few Member States smoothly proceeding in integration, as enhanced cooperation is often depicted. On the other hand, especially for anyone who sees enhanced cooperation as an instrument of a 'multi-speed Europe', it can also be seen as a success: The project, which features high internal benefits and a high degree of excludability, developed centripetal effects and convinced one of its two opponents, Italy, to join the enhanced cooperation in 2015.[120]

#### 2.3.1.2 Social Policy

The second principal area of shared competences is "social policy, for the aspects defined in this Treaty" (Art. 4 (2)(b) TFEU). It is apparent from the wording that the possibilities for the EU to act in the field of social policy are very limited, and largely constrained to coordination measures.[121]

Details on the EU social policy are laid down in Art. 151–161 TFEU. In addition, the EU has a competence to take initiatives to coordinate Member State's social policies according to Art. 5 (3) TFEU. Of these legal bases, only Art. 153 and 157 (3) TFEU contain relevant legislative competences relevant for the application of enhanced cooperation.

---

[117] See Council Decision (2011/167/EU) of 10 March 2011 authorising enhanced cooperation in the area of the creation of unitary patent protection.

[118] Regulation (EU) No 1257/2012 of the European Parliament and of the Council of 17 December 2012 implementing enhanced cooperation in the area of the creation of unitary patent protection.

[119] Graf von Luckner, J. (2021), 'Stay home, stay healthy: Das „Ergänzungs- oder besondere Näheverhältnis zum Unionsrecht" in der BVerfG-Rechtsprechung und die europäische Integration durch Völkerrecht', *Europarecht*, No. 2, pp. 209–224.

[120] European Commission, Decision (EU) 2015/1753.

[121] Fischer-Lescano, A., Kommer, S. (2011), 'EU in der Finanzkrise: Zur Leistungsfähigkeit des Verfahrens der verstärkten Zusammenarbeit für eine Intensivierung der Wirtschafts- und Sozialpolitik', *KJ*, 412–433.

**Art. 153 TFEU** contains legislative competences in the field of labour law, ranging from mere knowledge exchange (Art. 153 (2)(a) TFEU) to establishing minimum requirement in several areas such as improvement of working environments, social protection and equal treatment of men and women in the labour market (Art. 153 (2)(b) TFEU). For several of these, decision-making in the Council is governed by unanimity.[122] Fields of potential future action can be found in the European Pillar on Social Rights.[123] In light of diverging views on social policy across the EU, especially where unanimity in the Council is required, Member States could look into the use of enhanced cooperation. However, as the subjects listed under this title mostly regard workers and their rights, it would seem difficult to introduce an instrument giving rights only to workers in certain Member States, as such an approach could spark anti-European sentiments in the outsider states' population.[124] The degree of externalities and rivalry in consumption depends largely on the specific project and could tilt in any direction. Due to this, Art. 153 (2)(b) TFEU could be the legal base for a future enhanced cooperation, but is not necessarily a "prime candidate".

It can be noted, however, that differentiation of social policy is repeatedly discussed as a means of stabilisation among the Euro-Member States.[125] It is argued that states with a shared currency need to be more integrated economically for the monetary union to work. In this context, economic integration includes social and

---

122 See Art. 152 (2)(subpar 3) TFEU: social security and social protection of workers; protection of workers where their employment contract is terminated; representation and collective defence of the interests of workers and employers; conditions of employment for third-country nationals legally residing in Union territory.

123 European Commission (2017), 'Establishing a European Pillar of Social Rights', COM(2017) 250 final; see also: Hendrickx, F. (2018), 'The European Social Pillar', *European Labour Law Journal*, Vol. 9, No. 1, pp. 3–6; Kingreen, T. (2017), Ein verbindlicher EU-Rechtsrahmen für soziale Grundsicherungssysteme in den Mitgliedstaaten, FORSCHUNGSBERICHT.

124 In the context of a equal treatment-related proposal, it was untypically decided to *explicitly* exclude enhanced cooperation because of the sensitive interplay between individual rights and differentiation: "A number of delegations felt that enhanced cooperation was not the right way forward, citing, in particular, the importance of ensuring consistency in the protection of basic rights and possible negative implications for the functioning of the internal market. Recalling that equal treatment was one of the objectives of the European Union, as defined in the Treaties, the Commission also urged the need to seek unanimous agreement on the Directive." Council Doc. 15819/14 of 21 November 2014, p. 7.

125 See already Thym, D. (2004), *Ungleichzeitigkeit und europäisches Verfassungsrecht*, Schriftenreihe europäisches Verfassungsrecht, Baden-Baden, Nomos, p. 148; European Commission, Strengthening the Social Dimension of the Economic and Monetary Union, COM(2013) 690 final.

welfare policies as they influence the economic performance and mitigate shocks and crises.[126] For this reason, the idea of introducing social enhanced cooperation for EMU-Member States was included in the Juncker-Commission's 'White Paper on the Future of Europe'.[127] Given that the differentiation would move along the lines of existing differences within the EU, such an approach would not arbitrarily "leaving outsiders behind" (after all, non-participation in the Euro is either voluntary or temporary) and therefore seems considerably more likely. One of the most prominent ideas brought forward is that of a Eurozone Unemployment Benefit System.[128] Such a system would prima facie have neutral externalities, have a high degree of excludability and a low degree of rivalry of consumption, all of which points towards the possibility of using enhanced cooperation.

Beyond the Eurozone, it has been proposed to use enhanced cooperation to create "'pools' for health care provision among countries sharing borders".[129] This alludes to the compensation of costs when Union citizens make use of social security-covered medial services in other MS, e.g. by seeing a doctor when abroad, which is covered by the European Health Insurance Card. There is a compensation mechanism for this between MS, but neighbouring MS (especially such with similar cost structures) could go beyond this to facilitate the process and thus lower administrative costs for the participants without, however, affecting the entitlements of citizens to cross-border health care. It would not, therefore, "undermine the [...] social cohesion" within the EU, as prohibited by Art. 326 TFEU. Yet, Art. 35 (3) of the Regulation on the Coordination of Social

[126] See e.g. "Five Presidents' Report": https://ec.europa.eu/info/sites/default/files/5-presidents-report_en.pdf (last access 02/11/2021), p. 8 f.; European Commission, Reflection Paper on the Deepening of the Economic and Monetary Union, COM(2017) 291.

[127] COM(2017) 260, p. 29.

[128] European Commission, COM(2013) 690 final, p. 11; Meseberg Declaration of France and Germany, 19/06/2019, https://www.diplomatie.gouv.fr/de/frankreichs-beziehungen-zu-deutschland-osterreich-und-der-schweiz/bilaterale-beziehungen-mit-deutschland/neuigkeiten/article/europa-gemeinsame-erklarung-deutschlands-und-frankreichs-19-06-2018 (last access 21/01/2020); Fischer-Lescano, A., Kommer, S. (2011), 'EU in der Finanzkrise: Zur Leistungsfähigkeit des Verfahrens der verstärkten Zusammenarbeit für eine Intensivierung der Wirtschafts- und Sozialpolitik', *KJ*, 412–433 Scholars agree, however, that a Eurozone Unemployment Benefit Scheme could not be based entirely on the narrow legal base of Art. 153 TFEU. Whether a permanent scheme would at all be disputed without a Treaty change is disputed, see Beblavý, M., Lenaerts, K. (2017), 'Feasibility and Added Value of a European Unemployment Benefit Scheme: Main findings from a comprehensive research project'.

[129] Schmidt, V. A. (2009), 'Re-Envisioning the European Union: Identity, Democracy, Economy*', *JCMS: Journal of Common Market Studies*, Vol. 47, No. 3, pp. 17–42, p. 29.

Security Systems[130] already foresees the possibility of adapting bi- or multilateral agreements among Member States to establish alternative systems of mutual compensation, which could be used by Member States in case such a differentiation is desired. Therefore, there is no need to resort to enhanced cooperation to achieve this aim.

**Art. 157 (3) TFEU** enables the EU to adopt measures aiming for equal treatment (including equal payment) between male and female workers. The adoption follows the ordinary legislative procedure. The EU shows significant differences in engagement with equal treatment measures as came to light when two family law (divorce related) measures were adopted via enhanced cooperation (though based on a different legal basis). This could lead to a certain interest in differentiation when it comes to passing further laws, e.g. a move towards equal representation of both sexes in management positions.[131] Moreover, the effects of new measures are largely limited to participating states and therefore have very limited externalities. On the other hand, the fact that a qualified majority suffices to pass measures under Art. 157 TFEU makes an enhanced cooperation in this area considerably less likely.

In conclusion, enhanced cooperation in social policy is possible, but not highly likely in practice. This may, however, be different for cases along the lines of existing differentiation, especially the Eurozone. In this case, enhanced cooperation might enable a deeper integration of the Euro Member States in social matters in future.

#### 2.3.1.3 Economic, Social and Territorial Cohesion

EU policy on economic, social and territorial cohesion is laid out in Art. 174–178 TFEU.[132] It is largely implemented by way of cohesion and structural funds. While EU funds are not necessarily outside scope of enhanced cooperation as laid out below (Chap. 4: The Principle of Openness), and the implementation of the funds is regulated by secondary legal acts (Art. 177 (1), 178 (1) TFEU), the pursuit of territorial, social, and economic cohesion is an obligation to both the EU and the Member States (Art. 175, 174 TFEU). Moreover, Art. 226 TFEU explicitly regulates that enhanced cooperation shall not undermine economic, social

---

130 Regulation (EC) No 883/2004 on the coordination of social security systems.

131 European Commission, 'Proposal for a DIRECTIVE OF THE EUROPEAN PARLIAMENT AND OF THE COUNCIL on improving the gender balance among non-executive directors of companies listed on stock exchanges and related measures', COM(2012) 614 final.

132 Obwexer, W. (2015), 'Art. 4 AEUV' in: Groeben, H. v. d., Schwarze, J., Hatje, A. (eds.), *Europäisches Unionsrecht,* Baden-Baden, Nomos, para 18.

and territorial cohesion. Therefore, differentiation within the funds established by the Treaties is not an option. They are therefore outside the scope of enhanced cooperation.

#### 2.3.1.4 Agriculture and Fisheries, Excl. the Conservation of Marine Biological Resources

The fourth principal area includes agriculture and fisheries, except for the conservation of marine biological resources, which is part of the exclusive competence in Art. 3 (1)(d) TFEU. This branch of EU policy, especially agriculture, has traditionally had the role of the second major EU policy field after the internal market. The funds relating to the Common Agriculture Policy (CAP) regularly make up over a third of the EU's total expenditure.[133]

The detailed provisions on the CAP and common fisheries policy (CFP) can be found in Art. 38–44 TFEU, but only Art. 43 (2) TFEU contains an actual legal base within the shared competences of the EU.[134]

Following the ordinary legislative procedure, Council and EP may lay down the provisions necessary to pursue the aims of CAP and CFP, especially for the common organisation of agricultural markets (Art. 43 (2) TFEU). Yet, it is governed by QMV in the Council and moreover agricultural policy is not generally known as an arena for political experiments. This makes enhanced cooperation in agriculture and fisheries overall unlikely.

#### 2.3.1.5 Environment

The EU environmental policy is based on Art. 191–193 TFEU. **Art. 191 TFEU** sets out its aims, namely EU-wide and international efforts to protect the environment and combat climate change. **Art. 193 TFEU** secures the possibility for Member States to go beyond the EU level of protection, an instance of pre-determined differentiation.

---

[133] https://ec.europa.eu/info/food-farming-fisheries/key-policies/common-agricultural-policy/cap-glance_en (accessed 14/11/2019).

[134] Art. 43 (3) TFEU is largely part of the exclusive EU competence on the conservation of marine biological resources under the common fisheries policy, Art. 3 (1)(d) TFEU. While the agricultural arm of Art. 43 (3) TFEU does not fall within the exclusive competences (see COM(2016) 653 final, Explanatory Memorandum, para 2), it has, so far, only been used once in this regard and this is not expected to change (Bouquet, A., Erlbacher, F., Lewis, A.-X.-P. (2019), 'Art. 43 TFEU' in: Kellerbauer, M., Klamert, M., Tomkin, J., Bogensberger, W., Bouquet, A., Erlbacher, F. (eds.), *The EU treaties and the Charter of Fundamental Rights: A commentary*, Oxford, Oxford University Press, para. 15 f.).

**Art. 192 TFEU** is the principal legal base for EU environmental action. It is generally governed by ordinary legislative procedure (Art. 192 (1) TFEU), yet Art. 192 (2) TFEU foresees unanimous decision-making in the Council for a number of sub-areas, including taxation, town and country management, water management, and energy sources and supply. Any implementing measures of these programmes must, again, be passed according to paragraphs 1 or 2 respectively.

In the past, different scholars,[135] but also former German minister of foreign affairs *Fischer*[136] have brought up the idea of Member States going ahead in the field of environmental policy by way of enhanced cooperation.

Environmental policymaking is usually affiliated with high immediate policy costs. Emission-reduction, both in terms of emissions with immediate negative effects (harmful sewage or exhaust etc.) and with long-term negative effects (CO2, methane, CFC etc.) require conversion efforts, active environmental protection such as the establishment of nature reserves require management and restrictions. The externalities of such policies, on the other hand, are positive as outsiders even profit from participants efforts (cleaner air, water, etc.) and the benefits from environmental policies tend to be non-excludable public goods.[137] This leads to a situation in which it would, in theory, be conceivable that Member States opposed to further environmental action would support action by interested peers to the extent that they could even green-light an enhanced cooperation in the areas governed by QMV decision-making: if other states went ahead, non-participants could profit from the benefits and potentially even profit from cost evasion movements in their direction. Yet, this free riding would be diametrically opposed to the interests of willing Member States. Therefore, both in the areas of qualified majority- and unanimous voting, it seems difficult to imagine enhanced cooperation in the field of environmental policy. This is further underlined by the fact that by virtue of Art. 193 TFEU, environmental policy consists of minimum harmonisation measures, and Member States can always opt for higher

---

135 Bär, S., Gehring, T., Homeyer, I. von, Kraemer, R. A., Mazurek, A.-G., Klasing, A., Tarasofky, R. G. (2002), 'Closer Co-operation, A New Instrument for European Environmental Policy?', *SSRN Electronic Journal*; Müller-Brandeck-Bocquet, G. (1997), 'Flexible Integration—eine Chance für die europäische Umweltpolitik?', *integration*, pp. 292–304, 302 f.; Bender, T. (2001), 'Die Verstärkte Zusammenarbeit nach Nizza: Anwendungsfelder und Bewertung im Spiegel historischer Präzedenzfälle der differenzierten Integration', *ZaöRV*, Vol. 63, No. 3, pp. 729–770, 747 ff.

136 Joschka Fischer (2000).

137 Kölliker, A. (2001), 'Bringing together or driving apart the union? Towards a theory of differentiated integration', p. 136.

domestic standard already. In this context, it would not seem logic to establish an enhanced cooperation, at the same time reducing the political pressure for a uniform solution. Moreover, the EU has taken significant steps in environmental policy, e.g. in the context of the European Green New Deal,[138] with the EU as a whole, especially the so-called 'European Climate Law', which builds a binding framework for the EU climate action and enshrines the EU's climate neutrality goal for 2050.[139] There have not even been proposals to advance the programme in a differentiated matter.

If anything, what might be an imaginable, though somewhat unorthodox, option is the adoption of an action programme under Art. 192 (3) TFEU by way of enhanced cooperation. The same idea was proposed by the European Parliament in the context of the initial introduction of enhanced cooperation to the Treaties.[140] Action programmes lay down priority objectives, i.e. the broad lines for the environmental policy in the years to come. Since the Treaty of Maastricht, they need to be passed by Parliament and Council in an ordinary legislative procedure.[141] If ambitious Member States, especially a majority of them, were to pass an action programme among themselves, which would mainly outline and coordinate aims to fulfil in additional individual Member States' measures admissible under Art. 193 TFEU, it could create political pressure on the non-participants without creating the same level of positive externalities. However, in this case, non-participants would be less likely to authorise an enhanced cooperation with the necessary qualified majority, as the result would face them with political pressure towards unwanted policy measures. Beyond this, the usage of enhanced cooperation with the aim of passing, essentially, a policy statement seems excessively burdensome.

Finally, one could imagine differentiated approaches regarding the environment in the form of sub-regional cooperation, for example common norms for all states connected by a certain river (e.g. Danube, Rhine,...) or with certain common environmental features (e.g. all Alpine states) with respect to this common

[138] See European Commission, The Green New Deal, COM(2019) 640 final.

[139] Regulation (EU) 2021/1119 of the European Parliament and the Council establishing the framework for achieving climate neutrality and amending Regulations (EC) No 401/2009 and (EU) 2018/1999 ('European Climate Law').

[140] The implementation of non-legislative action programmes by way of enhanced cooperation was explicitly suggested by the European Parliament: European Parliament, *Minutes of the Sitting of Thursday 16 July 1998*, O. J. C 292/144 (1998).

[141] Kahl, W. (2018), 'Art. 192 AEUV' in: Streinz, R. (ed.), *EUV/AEUV: Vertrag über die Europäische Union, Vertrag über die Arbeitsweise der Europäischen Union, Charta der Grundrechte der Europäischen Union,* München, C. H.Beck, para. 36 ff.

interest.[142] Yet, it seems more likely that such measures would either be passed via international law (as is already the case, though not limited to environmental questions, see e.g. the Upper Rhine Council)[143], by way of formally unilateral secondary law with a limited scope of application, or as a European Grouping for Territorial Cooperation based on Art. 175 TFEU.

#### 2.3.1.6 Consumer Protection

The TFEU provision on consumer protection, **Art. 169 TFEU**, is of a largely programmatic nature. Art. 169.2 (b) TFEU provides the EU with a legal base to pass harmonising legal acts, although they can only "support, supplement and monitor the policy pursued by the Member States". Due to this nature of the instruments, Art. 169.2 (b) TFEU does not play a very significant role in practice.[144] Yet, it also means that resulting legislation is necessarily somewhat distinct from the core of the internal market. It is therefore more likely to pass the threshold of Art. 326 (2) TFEU, according to which an enhanced cooperation shall not undermine the internal market. Thus, in terms of the subject-matter, enhanced cooperation does not seem out of the question in this area—topics with a sufficient distance from internal market law entail consumer information and education, over-indebtedness of consumers, protection of weaker consumer groups.[145] However, all measures of consumer protection are subject to the ordinary legislative procedure, which would in many scenarios allow—and motivate, due to the subject matter—Member States to vote down sceptical Member States,

---

[142] See Milner, F., Kölliker, A. (1999), How to Make Use of Closer Cooperation?, Working Paper, Fn. 79. Note that none of the examples given would fulfil the minimum number of nine Member States necessary for an enhanced cooperation. Doubtful: Böttner, R. (2021), *The Constitutional Framework for Enhanced Cooperation in EU law*, Nijhoff studies in European Union law, Leiden The Netherlands, Koninklijke Brill NV.

[143] https://www.conseilrhenan.org/fr/le-conseil-rhenan/convention-de-creation.html?file=files/assets/oberrheinrat/1997-12-16-de-fr-gruendungsvereinbarung-convention-creation.pdf&cid=1339 (last access 07 December 2021); see e.g. Kotzur, M. (2004), *Grenznachbarschaftliche Zusammenarbeit in Europa: Der Beitrag von Art. 24 Abs. 1 a GG zu einer Lehre vom kooperativen Verfassungs- und Verwaltungsstaat*, Schriften zum öffentlichen Recht, Berlin, Duncker & Humblot.

[144] Garben, S. (2019), 'Art. 169 TFEU' in: Kellerbauer, M., Klamert, M., Tomkin, J., Bogensberger, W., Bouquet, A., Erlbacher, F. (eds.), *The EU treaties and the Charter of Fundamental Rights: A commentary,* Oxford, Oxford University Press.

[145] On the growing potential of Art. 169 (2)(b) TFEU as a legal base, see Lurger, B. (2018), 'Art. 169 AEUV' in: Streinz, R. (ed.), *EUV/AEUV: Vertrag über die Europäische Union, Vertrag über die Arbeitsweise der Europäischen Union, Charta der Grundrechte der Europäischen Union,* München, C. H.Beck, para. 33.

rather than resorting to enhanced cooperation. Should Member States decide to make use of the possibility of a QMV enhanced cooperation, with opposed Member States giving their willing peers the go-ahead by authorising an enhanced cooperation, the consumer law could legally be a possible field for this to happen. Its low degree of externalities, high excludability and low rivalry in consumption indicate that enhanced cooperation could happen if a group smaller than a qualified majority was sufficiently interested in a measure. It must be taken into account, however, that diverging levels of consumer protection within the Union would be politically unappealing as it would invoke the image of Union citizens left behind.

#### 2.3.1.7 Transport

EU policy on transport is defined in Art. 90–100 TFEU. **Art. 91 TFEU** contains the area's principal legal basis that all secondary legislation is based on.[146]

Within the title on transport, only **Art. 92 TFEU** on derogations features unanimous voting. As this allows, upon a unanimous Council decision, to change its laws in a less favourable way for non-national carriers, it would inevitably "undermine the internal market" (Art. 326 (2) TFEU) and is therefore banned for enhanced cooperation.

Legislation in the field of transportation is closely related to the fundamental freedom to provide services. This would make differentiated integration problematic (see above, internal market). Where there is a need to differentiate in terms of sub-regional regulation (e.g. to regulate the traffic along one specific river in several Member States), Member States previously decided to act by way of international rather than EU law,[147] resulting in a path dependency trend indicating towards more use of this avenue.

In sum, enhanced cooperation in the transport policy seems unlikely.

---

[146] For an overview of all articles, see Maxian Rusche, T. (2019), 'Art. 90–100' in: Kellerbauer, M., Klamert, M., Tomkin, J., Bogensberger, W., Bouquet, A., Erlbacher, F. (eds.), *The EU treaties and the Charter of Fundamental Rights: A commentary,* Oxford, Oxford University Press, Introduction, para. 5.

[147] See the *Moselle Convention*; *Mannheim Act for the Rhine*, which even secondary European legislation builds on: Council Regulation (EEC) No 2919/85 laying down the conditions for access to the arrangements under the Revised Convention for the navigation of the Rhine relating to vessels belonging to the Rhine Navigation; Maxian Rusche, T. (2019), 'Art. 91 TFEU' in: Kellerbauer, M., Klamert, M., Tomkin, J., Bogensberger, W., Bouquet, A., Erlbacher, F. (eds.), *The EU treaties and the Charter of Fundamental Rights: A commentary,* Oxford, Oxford University Press, para. 10.

#### 2.3.1.8 Trans-European Networks

The competences on Trans-European networks are laid down in Art. 170–172 TFEU. The idea of Trans-European networks is to set up interconnections in terms of transport, communications, and energy infrastructure (**Art. 170 TFEU**) to strengthen the Union, the internal market and economic, social, and territorial cohesion. Moreover, the networks are supposed to allow citizens and businesses to benefit directly from the EU as an area without internal frontiers.

The EU competences in the area of Trans-European networks comprise standardisation and similar measures, the establishment of guidelines, and funding through the EU cohesion fund (**Art. 171 TFEU**). As the latter is established by the TFEU itself, it is not eligible for enhanced cooperation (see above, cohesion). The introduction of technical standards is, according to the public goods theory, a field that could see differentiation (non-excludable network good) as participants do not suffer disadvantages from free-riders (the more a technical standard is used, the better for all users).[148] However, the entire field of Trans-European networks is regulated by the ordinary legislative procedure, and thus by QMV (**Art. 172 TFEU**), making enhanced cooperation unlikely. Precisely because technical standardisation tends to be beneficial for all participants, it does not seem likely that Member States could be so divided over this issue that even a qualified majority cannot be found. Guidelines, finally, have the effect that only projects laid out therein can receive European funding.[149] Differentiation would therefore be unfavourable for non-participants. In addition, Trans-European networks are intrinsically linked to the "setting-up of an area without internal frontiers" in the Union. This aim would be jeopardized by differentiated action in this field, which would be inadmissible according to Art. 326 (2) TFEU ("shall not undermine the internal market or economic, social and territorial cohesion"). This largely excludes the Trans-European Networks from the factual scope of enhanced cooperation.

#### 2.3.1.9 Energy

Only **Art. 194 TFEU** deals with energy specifically. It concerns all kinds and sources of energy and sets out the aims of the European energy policy, namely a functioning energy market, energy security,—efficiency and interconnectedness.

---

[148] Kölliker, A. (2001), 'Bringing together or driving apart the union? Towards a theory of differentiated integration', p. 132.

[149] Gundel, J. (2018), 'Art. 171 AEUV' in: Grabitz, E., Hilf, M., Nettesheim, M. (eds.), *Das Recht der Europäischen Union,* München, Beck, para. 3.

The Member States' choices between different energy sources, the general structure of their energy supply, and the conditions for the exploitation of their energy resources are excluded from its scope by Art. 194 (2) (2nd sub para) TFEU. Primarily fiscal measures in the field of energy policy must be decided unanimously (Art. 194 (3) TFEU), while all other decisions are taken by the ordinary legislative procedure. Concerning the fiscal aspects, what has been said above on taxation is valid in this field as well.

Large parts of the legislation under discussion in the energy sector regard the internal market.[150] The fact that consumer- and free movement-related legislation will hardly ever see an enhanced cooperation for political, but more importantly for legal reasons (Art. 326 TFEU) has been laid out above. In addition, in light of the interconnected European energy system, the field of energy is good with low excludability, making differentiation unattractive. Finally, the leftover field is governed by QMV voting in the Council, making enhanced cooperation unlikely.

Hence, an enhanced cooperation in the field of energy, despite having been discussed in the past,[151] seems overall unlikely.

#### 2.3.1.10 Area of Freedom, Security and Justice

Title V on the Area of Freedom, Security and Justice (AFSJ) comprises four chapters and covers topics ranging from migration, border checks, judicial cooperation civil and criminal matters, and police cooperation (Art. 67–89 TFEU).[152]

Chapter 1 (**Art. 67–76 TFEU**) of said title covers general aspects. The only competences conferred either concern cooperation between authorities

---

[150] Garben, S. (2019), 'Art. 194 TFEU' in: Kellerbauer, M., Klamert, M., Tomkin, J., Bogensberger, W., Bouquet, A., Erlbacher, F. (eds.), *The EU treaties and the Charter of Fundamental Rights: A commentary,* Oxford, Oxford University Press, para 6. All energy sources including electricity are goods in the sense of Art. 28 TFEU and therefore subject to the free movement of goods.

[151] See Fischer-Lescano, A., Kommer, S. (2011), 'EU in der Finanzkrise: Zur Leistungsfähigkeit des Verfahrens der verstärkten Zusammenarbeit für eine Intensivierung der Wirtschafts- und Sozialpolitik', *KJ*, 412–433, p. 419 with reference to the EP; European Commission, 'Tax policy in the European Union—Priorities for the years ahead', COM(2001) 260 final, p. 23; López-Ibor Mayor, V. (2009), 'Enhanced Cooperation and energy' in: Beneyto Pérez, J. M., Baquero Cruz, J. (eds.), *Unity and flexibility in the future of the European Union: The challenge of enhanced cooperation,* Madrid, CEU Ediciones, pp. 23–39.

[152] For an instructive introduction, see Blanke, H.-J., Bunse, S. R. (2019), 'Der Raum der Freiheit, der Sicherheit und des Rechts—ein Integrationswert?' in: Nitschke, P. (ed.), *Gemeinsame Werte in Europa?: Stärken und Schwächen im normativen Selbstverständnis der Europäischen Integration,* Baden-Baden, Bonn, Nomos; Konrad Adenauer Stiftung.

(Art. 74 TFEU, which is usually applied in conjunction with other substantive legal bases[153]) or administrative action to combat terrorism (Art. 75 TFEU, a subject in which ununified action could hardly be justified). Both legal bases make use of qualified majority voting in the Council. In sum, both are not likely to see any differentiation attempts.

#### 2.3.1.10.1 Migration

Chapter 2 regards border checks and migration in a wider sense, i.e. immigration and asylum. **Art. 77 (2) TFEU** enables the EU to legislate for the purpose of ensuring the absence of border controls at the internal borders, to implement a common management system for external borders, as well as to regulate short-term visas and travel rules for third country nationals. As all matters are regulated through the ordinary legislative procedure, the likelihood for enhanced cooperation is low from the outset. In the absence of internal borders, the external borders are a matter of common interest for all Member States, which is why also Member States without external borders would want to have equal say and would not let enhanced cooperation happen. As regards internal borders, there is already a significant degree of differentiation especially with a view to the Schengen area, which, on the one hand, extends to non-EU states such as Switzerland and Norway while on the other hand not being applicable in its entirety in the Member States Ireland and Denmark (as well as the UK when it still was a Member State). Schengen itself is legally construed as an atypical enhanced cooperation,[154] which was authorised by Art. 1 Protocol (No 19) on the Schengen Acquis Integrated into the Framework of the EU. This shows that the regulatory framework on the absence of internal border controls is already fragmented and differentiated as it is, which poses challenges for further differentiation, but also serves as an example, as the example of the European border surveillance system (EUROSUR) shows. EUROSUR was introduced first by six Schengen members in 2010, expanded to twelve members in 2012 and only in 2013 was turned into a regulation that eventually covered all Member States participating in Schengen.[155]

---

[153] Wilderspin, M. (2019), 'Art. 74 TFEU' in: Kellerbauer, M., Klamert, M., Tomkin, J., Bogensberger, W., Bouquet, A., Erlbacher, F. (eds.), *The EU treaties and the Charter of Fundamental Rights: A commentary,* Oxford, Oxford University Press.

[154] More precisely a "closer cooperation", as the legal design was conceived under the Maastricht Treaty.

[155] Regulation (EU) No 1052/2013 of the European Parliament and of the Council of 22 October 2013 establishing the European Border Surveillance System (Eurosur). On the developments Capitani, E. de (2014), 'The Schengen system after Lisbon: from cooperation

Thus, what occurred was a further sub-differentiation among the Schengen members with a vanguard group that went ahead and the others joining in eventually. Such sub-differentiations could be conceivable also in future. What seems more difficult to imagine, on the other hand, is a new enhanced cooperation independent from and thus overlapping Schengen, as it would have to pass the threshold of being consistent with the policies of the Union (Art. 334 TFEU), including the existing differentiated Schengen framework, which would further complicate the matter legally.

Other legal bases of Chap. 2 seem unlikely to see enhanced cooperation attempts, be it because they affect all MS too much (Art. 79.2 (c) TFEU on illegal immigration and unauthorised residence, Art. 77 (2) TFEU on short-term visas and travel rules, Art. 79 (2)(a)(b) TFEU on the conditions of entry and residence), for political reasons (Art. 79.2 (d) TFEU, different standards for combatting human trafficking seem politically hard to sell), or because the EU has already legislated jointly (Art. 77 (3) TFEU, rules concerning travel documents like ID cards or passports).

**Art. 78 TFEU**, finally, deals with asylum and the related statuses of subsidiary and temporary protection. All competences are governed by QMV. Art. 78 (2)(a) and (b) TFEU concern uniform statuses of asylum and other protection forms. The former is predetermined by the Geneva Convention Relating to the Status of Refugees, the latter seems to be one of the less controversial aspects in the very controversial field of asylum law.[156] Other competences concern common procedures (on both granting and withdrawing asylum) (Art. 78 (2)(d) TFEU) and reception standards (Art. 78 (2)(f) TFEU), the important question of which Member State is responsible for an application (Art. 78 (2)(e) TFEU, the legal base for the controversial 'Dublin Regulations'), cooperation with third countries (Art. 78 (2)(g) TFEU), and, finally, rules for the event of a massive inflow of asylum seekers (Art. 78 (2)(c) and (3) TFEU). The latter legal base was the foundation for a Council decision on the relocation of 120 000 asylum seekers in 2015, passed with QMV. Despite the fact that this decision sought to organise the relocation of a mere 10% of the people who applied for asylum in

---

to integration', *ERA Forum*, Vol. 15, No. 1, pp. 101–118 On differentiation and Eurosur, see CJEU Case C-44/14, *Spain v. European Parliament and Council of the European.*

*Union (Eurosur)*, EU:C:2015:554 and Hanf, D. (2017), 'Balancing openness and coherence of enhanced cooperation: The principle of coherence affirmed by drawing its outer limits: *Spain v. Parliament and Council (Eurosur)*', *Common Market Law Review*, Vol. 54, No. 3, pp. 873–898.

[156] Directive 2011/95/EU.

2015,[157] it led to turmoil amongst the Member States, after Hungary, Czechia and Poland refused to fulfil their duties under the quota system.[158] Regarding this latter aspect, it was proposed in academia that enhanced cooperation should have been used instead of QMV decision making in the Council[159] or that enhanced cooperation could be used for similar reforms of asylum law in future.[160] The same claim was also made in the European Parliament by the GUE/NGL group.[161] However, this ignores several aspects. Firstly, in a situation where only a qualified majority is necessary and the opposed Member States do not reach the numbers necessary to block such a qualified majority, an enhanced cooperation could never be a *last resort* (Art. 20 (2) TEU), which is a necessity for the mechanism to be put in action.[162] Beyond the single case in question,

---

157 Over 1.2 Million first time asylum seekers were registered in the EU in 2015: https://ec.europa.eu/eurostat/documents/2995521/7203832/3-04032016-AP-EN.pdf/790eba01-381c-4163-bcd2-a54959b99ed6.

158 See joint CJEU Cases C-715/17 (*Commission v Poland*), C-718/17 (*Commission v Hungary*), C-719/17 (*Commission v Czech Republik*), ECLI:EU:C:2020:257; see also Blanke, H.-J., Bunse, S. R. (2019), 'Der Raum der Freiheit, der Sicherheit und des Rechts—ein Integrationswert?' in: Nitschke, P. (ed.), *Gemeinsame Werte in Europa?: Stärken und Schwächen im normativen Selbstverständnis der Europäischen Integration,* Baden-Baden, Bonn, Nomos; Konrad Adenauer Stiftung.

159 Kreilinger, V., Jacques Delors Institut Berlin (2015), *Proposal to use Enhanced Cooperation in the Refugee Crisis*, available at: www.delorsinstitut.de/en/publications/topics/institutions-and-democracy/proposal-to-use-enhanced-cooperation-in-the-refugee-crisis/. For a similar proposal beyond the 2015 situation, see Blanke, H.-J., Johr, M. (2019), 'Rechtliche Vorkehrungen für die zivile Seenotrettung im Mittelmeer: „Sichere Häfen“ und „verlässliche Ausschiffungsregelungen“ in der EU zur Überwindung völkerrechtlicher Ungewissheit', *DÖV*, No. 23, pp. 929–939.

160 Jungfleisch, J. (2019), 'Verstärkte Zusammenarbeit im Rahmen der Flüchtlingspolitik: Ein Ausweg aus der Krise oder die endgültige Aufgabe eines einheitlichen Europas?' in: Kopetzki, M., Lanser, C., Leitner, P. (eds.), *Autoritäres vs liberales Europa: Tagung Junger Europarechtler*innen, Band 2, Wien 2019,* Wien, Jan Sramek Verlag.

161 Motion for a Resolution to wind up the debate on the statements by the Council and the Commission pursuant to Rule 123(2) of the Rules of Procedure on migration and the situation of refugees (2015/2833(RSP)), B8-0835/2015, http://www.europarl.europa.eu/doceo/document/B-8-2015-0835_EN.html (accessed 12/12/2019).

162 *Kreilinger*'s argument (p. 8 ff.) that despite its illegality no actor would be likely to bring a case to the CJEU firstly unveils a more than questionable approach towards the rule of law, secondly underestimates the willingness of Member States to establish a fair burden-sharing among themselves (a single Member State opposed to an enhanced cooperation would suffice to make the CJEU declare the act illegal), and thirdly ignores the fact that the Commission would not be able to propose an authorisation decision for an illegal enhanced cooperation. Böttner, R. (2021), *The Constitutional Framework for Enhanced Cooperation in EU*

however, the call disregards the nature of the decision to take in refugees, particularly in times of massive inflow of asylum seekers. While societies may be able to benefit from well-managed migration, and therefore also from refugees,[163] on the long run, especially during the refugee crisis in 2015, the costs—pecuniary and political—of accepting asylum seekers into one's country were clearly at the centre of the debate. Yet, hundreds of thousands of refugees where there, within the EU, with hundreds more arriving every day. In this case, the reception of refugees was a public good that was complimentary in consumption (the more Member States participated, the lower the numbers and consequently the costs were for each state) with low excludability (by not taking in refugees, Member States could save on the immediate costs and therefore free-ride on the commitments of other states). This means, according to the theory of *Kölliker* laid out above, that while cooperating is attractive *per se* (complimentary consumption), once a smaller group agreed to act, the *centripetal effect*, the likelihood of non-participants to join the effort, is equal to zero. This is due to the fact that non-participants would have all the benefits of the cooperation (refugees are being received, crisis is solved), without sharing any of the costs. A binding mechanism of relocation of refugees established via enhanced cooperation would have only led to a situation in which uncooperative Member States would have ceased to be in need to justify their position and political pressure would have been deflected from them towards the participating states. Thus, although a binding legal mechanism established through enhanced cooperation would have helped the participating Member States to honour their humanitarian obligations, they would have agreed to pay the costs also for those states unwilling to cooperate. Such an approach was politically out of the question as it would have only encouraged a behaviour lacking solidarity.[164] It must be reminded, once again,

*law*, Nijhoff studies in European Union law, Leiden The Netherlands, Koninklijke Brill NV and Jungfleisch, J. (2019), 'Verstärkte Zusammenarbeit im Rahmen der Flüchtlingspolitik: Ein Ausweg aus der Krise oder die endgültige Aufgabe eines einheitlichen Europas?' in: Kopetzki, M., Lanser, C., Leitner, P. (eds.), *Autoritäres vs liberales Europa: Tagung Junger Europarechtler*innen, Band 2, Wien 2019,* Wien, Jan Sramek Verlag argue that in the *factual* restistence that can be expected against the implementation of a quota introduced by QMV in the light of the past experiences suffices to admit an enhanced cooperation as a last resort.

[163] See also the aspects brought up in Betts, A. (2003), 'Public Goods Theory and the Provision of Refugee Protection: The Role of the Joint-Product Model in Burden-Sharing Theory', *Journal of Refugee Studies*, Vol. 16, p. 274, who stresses that helping refugees can have an abstract value of its own ("excludable benefit") for states.

[164] Agreeing: Böttner, R. (2021), *The Constitutional Framework for Enhanced Cooperation in EU law*, Nijhoff studies in European Union law, Leiden The Netherlands, Koninklijke Brill NV.

that enhanced cooperation can only put obligations on the participants, and therefore cannot equip non-participants with other duties in a sort of burden-sharing agreement.

If that was not enough to exclude enhanced cooperation in receiving and distributing refugees, it should be recalled that decisions in this area can be taken by QMV. Thus, rather than constructing a legal framework that leaves unwilling states off the hook, Member States would predictably rather decide reception quotas binding for all Member States as occurred in 2015. If unwilling states—again—refused to fulfil their consequent obligations, they would be disobeying EU law, which can lead to infringement proceedings und thus at least pressure the non-participants.[165] For all of these reasons, willing Member States are much more likely to keep up the status quo and either organise help on a voluntary basis where an agreement for the EU as a whole cannot be found[166] or decide measures binding for all Member States by QMV—even if they face gross difficulties in their implementation. This prediction was confirmed in 2023 when finally, after year-long debates especially among Member States, the EU institutions came to an agreement on a reform of the asylum system in December 2023.[167]

Other policy areas within the field of migration may have dynamics in costs, benefits and excludability that would make differentiation seem more likely: A common system determining which Member State is responsible for considering an application, for example, has the potential to lower the number of applications in participating states, as there are ideally no more multiple applications. As all non-participants are excluded from this benefit, the system creates an 'excludable network good', making progress in legislation attractive with or without the participation of all states. In fact, Denmark, which has the possibility of opting out of AFSJ law, adopted the Dublin rules precisely because of the threat of being

[165] Although in the cases against Hungary, Czechia and Poland, the quota instrument expired long before the CJEU issued a judgement and the states' failure to fulfil EU law obligations therefore did not have relevant consequences. CJEU joint Cases C-715/17 (*Commission v Poland*), C-718/17 (*Commission v Hungary*), C-719/17 (*Commission v Czech Republik*), ECLI:EU:C:2020:257.

[166] See especially the 'Joint Declaration of Intent on a Controlled Emergency Procedure' by Germany, France, Italy and Malta', open to other states, which entails "voluntary commitments by Member States for a predictable temporary solidarity mechanism" (https://download.repubblica.it/pdf/2019/politica/joint-declaration.pdf last access 19 November 2021).

[167] https://www.consilium.europa.eu/en/press/press-releases/2023/12/20/the-council-and-the-european-parliament-reach-breakthrough-in-reform-of-eu-asylum-and-migration-system/ (last access 26 January 2024).

left behind.[168] Yet, as the Dublin rules are already in place, any future reform involving fewer Member States would mean a step back in integration,[169] and would therefore not be admissible as enhanced cooperation. Before the recent compromise, voluntary[170] cooperation such as the 'Joint Declaration of Intent on a Controlled Emergency Procedure' was therefore once again preferred by states, as it left the Dublin framework untouched and was therefore legally uncritical.

These examples show a tendency: while there can be examples of disagreements between Member States that can cause them to legislate in a differentiated manner, asylum and refugee policy does not seem to be a field in which this can be expected. Rather, one can expect single Member States to act going beyond their legal obligations on a voluntary basis (which can happen in semi-formal groups, see 'Joint Declaration of Intent on a Controlled Emergency Procedure' by Germany, France, Italy and Malta), while legislative reforms are developed by all Member States jointly—or not at all.[171] This is not to say that the migration and asylum system cannot see any further forms of differentiation at all: The recent compromise ('Pact on Migration and Asylum') include a division of labour and responsibilities among Member States. In case of increased migratory pressure on single states a system of mandatory solidarity is foreseen in which Member States, however, can choose themselves how to support the Member State(s) in need. This could involve receiving asylum seekers as well as financial contributions, deployment of personnel, etc.[172] This system will lead to unequal (though, as proponents argue, not unfair) bearing of responsibilities and will thus

[168] Kölliker, A. (2001), 'Bringing together or driving apart the union? Towards a theory of differentiated integration', p. 146.

[169] Although this happened in practice anyway, Schmidt, V. A. (2019), 'The future of differentiated integration: a 'soft-core,' multi-clustered Europe of overlapping policy communities', *Comparative European Politics*, Vol. 17, No. 2, pp. 294–315, p. 298.

[170] The degree to which the action is 'voluntary' from a human rights point of view (see Art. 21.1 (1) TEU) and/or the law of the sea is debatable (see also Blanke, H.-J., Johr, M. (2019), 'Rechtliche Vorkehrungen für die zivile Seenotrettung im Mittelmeer: „Sichere Häfen" und „verlässliche Ausschiffungsregelungen" in der EU zur Überwindung völkerrechtlicher Ungewissheit', *DÖV*, No. 23, pp. 929–939).

[171] Agreeing: Schmidt, V. A. (2019), 'The future of differentiated integration: a 'soft-core,' multi-clustered Europe of overlapping policy communities', *Comparative European Politics*, Vol. 17, No. 2, pp. 294–315, 308.

[172] https://www.consilium.europa.eu/en/press/press-releases/2023/12/20/the-council-and-the-european-parliament-reach-breakthrough-in-reform-of-eu-asylum-and-migration-system/ (last access 25 January 2024).

to some degree be differentiating. Crucially, however, it will still address all Member States alike as a measure of the Union as a whole, and thus have nothing to do with enhanced cooperation.

Enhanced cooperation is, in conclusion, highly unlikely in asylum matters.

#### 2.3.1.10.2 Judicial Cooperation in Civil Matters

Chapter 3 on Judicial Cooperation in Civil Matters, despite its practical relevance, consists of only one Article, **Art. 81 TFEU**. Its aim is to foster judicial cooperation on the basis of mutual recognition of judgments and extrajudicial decisions. The largest part of the competences conferred to the EU through Art. 81 TFEU is based on the ordinary legislative procedure (para. 2). It concerns the mutual recognition and enforcement of judgments and decisions, rules on conflicts of laws and jurisdiction, evidence-taking, the compatibility of procedural rules, alternative dispute settlement and judicial training. Paragraph 3 concerns measures on "family law with cross-border implications". In contrast to the other fields, the Council needs to act unanimously in order to legislate here.

As a matter of fact, it is Art. 81 (3) TFEU that two of the five enhanced cooperation enacted until today are based on. In 2010, 14 Member States were authorised to establish an enhanced cooperation on the law applicable to divorce and legal separation, which laid down a binding framework to determine the Member State responsible for divorces of international couples.[173] In 2016, 18 Member States got the authorisation to launch an enhanced cooperation in the field of property disputes of international couples, again focussing on determining jurisdiction and applicable law.[174] Given these successful predecessors, in light of the principle of path dependency, it appears rather likely that another enhanced cooperation occurs, should the Council again face a situation in which Member States cannot agree on family law legislation. This seems particularly likely, as in the previous cases, disagreements did not arise in principle about the implementation details of the legislative projects, but about the very need to introduce such reforms. In case of the enhanced cooperation on divorce and legal separation, for example, very conservative (Malta) and very liberal (Sweden) Member States opposed the project from opposite angles as they did not,

[173] Council Decision (2010/405/EU) authorising enhanced cooperation in the area of the law applicable to divorce and legal separation; see Kuipers, J.-J. (2012), 'The Law Applicable to Divorce as Test Ground for Enhanced Cooperation', *ELJ*, Vol. 18, pp. 201–229.

[174] Council Decision (EU) 2016/954 authorising enhanced cooperation in the area of jurisdiction, applicable law and the recognition and enforcement of decisions on the property regimes of international couples, covering both matters of matrimonial property regimes and the property consequences of registered partnerships.

respectively, want *progressive* (Malta) or *retrogressive* (Sweden) laws from other Member States to be applied in their own jurisdictions.[175] Family law is even referred to as part of the 'cultural identity' of Member States.[176] As such societal attitudes tend to change only slowly, if ever, further disputes of a similar kind are likely. In fact, after 2009, no legislative proposals were adopted by the Union as a whole for ten years.[177] In 2019, however, the Union as a whole adopted a Regulation on the recognition of decision in matrimonial matters, international child abduction and parental responsibility.[178]

At the same time, the two enhanced cooperations on family law were authorised and implemented rather calmly, as compared to the controversial attempts on the Unitary patent and Financial Transaction Tax. This shows that in the presence of fundamental disagreements on basic societal values, Member States can reach a point at which they "agree to disagree". As a result, interested Member States proceed and opposed Member States stay out, both acting in full sovereignty in a manner that is akin to intergovernmental negotiations.

Reform ideas concerning European family law were brought up in the fields of parentage and adoption, name law, or even the creation of a single EU Private International Law Code including family law.[179] Should these or other topics in the field of European family law be discussed as further reform attempts, further enhanced cooperations would be a likely outcome.Should these or other topics in the field of European family law be discussed as further reform attempts, further enhanced cooperations would be a comparatively likely outcome.

---

[175] Kuipers, J.-J. (2012), 'The Law Applicable to Divorce as Test Ground for Enhanced Cooperation', *ELJ*, Vol. 18, pp. 201–229.

[176] Hein, J. von (2017), 'EU Competence to Legislate in the Area of Private International Law and Law Reforms at the EU Level' in: Beaumont, P., Danov, M., Trimmings, K., Yüksel, B. (eds.), *Cross-Border Litigation in Europe,* Bloomsbury Publishing, p. 24.

[177] Wilderspin, M. (2019), 'Art. 81 TFEU' in: Kellerbauer, M., Klamert, M., Tomkin, J., Bogensberger, W., Bouquet, A., Erlbacher, F. (eds.), *The EU treaties and the Charter of Fundamental Rights: A commentary,* Oxford, Oxford University Press, para. 38.

[178] Council Regulation (EU) 2019/1111 on jurisdiction, the recognition and enforcement of decisions in matrimonial matters and the matters of parental responsibility, and on international child abduction; see also Wilderspin, M. (2011), 'Derechos fundamentales en materia de derecho de familia: en particular, la sustracción de menores', *Anuario español de derecho internacional privado,* No. 11, pp. 527–558Wilderspin derechos.

[179] See list in Kramer, X. (2012), 'A European framework for private international law: current gaps and future perspectives', Bruxellesp. 11; Hein, J. von (2017), 'EU Competence to Legislate in the Area of Private International Law and Law Reforms at the EU Level' in: Beaumont, P., Danov, M., Trimmings, K., Yüksel, B. (eds.), *Cross-Border Litigation in Europe,* Bloomsbury Publishing, p. 33 f.

#### 2.3.1.10.3 Judicial Cooperation in Criminal Matters and Police Cooperation

If there is a field in which enhanced cooperation comes close to being a default scenario, it is Chaps. 4 (Art. 82–86 TFEU) and 5 (Art. 87–89 TFEU) on judicial cooperation in criminal matters and police cooperation.[180] They are the cornerstone of the EU's aim to ensure a high level of security within the Union (Art. 67 (3) TFEU). Measures passed in this area concern both procedural criminal law (European Arrest Warrant, mutual recognition of criminal judgments, European Criminal Record Information System (ECRIS), protection of victim's and fair trial rights, etc.) and substantive criminal law (approximation of laws on environmental crimes, crimes against the EU budget, etc.). What makes the field particularly likely to see enhanced cooperations are the clauses on *facilitated enhanced cooperation.* Most of the competences in Chap. 4 (Articles 82, 83, 86, 87 TFEU) foresee clauses on a modified procedure in case of disagreements among Member States on specific aspects. According to these provisions, Member States can refer controversial proposals to the European Council. If the Presidents and Heads of States in the European Council fail to find a compromise among all states, nine Member States may notify the institutions of their wish to establish an enhanced cooperation, which is then automatically deemed to be authorised. Hence, without the need for an authorising decision taken by a qualified majority in the Council, Member States can proceed using enhanced cooperation.[181] As such, the hurdle to launch enhanced cooperation is lowered substantially. Beside the facilitated enhanced cooperation, groups of Member States can still, however, opt for the regular enhanced cooperation procedure even where facilitated enhanced cooperation is foreseen.

Chapter 4 contains two general types of provision: Art. 82, 83 TFEU deal with legislation, Art. 84–86 TFEU concern institutions, actors, and coordination.

**Art. 85 TFEU** concerns the establishment, mission and implementing legislation of Eurojust, the EU agency supporting and coordinating investigation and prosecution services in cross-border cases. It was established in 2000 by the EU as a whole (Denmark has an opt-out and does not participate).[182] Hence, there is

---

[180] See Weyembergh, A. (2018), 'Enhanced cooperation in criminal matters: past, present and future' in: Kert, R., Lehner, A. (eds.), *Vielfalt des Strafrechts im internationalen Kontext: Festschrift für Frank Höpfel zum 65. Geburtstag,* Wien, Graz, NWV, pp. 605–624.

[181] For more detail on the different facilitated enhanced cooperation clauses, see Sect. 5.2.3.

[182] Regulation (EU) 2018/1727 on the European Union Agency for Criminal Justice Cooperation (Eurojust); see also Nilsson, H. Moreover, its implementing legislative act was renewed, again by the EU as a whole, in 2018.Regulation (EU) 2018/1727 on the European Union Agency for Criminal Justice Cooperation (Eurojust); see also Nilsson, H. G. (2021),

no space for any future differentiation, which would mean a step backwards in integration. The same can be said about **Art. 88 TFEU** introducing the policing agency Europol.

**Art. 84 TFEU** is a legal base to promote and coordinate crime prevention, without however harmonising Member States' laws. It is not per se an institutional provision, however, as Council Decision 2009/902/JHA establishes a European Crime Prevention Network (EUCPN), it is used institutionally.[183] A current plan based on Art. 84 TFEU is the establishment of an Internal Security Fund.[184] None of this is particularly likely to see differentiation attempts, be it because of the rather uncontroversial nature of crime prevention as an aim, be it because of financial interests (security fund) or because the area is governed by QMV.

**Art. 86 TFEU** enables the Council—acting unanimously—to set up a European Public Prosecutor's Office (EPPO). The EPPO can investigate and prosecute crimes affecting the EU's financial interests and bring them before national Courts itself. Again requiring unanimity in the Council, the EPPO's powers can be extended to other serious cross-border crimes (Art. 86 (4) TFEU). The EPPO is the first case of an enhanced cooperation established in the field of AFSJ: In 2013, the Commission proposed the establishment of the EPPO by way of a regulation.[185] As no unanimity could be reached, the proposal was referred to the European Council in 2017, which also failed to reach a compromise. Subsequently, 16 Member States expressed their wish to launch an enhanced cooperation, which was deemed to be authorised because of the facilitated enhanced cooperation clause in Art. 86 (1)(3rd subpara) TFEU.[186] It is therefore also the first facilitated enhanced cooperation adopted. EPPO developed significant centripetal effects and nowadays, has 24 members.[187]

**Art. 82 TFEU** concerns the procedural criminal law branch of AFSJ. It contains a broad list of enumerated single competences (e.g. mutual recognition

'Art. 85 TFEU' in: Blanke, H.-J., Mangiameli, S. (eds.), *Treaty on the Functioning of the European Union—A Commentary*.

183 Bogensberger, W. (2019), 'Art. 84 TFEU' in: Kellerbauer, M., Klamert, M., Tomkin, J., Bogensberger, W., Bouquet, A., Erlbacher, F. (eds.), *The EU treaties and the Charter of Fundamental Rights: A commentary*, Oxford, Oxford University Press, para. 3.

184 Proposal for a Regulation establishing the Internal Security Fund, COM/2018/472 final.

185 Proposal for a Regulation on the establishment of the European Public Prosecutor's Office, COM (2013) 534 final.

186 Council Regulation (Eu) 2017/1939 implementing enhanced cooperation on the establishment of the European Public Prosecutor's Office ('the EPPO'), para. 4 ff.

187 https://www.eppo.europa.eu/en/members (last access 14 September 2025 2021).

of judgments and judicial decisions, conflicts of jurisdiction, judicial training, Art. 82 (1) TFEU) in which QMV applies as well as a blanket clause (requiring unanimity) which enables the Council to identify fields with need for EU legislation that are not enumerated.

Callscalls for reforms and legislation are frequent. A popular idea is to propose proposal common minimum standards of pre-trial detention.[188] As the standards differ largely within the Union,[189] and unanimity might be required in the Council depending on the precise content of the proposal (blanket clause of Art. 82 (2)(d) TFEU or Art. 82 (2)(d) TFEU), enhanced cooperation could be a possible outcome.

It is worth mentioning that in the field of procedural criminal law, two proposals were *almost* passed as enhanced cooperations: When the EAW was debated, Italy opposed the draft legislation. It was only when the other Member States threatened to use enhanced cooperation that Italy gave in and the EAW was adopted for the Union as a whole.[190] This was seen as a proof of enhanced cooperation's capacity as a 'veto buster'. Second, legislation on a Framework Decision on certain procedural rights in criminal proceedings was proposed in 2004. By 2007, the Commission and some Member States were ready to proceed using enhanced cooperation. Even after this, the proposal as such was not adopted neither uniformly nor by enhanced cooperation, but the main contents of the proposal were subsequently passed in single instruments.[191] This underlines the hypothesis of the influence of excludability and consumption on Member States' behaviour

---

[188] See e.g. European Parliament resolution of 2 April 2014 on the mid-term review of the Stockholm Programme (2013/2024(INI)), para. 47, 49.

[189] Van Kalmthout, Anton M.; Knapen, Marije M.; Morgenstern, Christine, eds. (2009), *Pre-trial detention in the European Union: An analysis of minimum standards in pre-trial detention and the grounds for regular review in the member states of the EU*, Nijmegen, Wolf Legal Publ; Fair Trials Europe, 'A Measure of Last Resort? The practice of pre-trial detention decision making in the EU'.

[190] Kroll, D. A., Leuffen, D. (2015), 'Enhanced cooperation in practice. An analysis of differentiated integration in EU secondary law', *Journal of European Public Policy*, Vol. 22, No. 3, pp. 353–373, p. 366 f.

[191] Kroll, D. A., Leuffen, D. (2015), 'Enhanced cooperation in practice. An analysis of differentiated integration in EU secondary law', *Journal of European Public Policy*, Vol. 22, No. 3, pp. 353–373, p. 365; Proposal for a council framework Decision on certain procedural rights in criminal proceedings throughout the European Union, COM/2004/0328 final; Heber, C. (2021), *Enhanced Cooperation and European Tax Law*, Oxford University Press; https://data.consilium.europa.eu/doc/document/ST-10699-2007-INIT/fr/pdf (accessed 19/12/2019) p. 12; For a list of the instruments passed, see https://ec.europa.eu/info/policies/justice-and-fundamental-rights/criminal-justice/rights-suspects-and-accused_en (accessed 18/12/2019).

when confronted with potential enhanced cooperations: Measures like the EAW are highly excludable, but tend to benefit from more participants (complementary consumption). As a result, they are excludable network goods, in which differentiation is interesting for willing states, but in which unwilling states might rather change their minds and participate than to stay out.

It can be added, finally, that in the EPPO regulation, some of the aspects under debate for future EU legislation necessarily had to be implemented for proceedings in which the EPPO prosecutes a case in a participating Member States (see e.g. Art. 37 EPPO Regulation on the admissibility of evidence gathered in another Member State, which in an EPPO proceeding is accepted more easily than in case of a regular cross-border prosecution). If these measures turn out to function sufficiently, not only could they increase the pressure to pass similar legislation for all criminal proceedings, but path dependency could also make Member States favour a differentiated approach among the lines of EPPO Member States. This is even more likely due to the presence of the facilitated enhanced cooperation clause in Art. 82 (3) TFEU.

In conclusion, the field of European procedural criminal law is among the areas where a future enhanced cooperation seems most likely.

**Art. 83 TFEU** covers substantive criminal law. The EU may only act by way of directives. These can define minimum standards on the definition of crimes and offenses for particularly serious crime with a cross-border dimension. A list of such crimes is spelled out in Art. 83 (1)(2$^{nd}$ subpara) TFEU.[192] Other areas of crime may be added by a unanimous Council decision with the consent of the EP. Moreover, Member States may adopt minimum definition rules necessary for the effective implementation of EU policy that resulted in harmonising law (Art. 83 (2) TFEU). The legislative procedure to be applied is the same that is applicable for the underlying harmonising measure. Art. 83 TFEU, like Art. 82 TFEU, contains a facilitated enhanced cooperation clause.

Art. 83 TFEU offers wide-reaching options for legislation in the area of cross-border criminal activity. While many acts have already been adopted,[193] the fields named in Art. 83 TFEU are not exhaustive, and new types of criminal activity

[192] "These areas of crime are the following: terrorism, trafficking in human beings and sexual exploitation of women and children, illicit drug trafficking, illicit arms trafficking, money laundering, corruption, counterfeiting of means of payment, computer crime and organised crime." Art. 83 (1)(2$^{nd}$ subpara) TFEU.

[193] See list in Bogensberger, W. (2019), 'Art. 83 TFEU' in: Kellerbauer, M., Klamert, M., Tomkin, J., Bogensberger, W., Bouquet, A., Erlbacher, F. (eds.), *The EU treaties and the Charter of Fundamental Rights: A commentary,* Oxford, Oxford University Press (only post-Lisbon acts).

may arise. Adding to the list in Art. 83 (1) TFEU requires unanimity, which may rise the likelihood of enhanced cooperation. Regarding Art. 83 (2) TFEU, criminal law accompanying harmonising measures,measure e.g. fiscal provisions based on Art. 115 TFEU, might also require unanimous decision-making in the Council. Even where decisions are taken by qualified majority, the facilitated enhanced cooperation clause raises the probability of an enhanced cooperation. As the definition of substantive criminal law is mostly a Member State competence, and thus already very different throughout the Union, a future harmonization of single criminal offenses would in any case lead to more integration, even if some Member States did—for whatever reason—not participate. Needless to say, the offenses that already have been harmonized would have to be left untouched, as this would mean a fragmentation in comparison to the status quo, and would thus be prohibited by Art. 326 TFEU. Much like technical standards, the harmonization of criminal offenses is *complementary in consumption*, meaning that more participants lead to higher benefits of the policy and there is no risk of free-riding. Non-participants are largely left untouched by such measures (neutral externalities). This means that enhanced cooperation is in principle an interesting avenue for willing states, but initially uninterested states are likely to see the benefits themselves and join the project rather than staying out, which lowers the likelihood of enhanced cooperation occurring. In fact, not only has Art. 83 TFEU not seen an enhanced cooperation attempt yet, even the referral to the European Council, sometimes referred to as 'emergency brake', that is needed prior to activating a facilitated enhanced cooperation has not been invoked as of today. Assuming that this is indeed caused by a lack of controversy in the Council, there might, however, be a case left in which enhanced cooperation could occur despite a general willingness among Member States to introduce a measure: A situation in which a state would like to, but cannot give its consent in the Council. As a decision according to Art. 83.1 (2) TFEU factually amends Art. 83.1 (1) TFEU, it can be regarded as a Treaty change. This can mean that consent in the Council requires special national processes for reasons of national constitutional law.[194] Consequently, a situation could arise in which a Member State government would like to join its peers in a unanimous decision in the Council but cannot due to procedural reasons or a lack of specific majorities at home. The other states could

[194] BVerfG, 2 BvE 2/08 et al. (*Lissabon*), para. 363; see Blanke, H.-J., Bunse, S. R. (2019), 'Der Raum der Freiheit, der Sicherheit und des Rechts—ein Integrationswert?' in: Nitschke, P. (ed.), *Gemeinsame Werte in Europa?: Stärken und Schwächen im normativen Selbstverständnis der Europäischen Integration,* Baden-Baden, Bonn, Nomos; Konrad Adenauer Stiftung.

then decide to go ahead with enhanced cooperation and wait for the domestically blocked member to join once it can.

**Art. 89 TFEU** enables the Council to unanimously lay down conditions and limitations under which policy and judicial authorities may operate in the territory of another Member State. As the topic is particularly sensitive and requires a special level of mutual trust, it does not seem to be out of the question that an enhanced cooperation could prove to be necessary in future. Differentiation could move along the lines of the Schengen participants.

**Art. 87 TFEU** concerns the cooperation of national police authorities. According to Art. 87 (2) TFEU, measures concerning the collection and exchange of information, staff training and exchange, and common investigative techniques may be passed via the ordinary legislative procedure. Except for the fact that QMV decision making lowers the likelihood, enhanced cooperation could be expected in this field. Moreover, some particularities in majority arithmetics could favour an enhanced cooperation (see below). Under Art. 87 (3) TFEU, the Council may unanimously establish measures concerning operational cooperation between the authorities. If unanimity cannot be reached, there is a facilitated enhanced cooperation clause, which makes an eventual enhanced cooperation seem somewhat likely.

#### 2.3.1.10.4 Excursus: Exceptions and Specialties in Majority Arithmetics

In the field of judicial cooperation in criminal matters and police cooperation (Chaps. 4 and 5), and for Art. 74 TFEU, a special situation arises in terms of majority arithmetics. According to Art. 76 (b) TFEU, contrary to the usual monopoly of initiative of the Commission, acts can be adopted on the initiative of a quarter of the Member States. However, according Art. 238 (2) TFEU, in such cases, the qualified majority necessary to adopt acts no longer consists of 55% of the Members of the Council representing 65% of the population (Art. 16 (4) TEU), but of 72% of the Members of the Council representing 65% of the population. This could give rise to a situation in which a quarter of the Member States launches an initiative, and the number of Member States approving is between 65% (i.e. 15 for an EU-27) and the necessary majority of 72% (i.e. 21 for an EU-27). In this case, Member States could opt for enhanced cooperation, and authorise it with the necessary qualified majority. As the authorising decision for this would have to be based on a Commission proposal (see Art. 329 TFEU) the regular QMV calculation would apply, and 65% of the Member States would suffice for the authorisation.

In this scenario, a QMV enhanced cooperation would, contrary to other cases, not require the inconsistent behaviour of at least one Member State ('helper-state') blocking an QMV decision on the proposal but authorising an enhanced cooperation with the same majority that would have sufficed for the adoption of the main act (see above). This moves the scenario of a QMV enhanced cooperation closer to being a realistic option. It should be added that there is not a whole lot of legal bases that this would be interesting for: in fact, most legal bases in Chaps. 4 and 5 comprise facilitated enhanced cooperation clauses (Art. 82 (3), 83 (3), 86 (1), 87 (3) TFEU): Where the necessary majority in the Council cannot be attained, interested Member States may, after a procedure to be followed, inform the institutions of their will to launch an enhanced cooperation. In this case, the authorisation shall be deemed to be granted. This would be a much more obvious way to reach an enhanced cooperation than juggling between majorities of 55% and 72%. Of course, if the Commission, which is side-lined by the facilitated enhanced cooperation authorisation, withdrew its proposal in order to prevent enhanced cooperation, Member States could use Art. 76 (b) TFEU to revive it.[195] In any case, the important legal base in Art. 87 (1) TFEU on police cooperation is not covered by facilitated enhanced cooperation, as the facilitated enhanced cooperation clause in this article only concerns measures the basis of it Art. 87 (3) TFEU. Hence, in this case the strategy laid out before would remain relevant.

The latter is not to say, moreover, that facilitated enhanced cooperation is not affected by the possibility to launch legislative proposals by a quarter of Member States. In fact, Member States could put forward proposals on the basis of Art. 82, 83, 86, and 87 (3) TFEU. In the absence of a modified qualified majority (72% of Council members), they could refer the proposals to the European Council according to the respective legal bases. Without a consensus there, they could notify the institutions of their interest to launch an enhanced cooperation, and the authorisation would automatically be deemed to be granted.[196] As a consequence, a minority of as few as nine Member States could, theoretically, launch an enhanced cooperation without the factual participation of the Commission. This is a striking contrast to the usual role of the Commission as depicted in Art. 334 TFEU.

It must be noted, however, that this possibility is not unlimited, as in particular, Member States need to observe the principle of sincere cooperation (Art. 4 (3) TEU). Moreover, most acts legal act implementing the enhanced

[195] Thym, D. (2009), The Evolution of Supranational Differentiation, WHI-Paper.

[196] See Art. 82 (3), 83 (3), 86 (1), 87 (3) TFEU.

cooperation would need the approval of the Parliament (not Art. 87 (3) TFEU), which would hardly be tempted to join such tactics. This notwithstanding, both manoeuvres laid out here are striking options that the Treaty makers knowingly or unknowingly left to the disposal of Member States, within the limits of sincere cooperation.

#### 2.3.1.11 Common Safety Concerns in Public Health Matters

The last "principal area" spelled out in Art. 4 TFEU as part of the EU's shared competences are "common safety concerns in public health matters, for the aspects defined in this Treaty". The corresponding Treaty provision is **Art. 168 TFEU**. It regulates a number of EU competences. Among these, only Art. 168 (4) TFEU is a shared competence, the others are part of the coordinative competences described in Art. 6 (a) TFEU, precluding any harmonisation (Art. 2 (5) TFEU).[197] Action in this area may aim at subgroups of Member States, especially neighbouring states, as laid down in Art. 168 (2) TFEU, 2nd sentence.[198] Hence, differentiation is possible without needing to resort to enhanced cooperation.

**Art. 168 (4) TFEU** applies the ordinary legislative procedure to legislate mostly in the area of common safety standards, e.g. for handling blood and organs or for medical devices. Be it because of this—different standards for medical devices would be very hard to handle within the single market—or because of the critical image that differentiated approaches concerning the public health would invoke: Enhanced cooperation attempts in this field seem unlikely.

#### 2.3.1.12 Research, Technological Development and Space; Development Cooperation and Humanitarian Aid

According to Art. 4 (3) TFEU, the EU further has the non-exclusive competence "to carry out activities, in particular to define and implement programmes" in the areas of research, technological development and space. However, this competence and its exercise "shall not result in Member States being prevented from exercising theirs". The latter aspect gives the EU's 'R&D competences' an odd position within the article on shared competences, which can be explained

[197] Obwexer, W. (2015), 'Art. 4 AEUV' in: Groeben, H. v. d., Schwarze, J., Hatje, A. (eds.), *Europäisches Unionsrecht,* Baden-Baden, Nomos.

[198] For examples of such coordinated cooperation, see Niggemeier, F. (2015), 'Art. 186 AEUV' in: Groeben, H. v. d., Schwarze, J., Hatje, A. (eds.), *Europäisches Unionsrecht,* Baden-Baden, Nomos, para. 22.

by disagreements during the treaty negotiations.[199] The actual competences in Art. 179–190 TFEU mostly concern support of research activities, which are largely of a financial nature (an illustrative example was the 80 billion Euro Horizon2020 programme[200]). Besides the fact that all decisions are taken with majority voting, there is little reason for Member States not to participate in these programmes.

As regards in particular the European space activities, the framework is already rather differentiated: The European Space Agency (ESA), which implements large parts of the EU's space policy, is not an EU body, but an international organisation with merely 22 member states.[201] In the light of this, further differentiation does not seem to be on the EU's agenda.

According to Art. 4 (4) TFEU, the EU is competent to carry out activities and conduct a common policy in the fields of development cooperation and humanitarian aid, again without affecting the Member States' competences in these areas.

As in the areas of research, technology and space, development cooperation and humanitarian aid are hardly apt for differentiation on the EU level.

### 2.3.2 Other Areas

Art. 4 TFEU on shared competences states clearly that the areas listed in it are exemplary and not a complete list. In fact, all competences not listed explicitly in Articles 3 and 6 are shared (Art. 4(1) TFEU). In order to avoid a discussion of each and every EU competence for reasons of space, in the last step I will assess areas that do not fall within the principal areas but have been discussed as possible candidates to see an enhanced cooperation.

---

[199] Calliess, C. (2016), 'Art. 4 AEUV' in: Calliess, C., Ruffert, M. (eds.), *EUV/AEUV: Das Verfassungsrecht der Europäischen Union mit Europäischer Grundrechtecharta: Kommentar,* München, C. H. Beck, para. 21.

[200] https://ec.europa.eu/programmes/horizon2020/what-horizon-2020 (last access 15/01/2020).

[201] EU-Member States: Austria, Belgium, Czech Republic, Denmark, Estonia, Finland, France, Germany, Greece, Hungary, Ireland, Italy, Luxembourg, the Netherlands, Poland, Portugal, Romania, Spain, Sweden. Non-EU-Member States: Norway, Switzerland and the United Kingdom.

#### 2.3.2.1 EMU

The Economic and Monetary Union (EMU) is a strange animal within the EU legal framework. It is technically 'normal' EU law, even established on the Treaty level. Yet, there are no less than three categories of non-participating states: Some Member States have extensive opt-outs (formerly UK, Denmark), which means that they do not have to participate in it and consequently do not need to introduce the Euro as their currency. The second group is led by Sweden: Although it would easily fulfil all economic requirements for joining, it actively refrains from completing all formal requirements and thus avoids its obligation to join the Euro voluntarily. The last category of non-participating states foreseen are such that would like to join to EMU but do not yet fulfil all economic requirements (e.g. Bulgaria until 31 December 2025).

This could lead to the question why anyone could be interested in adding further levels of differentiation to this already complicated picture. The truth is, however, that the EU competences for EMU governance do not completely match the differentiated participation picture. There are some legal bases allowing the Eurozone Member States to pass EMU law only they are allowed to vote on (Art. 136 (2) TFEU). However, this enhanced cooperation-*esque* approach does not cover all areas of Eurozone governance. Thus, wherever the EMU Member States deem legislative action necessary in an area not covered by this exception, they need to find different approaches. One possibility is to pass law with the EU as a whole and limit its applicability to the Eurozone Member States.[202] This puts the interested states in the difficult position of being dependent on the votes of states to whom the laws passed would not even apply. In cases requiring unanimity, this may even lead to vetoes by non-participating states. The alternative to this, regularly applied during the financial crisis, is to leave the EU law framework altogether and legislate via international law instruments.[203] While

[202] See e.g. the proposal COM(2017) 824 final, Art. 1 (2) and 4; the legality of this approach is put in question by Becker, J., Kornwachs, L., Zembala-Börner, K. (2016), *Die gemeinsame Europäische Bankenaufsicht als Reformmodell für die verstärkte Zusammenarbeit?*, Heidelberger Beiträge zum Finanz- und Steuerrecht.

[203] See e.g. the Treaty on Stability, Coordination and Governance (TSCG), a. k. a. Fiscal Compact Treaty; the European Stability Mechanism (ESM); etc. On this development, see e.g. Clelia Lacchi (2017), 'How Much Flexibility Can European Integration Bear in Order to Face the Eurozone Crisis? Reflections on the EMU inter se International Agreements Between EU Member States' in: Giegerich, T., Schmitt, D. C., Zeitzmann, S. (eds.), *Flexibility in the EU and beyond: How much differentiation can European integration bear?*, Oxford, Hart Publishing, pp. 225–250; Peers, S. (2013), 'Towards a New Form of EU Law?: The Use of EU Institutions outside the EU Legal Framework', *European Constitutional Law Review*, Vol. 9, No. 01, pp. 37–72; CJEU C-370/12 (*Pringle*), ECLI:EU:C:2012:756.

this approach promises fast progress[204] and a bespoke group of participants, it lacks the primacy and enforceability of EU law. In the light of these issues, scholars have repeatedly called for the use of enhanced cooperation in the EMU.[205] Enhanced cooperation would offer the Eurozone Member States a possibility to pass binding, enforceable EU law without having to take into account objections from non-Euro countries. Member States would in principle[206] under the principle of openness always be able to join these instruments. This would, however, neither be problematic nor a novelty.[207] In order to strengthen the economic side of the EMU, which is a frequent demand in order to stabilise the Eurozone,[208] Member States could even pass legislation among themselves in a in a wider field than just the governance of the EMU, and for example harmonise their tax or social policy (see above).[209]

Economic coordination in the EMU would stabilise the Eurozone more, the more Member States participated.[210] Therefore, an EMU enhanced cooperation

---

[204] Putting this into question in the light of recent *Bundesverfassungsgericht* jurisprudence: Graf von Luckner, J. (2021), 'Stay home, stay healthy: Das „Ergänzungs- oder besondere Näheverhältnis zum Unionsrecht" in der BVerfG-Rechtsprechung und die europäische Integration durch Völkerrecht', *Europarecht*, No. 2, pp. 209–224.

[205] Graf von Luckner, J. (2018), 'How to Bring It Home—The EU's Options for Incorporating the Fiscal Compact into EU Law', *European Law Blog*; Schwarz, M. (2014), 'A Memorandum of Misunderstanding—The doomed road of the European Stability Mechanism and a possible way out: Enhanced cooperation', *CMLRev*, Vol. 51, pp. 389–423; Thym, D. (2004), *Ungleichzeitigkeit und europäisches Verfassungsrecht*, Schriftenreihe europäisches Verfassungsrecht, Baden-Baden, Nomos, p. 45, 147 ff.; Selmayr, M. (2013), 'Die "Euro- Rettung" und das Unionsprimärrecht: Von putativen, unnötigen und bisher versäumten Vertragsänderungen zur Stabilisierung der Wirtschafts- und Währungsunion' 2013, 68(2), Zeitschrift für Öffentliches Recht, 259', *ZÖR*, Vol. 68, No. 2, pp. 259–318.

[206] Art. 328.1 TFEU would allow to make participation depend on the condition of EMU membership.

[207] E.g. Non-Eurozone states Poland and Denmark joined the TSCG; Ondarza, N. von (2014), 'Die vertragliche und außervertragliche verstärkte Zusammenarbeit als Katalysator einer engeren Integrationsgemeinschaft' in: Blanke, H.-J., Pilz, S. (eds.), *Die „Fiskalunion": Voraussetzungen einer Vertiefung der politischen Integration im Währungsraum der Europäischen Union,* Tübingen, Mohr Siebeck, 149–169, p. 154 f. If they did want to limit an enhanced cooperation to Eurozone Member States, they could the use of the Euro as a currency as a condition for joining the enhanced cooperation, Art. 328 (1) TFEU.

[208] See e.g. Art. 1 TSCG.

[209] Thym, D. (2004), *Ungleichzeitigkeit und europäisches Verfassungsrecht*, Schriftenreihe europäisches Verfassungsrecht, Baden-Baden, Nomos, p. 148.

[210] In this sense e.g. the "Five Presidents' Report": https://ec.europa.eu/info/sites/default/files/5-presidents-report_en.pdf (last access 02/11/2021), p. 9.

would be a case of complementary consumption. The benefits would be relatively excludable (the entire EU economy can benefit from a stable Eurozone, particularly in times of economic crisis; however, only participating states would directly participate in and profit from the programmes undertaken within such a cooperation). This would make EMU enhanced cooperation a case of an excludable network good, having the highest likelihood of seeing enhanced cooperations.[211]

The theory of path dependency *prima facie* contradicts the finding that the EMU is an area suited for an enhanced cooperation in future, as there have not been any enhanced cooperations in the past and differentiation has been organised first and foremost on a Treaty level. However, the treaty on the Fiscal Compact (Treaty on Stability, Coordination and Governance, TSCG), raises the curtain on a different impression. First of all, the TSCG itself, an international law instrument of EMU governance, the parties of which are all EU Member States, is an example of a different kind of differentiation than that usually governing the EMU. Secondly, and more importantly for the use of *enhanced cooperation* as opposed to mere *differentiation*, in the treaty, the parties made direct reference to the use of enhanced cooperation:

> *"In accordance with the requirements of the Treaties on which the European Union is founded, the Contracting Parties stand ready to make active use, whenever appropriate and necessary, of [...] enhanced cooperation" (Art. 10 TSCG).*

This proves that policy makers are very much aware of the possibility to use enhanced cooperation in the context of EMU governance. Should it be decided to incorporate the TSCG into EU law[212] by way of enhanced cooperation as outlined in Art. 10 TSCG,[213] a repeated use of the instrument in EMU law seems very likely. Moreover, former French prime minister Jospin mentioned the Eurozone governance as an "obvious" case for enhanced cooperation as early as

---

[211] Kölliker, A. (2001), 'Bringing together or driving apart the union? Towards a theory of differentiated integration', p. 4.

[212] This is an obligation of the parties to the TSCG, see Art. 16 TSCG, although looking increasingly unlikely as time passes.

[213] In detail on this possibility: Graf von Luckner, J. (2018), 'How to Bring It Home—The EU's Options for Incorporating the Fiscal Compact into EU Law', *European Law Blog*.

2001,[214] the Commission made similar statements.[215] The repeated mention of enhanced cooperation in the EMU field can be seen as a sign that the mechanism is on the radar of crucial actors, and it almost seems a matter of time until it is put to use.

#### 2.3.2.2 Enhanced Cooperation Based on 'Competence-Competence', Art. 352 TFEU

While the EU's competences are based on the principle of conferral, meaning that competences must explicitly be conferred on the EU by the Member States (Art. 5.2 TEU), there is one major exception to this rule, namely Art. 352 TFEU. According to this rule, the EU may, within the general framework of the competences conferred on the EU, adopt the appropriate measures if EU action proves necessary attain one of the objectives set out in the Treaties, and the Treaties have not provided the necessary powers.[216] Procedurally, this entails the Council acting unanimously on a proposal from the Commission and after obtaining the consent of the European Parliament. Art. 352 TFEU may not be used to harmonise Member States' laws or for obtaining objectives in the field of CFSP. For the reason that on the one hand, Art. 352 TFEU allows the EU to take action in fields in which it has not been conferred powers upon, but on the other hand only in a strictly regulated manner, it has been labelled a bounded or partial competence-competence with a view to the term *Kompetenz-Kompetenz* from German constitutional theory, which describes the power of a legal body to designate its own competences.[217] Whether enhanced cooperation may be used in projects based on Art. 352 TFEU is disputed. Supporters cite Article 20(1) TEU which states that Member States may establish enhanced cooperation "within the framework of the Union's non-exclusive competences" and "by applying the relevant provisions of the Treaties", including Art. 352 TFEU,[218] while opponents

[214] Lionel Jospin, "L'avenir de l'Europe élargie", Paris, 28/07/2019, https://www.cvce.eu/content/publication/2005/1/17/642dc4c9-b224-4ea7-a77b-7e4d894b3077/publishable_fr.pdf (last access 16/01/2020).

[215] Commission communication on strengthening economic policy coordination within the euro area (COM(2001)82.

[216] See also Declarations 41 and 42 on Article 352 of the Treaty on the Functioning of the European Union.

[217] Schütze, R. (2009), 'The European Community's Federal Order of Competences—A Retrospective Analysis' in: Dougan, M., Currie, Samantha,—(eds.), *50 Years of the European Treaties Looking Back and Thinking Forward.*, Hart, pp. 63–92.

[218] Böttner, R. (2021), *The Constitutional Framework for Enhanced Cooperation in EU law*, Nijhoff studies in European Union law, Leiden The Netherlands, Koninklijke Brill NV.

argue that the enhanced cooperation mechanism's "emphasis on inclusivity" keep it from becoming "a form of *de-facto* Treaty amendment" valid only for a limited number of Member States.[219] A majority of scholars, however, seem to argue in favour of the possibility of using Art. 352 TFEU for enhanced cooperation.[220] In light of the remaining legal doubts, however, a proposal to create a European Foundation by way of an enhanced cooperation on the basis of Art. 352 TFEU was not pursued.[221] In the light of this and considering that a large number of contributions on the question were brought forward in the context of the financial and Eurozone crisis, it seems most likely that if enhanced cooperation and Art. 352 TFEU were to be used together, it would be in a moment of crisis. In such a scenario, the joint use does not seem to be out of the question.

### 2.3.2.3 Foreign Action

#### 2.3.2.3.1 CFSP Enhanced Cooperation

The EU competence on foreign action is first mentioned in Art. 2 (4) TFEU, alongside the competence categories of exclusive, shared, and coordinating competences. It is therefore an 'odd' competence which on first sight is hard to categorise. However, since for the use of enhanced cooperation it is only important whether a competence is exclusive, it can easily be concluded that the Member States had no intention to transfer a general foreign action competence to the EU.[222] On the contrary, the lacking categorisation can be seen as a sign of a particularly cautious approach to EU foreign action competence, which is also visible in the single competences. Following the fact that foreign policy

---

219 Cremona, M. (2009), 'Enhanced Cooperation and the Common Foreign and Security and Defence Policies of the EU', *EUI Working Papers*, No. 21 (though arguing on the basis of the pre-Lisbon legal framework).

220 Hinarejos, A. (2015), 'An Asymmetric EMU' in: Hinarejos Parga, A. (ed.), *The Euro area crisis in constitutional perspective,* Oxford University Press, pp. 3–10; Tosato, G. L. (2013), 'New institutional solutions for multi-tier governance?' in: *Challenges of multi-tier governance in the European Union: Effectiveness, efficiency and legitimacy*, pp. 152–160; Zeitzmann, S. (2015), 'Zuviel gewollt, zu wenig geregelt? Das komplizierte Verhältnis der Verstärkten Zusammenarbeit zum aquis communautaire' in: Stratenschulte, E. D. (ed.), *Der Anfang vom Ende?: Formen differenzierter Integration und ihre Konsequenzen,* Nomos, pp. 103–134; Böttner, R. (2021), *The Constitutional Framework for Enhanced Cooperation in EU law*, Nijhoff studies in European Union law, Leiden The Netherlands, Koninklijke Brill NV.

221 Heber, C. (2021), *Enhanced Cooperation and European Tax Law*, Oxford University Press.

222 Nettesheim, M. (2018), 'Art. 4 AEUV' in: Grabitz, E., Hilf, M., Nettesheim, M. (eds.), *Das Recht der Europäischen Union,* München, Beck, para. 43 f.

can under no circumstances be understood as an exclusive competence, enhanced cooperation is a viable approach.

This finding is mirrored in a number of provisions that regulate foreign and security policy enhanced cooperation (CFSP enhanced cooperation).[223] In particular, Art. 329 (2) TFEU significantly modifies the procedure to launch an enhanced cooperation. Rather than to the Commission, a CFSP enhanced cooperation request is addressed directly to the Council. In contrast to Art. 329 (1) TFEU on establishing a regular enhanced cooperation, Art. 329 (2) TFEU on establishing a CFSP enhanced cooperation does not explicitly mention the need to "specify[...] the scope and objectives of the enhanced cooperation proposed", which has been interpreted as making such specification unnecessary.[224] However, the wording "The request of the Member States which wish to establish enhanced cooperation between themselves within the framework of the common foreign and security policy" (rather than "a request") implies a referral to the request as defined in paragraph 1, i.e. a request containing scope and objectives. The only change therefore concerns the addressee of the request, which is the Council and not the Commission. Before a foreign policy enhanced cooperation can be authorised, the High Representative for Foreign Affairs and Security Policy and the Commission need to give their opinion on whether the proposed cooperation is consistent with other Union policies. However, a Commission proposal is not required, nor is any of the opinions binding. Rather than the qualified majority authorisation decision in the regular enhanced cooperation procedure, the CFSP enhanced cooperation needs to be authorised by a *unanimous* Council decision.

The Parliament is only informed. Similarly, joining a CFSP enhanced cooperation is subject to a unanimous Council decision of the participating Member States (Art. 331 (2) TFEU), rather than a Commission decision as in the regular enhanced cooperation procedure. Importantly, Art. 24 (1) TEU prohibits the adoption of legislative acts in the CFSP. Therefore, a CFSP enhanced cooperation would be limited to non-legislative action such as joint programmes. The *passarelle*-clause laid down in Art. 333 TFEU that allows enhanced cooperation participants to move from unanimous to QMV voting is specifically excluded from having military and defence implications (Art. 333 (3) TFEU) and could therefore not be applied in all CFSP decision. As the Court of Justice does not

[223] See Cremona, M. (2009), 'Enhanced Cooperation and the Common Foreign and Security and Defence Policies of the EU', *EUI Working Papers*, No. 21.

[224] Cremona, M. (2009), 'Enhanced Cooperation and the Common Foreign and Security and Defence Policies of the EU', *EUI Working Papers*, No. 21, p. 10.

have jurisdiction over matter regarding CFSP, enhanced cooperations in this area would not fall under its control. All of these modifications to the regular procedure move the enhanced cooperation well into the area of intergovernmentalism: The involvement of supranational bodies is reduced to providing and receiving information and no decision can be taken against the will of any Member State.[225] However, the mere existence of the particular CFSP enhanced cooperation rules, rather than an outright ban, constantly reminding decision makers of the option to opt for enhanced cooperation, moves it towards being imaginable. CFSP enhanced cooperation would, however, require a very particular political setting, as all non-participants would have to vote in favour of the project to authorise it (Art. 20.2 (2) TEU, Art. 329 TFEU.

#### 2.3.2.3.2 PESCO

Permanent Structured Cooperation (PESCO) was famously dubbed "the Sleeping Beauty of the Lisbon Treaty" by former Commission President *Jean-Claude Juncker*.[226] PESCO is a somewhat similar procedure to CFSP enhanced cooperation and enhanced cooperation in general, but at the same time features stark contrast to the latter. Introduced in Art. 42 (6), 46 TEU, PESCO gives Member States a possibility to cooperate more closely in the area of defence, while explicitly staying within the EU law framework (Art. 42 (6) TEU). An undetermined number of Member States may, at any time, inform the Council of their intention to form such a cooperation. As in the case of CFSP enhanced cooperation, the Council consults the High Representative, following which the Council can establish PESCO by way of an ordinary qualified majority decision. Joining PESCO once it has been established is subject to a QMV Council decision of participating Member States (Art. 46 (3) TEU). Contrary to enhanced cooperation, a Member States can unilaterally withdraw from PESCO (Art. 46 (5) TEU), but participation can also be suspended by a decision of the remaining participating states (Art. 46 (4) TEU) if the criteria of participation are no longer met.

---

[225] Blanke, H.-J. (2018), 'Art. 329 AEUV' in: Grabitz, E., Hilf, M., Nettesheim, M. (eds.), *Das Recht der Europäischen Union,* München, Beck, para 7.

[226] Speech by President *Jean-Claude Juncker* at the Defence and Security Conference Prague: In defence of Europe, 09/06/2017, https://ec.europa.eu/commission/presscorner/detail/en/SPEECH_17_1581 (last access 21/01/2020); on PESCO, see Biscop, S. (2017), European Defence: What's in the CARDs for PESCO?, EGMONT Security Policy Brief, Brussels Nováky, N. (2018), 'The EU's Permanent Structured Cooperation in defence: Keeping Sleeping Beauty from snoozing', *European View*, Vol. 17, No. 1, pp. 97–104; Wolfstädter, L. M., Kreilinger, V. (2017), European Integration via Flexibility Tools: The Cases of EPPO and PESCO, Policy Paper.

In 2017, 25 Member States[227] decided to trigger PESCO.[228] This was a surprisingly high number: the only states which did not participated were the UK (after its Brexit decision), Denmark (opt-out, but has nonetheless joined PESCO in 2023[229]), and Malta (which considers joining depending on actual implementation[230]). Four of the participating states considered themselves neutral when choosing to participate (Austria, Finland, Ireland and Sweden). Within the cooperation, Member States have decided dozens of projects to be implemented.[231] Interestingly, Member States can choose which PESCO projects they want to participate in—none of the projects was joined by all participating countries. As a consequence, PESCO features significant differentiation within the differentiation. What unites the PESCO Members is the overarching list of 21 binding commitments made by all participants.[232]

Just like in CFSP enhanced cooperation, no explicit role is foreseen for the Commission in PESCO. The practical application has shown, however, that this does not mean that the Commission stays out of the project: For instance, PESCO projects can receive higher funding from the (Commission administered) European Defence Fund,[233] which inevitably means that the Commission is involved in the practical application of PESCO. The establishment of a Directorate-General for Defence Industry and Space at the Commission in 2020 can be seen as part of this development.

In conclusion, while PESCO is *not* a form of enhanced cooperation, it is in some respects more similar to enhanced cooperation than CFSP enhanced cooperation. And in contrast to CFSP enhanced cooperation, it is up and running,

---

227 Austria, Belgium, Bulgaria, Czech Republic, Croatia, Cyprus, Estonia, Finland, France, Germany, Greece, Hungary, Italy, Ireland, Latvia, Lithuania, Luxembourg, the Netherlands, Poland, Portugal, Romania, Slovenia, Slovakia, Spain and Sweden.

228 Council Decision 14866/17; Biscop, S. (2018), 'European Defence: Give PESCO a Chance', *Survival*, Vol. 60, No. 3, pp. 161–180; https://pesco.europa.eu/ (last access 22/01/2020).

229 https://www.consilium.europa.eu/en/press/press-releases/2023/05/23/eu-defence-cooperation-council-welcomes-denmark-into-pesco-and-launches-the-5th-wave-of-new-pesco-projects/ (last access 22/08/2023).

230 https://www.maltatoday.com.mt/news/europe/83085/malta_to_wait_and_se e_before_deciding_on_pesco_defence_pact_muscat_says#.Wje3pN9l-Co (last access 21/01/2020).

231 https://www.consilium.europa.eu/media/41333/pesco-projects-12-nov-2019.pdf (last access 21/01/2020).

232 Council Decision 14866/17, Annex.

233 https://ec.europa.eu/commission/sites/beta-political/files/budget-may2018-eu-defence-fund_en.pdf (last access 21/01/2020).

leading to an instance well-balanced differentiated policy-making in the field of defence.

## 2.4 Conclusions on the Scope of Application of Enhanced Cooperation

Enhanced cooperation can reasonably be expected in fields such as the harmonisation of taxes (indirect taxes, Art. 113 TFEU or direct taxes, Art. 115 TFEU). In particular, company taxation (CCCTB/CCTB) or a digital tax seem fit for differentiated approaches. Social policy could also be a candidate for enhanced cooperation attempts if established along the lines of the EMU (e.g. European Unemployment Benefit Scheme). EMU governance in the narrower sense, i.e. monetary and fiscal policy regarding the Eurozone, is also a field that would be apt for enhanced cooperation. Moreover, judicial cooperation in civil matters, in particular regarding family law, is a prime candidate for future enhanced cooperations, as is judicial cooperation in criminal matters. The related field of police cooperation could also see differentiation in future the mechanism in future. Finally, the usage of the provisions on CFSP enhanced cooperation cannot be ruled out, nor could, especially in a moment of crisis, the resort to enhanced cooperation in the context of Art. 352 TFEU.

Among the QMV legal bases that would require a novel approach in the Council to see an enhanced cooperation, Art. 66 TFEU on protective measures against capital from third states to protect the EMU seems like a case apt for enhanced cooperation. QMV arithmetics would enable Member States to pass an enhanced cooperation without Commission involvement in the case of Art. 87 (2) TFEU on police cooperation. Consumer protections might also be a field where Member States could come to the result of an enhanced cooperation, which could also lead project like the Common European Sales Law to implementation. Finally, non-legislative measures like Environment Action Plans would be an imaginative, yet possible usage of enhanced cooperation. It remains to be said that in non-unanimity areas, enhanced cooperation it not excluded, but would require an overhaul of the EU's (or the Member States') general approach to policymaking in the Council, being more open to agreeing to disagree, and lowering the abstract value of unity as principle. As such, QMV enhanced cooperation would be a move away from the "culture of legislative compromise in the process of European integration."[234]

On the other side of the spectrum, many other areas brought up in the past, such as legislation on environmental matters or on migration matters in general and asylum in specific, seem rather unlikely to see an application of enhanced cooperation in the future. Despite all calls for enhanced cooperation in these particularly disputed policy fields, the problematic incentive structures at play suggest that binding differentiated lawmaking is unattractive for Member States—a finding that is confirmed by the absence of any enhanced cooperation attempts in these areas in practice.

234 Blanke, H.-J. (2021), 'Art. 27 TFEU' in: Blanke, H.-J., Mangiameli, S. (eds.), *Treaty on the Functioning of the European Union—A Commentary*.

# 3 The Principle of Last Resort—Do Procedural Legal Constraints Stand in the Way of a More Thorough Use of Enhanced Cooperation?

In the beginning of this thesis (Sect. 1.1), it was described how any instance of differentiated integration within the EU is automatically and by default situated between the poles of two conflicting interests, namely between the principle of unity dogmatically underlying all EU action and the interest of individual Member States of progressing in integration. This is particularly true for the most standardised form of differentiated integration, enhanced cooperation. When enhanced cooperation is resorted to, or—much more often—called for, it is in situations in which a number of Member States pushes towards an integration step but cannot proceed as desired because they do not fulfil the necessary majority requirement—in practice usually unanimity—because one or more Member States refuse the same step. In this scenario, the default solution is that principle of unity prescribes that nobody moves until everybody moves. The principle of unity, as laid out in Sect. 1.1, is not just a rule of EU law but a true principle, a dogma underlying EU integration and an objective of EU integration. It is only by way of an exception to the rule that this principle is ever deviated from, be it in an opt-out for individual Member States, temporal inapplicability of certain rules to certain Member States or the non-participation of Member States in secondary law acts, as enabled by enhanced cooperation. It is for this exceptional nature of differentiated integration mechanisms in general and enhanced cooperation in particular that they are meant to be used reluctantly only and are restrained by strict formal hurdles. At the same time, it is the very aim of enhanced cooperation to overcome political blockades in the Council and allow Member States

An earlier version of this chapter was part of my thesis to obtain the Master in Comparative, European and International Laws (LL.M.) at the European University Institute in Florence, Italy.



J. Graf von Luckner, *Enhanced Cooperation Revisited*,
https://doi.org/10.1007/978-3-658-51063-3_3

to pioneer and form a vanguard of states which integrate more deeply. As such, the enhanced cooperation legal framework is in itself weighing up the integration policy interests of progress and unity.

In the case of the enhanced cooperation mechanism, the formal hurdles performing this task of conciliating the diverging policy interests are visible first and foremost in the authorisation procedure that groups of Member States interested in forming an enhanced cooperation must pass in order to proceed with their joint project. In this procedure, Member States submit a request to the Commission, which may submit a proposal to that effect to the Council (Art. 329.2 TFEU). The Council, after obtaining the consent of the European Parliament, may then decide to authorise the enhanced cooperation by qualified majority (Art. 329.1 (2) TFEU, Art. 20 TEU). One of the most central requirements that need to be fulfilled in order for the Council to activate enhanced cooperation, i.e. to issue the authorisation decision, is the 'last resort' criterion (Art. 20.2 TEU). Differentiated legislation can only be used as a last resort when it has been established that a legislative project does not find the necessary majority among the Council members within a reasonable period of time. This cornerstone rule of the enhanced cooperation mechanism ensures that seeking a compromise among all Member States remains the default option, and enhanced cooperation is not used on an everyday basis but as an exception, as it is meant to be. Preventing arbitrary exclusion of Member States from certain projects, the last resort criterion is a defining feature and a crucial foundation of the enhanced cooperation mechanism. The inability to come to a solution with the Union as a whole must therefore be stated explicitly by the Council.[1]

[1] The inability to come to a solution with the Union as a whole must eventually be stated explicitly by the Council. It can, but does not have to be stated in a separate Council decision (although some Treaty versions, like the German language version, might suggest otherwise), see: Becker, U. (2015), 'Art. 20 EUV, Art. 326–334 AEUV' in: Groeben, H. v. d., Schwarze, J., Hatje, A. (eds.), *Europäisches Unionsrecht,* Baden-Baden, Nomos, Art. 20 EUV, 50; Linke, G. (2006), *Das Instrument der verstärkten Zusammenarbeit im Vertrag von Nizza: Möglichkeiten eines Europas der differenzierten Integration,* Interdisziplinäre Europa Studien, Frankfurt am Main, Lang, p. 113; Thym, D. (2004), *Ungleichzeitigkeit und europäisches Verfassungsrecht*, Schriftenreihe europäisches Verfassungsrecht, Baden-Baden, Nomos, p. 53; Heber, C. (2021), *Enhanced Cooperation and European Tax Law*, Oxford University Press.

The legal content of the last resort criterion is subject to a considerable range of different interpretations. Whereas the basic idea of the criterion is fairly clear,[2] the Treaties do not foresee any provisions on its practical application. Over the years, due to this ambiguity as well as earlier, more restrictive Treaty versions, the last resort criterion was often considered the biggest obstacle hindering Member States from using enhanced cooperation. This has resulted in calls to abolish the criterion altogether, both in the past[3] and more recently[4] in order to finally unleash the enhanced cooperation mechanism's full potential. In the following, I will take a different approach. I will set out to reveal in detail how big an obstacle the last resort criterion really is and what room for manoeuvre Member States have in this respect under the current Treaties. This aims to, once again, highlight which possibilities the enhanced cooperation mechanism offers to Member States, in particular in difficult situations such as the numerous crises the EU has been encountering as of late, and where the Treaty restrictions do stop Member States from resorting to enhanced cooperation. In particular, matters of concern in such situations are whether the last resort criterion keeps Member States from passing legislation by way of enhanced cooperation that they deem necessary or even vital to address a crisis situation if not all Member States agree on the short term. In certain cases, this could even lead to Member States looking for a 'fast track' enhanced cooperation, which leads to the question if the last resort criterion allows, in specific situations, to largely skip the regular legislative procedure and very quickly turn to enhanced cooperation in times of crisis.

In order to be able to address these issues, I will first conduct a detailed analysis of the last resort criterion. Some particularly relevant and ambiguous questions guiding this analysis this are:

- What does the term "last resort" mean, and what is a "reasonable period"? Which Council actions can be taken into account when assessing it, and what is the minimum activity necessary in the Council prior to resorting to enhanced cooperation, if any?
- To what extent does the Court of Justice scrutinize the last resort criterion, potentially limiting its application?

---

[2] Blanke, H.-J. (2013), 'Art. 20 TEU' in: Blanke, H.-J., Mangiameli, S. (eds.), *The Treaty on European Union (TEU): A commentary*, Berlin, Springer, pp. 787–830.

[3] CONFER 4783/00 (Germany and Italy), p. 5.

[4] Blanke, H.-J., Pilz, S. (2020), 'Europa 2019 bis 2024—Wohin trägt uns der Stier?: Sieben Thesen zu den Herausforderungen der Europäischen Union', *EuR*, pp. 270–300; Duff, A. (2022), *Constitutional change in the European Union: Towards a federal Europe*, Basingstoke, Palgrave Macmillan.

In the following, I will aim to find answers to these questions by combining findings from the literature and well-explored sources with previously unexplored materials.

As a first step, I will trace back the last resort criterion in the previous Treaty versions to gain insights into the aims of the Treaty legislator. Secondly, I will analyse the second main source of information when interpreting the Treaties, namely judgments, especially by the Court of Justice (CJEU). Only one of the four judgments on enhanced cooperation explicitly scrutinized the last resort criterion and will therefore be analysed. However, the final judgments are not the only revealing document type produced during Court proceedings. In addition to them, I applied for and gained access to the pleadings of all parties intervening in the proceedings under the EU Access to Documents-Regulation.[5] These pleadings from EU Institutions and several Member States, acting as defendant, applicants, and interveners contain a vast set of different arguments on and interpretations of the subject. The CJEU regularly reiterates the main arguments of the involved parties but does so only briefly and only in terms of arguments which it takes a stance on itself within the judgment. Therefore, analysing the pleadings provides new insights on known arguments and unveils points which have been raised but not addressed by the Court. In doing so, the research can also show which arguments were neglected without even mentioning them (which can be a stronger reaction than explicitly disregarding) and invalidate accusations of the Court having overlooked aspects of a case.

## 3.1 The Last Resort Criterion

### 3.1.1 The Role of the Last Resort Criterion

The 'last resort' criterion is one of the most central requirements that need to be fulfilled in order to activate enhanced cooperation. It is introduced to the Treaties in Art. 20.2 TEU:

> *The decision authorising enhanced cooperation shall be adopted by the Council as a last resort, when it has established that the objectives of such cooperation cannot be attained within a reasonable period by the Union as a whole [...]*

[5] Regulation (EC) No 1049/2001.

Beyond being a legal condition, the last resort criterion (also referred to as *ultima ratio* principle[6]) is considered to reveal the *ratio essendi*, the reason for the existence of enhanced cooperation. Since it can only be used as last resort, enhanced cooperation is necessarily a secondary option to which a solution including all Member States is to be preferred, making enhanced cooperation subsidiary to uniform legislation.[7]

However, the term 'last resort' is ambiguous,[8] with interpretations varying considerably. Art. 20 TEU is the only occasion in which the term last resort is used in the Treaties; the lack of points of reference adds to its ambiguity.

In the following, and as a preparation for a thorough interpretation, I will trace back the history of the last resort criterion in the different Treaty versions. Afterwards, I will reiterate the CJEU's findings on the criterion.

## 3.1.2 Treaty History

### 3.1.2.1 Treaty of Maastricht

The Treaty of Maastricht (1993) foresaw the possibility of legal differentiation by means of 'closer cooperation' in the fields of common foreign and security policy (Art. J.4 (5) TEU–Maastricht) and justice and home affairs (Art. K.7 TEU–Maastricht). However, this was meant as a cooperation *outside* of the Treaties. Thus, the conditions for such cooperation are limited to not conflicting with or impeding the provisions of the TEU. For this reason, a last resort criterion is not foreseen.

---

[6] Ruffert, M. (2016), 'Art. 20 EUV' in: Calliess, C., Ruffert, M. (eds.), *EUV/AEUV: Das Verfassungsrecht der Europäischen Union mit Europäischer Grundrechtecharta: Kommentar,* München, C.H. Beck, Art. 20 EUV para 19.

[7] Blanke, H.-J. (2018), 'Art. 20 EUV' in: Grabitz, E., Hilf, M., Nettesheim, M. (eds.), *Das Recht der Europäischen Union,* München, Beck, Art. 20 EUV para 43; Thym, D. (2004), *Ungleichzeitigkeit und europäisches Verfassungsrecht*, Schriftenreihe europäisches Verfassungsrecht, Baden-Baden, Nomos, p. 247; Cannone, A. (2005), *Le cooperazioni rafforzate: Contributo allo studio dell'integrazione differenziata,* Pubblicazioni della Facoltà giuridica dell'Università di Bari, Bari, Cacucci, p. 73.

[8] Philippart, E. (2003), *A new mechanism of enhanced co-operation for the enlarged European Union,* Notre Europe, p. 12.

#### 3.1.2.2 Treaty of Amsterdam

The Treaty of Amsterdam, which entered into force in 1999, picked up the term 'closer cooperation'[9], although changing its meaning and introducing for the first time the concept nowadays referred to as enhanced cooperation, i.e. an integration procedure *within* the EU framework without all Member States participating.

In doing so, it also introduced for the first time the notion of last resort, Art. 43 (1)(c) TEU (Amsterdam):

> *[T]he cooperation [...] is only used as a last resort, where the objectives of the [...] Treaties could not be attained by applying the relevant procedures laid down therein;*

By referring to the objectives of the Treaties, rather than the objectives of a single legislative project, the Treaty set a high bar for the application of the procedure: If a single legislative project fails to attain a majority, it does not necessarily mean that the Treaty objective lying *behind* it cannot be reached.[10] This may have been one of the reasons why the closer cooperation under the Treaty of Amsterdam was never put into action. Another reason for this may have been the referral to the "relevant procedures": This expression shows that a legislative procedure must have necessarily been brought to an unsuccessful conclusion before Member States could resort to closer cooperation. This, on the other hand, could be delayed willingly by uncooperative Member States in order to prevent a differentiated approach altogether or to "put a price on their vote in the authorisation procedure",even on a negative vote.[11] Furthermore, in the Amsterdam version of the TEU, it is not explicitly clear who is responsible for assessing whether the last resort criterion is fulfilled.[12]

These difficulties made the procedure practically impossible to use and led to reform debates during the negotiations for the Treaty of Nice.[13] When it came to the last resort criterion, Member States realized the difficulties it caused, and Italy

---

[9] This applies for the English language version. Interestingly, other versions such as Italian and German already changed the name of the mechanism to what in English later became 'enhanced cooperation' ('verstärkte Zusammenarbeit' and 'cooperazione rafforzata' as opposed to 'engere Zusammenarbeit' and 'cooperazione più stretta').

[10] Philippart, E. (2003), *A new mechanism of enhanced co-operation for the enlarged European Union*, Notre Europe, p. 18.

[11] Philippart, E. (2003), *A new mechanism of enhanced co-operation for the enlarged European Union*, Notre Europe.

[12] Philippart, E. (2003), *A new mechanism of enhanced co-operation for the enlarged European Union*, Notre Europe.

[13] For a thorough summary of the process and the different positions, see Linke, G. (2006), *Das Instrument der verstärkten Zusammenarbeit im Vertrag von Nizza: Möglichkeiten eines*

and Germany, in a joint position paper on enhanced cooperation, even proposed its deletion due to its ambiguities and the risk of juridical disputes to clarify the criterion.[14]

#### 3.1.2.3 Treaty of Nice

In the Treaty of Nice, the term 'enhanced cooperation' was introduced to replace 'closer cooperation'.[15] In this process, the last resort criterion was given an exposed position in a whole article on the matter:

> *Article 43a TEU (Nice)*
>
> *Enhanced cooperation may be undertaken only as a last resort, when it has been established within the Council that the objectives of such cooperation cannot be attained within a reasonable period by applying the relevant provisions of the Treaties.*

The new wording meant a significant lowering of the last resort-threshold: Instead of demanding that an objective of the Treaties cannot be attained otherwise, the Nice-version focuses on the specific legislative project that Member States want to conclude. Moreover, instead of explicitly calling for a concluded legislative process, Art. 43a TEU--Nice stresses that it is sufficient if the objectives of the project cannot be attained "within a reasonable period by applying the relevant provisions of the Treaties", disempowering states wanting to prevent differentiated integration through delaying tactics.[16] However, the referral to the application of the relevant Treaty provisions still points towards a regular legislative procedure.

Finally, the Council was exclusively entrusted with establishing whether the criterion was fulfilled.

Despite some remaining ambiguities, the negotiations for the Treaty of Nice resulted in a last resort-formula that was considered to be lighter, less fragmenting and to leave more liberty to the willing.[17]

---

*Europas der differenzierten Integration*, Interdisziplinäre Europa Studien, Frankfurt am Main, Lang, p. 67 ff.

[14] CONFER 4783/00, p. 5.

[15] In the English language version. For other versions, see above, Treaty of Amsterdam.

[16] Philippart, E. (2003), *A new mechanism of enhanced co-operation for the enlarged European Union*, Notre Europe, p. 18 f.

[17] Philippart, E. (2003), *A new mechanism of enhanced co-operation for the enlarged European Union*, Notre Europe, p. 18; see also Thym, D. (2004), *Ungleichzeitigkeit und europäisches Verfassungsrecht*, Schriftenreihe europäisches Verfassungsrecht, Baden-Baden, Nomos, p. 52.

#### 3.1.2.4 Constitutional Treaty and Treaty of Lisbon

As far as the last resort criterion is concerned, the Constitutional Treaty, rejected in 2005, and the Lisbon Treaty which has been in force since 2009, are identical. Art. I-44 Constitutional Treaty and Art. 20 TEU read:

> *The [...] decision authorising enhanced cooperation shall be adopted by the Council as a last resort, when it has established that the objectives of such cooperation cannot be attained within a reasonable period by the Union as a whole [...]*

The main change of the formula is the deletion of the phrase "by applying the relevant provisions of the Treaties", which as described above, lead to uncertainties as to which procedural steps are necessary in the Council concerning a uniform approach. The rationale for this change, according to the presidium of the European Convention drafting the Constitutional Treaty, was to "make[...] it clearer that the last resort condition does not necessarily mean the failure of a previous procedure, or even that any such decision-making procedure has been initiated".[18]

### 3.1.3 Court of Justice Interpretation

Of the four cases brought to the CJEU concerning enhanced cooperation,[19] only one dealt with the last resort criterion, namely *Spain/Italy v. Council* on the EU unitary patent.[20]

#### 3.1.3.1 The Case

In *Spain/Italy v. Council*, Spain and Italy sought annulment of the Council decision authorising enhanced cooperation in the field of a unitary patent. The dispute arose after the patent system, which all Member States agreed on in principle, was passed as an enhanced cooperation due to the Council's inability to find a language regime that contented all Member States. Italy and Spain wanted their respective languages to be official languages of the patent, or to only resort to English as an official language. When the final solution foresaw English, French,

---

[18] CONV 723/03, p. 18; c.f. Martenczuk, B. (2013), 'Enhanced Cooperation: The Practice of Ad Hoc Differentiation in the EU since the Lisbon Treaty', *StudDipl*, pp. 83–100, p. 88.

[19] ECJ C-274/11, 295/11 (*Spain/Italy v Council*), ECLI:EU:C:2013:240; C-146/13 (*Spain v Parliament and Council*), ECLI:EU:C:2015:298, C-147/13 (*Spain v Council*), ECLI:EU:C:2015:299; C-209/13 (*UK v Council*), ECLI:EU:C:2014:283.

[20] ECJ C-274/11, 295/11 (*Spain/Italy v Council*), ECLI:EU:C:2013:240.

and German, they refused to become part of the system and eventually brought the case to the Court. In the CJEU case, in addition to Spain and Italy as applicants and the Council as defendant, 13 Member States and institutions[21] acted as interveners, all of them in favour of the decision.

#### 3.1.3.2 Judgment of the Court of Justice

The Court of Justice (Grand Chamber), in its judgment, pointed out that the last resort criterion is a "particularly important" condition and must be read in the light of Art. 20.1 TEU insofar as it provides that enhanced cooperation aims to further the objectives of the union, protect its interests, and reinforce the integration process. In this context, the Court stressed that it would not be in the Union's interests if all fruitless negotiations could lead to an (or several) enhanced cooperation(s).[22]

In terms of its own role, the Court stated that it is its task to "ascertain whether the Council has carefully and impartially examined those aspects that are relevant [...] and whether adequate reasons have been given" and confirmed that the Council is best placed to determine whether an agreement among all Member States can be reached in a reasonable period.[23]

In terms of the unitary patent case, it held that several attempts were conducted to find a compromise in terms of the patent's language regime. Given this, and the appropriate reasoning on this by the Council, the Court stated that it could not find any evidence that could disprove the Council's evaluation of the enhanced cooperation being a last resort.[24] Moreover, it pointed out that last resort is not limited to cases in which the Members States declare that they are not willing or ready to take an integration step, but it can also be caused by the inability to agree on the implementation of a measure.[25]

---

[21] Namely Belgium, the Czech Republic, Germany, Ireland, France, Latvia, Hungary, the Netherlands, Poland, Sweden, the United Kingdom, the European Parliament, and the Commission.

[22] ECJ C-274/11, 295/11 (*Spain/Italy v Council*), ECLI:EU:C:2013:240, para 48, 49.

[23] ECJ C-274/11, 295/11 (*Spain/Italy v Council*), ECLI:EU:C:2013:240, para 54.

[24] ECJ C-274/11, 295/11 (*Spain/Italy v Council*), ECLI:EU:C:2013:240, para 55.

[25] ECJ C-274/11, 295/11 (*Spain/Italy v Council*), ECLI:EU:C:2013:240, para 36.

## 3.2 Interpretation

As stated in the introduction, the last resort criterion is still subject to debates and unclarity. This has a potential to keep Member States from applying enhanced cooperation when needed. Moreover, so far, the insecurity about its precise content led to lengthy processes prior to resorting to enhanced cooperation, which made the mechanism less suitable as a measure to react to imminent problems.

In the following, I will bring together findings from the literature, the material above, and the before-mentioned pleadings from *Spain/Italy v. Council* to produce new insights on the two most contested areas of questions: the level scrutiny of the CJEU and the substantial content of the criterion, as described in the questions above. In doing so, I aim to clarify some of the open questions which could help make the enhanced cooperation procedure easier to use in the future.

### 3.2.1 Level of Scrutiny

After the CJEU judgment in *Spain/Italy v. Council*, many were unpleased with how the Court had scrutinized the last resort criterion.

*Jäger* and *Lamping* both regard the CJEU judgment on the unitary patent as a significant weakening of the last resort criterion. The last resort criterion, they say, is "reduced to a mere requirement to state reasons",[26] while the Court is "hiding behind the separation of powers".[27] This was drawn from the Court's statements that the Council is "best placed to determine whether the Member States have demonstrated any willingness to compromise and are in a position to put forward proposals capable of leading to the adoption of legislation for the Union as a whole in the foreseeable future"[28], and "[t]he Court [...] should therefore ascertain whether the Council has carefully and impartially examined those aspects that are relevant to this point and whether adequate reasons have been

[26] Jaeger, T. (2017), 'The End to a Never-Ending Story? The Unitary Patent Regime' in: Giegerich, T., Schmitt, D. C., Zeitzmann, S. (eds.), *Flexibility in the EU and beyond: How much differentiation can European integration bear?,* Oxford, Hart Publishing, pp. 269–281, p. 278.

[27] Lamping, M., 'Enhanced Cooperation in the Area of Unitary Patent Protection: Testing the Boundaries of the Rule of Law', *Working Paper*, p. 10.

[28] ECJ C-274/11, 295/11 (*Spain/Italy v Council*), ECLI:EU:C:2013:240, para 53.

given for the conclusion reached by the Council." In doing so, both clearly interpret the Court's statements as excluding any further scrutiny. Especially *Lamping* does not seem to see this approach as a legal obligation but as a way of avoiding a (hence theoretically possible) scrutiny of political assessments.[29]

*Pistoia*, in this context, points out that in her opinion "such control totally left aside a review of the merits of last resort as such",[30] and that the Court does not only put a focus on, but limits itself to only reviewing carefulness and impartiality together with the adequacy of the given reason.[31] However, in contrast to *Jäger* and *Lamping,* she agrees with the legal necessity of such limited scrutiny of political assessments.

These interpretations, although founded in the *Spain/Italy v. Council* case and previous case law, may not be having regard to the whole picture as presented above.

In fact, taking into account the materials that the Court had at its disposal, it seems that interpreting the judgment as a Court's withdrawal from substantial scrutiny of the last resort criterion is premature. Firstly, it may be true that the Court assessed the criterion in a limited way. However, its language when doing so is remarkably open: "[The Court] should therefore ascertain whether the Council has carefully and impartially examined those aspects […] and whether adequate reasons have been given […]"—Nowhere does it state that it actually *must limit* itself to that. Isolated, this may not seem like a major finding. However, considering the arguments that the different parties equipped the Court with, allows for this phrasing to be seen in a new light:

---

[29] Lamping, M. (2011), 'Enhanced Cooperation—A Proper Approach to Market Integration in the Field of Unitary Patent Protection?', *IIC*, No. 42, p. 879; Lamping, M. (2013), 'Enhanced Cooperation in the Area of Unitary Patent Protection—Testing the Boundaries of the Rule of Law', *Maastricht J. Eur. Comp. L.*, pp. 589–600.

[30] Pistoia, E. (2014), 'Enhanced Cooperation as a tool to…enhance integration?: Spain and Italy v. Council', *CMLRev*, pp. 247–260, p. 254.

[31] Pistoia, E. (2014), 'Enhanced Cooperation as a tool to…enhance integration?: Spain and Italy v. Council', *CMLRev*, pp. 247–260, p. 259.

Several interveners, including even the applicant Italy,[32] but also the AG,[33] the Council,[34] the European Parliament[35], and Ireland,[36] proposed a set programme for the CJEU scrutiny of the last resort criterion indicating plenty of relevant case law which pointed in this direction.[37] This would have meant that the Court would have, once and for all, limited its scrutiny exclusively to manifest errors of assessment, misuse of powers, and the Council manifestly exceeding the boundaries of its discretion. While this would have provided the Court with fixed and easy to handle guiding lines for future cases, it would have largely limited it in its ability to scrutinize future enhanced cooperation attempts: It takes a lot for Council action to qualify as *manifestly* exceeding its admissible discretion. For the same reason, had the Court intended to disregard the last resort criterion, as argued by the authors mentioned above, this solution would have provided a convenient strategy to do so.

The Court, however, stayed away from such a set scrutiny programme and did not quote any earlier cases. Rather, it seems to point to a strong focus on, but not necessarily a fixed limitation of, its scrutiny.

Also, some interveners like the European Parliament, implicated that the last resort criterion was so purely political (or the margin of appreciation so wide) that they did not even discuss the merits of the case and just declared it to be met.[38] Had the Court really wanted to point out that the last resort was a purely political criterion, it could have followed suit. However, the Court did explore the situation underlying the Unitary Patent Case,[39] showing that it does not simply disregard the last resort principle.

---

[32] Complaint of the Italian Republic in C-295/11, Court register no. 876261, para 100.

[33] Opinion of AG *Bot* in C-274/11, C-295/11 (*Spain/Italy v. Council*), ECLI:EU:C:2012:782, para 115 f.

[34] Council of the European Union, Escrito de Contestacíon in C-274/11, para 52; Council of the European Union, Controricorso in C-295/11, para 47.

[35] Statement in intervention of the European Parliament in C-295/11, Court Register no. 893668, para 20; Statement in intervention of the European Parliament in C-274/11, Court Register no. 893544, para 29.

[36] Statement in intervention of Ireland in C-274/11, Court Register no. 894401, para 14; Statement in intervention of Ireland in C-295/11, Court Register no. 894479, para 10.

[37] See ECJ C- 435/08, (*Enviro Tech (Europe)*) ECLI:EU:C:2009:635, para 47; C-326/05 P (*Industrias Químicas del Vallés v Commission*) ECLI:EU:C:2007:443, para 75–77.

[38] Statement in intervention of the European Parliament in C-295/11, Court Register no. 893668, para 20 ff.; Statement in intervention of the European Parliament in C-274/11, Court Register no. 893544, para 29 ff.

[39] ECJ C-274/11, 295/11 (*Spain/Italy v Council*), ECLI:EU:C:2013:240, para 55–57.

All of this can be interpreted as the Court staying on alert. It is apparent from *Spain/Italy v. Council* that in fact the Court did not intend to stand in the way of enhanced cooperation as a matter of principle. However, the Court seems to see the risks of this integration mechanism and, therefore, stays vague enough to be able to intervene if necessary—also by means of the last resort criterion. These findings give rise to quite a different interpretation than the one pointed out above: In fact, despite the Court's limited scrutiny in *Spain/Italy v. Council*, it did not establish a set programme for assessing the last resort criterion and did not retreat from scrutinizing the last resort for good. Thus, the Court's strategy should be interpreted as an approach of *abuse control*. It does—at least for the time being—grant the Council a wide margin of appreciation when assessing whether an agreement can still be reached. This also means that the Court sees the possibility that enhanced cooperation may develop further and that it is not yet decided how the mechanism will be used in future. However, should a majority of the Member States misuse enhanced cooperation, the Court stays ready to step in.

### 3.2.2 Content of 'Last Resort' and a "Reasonable Period"

The term 'last resort' is a vague legal concept. After being completely open in the Treaty of Amsterdam, it was made slightly more concrete by the Treaty of Nice, which pointed out that enhanced cooperation was to be used as "last resort, when [...] the objectives of such cooperation cannot be attained within a reasonable period by applying the relevant provisions of the Treaties" (Art. 43a TEU–Nice), emphasising that the criterion is to be understood essentially as a temporal factor. Finally, the wording was changed to "when [the Council] has established that the objectives of such cooperation cannot be attained within a reasonable period by the Union as a whole" (Art. 20 TEU), deleting the reference to the relevant Treaty provision in order to point out that "the last resort condition does not necessarily mean the failure of a previous [legislative] procedure".[40] However, the content of the criterion was still far from clear, especially before *Spain/Italy v. Council* was decided.

[40] CONV 23/03, p. 18.

The Court, in its judgment on the matter, pointed out that this means "only those situations in which it is impossible to adopt such legislation in the foreseeable future".[41] Nonetheless, it also stressed that "[t]he Union's interests and the process of integration would, quite clearly, not be protected if all fruitless negotiations could lead to one or more instances of enhanced cooperation",[42] making clear that the temporal unforeseeability of a uniform legislation must be backed by a certain substance of the negotiations. Therefore, it will in any case depend on the details of the specific case whether an enhanced cooperation can be implemented as 'last resort':[43] The more states agree to disagree, the less discussion is needed.[44]

However, it does seem possible to give some more substance to the criterion.

#### 3.2.2.1 Council Activity to Consider

The first question to discuss may not be an obvious one and was therefore not discussed in the literature so far. However, in the context of the Unitary Patent proceedings, it became very clear that the question of which Council activity on a given subject even counts as attempts to find a uniform solution is a controversial issue and can have a major impact on the outcome.

The idea of establishing a unitary patent dates back to the 1970 s, including discussions in the Council. A first draft regulation was tabled significantly later in 2000.[45] On the other hand, the final act that eventually led to enhanced cooperation was different from this first proposal and had only been discussed for a few months (from 30 June to 10 December 2010) when the Council decided that unanimity could not be reached. This divergence illustrates the impact of the question. Given the absence of literature on the topic, the Court materials in the only case in which the question was addressed have particular importance in answering the question.

---

[41] ECJ C-274/11, 295/11 (*Spain/Italy v Council*), ECLI:EU:C:2013:240, para 50; Zeitzmann, S. (2013), 'Patentrecht: Ermächtigung zur Verstärkten Zusammenarbeit', *EuZW*, pp. 475–480, p. 475, 480.

[42] ECJ C-274/11, 295/11 (*Spain/Italy v Council*), ECLI:EU:C:2013:240, para 49.

[43] Blanke, H.-J. (2018), 'Art. 20 EUV' in: Grabitz, E., Hilf, M., Nettesheim, M. (eds.), *Das Recht der Europäischen Union,* München, Beck, para 44.

[44] Peers, S. (2017), 'Enhanced Cooperation: the Cinderella of differentiated integration' in: Witte, B. de, Ott, A., Vos, E. (eds.), *Between Flexibility and Disintegration: The Trajectory of Differentiation in EU Law,* Edward Elgar Publishing Limited, pp. 76–91, p. 87.

[45] Proposal for a Council Regulation on the Community patent, COM(2000) 412 final, 2000/0177(CNS).

The possible approaches to the topic differ mostly in the degree of formality that is required for Council activity to be regarded as part of a decision-making and compromise-finding process. The most informal approach was chosen by the UK[46] and Poland[47]. Both argued that every discussion that has ever taken place on an abstract topic (in the patent case, the talks during the past 40 years) plays a role and must be taken into account when assessing whether a solution cannot be found in a reasonable period.

Other parties, like the Council,[48] Commission,[49] Germany,[50] and AG *Bot*,[51] claimed that only formal discussions on legislative proposals can be regarded, even when they are not identical with the proposal that was debated before resorting to enhanced cooperation. This would, in the unitary patent case, mean that proposals like the one from 2000 are relevant, whereas prior discussions on the broader topic of a European Unitary Patent must not be considered. The defendants Spain[52] and Italy,[53] on the other side of the spectrum, took the most formal stand, only taking into account work on the very proposal that the Council debated before concluding that unanimity could not be reached.

The Court, although not explicitly deciding on the issue, did not take into account the discussions from decades ago. When assessing the Council's attempts to find a solution for the Union as a whole, it refers to the fact that "the legislative process undertaken [...] was begun during the year 2000" and marks this as starting point of the proceedings that must be taken into account.[54] Hence, the Court chose a semi-formal approach, still closely related to legislative processes. While refusing to take into account every debate on the broad, abstract topic in question, the court assesses the formal Council activity that has a clear internal

---

[46] Statement in intervention of the United Kingdom in C-274/11, Court Register no. 894567, para 32.

[47] Statement in intervention of Poland in C-295/11, para 30.

[48] Council of the European Union, Escrito de Contestacíon in C-274/11, para 55 f., Council of the European Union, Controricorso in C-295/11, para 49 f.

[49] Statement in intervention of the Commission in C-295/11, Court Register no. 894482, para 64.

[50] Statement in intervention of Germany in C-274/11, p. 7 para 17 f.; Statement in intervention of Germany in C-295/11, para 18 f.

[51] Opinion of AG *Bot* in C-274/11, C-295/22 (*Spain/Italy v. Council*), ECLI:EU:C:2012:782, para 119 ff.

[52] Complaint of the Kingdom of Spain in C-274/11, Court Register no. 875676, para 54 ff.

[53] Complaint of the Italian Republic in C-295/11, Court Register no. 876261, para 95 ff.

[54] ECJ C-274/11, 295/11 (*Spain/Italy v Council*), ECLI:EU:C:2013:240, para 55.

connection to the eventual proposal. This approach is very likely to be the guideline for future enhanced cooperation projects. Hence, it is advisable for involved parties to start working on a concrete proposal, not despite, but because of a possible need to resort to enhanced cooperation and even if such a proposal is far away from what Member States eventually want to be passed by the Council. This is also affirmed by all other occasions of enhanced cooperation: In all cases, enhanced cooperation was only started after discussion on the basis of a proposal issued by the Commission had taken place.[55]

However, especially in the light of the drafting history in which the need for a formal legislative procedure was specifically rejected[56] and the Court also taking into account discussions on an outdated draft regulation, a relevant discussion may not always have to be about a Commission legislation draft:[57] In legislative procedures, the Council has what is sometimes referred to as 'indirect right of initiative'. Under Art. 241 TFEU, the Council can, with simple majority, request the Commission to submit proposals for legislation. If a Council discussion in preparation of such a request is conducted in a sufficiently detailed and substantive manner, it constitutes formal Council activity and has a sufficiently clear internal connection with a legislative procedure. Under the standards set by the CJEU, this should without a doubt be able to constitute a valid and adequate attempt of finding a compromise among all Member States. Council action should, in conclusion, be serious, determined and focussed on possible Council action, but does not necessarily need to be part on an ongoing legislative procedure.

#### 3.2.2.2 Required Intensity of Council Engagement

When it comes to the central question, finally, of what the Council proceedings must comprise substantially to rule out the option of finding a uniform legislative solution, opinions still vary significantly. First and foremost, it should be reminded that the Treaties do not foresee any type of minimum threshold for the last resort criterion to be met. When it comes to the question of what the Member States need to try before resorting to enhanced cooperation, there is disagreement about the necessary Council activity in both legal literature and practice.

---

[55] Enhanced cooperation on divorce and legal separation: Council Decision 2010/405/EU, para. 3; financial transaction tax: Council Decision 2013/52/EU para. 4; international couples' property regimes: Council Decision (EU) 2016/954, para. 3.

[56] CONV 23/03, p. 18: "the last resort condition does not necessarily mean the failure of a previous [legislative] procedure".

[57] See also Peers, S. (2010), 'Divorce, European Style: The First Authorization of Enhanced Cooperation', *Eur. Const. L. Rev*, pp. 339–358.

Maybe the most extensive interpretation was offered by *Kuipers*. In the context of the first enhanced cooperation on divorce and legal separation, he claimed that "it cannot be maintained that enhanced cooperation was the instrument of last resort" because the Institutions had not made use of the '*passerelle*-clause' in Art. 81 (3) TFEU.[58] This clause gives the Council the opportunity to change the procedure for legislation regarding "family law with cross-border implications" from unanimous to qualified majority voting (QMV). It can do so with a unanimous vote after consulting the European Parliament and giving all national parliaments the possibility to object within six months.

Art. 81 (3) TFEU is, however, not the only *passerelle*-clause in the Treaties. Art. 48 (7) TEU allows the same, applying the similar procedural hurdles (decisions have to be taken by the European Council) for all unanimity decisions in the TFEU and in Title V TEU, except for those which concern military or defence matters. Hence, following *Kuiper*'s reasoning, the Council would have to try to use *passerelle*-clauses in virtually *all* legislative projects before resorting to enhanced cooperation. This would, among other things, regularly lead to a six month pause for national parliamentary assessment, significantly slowing down the processes. Moreover, in some Member States, the approval of a *passarelle* by its Council or European Council representative can be subject to special majorities in their respective parliaments, decisions in several parliamentary chambers, or even a referendum (possible in Denmark).[59] As such procedures can take very long, *Kuiper*'s interpretation, if taken seriously, would realistically halt enhanced cooperation projects for years in a vast number of fields. Finally, since the Council is best placed to determine whether an agreement between all Member States can be reached, it seems fair to say the Council can, in this process, also rule out the possibility that Member States could agree to QMV, without putting this to a

[58] Kuipers, J.-J. (2012), 'The Law Applicable to Divorce as Test Ground for Enhanced Cooperation', *ELJ*, Vol. 18, pp. 201–229, p. 216; on this clause: Zeitzmann, S. (2015), 'Zuviel gewollt, zu wenig geregelt? Das komplizierte Verhältnis der Verstärkten Zusammenarbeit zum aquis communautaire' in: Stratenschulte, E. D. (ed.), *Der Anfang vom Ende?: Formen differenzierter Integration und ihre Konsequenzen,* Nomos, pp. 103–134.

[59] Böttner, R. (2017), 'Brückenklauseln im europäischen Verfassungsrecht', *EuR*, Vol. 52, No. 3, pp. 381–400; see also with a similar conclusion on *passarelle* clauses and the last resort criterion, Böttner, R. (2021), *The Constitutional Framework for Enhanced Cooperation in EU law*, Nijhoff studies in European Union law, Leiden The Netherlands, Koninklijke Brill NV. Böttner rightly stresses that the respective national processes are not a matter of concern for EU law; however, in practice it cannot be denied that they would significantly slow down the process.

formal vote. The interpretation that an enhanced cooperation is only a last resort after having resorted to possible *passerelle*-clauses can therefore be disregarded.[60]

Another seemingly very broad interpretation (which, like *Kuiper*'s proposal, dates back to the time before the Unitary Patent judgment) is offered by *Brackhane*, who states that through the last resort criterion, cases in which a Member State is kept from participating in a legislative project for *objective reasons*, not lying within its power, are excluded from enhanced cooperation. Thus, only cases in which a state subjectively does not want to participate fall into the scope of enhanced cooperation. Such an objective obstacle, according to *Brackhane*, could be the economic weakness of a Member State.[61] *Becker* understands this as meaning that the Member States must first try to overcome all disagreements caused by economic doubts by offering financial aid, resulting in "immeasurable duties to provide assistance".[62] Such an interpretation would indeed be problematic. However, first of all, the idea of a duty for the participating Member States to provide assistance to promote the participation in an enhanced cooperation was discussed already in the drafting process of the Treaty of Amsterdam, brought forward by the European Parliament.[63] While this idea seems to have intended assistance to join *after* the start of an enhanced cooperation, the arguments can be transferred also to assistance *before* joining, since one case would necessarily lead to the other. Hence, (financial) assistance to promote participation was considered but actively disregarded and is therefore not part of the duties imposed by the last resort criterion.[64] Beyond that, *Becker* seems to overstate the idea of an "objective" hindrance. In fact, when is a state *objectively* hindered from participating in a measure? When it would cost more money than the state has at its disposal? Or more than a certain percentage of its budget? Whether or not a state can afford something is a political question. Although *Becker*'s criticism seems to miss the core of the idea, the disagreement shows that the criterion "objective

[60] Agreeing: Heber, C. (2021), *Enhanced Cooperation and European Tax Law*, Oxford University Press.

[61] Brackhane, B. (2008), *Differenzierte Integration im Recht der Europäischen Union*, Ius Europaeum, Baden-Baden, Nomos, p. 179; on similar proposals of including financial aids in enhanced cooperation: Linke, G. (2006), *Das Instrument der verstärkten Zusammenarbeit im Vertrag von Nizza: Möglichkeiten eines Europas der differenzierten Integration*, Interdisziplinäre Europa Studien, Frankfurt am Main, Lang, p. 166 ff.

[62] Becker, U. (2015), 'Art. 20 EUV, Art. 326–334 AEUV' in: Groeben, H. v. d., Schwarze, J., Hatje, A. (eds.), *Europäisches Unionsrecht*, Baden-Baden, Nomos, Art. 20 EUV, para 51.

[63] EP, OJ 1997 C 115/167, para 20.

[64] See Ehlermann, C.-D. (1997), 'Engere Zusammenarbeit nach dem Amsterdamer Vertrag: ein neues Verfassungsprinzip?', *EuR*, pp. 362–397, p. 379;, Art. 327 AEUV para 2.

hindrance" hardly works legally in a politically determined question. Therefore, it is necessary to find landmarks within the political process, rather than seemingly scientific ('objective') criteria.

According to *Becker*, a failed legislative procedure is an "indispensable formal requirement" despite the evolution of the Treaty provisions (see above), since the TEU refers to an agreement of all Member States as a preferential scenario, and this always implies passing legal norms.[65] Although it may be true that uniform legislation attempts generally comprise such a procedure, it is the stated intention of the Treaty legislator,[66] manifested in a clear Treaty evolution, that specific procedural steps should not be formally required to fulfil the last resort criterion. This seems like an indication too strong for Art. 20 TEU to still require a failed legislative procedure, especially in light of the above-mentioned 'indirect right of initiative', which allows Member States to thoroughly discuss a matter before Commission proposal has been tabled.[67]

Moreover, formally requiring a failed legislative proposal would lead to additional confusion: The course of action for legislation through an enhanced cooperation is to first of all issue a Council decision allowing the enhanced cooperation *per se* in a specific field (i.e. creating a unitary patent, a financial transaction tax, etc.). Then, in a second decision, secondary law, which introduces the new substantial rules for that field, is passed. This approach is embedded in the Treaties[68] and was repeatedly reviewed without any objection by the CJEU.[69] If the Member States, before resorting to enhanced cooperation, were to conclude a legislative procedure, the question would arise to what extent the new secondary legal acts are still bound to the old, refused proposal. If a failed proposal was

---

[65] Ibid.; Similarly Martenczuk, B. (2013), 'Enhanced Cooperation: The Practice of Ad Hoc Differentiation in the EU since the Lisbon Treaty', *StudDipl*, pp. 83–100, p. 88.

[66] CONV 23/03, p. 18.

[67] See also Peers, S. (2010), 'Divorce, European Style: The First Authorization of Enhanced Cooperation', *Eur. Const. L. Rev*, pp. 339–358; Thym, D. (2018), 'Supranational Differentiation and Enhanced Cooperation' in: Schütze, R., Tridimas, T. (eds.), *Oxford principles of European Union law,* Oxford, Oxford University Press, pp. 849–883 Disagreeing, and demanding a Commission proposal in any case: Böttner, R. (2023), 'The Instrument of Enhanced Cooperation: Pitfalls and Possibilities for Differentiated Integration'.

[68] Art. 329 TFEU: "Authorisation to *proceed* with the enhanced cooperation"; also, the authorising decision is taken by QMV, even in fields where unanimity is required (Art. 329 (1) TFEU); hence, there must be two distinct decisions.

[69] ECJ, C–146/13 (*Spain v Parliament/Council*), ECLI:EU:C:2015:298; C-147/13 (*Spain v Council*), ECLI:EU:C:2015:299; Pistoia, E. (2016), 'Outsourcing EU Law While Differentiating European Integration: The Unitary Patent's Identity in the Two "Spanish Rulings" of 5 May 2015.', *European Law Review*, No. 4, pp. 711–726.

an absolute necessity, the new acts would have to be predetermined by the old proposal, since otherwise the failed procedure could be on one subject and the enhanced cooperation on another. Thus, the participating Member States would (to some extent) be bound to a proposal that was potentially influenced by positions of non-participating Member States—a situation that contradicts the very idea of enhanced cooperation.

Finally, although enhanced cooperation is most likely in fields where unanimity is required and accordingly with limited Parliament involvement, it could as well occur in fields with obligatory Parliament involvement or even ordinary legislative procedure.[70] Since the Council is allowed and encouraged to work on proposals before the Parliament adopts its position,[71] there is no reason why it should be obliged to first officially let a procedure fail, significantly slowing down the process due to potential delays when waiting for the Parliament's position, if it is sufficiently clear that the necessary majority for a uniform solution will not be reached.

Hence, it becomes clear that a complete, formal legislative procedure cannot be considered obligatory under the Treaties.[72] At the same time, in order to rule out the possibility of a solution by the Union as a whole, *some procedure* in the Council needs to precede enhanced cooperation authorisation.

This view is generally shared. *Cannone,* for example, considers a "general discussion on the subject" in the Council to be sufficient,[73] which hardly provides working guidelines, and seems like a very low definition of the hurdle. The *European Parliament*, on the other side of the spectrum, in its 2019 Report on the implementation of the Treaty provisions on enhanced cooperation provided a more defined interpretation of when it can be regarded as "established" in the sense of Art. 20 (2) TEU that a uniform solution cannot be found: if during two consecutive Council presidencies, no substantive progress has been made in the Council.[74] This approach can be criticized from two angles. On the one hand,

[70] See Sect. 2.2.1.

[71] ECJ C-412/93 (*Parliament v Council)*, ECLI:EU:C:1995:127, para 10–11.

[72] Agreeing in this sense: Böttner, R. (2023), 'The Instrument of Enhanced Cooperation: Pitfalls and Possibilities for Differentiated Integration'.

[73] Cannone, A. (2005), *Le cooperazioni rafforzate*: *Contributo allo studio dell'integrazione differenziata*, Pubblicazioni della Facoltà giuridica dell'Università di Bari, Bari, Cacucci, p. 74.

[74] European Parliament resolution of 12 February 2019 on the implementation of the Treaty provisions concerning enhanced cooperation (2018/2112(INI)), p. 5; see also Heber, C. (2021), *Enhanced Cooperation and European Tax Law*, Oxford University Press.

it can be argued that the new formula merely shifts the problem of the undefined 'last resort' concept to that of 'substantive progress'. This term is just as undefined and could mean anything from a rough agreement on a single article of a proposal to negotiation mandates that all Member States agree on. The formula therefore does not offer the clarification it suggests at first sight. Even then, the number of two consecutive Council presidencies is completely arbitrary. Two Council presidencies can be made up of one very determined presidency pushing for a project to be adopted and another one that has no interest in it—in this case, the second presidency is useless in the formula. Council presidencies are divided into groups of three, known as trios, which work together and which, wherever possible, synchronize their programmes and efforts.[75] Why would a threshold of a defined number of Council presidencies not cover the whole duration of a presidency trio? Finally, the list of legislative projects which took longer than a year of Council deliberations, but where eventually passed by the Union as a whole is excruciatingly long. At the same time, there are projects that must be decided in a much shorter period than a year. Thus, it can be concluded that the EP's formula, though well-meaningly trying to simplify the last resort criterion, is not fit for purpose and not covered by the Treaties.

A more convincing interpretation of the last resort criterion is offered by *Martenczuk*. He argues in this context that it seems difficult to claim that all possibilities for compromise have been exhausted without a substantive discussion in *all instances* of the Council, including the political level.[76] As laid out above, it must be possible to resort to enhanced cooperation without unsuccessfully concluding an entire legislative procedure, taking into account the will of the Treaty legislators and the CJEU interpretation. Yet, even then, to respect the Court's requirement that not all fruitless negotiations can lead to enhanced cooperation and to ensure the necessary level of security that a compromise cannot be reached, the last resort criterion should be interpreted as requiring discussions in the various instances of the Council, including *at least one discussion on the ministerial level*, provided that this brings about sufficient clarity on the Member States' positions.[77] Given the working methods of the Council, the discussions

[75] Art. 1 (2) Council Decision 2009/908/EU laying down measures for the implementation of the European Council Decision on the exercise of the Presidency of the Council, and on the chairmanship of preparatory bodies of the Council.

[76] Martenczuk, B. (2013), 'Enhanced Cooperation: The Practice of Ad Hoc Differentiation in the EU since the Lisbon Treaty', *StudDipl*, pp. 83–100, p. 89; however, Martenczuk considers a Commission proposal to be obligatory.

[77] Martenczuk, B. (2013), 'Enhanced Cooperation: The Practice of Ad Hoc Differentiation in the EU since the Lisbon Treaty', *StudDipl*, pp. 83–100, p. 89.

and decisions of which are thoroughly prepared by working parties, bodies and committees,[78] this appears to be a convincing, stringent middle way to ensure that the Council can soundly establish the impossibility of a uniform solution without being bound to excessive procedural requisites not foreseen in nor intended by the Treaties.[79] What should be added to this observation, however, is the level of the European Council. As Art. 15.1 TEU stresses, the European Council, while being an EU institution, does not exercise any legislative functions, but "define[s] the general political directions and priorities" of the Union. It could therefore be seen as unfit to determine the chances of a legislative project. Yet, as was repeatedly pointed out above, the history of the Treaties shows very clearly that the last criterion is not supposed to be tied exclusively to a failed legislative procedure. The Treaties do, on the contrary, confer upon the European Council the task of determining red lines and overall chances of finding agreements among Member States. This is the case in particular in the 'emergency brake' and'break and accelerator' procedures in Art. 82 (3), 83 (3), 86 (1), 87 (3) TFEU. Indeed, who would be better suited to establish whether its country's position contains room for compromise than its Head of State or Government, as represented in the European Council? This is further underlined by the fact that the mentioned clauses can, if the European Council fails to find a compromise, lead to facilitated enhanced cooperation procedures,[80] which, among other facilitations, replace the last resort criterion. Of course, the *ratio legis* of the criterion, ensuring an overall cohesiveness in the integration process remains just as important also in the policy fields that entail facilitated enhanced cooperation clauses. This fact demonstrates that implicitly, the Heads of State and Government are already tasked with ensuring that "the objectives of such cooperation cannot be attained within a reasonable period by the Union as a whole" as demanded by Art. 20 TEU in certain cases. If the European Council cannot agree at least to include a project in the general political directions and priorities of the Union that it are responsible for, any subsequent legislative procedure would be doomed from the outset. Thus, *Martenczuk*'s convincing formula can be completed by saying that to establish that an enhanced cooperation is, in fact, a last resort, it must be concluded that a substantive discussion was conducted in all instances of the Council, including

---

[78] Zbíral, R., Pivoda, M. (2021), 'Art. 240 TFEU' in: Blanke, H.-J., Mangiameli, S. (eds.), *Treaty on the Functioning of the European Union—A Commentary* [forthcoming].

[79] See also Böttner, R. (2021), *The Constitutional Framework for Enhanced Cooperation in EU law*, Nijhoff studies in European Union law, Leiden The Netherlands, Koninklijke Brill NV, also stressing the importance of the Council's preparatory bodies when concluding that unanimity cannot be reached.

[80] See in particular Sects. 5.2.3.2, 5.2.3.3.

the political level, *or* the European Council deliberated and concluded that an agreement cannot possibly be reached.

#### 3.2.2.3 A 'Fast Track' Enhanced Cooperation?

The prior conclusions allow to take a look into situations that could have, but never actually have led to the application of the enhanced cooperation mechanism: Situations with an urgent need for EU action but a lack of unity among Member States. It is no coincidence that the enhanced cooperation mechanism has recently made headlines in a number of situations, all of which were labelled as crises or characterised by urgency and/or particular necessity to act. Proposals for using enhanced cooperation could be witnessed in the financial crisis,[81] the migration crisis,[82] or the Covid-19 pandemic.[83] Accordingly, the European Parliament in its 2019 Report on the implementation of the Treaty provisions concerning enhanced cooperation describes the need for "fast-track authorisation of enhanced cooperation in fields of high political salience".[84]

The scenario of a fast-track enhanced cooperation may best be described in an example, namely that of the Eurozone/financial crisis:

---

[81] Several authors proposed to introduce measures such as the ESM or the Fiscal Compact as enhanced cooperations, see e.g. Selmayr, M. (2013), 'Die "Euro- Rettung" und das Unionsprimärrecht: Von putativen, unnötigen und bisher versäumten Vertragsänderungen zur Stabilisierung der Wirtschafts- und Währungsunion' 2013, 68(2), Zeitschrift für Öffentliches Recht, 259', *ZÖR*, Vol. 68, No. 2, pp. 259–318; Schwarz, M. (2014), 'A Memorandum of Misunderstanding—The doomed road of the European Stability Mechanism and a possible way out: Enhanced cooperation', *CMLRev*, Vol. 51, pp. 389–423.

[82] Kreilinger, V., Jacques Delors Institut Berlin (2015), *Proposal to use Enhanced Cooperation in the Refugee Crisis*, available at: www.delorsinstitut.de/en/publications/topics/institutions-and-democracy/proposal-to-use-enhanced-cooperation-in-the-refugee-crisis/; Blanke, H.-J., Johr, M. (2019), 'Rechtliche Vorkehrungen für die zivile Seenotrettung im Mittelmeer: „Sichere Häfen" und „verlässliche Ausschiffungsregelungen" in der EU zur Überwindung völkerrechtlicher Ungewissheit', *DÖV*, No. 23, pp. 929–939; Jungfleisch, J. (2019), 'Verstärkte Zusammenarbeit im Rahmen der Flüchtlingspolitik: Ein Ausweg aus der Krise oder die endgültige Aufgabe eines einheitlichen Europas?' in: Kopetzki, M., Lanser, C., Leitner, P. (eds.), *Autoritäres vs liberales Europa: Tagung Junger Europarechtler*innen, Band 2, Wien 2019,* Wien, Jan Sramek Verlag.

[83] EU Commission proposal to establish the recovery fund 'Next Generation EU' by way of enhanced cooperation to overcome vetoes by Poland and Hungary connected to rule of law-related issues: see Graf von Luckner, J. (2020), *A Novel "Reinforced Cooperation" in the EU*, available at: verfassungsblog.de/a-novel-reinforced-cooperation-in-the-eu/.

[84] European Parliament resolution of 12 February 2019 on the implementation of the.

Treaty provisions concerning enhanced cooperation (2018/2112(INI), Recommendation No. 35.

As the interest rates for Eurozone governments bonds were reaching unprecedented and unsustainable highs between 2010 and 2012, it was considered to be decisive for politics to react on market turbulences swiftly. However, not all Member States were affected equally: The states that were not part of the Eurozone were much less exposed to the risks emanating from unsustainable sovereign debt levels in some Eurozone countries. In this situation, when the discussions in the European Council turned to what would later become the 'Fiscal Compact', it quickly became clear that the necessary unanimity among the Member States could not be reached due to resistance mainly from the UK and Czechia.[85] In situations such as this, enhanced cooperation could provide a way out of the logjam. The interested states could have concluded that the necessary majority could not be found, authorised an enhanced cooperation and passed the necessary legislation among the participants. However, the Member States decided to resort to international law instead and concluded a treaty among themselves, namely the Treaty on Stability, Coordination and Governance in the Economic and Monetary Union (informally named the 'Fiscal Compact'). Ironically, enhanced cooperation was considered as a possibility to reincorporate the Treaty into EU law at a later point of time,[86] but seemingly not to conclude it in the first place—possibly because of doubts on the last resort criterion. However, if interpreted as stated above, enhanced cooperation would have indeed been a way out of the blockage, despite its *ultima ratio* character: The decisive question is, once again, what is necessary for the political process to "establish[...] that the objectives of such cooperation cannot be attained within a reasonable period by the Union as a whole". In the case of the Fiscal Compact, discussions took place directly in the European Council.[87] It was there that UK Prime Minister Cameron "deployed the ultimate weapon", as UK media reported at the time, and vetoed the discussed instrument.[88] As discussed above, a failure to find a compromise on the highest

[85] https://www.theguardian.com/world/2011/dec/09/david-cameron-blocks-eu-treaty (last access 22 December 2021).

[86] Graf von Luckner, J. (2018), 'How to Bring It Home—The EU's Options for Incorporating the Fiscal Compact into EU Law', *European Law Blog*.

[87] Treaty on Stability, Coordination and Governance in the Economic and Monetary Union (TSCG), recital 6. Note that during these discussions, the subject of the discussions was a Treaty change. However, the fact that the Commission proposal to incorporate the substance of the Fiscal Compact into EU law (on this Art. 16 TSCG; Graf von Luckner, J. (2018), 'How to Bring It Home—The EU's Options for Incorporating the Fiscal Compact into EU Law', *European Law Blog*) is based on secondary law (COM(2017) 824 final) shows that there were feasible alternatives to action on a primary law level.

[88] https://www.theguardian.com/world/2011/dec/09/david-cameron-blocks-eu-treaty (last access 22 December 2021).

political level is a very strong indicator that indeed, a uniform solution cannot be found. In addition, given that the term "a reasonable period" (Art. 20.2 TEU) is not further defined, it should be seen in light of the situation at hand. When the European Council discussed the Fiscal Compact, it was a matter of extreme urgency given the situation on the financial markets. Thus, a period that was 'reasonable' to find a solution simply was a lot shorter than it would be for everyday legislative business. Under these circumstances, it seems reasonable to conclude that the Fiscal Compact could have indeed been passed as a 'last resort' within an enhanced cooperation.

Yet, not every urgent or semi-urgent project ends up right at the level of the European Council straight away. In such a scenario, it was described above that an unsuccessful discussion in all Council instances including the political level is required to establish that an enhanced cooperation would be a last resort. Does this block altogether the option of a 'fast track' enhanced cooperation with swift results established in the Council? This question is particularly relevant if Member States simply agree to disagree from the start, or a Member State makes clear right away that it would agree to a measure only "over my dead body"[89]—how long does it take for this position to be turned into an enhanced cooperation if desired by the interested states? This last question centres around the issue of how fast a policy project can move through the legislative process, particularly through the Council instances, if need be. For this matter, it is instructive to look into one of the measures taken in response to the Covid-19 pandemic in 2021, namely the 'EU Digital COVID Certificate', which entered into force as a regulation.[90] While the overall legislative procedure was completed in just three months, the Portuguese Council presidency took pride in noting that it had completed preparatory work on the file in "record time" of less than a month.[91] This exemplifies that, political willingness permitting, political and legislatives processes *can* be quick if need be. As such processes are the precondition of a thorough determination of whether an agreement can be reached at all, this includes implicitly the possibility of a quick resource to enhanced cooperation in particular situations.

---

[89] Peers, S. (2010), 'Divorce, European Style: The First Authorization of Enhanced Cooperation', *Eur. Const. L. Rev*, pp. 339–358.

[90] Regulation (EU) 2021/953 of 14 June 2021 on a framework for the issuance, verification and acceptance of interoperable COVID-19 vaccination, test and recovery certificates (EU Digital COVID Certificate) to facilitate free movement during the COVID-19 pandemic.

[91] https://www.politico.eu/newsletter/brussels-playbook/politico-brussels-playbook-afghanistan-controversy-more-eu-blunders-pfizer-to-the-rescue/ (last access 30 December 2021).

At the same time, this finding counters the idea that action outside of the EU law framework is necessarily the quicker alternative in time-sensitive situations.[92]

Thus, a 'fast track enhanced cooperation' is anything but impossible.[93] In a situation in which it becomes clear at an early stage that the necessary majority for uniform EU action cannot be found, and the willing Member States are nonetheless interested in a swift procedure leading to an EU law solution, the Council could, for example, combine a request to the Commission under Art. 241 TFEU (indirect right of initiative) and a request to start an enhanced cooperation according to Art. 329 (1) TFEU after thorough and detailed discussions up to the ministerial level in an attempt to 'fast-track' the enhanced cooperation procedure. If a Commission proposal is already on the table, it could be discussed in all necessary Council instances in as little time as a month before concluding that unanimity (if applicable) cannot be reached. Especially in situations in which prompt action is deemed essential, this could constitute a way to keep Member States from acting outside the Treaty framework and allow them to use and profit from the EU Institutions in the course of their project and its implementation. In light of the duty to respect other Member States in the enhanced cooperation procedure (Art. 326–327 TFEU), and enforceability of this duty via the CJEU, this option should be in the interest of both participating and non-participating Member States. Thus, in conclusion, a 'fast track' enhanced cooperation is legally possibly could indeed occur *very* fast for the standards of EU legislation; however, this prospect is, in any case, reserved for very particular situations characterised by urgency to act and a *disagreement to disagree* with clear political front lines and determined positions. In the realms of regular EU law making, finding compromises, which takes more time than the bare minimum-periods depicted above, by all means stays the preferable approach from the perspective of EU law and the finding above should not be read as undermining this principle.

[92] As argued e.g. by Della Cananea, G. (2019), 'Differentiated Integration in Europe After Brexit: An Institutional Analysis' in: Pernice, I., Guerra Martins, A. M. (eds.), *Brexit and the Future of EU Politics: A Constitutional Law Perspective,* Baden-Baden, Nomos Verlagsgesellschaft mbH & Co. KG, pp. 45–89; putting in question the speed of future satellite treaty making: Graf von Luckner, J. (2021), 'Stay home, stay healthy: Das „Ergänzungs- oder besondere Näheverhältnis zum Unionsrecht" in der BVerfG-Rechtsprechung und die europäische Integration durch Völkerrecht', *Europarecht*, No. 2, pp. 209–224.

[93] Doubtful in this regard: Heber, C. (2021), *Enhanced Cooperation and European Tax Law*, Oxford University Press.

## 3.3 Conclusions on the Principle of Last Resort

The last resort criterion makes it abundantly clear that "enhanced cooperation is not a normal mode of functioning of the EU".[94] It is crucial that Member States explore the possibilities to find a uniform solution as thoroughly as possible. However, requiring a previous, failed legislative procedure does not automatically guarantee such thorough exploration. In cases of urgency, such an approach can excessively slow down the process and lead to Member States legislating outside the Treaty framework.

While working jointly on a concrete commission proposal should continue to be the rule, in certain situations, Member States might have to, and can legally, choose a faster procedure if the Member States' positions (particularly of those not wanting to participate in a project) are sufficiently clear. Moreover, rather than awaiting a Commission proposal on a given topic to debate it, Member States can discuss it in the framework of the Council's 'indirect right of initiative'. If it becomes clear in such a setting that a given Member State would only approve a measure "over my dead body",[95] while others deem the measure indispensable, they can move on to enhanced cooperation already at this stage. In the light of these findings, it becomes clear that enhanced cooperation could indeed be used in times of urgency and crisis.

As shown above, such an approach will be complemented by the CJEU staying on alert and being ready to step in should a misuse of this possibility occur.

However, in what is probably the most difficult situation, namely a scenario in which Member States agree on a measure but not on its implementation, even more legal insights cannot take the burden of having to decide against certain fellow Member States off the shoulders of Council members. The Court of Justice pointed out that this is legally possible. Nevertheless, it remains in any case a politically highly problematic decision and needs thorough prior discussions—if not for legal reasons, then for the sake of preserving cohesion between the Member States of the EU.

Concluding, enhanced cooperation can, despite having to be used as a last resort only, be applied in a wider area of scenarios than it may seem at first glance. It is likely that it will continue to be used as a "veto-buster"[96] when, in

---

[94] Martenczuk, B. (2013), 'Enhanced Cooperation: The Practice of Ad Hoc Differentiation in the EU since the Lisbon Treaty', *StudDipl*, pp. 83–100, p. 87.

[95] Peers, S. (2010), 'Divorce, European Style: The First Authorization of Enhanced Cooperation', *Eur. Const. L. Rev*, pp. 339–358.

[96] Thym, D. (2005), 'United in Diversity: The Integration of Enhanced Cooperation into the European Constitutional Order', *GLJ*, pp. 1731–1747.

an advanced legislative process, Member States cannot agree on the details of a measure (like in the unitary patent case) or in cases where Member States 'agree to disagree', like in the family law related examples of the past. Moreover, as shown above, the mechanism could be applied in cases where there is particular urgency, as seen when the Member States had to react on the sovereign debt crisis. In all of these cases, the last resort criterion would not necessarily keep the Member States from resorting to enhanced cooperation.

One thing remains clear: The last resort criterion may be easier to work with than some think, but it still serves its main purpose to protect the EU from a too easy and too regular use of differentiation, leaving single Member States excluded from the integration process. Within the framework of differentiation in EU law, it is a safeguard for overall cohesiveness in the integration process. An abolishment of the criterion, as it has been demanded both in the past[97] and in more recent times,[98] would have the advantage of doing away with a hurdle that still is perceived as a knockout criterion for a more frequent use of enhanced cooperation. However, the analysis above has shown the last resort criterion is not per se a reason to shy away from the differentiation mechanism. What would be more efficient than an abolishment of the last resort criterion, which would require a Treaty change, is an informed discussion on enhanced cooperation as an alternative path in EU law making and on the limits that the last criterion really puts on it.

---

[97] CONFER 4783/00, p. 5.

[98] Blanke, H.-J., Pilz, S. (2020), 'Europa 2019 bis 2024—Wohin trägt uns der Stier?: Sieben Thesen zu den Herausforderungen der Europäischen Union', *EuR*, pp. 270–300.

# Rethinking the Procedural Principle of Openness Towards Innovative use of Enhanced Cooperation—Conditionality

# 4

The principle of openness of enhanced cooperation[1] is a defining element of the differentiation mechanism. Its aim is to ensure the possibility for all Member States to join an ongoing enhanced cooperation at all times.

In the discussion of flexibility and differentiation in the EU, repeated reference is made to the idea, or danger, of creating a 'core Europe' (as described earlier in Sect. 1.3).[2] This notion describes an inner circle of Member States, which reaches a deeper level of integration without all Member States participating. However, as opposed to notions such as multi-speed Europe or Europe of variable geometries, such a 'core Europe' would be defined by a certain degree of exclusiveness: It would not be for the non-participating Member States to decide whether or not they want to be part of the inner circle.[3] The principle of openness is the antithesis to this notion. According to it (Art. 20 (1) TEU, Art. 328 TFEU), enhanced cooperations shall be open for all non-participating Member States to join at all times, making the willingness to join and participate in the enhanced cooperation the main prerequisite. While some (objective) conditions can be applied, it

[1] Not to be confused with openness in the sense of Art. 1 (2) TEU, see Alemanno, A., Stefan, O. (2014), 'Openness at the Court of Justice of the European Union: Toppling a taboo', *CMLRev*, pp. 97–140, p. 97 ff.

[2] See e.g. Thym, D. (2004), *Ungleichzeitigkeit und europäisches Verfassungsrecht*, Schriftenreihe europäisches Verfassungsrecht, Baden-Baden, Nomos, p. 32 ff.

[3] Thym, D. (2004), *Ungleichzeitigkeit und europäisches Verfassungsrecht*, Schriftenreihe europäisches Verfassungsrecht, Baden-Baden, Nomos, p. 54.

An earlier version of this chapter was part of my thesis to obtain the Master in Comparative, European and International Laws (LL.M.) at the European University Institute in Florence, Italy.



J. Graf von Luckner, *Enhanced Cooperation Revisited*,
https://doi.org/10.1007/978-3-658-51063-3_4

is not for the Member States but for the Commission to decide upon the application of an interested Member State; a measure aimed at ensuring the neutral, non-political nature of the decision.[4] All of this shows that through its inherent openness, enhanced cooperation is designed to prevent Member States from creating exclusive cores within the EU. *By design*, which does not mean that this is how it plays out in practice (see Sect. 1.3.2.2), it may rather be considered a mechanism allowing a European integration in which everyone at least could reach the same level of integration eventually.[5]

The principle of openness does not only confer a right on non-participating Member States. According to Art. 328 (1) TFEU, participating Member States and the Commission "shall ensure that they promote participation by as many Member States as possible", obliging the involved actors at least in a limited way to encourage participation. The possibility to withdraw from an enhanced cooperation, although being discussed in academia,[6] it is not legally a part of the principle of openness. The principle of openness is, in this sense, a one-way valve into enhanced cooperation, guaranteeing only that Member States which have not yet joined can do so.

The principle of openness is subject to a number of formal and substantive constraints, namely procedures and conditions. Both have been explained before. However, the literature is still lacking a profound analysis of these constraints, as well as the implications that such an analysis reveals at the political level. Therefore, the following analysis will go deep into the details of the principle of openness while keeping an eye open for the broader picture of enhanced cooperation, its role in political processes and what chances it has to offer to EU policy making, especially in in moments of difficulty. This will be done by analysing in depth, first, the procedure of Member States joining enhanced cooperation and, second, the limits and criteria that joining Member States can face and how these can be active design choices of an enhance cooperation.

[4] Thym, D. (2004), *Ungleichzeitigkeit und europäisches Verfassungsrecht*, Schriftenreihe europäisches Verfassungsrecht, Baden-Baden, Nomos, 55.

[5] Cantore, C. (2011), 'We're One, but We're Not the Same: Enhanced Cooperation and the Tension between Unity and Asymmetry in the EU', *Perspectives on Federalism*, No. 3, E-1–E-21, p. 8 f.; Linke, G. (2006), *Das Instrument der verstärkten Zusammenarbeit im Vertrag von Nizza: Möglichkeiten eines Europas der differenzierten Integration*, Interdisziplinäre Europa Studien, Frankfurt am Main, Lang, p. 109.

[6] See e.g. Editorial Comments (2011), 'Enhanced cooperation: A Union à taille réduite or à porte tournante?', *CMLRev*, pp. 317–327.

## 4.1 Procedure

The general procedure to join an enhanced cooperation is laid down in Art. 331 TFEU.

> *Any Member State which wishes to participate in enhanced cooperation in progress in one of the areas referred to in Article 329(1) shall notify its intention to the Council and the Commission. […]*

However, this concerns enhanced cooperations "in progress", i.e. the situation after the decision authorising an enhanced cooperation has been issued by the Council.[7] This notwithstanding, there are several occasions prior to this in which Member States can undertake to join an enhanced cooperation procedure. Given that enhanced cooperation is designed to favour and promote participation by as many Member States as possible, it would contradict the mechanism's main philosophy if the principle of openness did not apply to Member States which wanted to join before the authorisation decision.

While Member States can, therefore, join enhanced cooperation procedures at any time during their trajectory from an initial request to the time after the passing of implementing legal acts, the procedure differs according to the exact phase in which the interest in participation is made known. Moreover, joining at different stages has different political implications for the joining Member States as they have more or less influence on the final legal nature of the enhanced cooperation, which comes with more or less certainty about what states commit to.

Existing literature mainly differentiates between the time before and after the enhanced cooperation is "in progress" (Art. 331 TFEU), that is after the authorising decision has been issued.[8] To get a full picture, I will analyse all different stages (distinguishing five phases), name them, and point out their legal and political implications. This analysis draws, on the one hand, on a closer look on the

---

[7] Martenczuk, B. (2013), 'Enhanced Cooperation: The Practice of Ad Hoc Differentiation in the EU since the Lisbon Treaty', *StudDipl*, pp. 83–100, p. 97.

[8] E.g. Martenczuk, B. (2013), 'Enhanced Cooperation: The Practice of Ad Hoc Differentiation in the EU since the Lisbon Treaty', *StudDipl*, pp. 83–100; Gerards, C., Wessels, W. (2019), Enhancing 'Enhanced Cooperation': constraints and opportunities of an inflexible flexibility clause, CEPOB, Bruges; Böttner, R. (2021), *The Constitutional Framework for Enhanced Cooperation in EU law*, Nijhoff studies in European Union law, Leiden The Netherlands, Koninklijke Brill NV speaks of "authorisation phase" and "implementing phase", somewhat similar to some of the terminology proposed here. However, the terms are not used in the same way.

factually different phases. On the other hand, the cases in which Member States joined enhanced cooperation projects in practice will be studied. Information on this can be obtained from the political situations in which Member States joined, the decisions confirming the participation, as well as application letters obtained through access to documents requests[9] from EU institutions. As a final overview at the end of this chapter, Table 4.2 illustrates all instances in which Member States joined enhanced cooperations.

Five different phases in which States can join an enhanced cooperation can be distinguished: the phase leading up to the initial request by the Member States ("Request Phase"); from the Member States' initial request to the issuing of a proposal for the authorising decision by the Commission ("Preparation Phase"); from the proposal for the authorising decision to its adoption by the Council ("Authorisation Phase");[10] from the authorising decision to the passing of implementing secondary law ("Legislative Phase"); after implementing secondary law has been passed ("Implementation Phase").

**Table 4.1** Different phases for joining an enhanced cooperation

| Phase 1 | Phase 2 | Phase 3 | Phase 4 | Phase 5 |
|---|---|---|---|---|
| Request | Preparation | Authorisation | Legislation | Implementation |
| Period until the initial request for an enhanced cooperation by at least nine Member States. | Phase between the initial request and the moment a proposal for the authorisation decision is decided by the Commission and presented to the Council. | Phase between the presentation of the draft authorisation decision and its adoption by the Council in enhanced cooperation setting. | Stage during which the implementing legislation is drafted and/or eventually passed in the Council. | Phase after the implementing law has been passed and is implemented and put to use in the Member States. |

[9] That is, under Regulation (EC) No 1049/2001 regarding public access to European Parliament, Council and Commission documents.

[10] Note that though using the same term, Böttner, R. (2021), *The Constitutional Framework for Enhanced Cooperation in EU law*, Nijhoff studies in European Union law, Leiden The Netherlands, Koninklijke Brill NV describes the entire period of phases 1–3 when calling it "authorisation phase".

### 4.1.1 Phase 1: Request

The request phase is the period leading up to the request for an enhanced cooperation, during which a minimum of nine Member States informally agree to launch the request jointly. Since joining an enhanced cooperation at this stage merely requires a letter to the Commission in which a state voices its interest to participate,[11] this phase is inherently open. Although a group of at least nine Member States is required, the established practice is that each Member State addresses an individual letter to the Commission, often (but not always) with identical content in different languages.[12] Access at this stage is therefore unrestricted. The only requirement for participation is that the request is similar enough to those of the other Member States that it can be considered a request for one and the same project. Whether this is the case is necessarily for the Commission as the addressee of the letters to decide.

### 4.1.2 Phase 2: Preparation Phase—From the Initial Request to the Proposal for an Authorising Decision

For the procedure to start formally, the Commission needs to present a proposal for a decision authorising enhanced cooperation to the Council (Art. 329.1 TFEU). This is exclusively at the Commissions' discretion. It can decide to publish a proposal right away, delay it, or not to publish the proposal at all, bringing the enhanced cooperation procedure to an early end. In this latter case, it has to give reasons for its decision to the requesting Member States (Art. 329.1 TFEU). So far, all requests were granted eventually, although the Commission significantly slowed down the process of adaptation of the first enhanced cooperation (divorce and legal separation).[13]

Before the Commission first publishes a proposal, Member States which want to join the ongoing procedure still only need to notify the Commission of their intention to participate. In this case, the Commission treats the new member the same as the initial Member States who originally requested enhanced cooperation.

---

[11] For examples, see Notification letters EPPO, Council, Doc. No. 8027/17.

[12] Ibid; see also Letters of Austria, Greece, Hungary, Italy, Luxembourg, Romania, Slovenia, Spain, and Bulgaria requesting enhanced cooperation on divorce and legal separation.

[13] See Kuipers, J.-J. (2012), 'The Law Applicable to Divorce as Test Ground for Enhanced Cooperation', *ELJ*, Vol. 18, pp. 201–229, p. 210.

This procedure was used in all enhanced cooperations except the one on a financial transaction tax (for details, see Table 4.2). As joining states are treated the same as the original states, they still have a maximum amount of influence on the procedure (except for a certain level of path-dependency that may be triggered by the first letters initiating the procedure). Through their letters, they could try to make an influence on the content of the Commission's authorising decision, which predetermines the eventual enhanced cooperation and can be changed by the Council only by a unanimous decision (Art. 293.1 TFEU, see below). An example of such influence could be an attempt to convince the Commission to include conditions for participation at a later stage (Art. 328.1 TFEU). However, analysing the letters which could be obtained and which concern two of the five occasions (including the special case of the European Public Prosecutor's Office), no attempt to use this influence could be found. This could change, however, in more controversial cases in future.

As the example of the enhanced cooperation on divorce and legal separation showed,[14] the Request Phase can drag on for a long period of time (July 2008—March 2010), or be a matter of days as in the case of the unitary patent (07 December 2010—14 December 2010) (on both see Table 4.2).

### 4.1.3 Authorisation—From the Proposal to the Adoption of the Authorising Decision

After the Commission first publishes its proposal for an authorising decision, the procedure changes slightly. The participating Member States are a crucial part of the authorisation decision. Therefore, to include further Member States, the proposed authorisation decision must be amended. Since the authorising decision is based on a Commission initiative, any change to the content of the proposed decision needs to be introduced through a formal amendment either by the Commission or the Council (Art. 293 TFEU).[15]

However, according to Art. 293.1 TFEU, where the Council acts on a proposal from the Commission (like in the case of the authorisation decision), the Council may change the proposal only by acting unanimously. As the authorising decision is taken by the Council as a whole (with qualified majority), this

---

[14] Cf. Peers, S. (2010), 'Divorce, European Style: The First Authorization of Enhanced Cooperation', *Eur. Const. L. Rev*, pp. 339–358, p. 346 f.

[15] See Editorial Comments (2011), 'Enhanced cooperation: A Union à taille réduite or à porte tournante?', *CMLRev*, pp. 317–327, p. 321 f.; Böttner, R. (2016), 'Ein scharfes Schwert der Kommission? Überlegungen zu Artikel 293 AEUV', *EuR*, Vol. 51, No. 1, pp. 105–122.

unanimity requirement means unanimity among all Council members, not unanimity among the enhanced cooperation states. However, enhanced cooperation is regularly used where there is no unanimity, which makes unanimously changing a Commission proposal an unlikely scenario. Furthermore, Art. 328.1 (1) TFEU obliges only the "Member States participating in enhanced cooperation" to ensure that they promote participation by as many Member States as possible—the non-participants are not obliged to facilitate the participation of another Member State in an enhanced cooperation they are not part of. As the facilitated way of finding majorities that enhanced cooperation promises cannot yet be utilized at this point, since the enhanced cooperation is not yet authorised, the procedure Art. 293.1 TFEU primarily leaves the willing Member States in the hands of the unwilling. In the ordinary legislative procedure, this is compensated by the opportunity to change the proposal later on, in interaction with the Parliament. However, the adoption procedure of an authorisation decision is not an ordinary legislative proceeding (see Art. 329.1 TFEU), which is why this option is not available either. Therefore, the remaining and significantly easier option is to change the proposal by a Commission decision according to Art. 293.2 TFEU. The Commission can change the proposal at any time before the Council acted on the basis of the proposal.[16]

Interested Member States can address a request to change the proposed authorisation decision to the Commission.

Although accession at this stage is not specifically foreseen in Art. 331 TFEU, states must have the same right to access (where applicable, subject to the same limitations) due to the general principle of openness introduced by Art. 20 TEU and Art. 328 TFEU.

This approach was followed by Member States in the enhanced cooperation on divorce and legal separation, as well as on international couples' property regimes. A particularly interesting case regarding the political motivation to join in a specific phase is the case of Malta joining the enhanced cooperation on divorce and legal separation. Malta joined the procedure after a proposal for the authorisation decision had been published (March 2010) but before it was passed by the Council (July 2010). Malta's legal system, at that point in time, did not in any event foresee the possibility to get a divorce. Because it feared that the legislative project could circumvent this prohibition, Malta opposed it in the Council

[16] See Böttner, R. (2016), 'Eine Idee lernt laufen—zur Praxis der Verstärkten Zusammenarbeit nach Lissabon', *ZEuS*, Vol. 19, No. 4, pp. 501–550; Böttner, R. (2016), 'Ein scharfes Schwert der Kommission? Überlegungen zu Artikel 293 AEUV', *EuR*, Vol. 51, No. 1, pp. 105–122; *Böttner* points out that the amendment can even be made orally.

and helped to block the procedure.[17] When the remaining Member States decided to continue using the enhanced cooperation procedure, it joined the project in an apparent attempt to at least have an influence on the content, and indeed, it did manage to negotiate an exception for itself in the final regulation.[18] Before March 2010, there had been no need for Malta to join the enhanced cooperation because it seemed unlikely that the Commission would propose an authorisation decision to the Council at all.[19] When the proposal was eventually published, the Maltese government (led by the same party and Prime Minister as during the initial negotiations) needed to act quickly to join and maintain a seat at the negotiating table: From the moment of the authorisation on, a different procedure (described below, Phases 4 and 5) would have applied, in which stricter conditions apply for participation. It is unlikely that, under these circumstances, the Commission would have or even legally could have approved Malta's participation given that they lacked the most essential prerequisite, i.e. allowing divorces at all. Malta had a period of four months between the publication of the proposed authorisation decision and its adoption (see Table 4.1) and used this short time frame strategically.

Another interesting insight stems from Germany's letter trying to join the same enhanced cooperation (divorce and legal separation). In this document, the German Minister of Justice claimed that her country played a "substantial" role in the initial Council deliberations for a solution applicable to all Member States. Since Germany had "great interest" in participating in the deliberations in the enhanced cooperation framework, she explicitly asked the Commission to change its proposal in a way that Germany is included among the initial Member States—i.e. to let it join while the Authorisation Phase is still ongoing.[20] From this phrasing, it can be seen that indeed Member States have a great interest in joining enhanced

[17] Kuipers, J.-J. (2012), 'The Law Applicable to Divorce as Test Ground for Enhanced Cooperation', *ELJ*, Vol. 18, pp. 201–229, p. 201.

[18] Art. 13 Council Regulation (EU) No 1259/2010.

[19] Kuipers, J.-J. (2012), 'The Law Applicable to Divorce as Test Ground for Enhanced Cooperation', *ELJ*, Vol. 18, pp. 201–229, p. 210.

[20] Letters of German Minister of Justice requesting to join the enhanced cooperation on divorce and legal separation, 15 April 2010; „Ich habe ein großes Interesse daran, auch an den jetzt im Rahmen der verstärkten Zusammenarbeit noch anstehenden Verhandlungen aktiv teilzunehmen. Ich bitte Sie daher, den vorliegenden Antrag noch in das gerade eingeleitete Verfahren einzubeziehen und Ihren Vorschlag für den Ermächtigungsbeschluss (COM (2010) 104), gegebenenfalls auch den Durchführungsbeschluss (COM (2010) 105), so zu ergänzen, dass auch Deutschland als Antrag stellender Mitgliedstaat erfasst wird."

cooperation while they still do not face any hurdles, as they would in the following phases. At the same time, like in the Maltese case, it is quite obvious that the German government wanted to see what the proposed authorisation decision looked like before joining the enhanced cooperation: Between the initial request and the publication by the Commission, almost two years passed in which Germany made no move towards joining the project. Once the draft authorisation decision was published, Germany requested to join within 20 days (see Table 4.2 below).

### 4.1.4 Phase 3.5: The Odd Case of Facilitated Enhanced Cooperation

In the case of the European Public Prosecutor's Office (EPPO),[21] one would think that Latvia, Italy, Estonia, and Austria chose the course of action described above in the Authorisation Phase when they joined the project soon after the initial states and before any other action had happened (see Table 4.2). However, the EPPO is a case of a facilitated enhanced cooperation and thus based on a modified enhanced cooperation procedure: Art. 86 (1)(3) TFEU refers to the enhanced cooperation procedure but facilitates it so that the authorisation is "deemed to be granted" if the procedure of Art. 86 TFEU has been completed without success and interested Member States notified the Parliament, Council, and Commission of their willingness to proceed with enhanced cooperation. From the moment the authorisation is deemed to be granted, the ordinary enhanced cooperation rules apply. Because of the automatic authorisation, Phases 3 and 4 are not as easily distinguishable as in the normal enhanced cooperation procedure. The same procedure used for the establishment of the EPPO is foreseen in Art. 82 (3) TFEU (mutual recognition in criminal matters), Art. 83 (3) TFEU (substantial criminal law harmonization), and Art. 87 (3) TFEU (police cooperation) which have, however, not yet been used in practice.

If Member States decide to join such a facilitated enhanced cooperation before implementing law is passed,[22] the Treaties do not specify an accession procedure. Following the wording of the Treaties, it could be argued that since the authorisation decision is considered to be taken automatically with notification by at

[21] On EPPO, see Geelhoed, Willem; Erkelens, Leendert H.; Meij, Arjen W.H, eds. (2018), *Shifting Perspectives on the European Public Prosecutor's Office*, T.M.C. Asser Press: Imprint: T.M.C. Asser Press.

[22] Once implementing law exists, it is clear that Art. 331 TFEU applies for accessions.

least nine interested Member States, the procedure automatically skips Authorisation Phase and goes straight to Implementation Phase. This would mean that the accession of Member States who want to join an enhanced cooperation just after the initial group (like Latvia, which joined the EPPO enhanced cooperation within the same month of the initial 16) would be subject to a positive decision of the Commission. However, it is the clear intention of the Treaty to facilitate enhanced cooperation in these instances by *avoiding* all kinds of authorisation or confirmation decisions. Hence, such an interpretation would hardly be in line with the *ratio* of the relevant Treaty provisions in the light of the principle of openness. Therefore, Art. 86 (1) TFEU as well as Art. 82 (3), 83 (3), and 87 (3) TFEU (all of which contain facilitated enhanced cooperation clauses) should be interpreted as allowing Member States to join ongoing facilitated enhanced cooperations which have not yet resulted in implementing legal acts by a notification of the Parliament, Council, and Commission.

This, indeed, was the practice of participating and interested Member States as well as the institutions pursued in the case of the EPPO when Latvia, Italy, Estonia, and Austria indicated their wish to participate before implementing legal acts were passed.[23]

### 4.1.5 Phase 4: Legislation—From the Authorising Decision to Secondary Law

Once the authorisation decision is passed, the enhanced cooperation can be considered to be “in progress”, triggering the applicability of the procedure laid out in Art. 331 TFEU.[24] Hence, interested Member States need to first notify their intention to the Council and the Commission. The Commission examines if all the conditions for participation (see below) are met and then, ideally, confirms the participation of new Member States within four months. If not, the Commission indicates measures to be taken by the concerned Member State and sets a deadline for the re-examination of the request. After this deadline, the Commission repeats its examination and either confirms the participation or, if negative, forwards the request to the Council. The Council can then confirm or decline the request, with the votes of the participating Member States only.

[23] Council Regulation (EU) 2017/1939, para. 8.

[24] Martenczuk, B. (2013), ‘Enhanced Cooperation: The Practice of Ad Hoc Differentiation in the EU since the Lisbon Treaty’, *StudDipl*, pp. 83–100, p. 97.

If the participation is confirmed before any implementing secondary law is passed, the affected Member State gains the opportunity to co-decide these measures and thus influence their content. This is a political advantage (though, as described before, it is even more favourable to join at an earlier stage). Moreover, states joining in the Legislative Phase do not fall under the Commission's jurisdiction to adopt transitional measures for the enactment of the implementing law. Despite this more favourable position compared to an accession in Phase 5, no Member State has joined an enhanced cooperation in the Legislative Phase yet. In some cases, this might be due to the fact that implementing legislation was passed shortly after the authorising decision (International Couples' Property). Moreover, it is to be noted that in the enhanced cooperation on a financial transaction tax, no implementing law has been passed yet, meaning that the procedure is still in the Legislative Phase, and states could join should there be movement in the negotiations.

### 4.1.6 Phase 5: Implementation Phase—After Passing Implementing Law

After the initial Member States have passed legal acts implementing the enhanced cooperation, the accession procedure is largely the same as in the Legislative Phase, before the existence of implementing law. The main difference is that now newcomers need to introduce the already existing implementing law to their legal systems. For this reason, the Commission may adopt transitional measures it deems necessary for the implementation (Art. 331.1 (2) TFEU). In the past, the adopted measures consisted of transition periods (delayed entry into force, initially limited application, etc.). In addition, the Commission may verify whether any conditions for participation (see below) are fulfilled (Art. 331.1 (2) TFEU).

After a repeated negative decision on the participation by the Commission due to the non-fulfilment of the participation requirements, the responsibility for the decision can be passed on to the Council (Art. 331.1 (3) TFEU). In this case, the Council equally gains the competence to adopt transitional measures although the Council can only adopt measures on a proposal from the Commission.

So far, Member States successfully joined regular enhanced cooperations in the Implementation Phase on four occasions: Lithuania, Greece, and Estonia were subsequently added to the list of states participating in the enhanced cooperation on divorce and legal separation, and Italy joined the unitary patent (see Table 4.2). These can most clearly be described as the cases in which states changed their mind and joined a project. In all of these cases, there were no general conditions for participation foreseen in the projects. The transitional measures in all cases mirrored, in substance and timespans, the transitional measures for the initial Member States in the implementing legal acts.[25] In addition, the Netherlands and Malta joined the facilitated enhanced cooperation on the European Public Prosecutor's Office. In both cases, no transitional measures were deemed necessary.[26]

A different situation might arise if enhanced cooperation were to be applied in a case governed by QMV. Even in the cases where unanimity is needed, Member States are staying away from participating in enhanced cooperation projects in order to first see the eventual implementing law and then decide on their participation.[27] Given this, Member States could fear all the more to be bound by implementation laws passed against their will in cases governed by QMV. Therefore, more Member States could decide to wait and see the final acts before making a decision about their accession to the enhanced cooperation.

[25] See Commission Decision 2012/714/EU, Commission Decision 2014/39/EU, Commission Decision (EU) 2016/1366, and Commission Decision (EU) 2015/1753.

[26] Commission Decision (EU) 2018/1094 and Commission Decision (EU) 2018/1103.

[27] See the example of Estonia in the EPPO, https://news.err.ee/591270/estonia-not-in-hurry-to-join-european-public-prosecutor-s-office (accessed 20.07.2018), and Malta in PESCO, https://www.maltatoday.com.mt/news/europe/83085/malta_to_wait_and_see_before_deciding_on_pesco_defence_pact_muscat_says (accessed 20.07.2018).

**Table 4.2** Participation in enhanced cooperation projects

| Project | Request Phase Initial Member States | Preparation Phase Before proposal for authorisation | Authorisation Phase After proposal, before authorisation | Legislative Phase After authorisation, before law | Implementation Phase After adoption of implementing law |
|---|---|---|---|---|---|
| **Divorce and Legal Separation** Authorisation Decision (Commission: March 2010) Council: July 2010 Implementing law: December 2010 | July 2008 Austria, (Greece,) Hungary, Italy, Luxembourg, Romania, Slovenia, and Spain[28] | August 2008: Bulgaria January 2009: France | April 2010: Germany, Belgium May 2010: Latvia, Malta June 2010: Portugal | – | November 2012: Lithuania January 2014: Greece August 2016: Estonia |
| **Unitary Patent** Authorisation Decision (Commission: December 2010) Council: March 2011 Implementing law: December 2012 | December 2010: Denmark, Germany, Estonia, France, Lithuania, Luxembourg, the Netherlands, Poland, Slovenia, Finland, Sweden, and the United Kingdom | December 2010: Belgium, Bulgaria, the Czech Republic, Ireland, Greece, Cyprus, Latvia, Hungary, Malta, Austria, Portugal, Romania, and Slovakia[29] | – | – | September 2015: Italy |

(continued)

[28] Note that this took place before the entry into force of the Lisbon treaty. Therefore, the initial number of 8 Member States was sufficient to launch enhanced cooperation. Greece withdrew its request in March 2010.

[29] All requests were submitted before the Commission adopted a proposal for the authorising decision.

**Table 4.2** (continued)

| Project | Request Phase Initial Member States | Preparation Phase Before proposal for authorisation | Authorisation Phase After proposal, before authorisation | Legislative Phase After authorisation, before law | Implementation Phase After adoption of implementing law |
|---|---|---|---|---|---|
| **Financial Transaction Tax** Authorisation Decision (Commission: December 2012) Council: January 2013 | September/ October 2012: Austria, Belgium, Estonia,[30] France, Germany, Greece, Italy, Portugal, Slovakia, Slovenia, and Spain | – | – | – | – |
| **International Couples' Property** Authorisation Decision (Commission: March 2016) Council: June 2016 Implementing law: June 2016 | December 2015: Malta, Croatia, Belgium, Germany, Greece, Spain, France, Italy, Luxembourg, Portugal, Slovenia, Sweden | January 2016: Czech Republic February 2016: The Netherlands, Bulgaria, Austria, and Finland | March 2016: Cyprus | – | – |

(continued)

[30] Estonia subsequently withdrew from participating in March 2016, https://www.europarl.europa.eu/legislative-train/theme-an-economy-that-works-for-people/file-financial-transaction-tax?sid=5201 (last access 03 August 2023).

**Table 4.2** (continued)

| Project | Request Phase Initial Member States | Preparation Phase Before proposal for authorisation | Authorisation Phase After proposal, before authorisation | Legislative Phase After authorisation, before law | Implementation Phase After adoption of implementing law |
|---|---|---|---|---|---|
| **EPPO** Notification replacing authorisation decision: April 2017 Implementing law: October 2017 | April 2017: Belgium, Bulgaria, Croatia, Cyprus, Czech Republic, Finland, France, Germany, Greece, Lithuania, Luxembourg, Portugal, Romania, Slovakia, Slovenia, Spain | April 2017: Latvia June 2017: Estonia, Austria, and Italy | – | – | August 2018: Netherlands, Malta |

Table 4.2–Sources:
Divorce and Legal Separation:
Authorisation Decision: Council Decision 2010/405/EU, esp. para 5.
Implementing Law: Council Regulation (EU) No 1259/2010.
Commission Decisions on Participation: Commission Decision 2012/714/EU (Lithuania); Commission Decision 2014/39/EU (Greece); Commission Decision (EU) 2016/1366 (Estonia)
Unitary Patent:
Proposal for Authorisation Decision: COM/2010/0790 final – NLE 2010/0384.
Authorisation Decision: Council Decision 2011/167/EU, esp. para 5.
Implementing Law: Regulation (EU) No 1257/2012 and No 1260/2012.
Commission Decisions on Participation: Commission Decision (EU) 2015/1753 (Italy).
Financial Transaction Tax:
Authorisation Decision: Council Decision 2013/52/EU, esp. para 6.
International Couples' Property Regimes:
Authorisation Decision: Council Decision (EU) 2016/954, esp. para 5.
Implementing Law: Council Regulation (EU) 2016/1103 and Council Regulation (EU) 2016/1104.
Commission Decisions on Participation: Commission Decision (EU) 2018/1094 (Cyprus).
European Public Prosecutor's Office:
Notification letters: Council, Doc. No. 8027/17.
Implementing Law: Council Regulation (EU) 2017/1939, esp. para 8.
Commission Decisions on Participation: Commission Decision (EU) 2018/1094 (Netherlands); Commission Decision (EU) 2018/1103 (Malta).

## 4.2 Limits on Openness—Compliance, Conditions... and Conditionalities?

Its inherent openness is fundamentally important for enhanced cooperation. Nevertheless, the openness is not unlimited—indeed, participation of interested Member States can be made dependent on three types of requirements. Firstly, newly joining Member States need to adapt their legal systems to the enhanced cooperation if any legal acts have already been passed in the differentiated framework. Secondly, conditions for participation can be introduced in the authorisation decision or the implementing legal acts. Thirdly, it can be argued that there is an unwritten category of requirements that revolves around a sincere willingness to cooperate.

While most of this has been written about before, many aspects have not been or not been sufficiently dealt with yet. Firstly, it was already suggested above that the different limits to the principle of openness have impacts on the moments in which the political will is strong enough to convince a Member State to join an ongoing enhanced cooperation. Therefore, the greater attention paid above to the phases in which Member States can join will now be reflected upon with a greater attention to the political implications of the different limits. Moreover, when it comes to unwritten requirements, the practical application of the enhanced cooperation mechanism has produced some new evidence of such limitations, which will be introduced below. Finally, the possibility for enhanced cooperation Member States to introduce conditions for participation could in future, especially in the light of the various crises the EU is facing, be used to incentivise other states in different ways. This would change the nature of the conditions towards being *conditionalities*. While this has not been discussed in the literature yet, it will be shown that the Treaties do not in principle prohibit such a use of the possibility to introduce conditions.

### 4.2.1 Compliance with Legislation

If Member States adopt law in the framework of an enhanced cooperation, it does not become part of the *acquis communautaire* as it is only applicable to the participating Member States. However, the purpose and advantage of enhanced cooperation is that for the participating states, the implementing law has the same value and function as regular EU law, becoming what has been referred to as "partial acquis".[31] Hence, first and foremost, new Members must comply with all legal acts already adopted in the enhanced cooperation (Art. 328.1 TFEU). The implementing law could be changed to accommodate new Member States; however, it is the norm that newcomers adopt the existing law as it stands and only get a say in future developments.[32]

The practice (Table 4.2) shows that the Commission routinely makes use of its jurisdiction to adopt transitional measures to this end. In all cases where such measures were adopted in practice, they mirrored, in substance and timespans, the transitional measures for the initial Member States, foreseen in the implementing legal acts. However, the open wording of Art. 331.1 TFEU and the fact that such measures are only for the Commission to decide, illustrate that the Commission has the power to influence when and how a Member State joins the enhanced cooperation through transitional measures. This can be an incentive for a Member State to join enhanced cooperations as soon as possible.

The example of Malta[33] (see above, Authorisation Phase) once more exemplifies the relevance of the need to comply with passed legislation for a newly joining state. Had Malta not joined the enhanced cooperation on divorce and legal separation before it was authorised and implementing law was adopted, it could not have negotiated an exception for it not allowing divorces. Under this circumstance, Malta could not have satisfied the accession condition to comply with implementing law because its legal system did not foresee a possibility to get a divorce and, hence, could not have joined the enhanced cooperation.[34]

### 4.2.2 Unwritten Limits

The Principle of Openness is designed as a safeguard against the misuse of enhanced cooperation by Member States which want to exclude another Member State from participating in a measure. However, the principle could itself be misused: The declared aim of enhanced cooperation is to have as many Member States as possible participate. Participating Member States must, wherever possible, promote participation, and the wording of the Treaties only

[31] Blanke, H.-J. (2013), 'Art. 20 TEU' in: Blanke, H.-J., Mangiameli, S. (eds.), *The Treaty on European Union (TEU): A commentary*, Berlin, Springer, pp. 787–830, para. 47.

[32] Ibid., para. 49.

[33] Kuipers, J.-J. (2012), 'The Law Applicable to Divorce as Test Ground for Enhanced Cooperation', *ELJ*, Vol. 18, pp. 201–229.

[34] At least until 2011 when Malta introduced the possibility of divorce after a referendum.

limits the openness in terms of conditions and compliance with passed law (Art. 328.1 TFEU). Given all this, it would be an obvious tactic for a Member State which is opposed to an enhanced cooperation to *join* it and influence it from the inside. In fact, enhanced cooperation has, until this day, only been used in cases which require unanimity in the Council. In such cases, dissenting Member States could join the enhanced cooperation and then continuously veto the implementing law. Such possible tactics have been labelled "Trojan horse" or "deadly embrace".[35] Given the possibility of such blockages, the question arises if the right to participate conferred by the principle of openness is really unlimited, or whether Member States or institutions can act to prevent such a "deadly embrace", or even to end it once it has occurred.

The purpose of enhanced cooperation is to allow flexibility. Member States are not supposed to be overly limited in their capacity to legislate on an EU level even if only a group of them can agree on any given path. While the procedure is not limited to unanimity situations, it is particularly in situations in which very few Member States impede progress that such a "veto-buster"[36] is necessary, and which lead to the introduction of enhanced cooperation in the first place. Therefore, a "deadly embrace" tactic would be an obvious contradiction to the purpose of enhanced cooperation. Rather than allowing flexibility, it would just move blockages to a different level. Therefore, it cannot be claimed that a limitless right to join enhanced cooperations reflects the *telos* or the history of the Treaties.

In the past, several authors thought about an unwritten limit on the openness of enhanced cooperation for this reason and came to similar, yet not identical results. What has not been done yet, however, is to look into the practice to investigate if there are signs confirming the existence of such an unwritten limit or how it would be used practically.

Therefore, it is useful to explore the ideas in the literature to understand what claims have been made exactly, which will follow in a first step. Afterwards, these claims will be confronted with findings from different documents issued in enhanced cooperation procedures as well as the political background of these to see if the initial claims can be upheld.

---

[35] Kuipers, J.-J. (2012), 'The Law Applicable to Divorce as Test Ground for Enhanced Cooperation', *ELJ*, Vol. 18, pp. 201–229 p. 221 ff.; Thym, D. (2004), *Ungleichzeitigkeit und europäisches Verfassungsrecht*, Schriftenreihe europäisches Verfassungsrecht, Baden-Baden, Nomos, p. 57;

[36] Thym, D. (2005), 'United in Diversity: The Integration of Enhanced Cooperation into the European Constitutional Order', *GLJ*, pp. 1731–1747, p. 1737.

#### 4.2.2.1 Unwritten Limit on Openness—Literature

*Von Buttlar* claims that the problem can only arise before implementing law has been passed in an enhanced cooperation, since afterwards Member States have to comply with the partial acquis already passed in the enhanced cooperation framework. Therefore, according to him, Member States have an unlimited right to join enhanced cooperations after implementing law was passed, while before that the project is only open to them if they are actually willing to accede to the project in the sense of the initial Member States.[37] However, this underestimates the variety of situations that can occur. In two out of five instances of enhanced cooperation, one legal act did not suffice to implement the enhanced cooperation (unitary patent and international couples' property regimes, see Table 4.2 sources above). Moreover, there could always be the need for further amendments or changes. In such a situation, an utterly uncooperative Member State could prove to be just as obstructive. Therefore, the limitation must be broader than depicted by *von Buttlar.* In this sense, *Thym* argues that the right to participate in an enhanced cooperation is limited in any stage, and that the EU organs in each accession have the possibility to verify if the interest in joining is due to a sincere willingness to participate or is only fuelled by the intention to block implementing law in the sense of a "deadly embrace".[38]

According to *Becker*, there is a limitation on the openness whenever participation in an enhanced cooperation would amount to misuse. In these cases, the concerned Member State does not have a right to participate. However, *Becker* recognises that in most cases, such misuse will only be established retrospectively. Therefore, *Becker* additionally acknowledges a possibility to exclude the misusing Member State. [39] The idea that an obstructive Member State cannot rely on a right to participate is seconded by *Böttner*, who also points out that the CJEU has developed a general principle according to which the exercise of a right shall be denied even if formal prerequisites are met if the exercise would be abusive, and that a similar principle exists in international law.[40] Participation

[37] Buttlar, C. von (2001), 'Rechtsprobleme der "verstärkten Zusammenarbeit" nach dem Vertrag von Nizza', *ZEuS*, pp. 649–688, p. 673 f. and 675.

[38] Thym, D. (2004), *Ungleichzeitigkeit und europäisches Verfassungsrecht*, Schriftenreihe europäisches Verfassungsrecht, Baden-Baden, Nomos, p. 57 and 249.

[39] Becker, U. (2015), 'Art. 20 EUV, Art. 326–334 AEUV' in: Groeben, H. v. d., Schwarze, J., Hatje, A. (eds.), *Europäisches Unionsrecht,* Baden-Baden, Nomos, Art. 328 para. 8. and Art. 331 para. 11; similarly Hatje, A. (2012), 'Art. 20 EUV, Art. 326–334 AEUV' in: Schwarze, J., Becker, U., Hatje, A., Schoo, J. (eds.), *EU-Kommentar,* Nomos Facultas.wuv.

[40] Böttner, R. (2021), *The Constitutional Framework for Enhanced Cooperation in EU law*, Nijhoff studies in European Union law, Leiden The Netherlands, Koninklijke Brill NV Note,

would, without a doubt, be abusive if a Member State pursued a *deadly embrace* tactic.

*Linke* points out that this creates a tension with Member States who sincerely want to participate in a measure but cannot agree with the other Member States on the way it is to be implemented (as seen for example in the enhanced cooperation on a unitary patent where Spain and Italy agreed on the need for a patent but not on its working languages—*Linke*'s argument was made well before that experience though). In such cases, the concerned Member State could join the enhanced cooperation and then block its implementation to force the others towards its favoured way of implementation. However, while the Member State may sincerely want the measure, the enhanced cooperation mechanism is based on the idea that in some cases, consensus cannot be reached among the Member States, either on a measure or its implementation. Given that under the last resort principle the states must do everything that is reasonable to try and find a compromise, in the absence of it, different views on the implementation of a measure are not a sign of lacking openness when a project is eventually implemented in one way and not the other.[41]

#### 4.2.2.2 Unwritten Limit on Openness—Practice

As usual, when enhanced cooperation is concerned, most literature is from the time before the procedure was actually enacted in practice for the first time. Consequently, the question arises if the practical application confirms the literature's claims that there is an unwritten limit on the principle of openness.

First of all, it must be noted that until now, the Commission confirmed participation or changed its proposal to this effect in all cases in which Member States wanted to join an enhanced cooperation. So, regardless of whether an unwritten limit exists, it did not need to be used until now.

That being said, most insights on this topic can be derived from the Commission's decisions in the cases in which it confirmed the subsequent participation of a Member State to an ongoing enhanced cooperation. In these decisions, the Commission had to describe what it verified beforehand. Among such decisions, the cases in which no implementing law was passed yet would surely be the most insightful, since in these cases the "deadly embrace" poses the biggest challenge

however, that Böttner expressly denies the possibility of expulsion of an obstructive Member States, Böttner, R. (2021), *The Constitutional Framework for Enhanced Cooperation in EU law*, Nijhoff studies in European Union law, Leiden The Netherlands, Koninklijke Brill NV.

[41] Linke, G. (2006), *Das Instrument der verstärkten Zusammenarbeit im Vertrag von Nizza: Möglichkeiten eines Europas der differenzierten Integration*, Interdisziplinäre Europa Studien, Frankfurt am Main, Lang, p. 110.

to the projects. However, as showed before, in most of these cases, the Commission merely changes its proposal and therefore does not issue a written decision confirming participation (this is true for the Request Phase, Preparation Phase, and Authorisation Phase). In the Legislative Phase, a written Commission decision would be required for a Member State to join, but this has not happened yet. Therefore, the available decisions are the ones from Member States joining in the Implementation Phase, i.e. after implementing law has successfully been passed. So far, four such decisions have been issued in regular enhanced cooperations and two in a facilitated enhanced cooperation.[42] If the Commission had stuck closely to the black letter legal requirements foreseen in Art. 328.1 TFEU, it would have only had to note the absence of (written) conditions in the authorisation decision and specific prerequisites in the implementing law, while the compliance with the implementing law would be ensured through transitional measures. However, the wording that the Commission used in every one of the four regular enhanced cooperation decisions was:

> *The Commission notes that neither [AUTHORISATION DECISION] nor [IMPLEMENTING LEGAL ACT] prescribe any particular conditions of participation in enhanced cooperation in the area of […] and that [MEMBER STATE]'s participation should strengthen the benefits of this enhanced cooperation.*[43] *(emphasis added)*

Given the continuous usage of the expression "that [Member State]'s participation should strengthen the benefits of this enhanced cooperation", the Commission apparently tested more than just the existence of written criteria.[44] In different language versions, this seems even clearer.[45] If an enhanced cooperation is to

[42] Three in the enhanced cooperation on divorce and legal separation, one on the unitary patent, and two in the facilitated enhanced cooperation on the establishment of the European Public Prosecutor's Office (EPPO).

[43] Commission Decision 2012/714/EU para 4 (in this case, the Commission only mentioned the authorisation decision); Commission Decision 2014/39/EU para 5; Commission Decision (EU) 2016/1366 para 6; Commission Decision (EU) 2015/1753 para 5.

[44] An interpretation of the provisions on joining an enhanced cooperation which grants the Commission a greater role was already proposed for the pre-Lisbon enhanced cooperation legal framework: Kochenov, D., Amtenbrink, F. (2009), 'Towards a More Flexible Approach to Enhanced Cooperation' in: Ott, A. (ed.), *Fifty years of European integration: Foundations and perspectives,* The Hague, Asser Press, pp. 181–199.

[45] German: "[…]dass die Teilnahme […] [an] dieser Verstärkten Zusammenarbeit förderlich wäre", that the participation would be benefitial; Italian: "[…]che la partecipazione […] rafforzerà i benefici di detta cooperazione rafforzata", that the participation *will* strengthen the benefits.

*benefit* from a Member State's participation, the State clearly cannot be planning a "deadly embrace" of the project. Apparently, the Commission carries out a benefit assessment of a Member State's participation in an enhanced cooperation, the core of which logically must be its sincere willingness to cooperate in the project, since its absence would pose the biggest conceivable *dis*benefit.

It needs to be added that no trace of such a benefit assessment can be found in the Commission decisions confirming the participation in the facilitated enhanced cooperation on EPPO. This could *prima facie* be understood as a more restrained approach by the Commission, mirroring its more limited role in setting up facilitated enhanced cooperations. However, in different, internal Commission documents, namely the notice of the launch of the inter-service consultation regarding the request to join (i.e. a consultation through which it is made sure that all services within the Commission agree with the decision to let a Member State join), the Commission, as in the confirmation decisions in the regular enhanced cooperation procedures, stresses the benefits of the participation of the requesting Member States.[46]

Regarding the Commission's approach in regular enhanced cooperations, however, it is again informative to look at the case of Malta in the enhanced cooperation on divorce and legal separation law (see above, Authorisation Phase and Compliance with passed legal acts). Malta's legal system did not foresee the possibility to get a divorce. To maintain this status, it vetoed the legislative project on harmonizing access to Courts in such cases. When the majority of the remaining Member States decided to proceed using the enhanced cooperation procedure, Malta joined and obliged the participating Member States to include an exception for its benefit in the implementing regulation.[47] Malta thus refrained from "deadly embracing" the project and settled for a special clause to protect its interest.

In its letter notifying its intention to join the enhanced cooperation, it pointed out that it would "seek assurance that its particular position on divorce is

[46] European Commission, Note to the Attention of Mr M. Selmayr (Secretary-General) Ms. I. Souka (Director-General, Human Resources) Mr L. Romero Requena (Director-General, Legal Service) Mr. S. Presa (Acting Director-General, Budget), INTERSERVICE CONSULTATION, Subject: Launch of an inter-service consultation for the adoption of a Commission Decision confirming the participation of Malta in the enhanced cooperation on the establishment of the European Public Prosecutor's Office (EPPO), p. 1: "The participation of Malta will further strengthen the benefits of the enhanced cooperation on the establishment of the EPPO."

[47] Art. 13 Council Regulation (EU) No 1259/2010.

safeguarded in the text of the Council regulation", which indeed happened eventually.[48] However, the Commission could not be sure of this at the time of confirming Malta's participation. On the one hand, this strengthens the expectation raised in the past that the Commission will be extremely careful when exercising its benefit assessment.[49] On the other hand, this could point towards the existence of a possibility to reverse the accession confirmation by the Commission (more on this just below).

#### 4.2.2.3 Conclusions on Unwritten Limits

In conclusion, both theory and practice point towards an unwritten limit on the principle of openness. The Commission tests broadly if the participation of a Member State benefits the project, and it remains somewhat unclear what is assesses in this context. It should be pointed out, though, that the Commission, like the Member States, is bound by (and, as shown for instance in the case of Malta, committed to) the duty to promote participation by as many Member States as possible (Art. 328.1 (2) TFEU). There are scenarios in which the participation of more Member States makes an enhanced cooperation objectively work less well, for example by creating less economic benefits.[50] In such cases, it can be said that the participation of certain states is not actually beneficial. However, the clear Treaty provision in Art. 328.1 TFEU bans the possibility of excluding the Member States in such a scenario. Hence, it becomes even clearer that the core of the benefit assessment, and thus of the unwritten limitation on the principle of openness, is the assessment of a sincere willingness to cooperate in the differentiated integration measure. The reason for this unwritten limit can be found, as described above, in the nature of enhanced cooperation and its aim to facilitate flexibility and circumvent persistent vetoes in certain scenarios. However, the legal foundation for it can be seen in the principle of sincere cooperation

---

[48] Letter by the Permanent Representation of Malta to the European Union (PR 550/10), 31 May 2010.

[49] Thym, D. (2004), *Ungleichzeitigkeit und europäisches Verfassungsrecht*, Schriftenreihe europäisches Verfassungsrecht, Baden-Baden, Nomos, p. 57 and 249; Gaja, G. (1998), 'How Flexible Is Flexibility Under the Amsterdam Treaty?', *Common Market Law Review*, Vol. 35, No. 4, pp. 855–870; Cremona, M. (2009), 'Enhanced Cooperation and the Common Foreign and Security and Defence Policies of the EU', *EUI Working Papers*, No. 21 ("weighted in favour of inclusion").

[50] See e.g. the different scenarios for a Common Consolidated Corporate Tax Base in Bettendorf, L., van der Horst, A., Mooij, R. A. D., Vrijburg, H., 'Corporate Tax Consolidation and Enhanced Cooperation in the European Union', *Fiscal Studies*, Vol. 31, No. 4, pp. 453–479.

(Art. 4.3 TEU)[51,52] Where Member States are obliged to cooperate sincerely and loyally with the Institutions and the other Member States,[53] they cannot block others when they legally choose a path that does not include all states to pursue the objectives of the Union.

The sincere willingness to cooperate entails a general willingness to participate, i.e. agreement on the necessity of the measure as well as a general agreement on the way it is thought to be implemented. The latter is particularly relevant if this was what led to the usage of enhanced cooperation (like in the unitary patent case). This shows that the unwritten limit always operates on a thin and delicate line between preventing "deadly embraces" by uncooperative Member States and the preclusion of a healthy political debate on the implementation of the enhanced cooperation.

In this context, it is particularly difficult to answer what happens when a Member State joins an enhanced cooperation without the sincere willingness to cooperate, i.e. when the Commission's benefit assessment fails and an enhanced cooperation member consistently blocks the progress of the procedure. *Becker* proposes that in this case, a Member State can be excluded from the enhanced cooperation.[54] He does not explain how this exclusion would come to be in practice, particularly who would decide on the measure.

It is true that an enhanced cooperation project could be jeopardized by Member States joining and blocking the adoption of implementing law, that this danger cannot be excluded completely by the benefit assessment that the Commission carries out beforehand, and that the Commission's behaviour in the case of Malta regarding the enhanced cooperation on divorces and legal separation might point toward it assuming to have a possibility to intervene at a later stage in the process, if necessary. However, the comparison with another differentiation mechanism

---

[51] Blanke, H.-J. (2013), 'Art. 4 TEU' in: Blanke, H.-J., Mangiameli, S. (eds.), *The Treaty on European Union (TEU): A commentary,* Berlin, Springer, para. 81 ff.

[52] Editorial Comments (2011), 'Enhanced cooperation: A Union à taille réduite or à porte tournante?', *CMLRev*, pp. 317–327, Fn. 13; Thym, D. (2004), *Ungleichzeitigkeit und europäisches Verfassungsrecht*, Schriftenreihe europäisches Verfassungsrecht, Baden-Baden, Nomos, p. 57; Böttner, R. (2021), *The Constitutional Framework for Enhanced Cooperation in EU law*, Nijhoff studies in European Union law, Leiden The Netherlands, Koninklijke Brill NV.

[53] Blanke, H.-J. (2013), 'Art. 4 TEU' in: Blanke, H.-J., Mangiameli, S. (eds.), *The Treaty on European Union (TEU): A commentary,* Berlin, Springer, para. 83.

[54] Becker, U. (2015), 'Art. 20 EUV, Art. 326–334 AEUV' in: Groeben, H. v. d., Schwarze, J., Hatje, A. (eds.), *Europäisches Unionsrecht,* Baden-Baden, Nomos, Art. 328 para. 8. and Art. 331 para. 11.

foreseen by the Treaties, PESCO, challenges the claim that there is an unwritten exclusion mechanism from enhanced cooperation. In PESCO ('Permanent Structured Cooperation' in defence policy), which is distinct from enhanced cooperation but largely resembles it,[55] the participating Member States can suspend the membership of another participant by a qualitative majority decision in the Council (Art. 46 (4) TEU).[56] Given this clear statement and a written Treaty basis in a similar procedure, it is difficult to argue that such a provision is intended but not explicitly included in the Treaties for enhanced cooperation.[57]

What could be conceivable, however, is a slightly different approach from a right to exclude an uncooperative Member State: Since the participation in enhanced cooperation is subject to the fulfilment of certain criteria, and one of them is the sincere willingness to cooperate, one could claim that where a Member State indeed uses its membership only to block an enhanced cooperation, the criteria were never fulfilled in the first place. In the light of this, and of the importance of this criterion, it can be argued that the conditions were just never met—and that, therefore, the Commission decision confirming the participation must be declared invalid *ex ante*, annulling the participation of the concerned state from the outset.[58] This is not an entirely new idea: In fact, a similar argument has been made for the participation of Greece in the EMU, which was based on inaccurate fiscal statistics.[59] Assuming that this is possible, *ex ante* invalidity of the participation would have to be established by the institution(s) responsible for the participation of the not sincerely willing Member State, i.e. the Commission, at any moment after the authorisation decision has been adopted by the Council

---

[55] In fact, enhanced cooperation could be used on defence matters (Art. 329.2 TFEU). However, PESCO provides Member States with more liberty and less rigid conditions than enhanced cooperation would.

[56] Biscop, S. (2018), 'European Defence: Give PESCO a Chance', *Survival*, Vol. 60, No. 3, pp. 161–180.

[57] Agreeing: Böttner, R. (2021), *The Constitutional Framework for Enhanced Cooperation in EU law*, Nijhoff studies in European Union law, Leiden The Netherlands, Koninklijke Brill NV.

[58] With a similar interpretation: Heber, C. (2021), *Enhanced Cooperation and European Tax Law*, Oxford University Press.

[59] Peers, S. (2015), The law of Grexit: What does EU law say about leaving economic and monetary union?, EU Law Analysis; see also: Proctor, C. (2006), 'The Future of the Euro—What Happens if a Member State Leaves?', *E.B.L.R.*, Vol. 17, No. 4, pp. 909–937; Blocher, J., Gulati, G. M., Helfer, L. (2016), 'Can Greece Be Expelled from the Eurozone? Toward a Default Rule on Expulsion from International Organizations' in: Allen, F., Carletti, E., Gray, J., Gulati, G. M. (eds.), *Filling the gaps in governance: The case of Europe,* San Domenico di Fiesole, European University Institute, pp. 127–150.

(Legislative Phase, Implementation Phase).[60] Before this, it could be argued that the decision must be taken by the actors involved in passing the authorisation decision which the concerned Member State becomes part of, i.e. the Commission, the Council (in an analogy to Art. 329.1 (2) TFEU with QMV), and with consent of the Parliament. Of course, this would only be possible if more than the nine Member States were left afterwards to make the enhanced cooperation continue. It goes without saying that the operation to conclude that a Member State's participation is only based on the intention to veto implementing legal acts would be extremely delicate and difficult. The only aid when doing so could be drawn from the Council material on the verification of the last resort-criterion. In fact, the only case in which it would be somewhat easy to verify that a state joined an enhanced cooperation for uncooperative purposes would be if a Member State brought back up the discussions which led to the conclusion that a uniform solution could not be found.

A Member State left out after such a decision could resort to an action for annulment before the Court of Justice (Art. 263 TFEU). Likewise, the Council could, at least in theory, seek to annul a Commission decision confirming the participation of a Member State before the CJEU.[61]

### 4.2.3 Written Conditions and Conditionality

The Treaty of Lisbon for the first time gave Member States the possibility to make participation dependent on the fulfilment of certain criteria. For that purpose, "conditions of participation" can be laid down in the authorising decision according to Art. 328 (1) TFEU. While limiting the openness of enhanced cooperations to some extent, this option is regarded as a means to strengthen the enhanced cooperation mechanism by giving participating Member States some control over accessions through objective criteria, while avoiding less objective, politicised Council decisions on accession.[62] Nevertheless, until today, no such condition was used in practice. All authorisation decisions were limited to the mere triggering of enhanced cooperation.

---

[60] Similarly for the older Art. 11 ECT: Hatje, A. (2000), 'Art. 11 EGV' in: Schwarze, J., Bär-Bouyssière, B. (eds.), *EU-Kommentar*, Baden-Baden, Nomos-Verl.-Ges.

[61] Zeitzmann, S. (2011), 'Das Verfahren der Verstärkten Zusammenarbeit und dessen erstmalige Anwendung: Ein Ehescheidungs- und Trennungsrecht für Europa', *ZEuS*, pp. 87–113.

[62] Blanke, H.-J. (2013), 'Art. 20 TEU' in: Blanke, H.-J., Mangiameli, S. (eds.), *The Treaty on European Union (TEU): A commentary*, Berlin, Springer, pp. 787–830, para 36.

However, unity in the EU has been under attack in recent times. This practice might therefore be bound to change in the future. Serious disagreement on various questions regarding the EU could lead to a more frequent use of enhanced cooperation. In an atmosphere of disunity and lacking cooperation, Member States might feel the need to ensure the functionality of such enhanced cooperation projects by introducing conditions to govern participation.

*Prima facie*, one would expect these conditions to be straight forward criteria, like the participation in the Euro or Schengen, to name but a few possibilities. However, the conditions could also be very different in nature. This is due to another topic that has been generating renewed interest in the light of the different recent European crises: the idea of conditionality, i.e. connecting a benefit to a country's fulfilment of certain policy requirements. In the Eurozone crisis, active use has been made of conditionality as a policy tool. In the ongoing rule of law crisis, voices from all directions demanded the use of conditionality to ensure core values, which was eventually introduced in a regulation to protect the EU budget.[63] Therefore, the current situation of the EU calls, on the one hand, for renewed attention to the *conditions* enhanced cooperation can be made dependent on. On the other hand, it is worth exploring if the *conditions* can amount to *conditionalities* and if so, how far enhanced cooperation conditionality can go.

Enhanced cooperation conditions have so far been living largely in the shadow, which is why there is little literature on the topic, making an analysis worthwhile. Using the conditions as conditionalities, on the other hand, has not been analysed at all to this day. However, conditionalities offer a great deal of political leverage. For this reason, it is well worth looking into the possibilities hidden in the enhanced cooperation mechanism.

#### 4.2.3.1 Conditions vs Conditionalities

As a first step, I want to explore the differences between conditions and conditionalities. A condition can be defined as "a situation that must exist before something else is possible or permitted".[64] A conditionality, on the other hand, is a condition that has additional features.

According to *Viţă*, two core features distinguish conditionalities from mere conditions: Firstly, the conduct prescribed by a conditionality must pursue a policy objective which goes beyond the primary purpose. Secondly, there must either

---

[63] Regulation (EU, Euratom) 2020/2092 on a general regime of conditionality for the protection of the Union budget.

[64] Stevenson, Angus, ed. (2010), *Oxford Dictionary of English*, Oxford, Oxford University Press.

be a sanction or an incentive attached to the (non-)fulfilment of the prescribed behaviour. It can occur as negative conditionality (deprivation of benefits in case of non-fulfilment), positive conditionality (provision of additional benefits in case of fulfilment), or a connection of the two ("carrot-and-stick conditionality").[65]

Hence, for enhanced cooperation 'conditions', the classification depends on the nature of the condition and of the enhanced cooperation. The two aforementioned criteria would have to be fulfilled in order for the condition to be classified as a conditionality. On the one hand, the enhanced cooperation project would have to be designed in a way that is particularly beneficial for the (or some of the) participating Member States, so that being able to participate acts as "carrot" incentivising Member States to join. On the other hand, the condition would have to go beyond what is indispensable for its functioning and pursue (at least *also* pursue) an additional, distinct policy objective. Under these circumstances, the condition might qualify and be used as a positive conditionality.

#### 4.2.3.2 Legal Framework of 'Conditions'[66]

The Treaties (Art. 328.1 TFEU) give little guidance about the nature of 'conditions':

> *When enhanced cooperation is being established, it shall be open to all Member States, subject to compliance with any conditions of participation laid down by the authorising decision.*

According to the wording "any conditions", it could follow that there is no limitation as to what enhanced cooperation parties can ask of interested Member States. However, such an interpretation would be incompatible with the importance of the principle of openness in the enhanced cooperation mechanism. Moreover, the provision must be read in the broader Treaty context, and particularly in the context of the other provisions on enhanced cooperation. Therefore, the conditions must respect rights and obligations of non-participating Member States (Art. 327 TFEU), cannot undermine internal market or cohesion in the EU, or establish trade barriers and discriminations.

---

[65] Viţă, V. (2017), 'Revisiting the Dominant Discourse on Conditionality in the EU: The Case of EU Spending Conditionality', *Camb. Yearb. Eur. Legal Stud.*, Vol. 19, pp. 116–143, p. 122. *Viţă* focuses particularly on spending conditionality.

[66] By 'conditions', here I mean conditions in a broad sense, including normal conditions and conditionalities.

Some more clarity can be drawn from the Treaty negotiations: According to the European Conventions'[67] explanatory documents, delegations were in agreement that Art. 328 TFEU referred to *objective* conditions.[68] According to the Convention, the conditions were introduced so that enhanced cooperation would "*no longer be designed basically as a substitute for unanimity*". Instead, "*[t]he enhanced cooperation mechanism could also be based on objective differences, or even reflect objective criteria for participation by particular Member States, as with the adoption of the Euro, participation in the Schengen system, or indeed some aspects of defence*".[69] Hence, it becomes clear that the Treaty drafters envisaged conditions that, in addition to being objective, are genuinely *linked* to the content of the enhanced cooperation. They intend requirements that an enhanced cooperation is "based on", i.e. fundamental for its functioning, or at least so beneficial for it that states can require their fulfilment as "criteria for participation". Arbitrary criteria, which basically aim to establish a core group of Member States within the EU but are disconnected from the content of the enhanced cooperation (say, requiring Euro membership for an enhanced cooperation in defence policy), would not fit this description and would therefore not be admissible under the principle of openness.

A detail that follows from the necessity of conditions to be "objective" is that they must be as clear and unambiguous as possible. In fact, for Member States which do not fulfil an enhanced cooperation criterion, the prerequisite leads to potentially *involuntary* differentiation. To justify a limitation on the principle of openness in this politically highly sensitive context, the question whether conditions are fulfilled should, to the maximum extent possible, be easy to clearly answer as either yes or no. Conditions that can be reached gradually are hardly workable and would guarantee opposition.

In the European Conventions' explanatory documents, it is notable that the given examples include conditions that might be able to permanently exclude certain Member States. An enhanced cooperation limited to Member States which are members of the Euro and Schengen excludes countries that opted out of these measures (one could also mention the voluntary but permanent non-fulfilment of the Euro convergence criteria by states like Sweden).[70] Moreover, the Convention

---

[67] Art. 328 TFEU was drafted in the process of drafting the European Constitutional Treaty but transferred to the Lisbon Treaty without changes.

[68] CONV 723/03, p. 22.

[69] CONV 723/03, p. 22.

[70] This fact was overlooked by Becker, J., Kornwachs, L., Zembala-Börner, K. (2016), *Die gemeinsame Europäische Bankenaufsicht als Reformmodell für die verstärkte Zusammenarbeit?*, Heidelberger Beiträge zum Finanz- und Steuerrecht, who conclude that the Single

must have been aware that enhanced cooperations in the area of defence could have the possibility to permanently exclude certain Member States because of national constitutional restraints (i.e. neutral Member States like Austria or Ireland and at the time also Sweden and Finland, or states with strict constitutional requirements for deployment of military, like Germany).

It follows from this that the conditions referred to in Art. 328.1 (1) TFEU must be objective, genuinely linked to and necessary for the purpose of the enhanced cooperation; they can, however, limit the openness of the cooperation to an extent that single Member States may even factually be excluded by them in a permanent way.

It is important to note that the conditions do not only apply to states interested in joining an enhanced cooperation, but also to the initial Member States.[71] This is crucial because it prevents the initial states from applying conditions that they themselves could not fulfil, effectively building a wall around a core of states via an enhanced cooperation. It follows from this that the Treaties prevent the Council—even if it has the support of the Commission—from retrospectively changing the authorisation decision to add such conditions. An exception to this could only be imaginable if all participating Member States had fulfilled them at the time of the authorisation.

The authorisation decision potentially containing participation conditions is drafted by the Commission and can only be amended by the Council with an unlikely unanimous decision (Art. 293.1 TFEU) or by the Commission itself. Hence, it is the Commission that is in charge of including conditions in the draft decision. However, given that the Council has an exclusive right of initiative, the Commission must, to a certain degree, be bound by the requests of the Member States since otherwise it could propose a substantially different enhanced cooperation and undermine the Council's initiative. This gives Member States a substantive possibility to influence the Commission when deciding whether or not to include conditions in the proposal.[72]

Despite the fact that the Treaties only refer to conditions in the authorisation decision, practice shows that in five out of six cases, i.e. in all but the very first

---

Supervisory Mechanism could neither be based legally on Art. 127 (6) TFEU alone because according to the authors it does not allow differentiation, nor be introduced via enhanced cooperation because the principle of openness, according to the authors, would not have been respected by an enhanced cooperation factually excluding non-Eurozone Member States.

[71] CONV 723/03, p. 22.

[72] Becker, U. (2015), 'Art. 20 EUV, Art. 326–334 AEUV' in: Groeben, H. v. d., Schwarze, J., Hatje, A. (eds.), *Europäisches Unionsrecht,* Baden-Baden, Nomos, Art. 328 AEUV para. 3 f., Art. 329 AEUV para. 8 f.

case, the Commission also examined conditions in the implementing acts when assessing the request for participation of an interested Member State.[73] Hence, it can be assumed that the Commission, as responsible legal actor, would regard a condition in the implementing legal act as binding like one in the authorisation decision.

In summary, conditions for the participation in an enhanced cooperation must be fulfilled by all participating Member States from the beginning and must be objective, which includes that they must be unambiguous (possible to be answered with yes or no beyond reasonable doubt). Moreover, they must be genuinely linked to the nature or the functioning of the measure introduced through enhanced cooperation. While they could be proposed by the Commission, it is likely that the Member States will take the initiative in case of future uses.

All of this is true for both mere conditions and potential conditionalities. However, especially the criterion of a genuine link between a criterion and the functioning of the enhanced cooperation can be problematic for a conditionality, which by definition has a purpose that goes beyond the primary purpose—here the functioning of the enhanced cooperation.[74] It follows from this that for an enhanced cooperation condition to work as a conditionality, it must be closely linked to the functioning of the enhanced cooperation, while at the same time furthering a policy objective that goes beyond its scope.

#### 4.2.3.3 Potential Conditions, Conditionalities and their Implications

As stated above, the possibility to introduce conditions (and therefore also conditionalities) to enhanced cooperation has not been used to this day. It is, however, a political tool that could be used in future, in particular in response to the many political crises of our time.

---

[73] Commission Decision 2014/39/EU para 5; Commission Decision (EU) 2016/1366 para 6; Commission Decision (EU) 2015/1753 para 5; the standard phrasing is "The Commission notes that neither [AUTHORISATION DECISION] nor [IMPLEMENTING LEGAL ACT] prescribe any particular conditions of participation in enhanced cooperation in the area of [...]. In the two cases of Member States (Commission Decision (EU) 2018/1094 para 5 and Commission Decision (EU) 2018/1103 para 7) joining the EPPO enhanced cooperation, the wording differs as there is no authorisation decision that could be checked, but the Commission confirms the absence of conditions in the implementing legislation.

[74] For a similar effect, see CJEU C-156/21 (Hungary v Parliament and Council), ECLI:EU:C:2022:97, para. 147, 176, 244, 267 on the genuine link, within the Rule of Law Conditionality Regulation, between the conduct of a state undermining the rule of law and the effects it has on the Union budget.

In the absence of real-life examples, I will introduce hypothetical examples of possible future enhanced cooperations to show how conditions and conditionalities would work in practice and to further illustrate the differences between the two. In doing so, I will apply the legal criteria established above to test their legal feasibility. Moreover, I will try to show which kind of political leverage could be gained by using enhanced cooperation conditionalities. To stay as close as possible to some of the real problems the EU has been facing recently, I will use the two main fields in which conditionality has been discussed recently as examples: the governance of the Economic and Monetary Union (EMU) and the rule of law crisis.

#### 4.2.3.3.1 Eurozone/EMU Governance

Any EU action regarding the Eurozone differentiates per definition. Therefore, legal action that does not include all Member States is the norm, and the Member States never had to resort to enhanced cooperation. To this end, Art. 136 ff. TFEU in connection with Art. 121 and 126 TFEU give the Eurozone Member States the possibility to legislate in a certain limited number of fields in an enhanced cooperation-*esque* way, with only the Eurozone Member States being able to vote. Beyond the scope of these provisions, if they want to legislate on questions regarding the single currency, the acts must be passed by the EU as a whole, while their scope of application is limited to the Member States whose currency is the Euro.[75]

The fact that such action often requires unanimity makes it apparent that sometimes this path is not viable.[76] In such situations, enhanced cooperation may provide a possible way forward.[77] To limit such a hypothetical enhanced cooperation to the Eurozone Member States, it would be an obvious choice to make

[75] See e.g. the proposal COM(2017) 824 final, Art. 1 (2) and 4; critical of the legality of this approach: Becker, J., Kornwachs, L., Zembala-Börner, K. (2016), *Die gemeinsame Europäische Bankenaufsicht als Reformmodell für die verstärkte Zusammenarbeit?*, Heidelberger Beiträge zum Finanz- und Steuerrecht.

[76] An example for this is the UK's veto against the Fiscal Compact, https://www.theguardian.com/world/2011/dec/09/david-cameron-blocks-eu-treaty (accessed 25.06.2018).

[77] Messina, M. (2014), 'Strengthening economic governance of the European Union through enhanced cooperation: a still possible, but already missed, opportunity', *ELRev*, Vol. 39, pp. 404–417; Schwarz, M. (2014), 'A Memorandum of Misunderstanding—The doomed road of the European Stability Mechanism and a possible way out: Enhanced cooperation', *CMLRev*, Vol. 51, pp. 389–423; Graf von Luckner, J. (2018), 'How to Bring It Home—The EU's Options for Incorporating the Fiscal Compact into EU Law', *European Law Blog*; see also Sect. 2.3.2.1.

participation dependent on having the Euro as a currency. While this would permanently exclude some Member States to whom the enhanced cooperation would not be *open*, the Treaty drafters explicitly foresaw this case, and the legality of this procedure could hardly be denied per se.[78] Having the Euro as a currency is an objective, unambiguous factor and therefore suitable to be an enhanced cooperation condition. Nevertheless, it must be stressed that not any legal measure could be passed and limited to the Eurozone this way. As set out above, the condition must have a genuine link with the content of the enhanced cooperation, i.e. with having the Euro as a currency.

In recent times, a frequently occurring policy proposal is that of a Eurozone budget.[79] There is wide agreement that the economic side of EMU governance needs to be strengthened.[80] Therefore, if such a budget was introduced using the enhanced cooperation mechanism,[81] it would not be hard to establish a link between a Eurozone budget and the condition of having the Euro as a currency to participate—Member States with their own currency are affected significantly less by the lack of economic governance in the EMU. When it comes to the proposal to establish a new tax to finance this budget,[82] the link is considerably less clear and can be challenged: The link to limiting the measure to Eurozone states would, again, be made through the necessity to strengthen the economic side of EMU. However, it would only be indirect since the measure to strengthen the EMU would not be the tax, but the Eurozone budget ("We need a new tax which must exclude all but Eurozone Member States because we need to strengthen the economic side of EMU"). Whether this link is still close enough is a question that would, in such a scenario, likely have to be decided by the Court of Justice eventually.[83]

---

[78] CONV 723/03, p. 22.

[79] https://www.euractiv.com/section/economy-jobs/news/macron-wins-merkels-backing-on-budget-for-eurozone/ (accessed 25.05.2018).

[80] Hinarejos, A. (2015), 'An Asymmetric EMU' in: Hinarejos Parga, A. (ed.), *The Euro area crisis in constitutional perspective,* Oxford University Press, pp. 3–10, p. 4 ff.

[81] Art. 332 TFEU could, in addition, be a particularly easy way to establish its funding separate from the EU budget.

[82] https://www.euractiv.com/section/economy-jobs/news/macron-wins-merkels-backing-on-budget-for-eurozone/ (accessed 25.05.2018); Iara, A. (2015), *Revenue for EMU: A contribution to the debate on Fiscal Union*, Taxation papers. Working paper, Luxembourg, Publications Office.

[83] It is indeed likely that such a project would end up at the Court as the proceedings against the Financial Transaction Tax even before the adoption of law implementing it shows; see CJEU C-209/13 (*United Kingdom v Council*), ECLI:EU:C:2014:283.

In any case, the purpose for introducing Eurozone membership as a condition as described would in all likelihood not aim to incentivise further Member States to join the Eurozone. Therefore, it would be a mere condition and not a conditionality. However, a substantial Eurozone budget in particular might also make participating in the EMU more attractive to outsiders—if this was the an additional aim of the measure, it could also qualify as a conditionality.

Another viable and conceivable condition could be a link to the intergovernmental aspects of the EMU which not all Member States participate in, like the Fiscal Compact or the ESM treaty.[84] EU action in this field could be passed as enhanced cooperation and limited to the Members who are party to one or all of these international law measures. If the reason for linking new, differentiating legal acts to the older intergovernmental measures is limited to necessities, such as the new measures making active use of the older ones, the genuine link would be easy to show, and the measure would qualify as a condition rather than a conditionality. However, if the aim of the linking were *also* to make a higher number of Member States participate in the older framework, and the new enhanced cooperation project would bring certain benefits, it could also qualify as a conditionality. As long as there is nevertheless a sufficiently strong link to the measure (e.g. the need for guaranteed financial stability to participate in the hypothetical new measure), limiting enhanced cooperation to participating Member States of said intergovernmental instruments would still be legally feasible.

Finally, it could be debatable whether to use a consistent fulfilment of budgetary rules as a condition for an enhanced cooperation in the EMU governance. What is complicated about this approach is that depending on the enhanced cooperation project, the policy goal pursued by a hypothetical enhanced cooperation and by the conditionality could both be EMU stability. Nevertheless, if the budgetary compliance is sufficiently relevant for the enhanced cooperation, this approach would not be excluded.

In conclusion, while many legal acts concerning the governance of the EMU can be passed on the basis of Art. 136 TFEU and thus be limited to the Eurozone Member States from the outset, in situations in which Art. 136 TFEU is not applicable, enhanced cooperation could be used while the measures could still be limited to certain groups of states. Beyond that, even where Art. 136 TFEU *is* applicable, Member States could choose to go for enhanced cooperation and use its conditionality clause to incentivise Member States to pursue certain conducts.

[84] Hinarejos, A. (2015), 'Institutional Responses to the Crisis' in: Hinarejos Parga, A. (ed.), *The Euro area crisis in constitutional perspective,* Oxford University Press, pp. 15–50.

#### 4.2.3.3.2 Rule of Law Conditionality

Another field in which conditionality is considered particularly often is the rule of law.[85] Internal practices in some Member States are increasingly seen as threats to the rule of law, and the procedure foreseen for such scenarios, Art. 7 TEU, is proving ineffective because of the unanimity requirement in paragraph 2 thereof. In this situation, Member States have been looking for alternative ways to protect the rule of law. After extensive debates and a lengthy procedure,[86] this led to a regulation applying negative spending conditionality to disbursements from the EU budget.[87] Following a political deal, its application was delayed until the CJEU had decided on the legality of the regulation by way of an action for annulment, which was decided in spring of 2022.[88] The CJEU declared the regulation legal. However, the conditionality regulation is limited in scope, as it only and exclusively serves the protection of the EU budget. Thus, breaches of the rule of law that do not have direct effects on the Union budget cannot lead to consequences under the new framework.[89] However, the precedent of the conditionality regulation has emboldened the institutions to use funding conditionality for the purpose of protecting the rule of law, which has, in the meantime, been introduced to a host of instruments, introduced by a qualified Council majority.[90] It is therefore more likely than not that further conditionality instruments will

---

[85] See e.g. Regulation (EU, Euratom) 2020/2092 on a general regime of conditionality for the protection of the Union budget; Halmai, G. (2019), 'The Possibility and Desirability of Rule of Law Conditionality', *HJRL*, Vol. 11, 171–188; Bogdandy, A. von, Ioannidis, M. (2014), 'Systemic deficiency in the rule of law: What it is, what has been done, what can be done', *CMLRev*, pp. 59–96; Pech, L., 'The EU as a global rule of law promoter: the consistency and effectiveness challenges', *Asia Europe Journal*, Vol. 14, No. 1, pp. 7–24; Fisicaro, M. (2020), 'Rule of Law Conditionality in EU Funds: The Value of Money in the Crisis of European Values'; Bonelli, M., Claes, M., Witte, B. de, Podstawa, K. (2022), 'Usual and Unusual Suspect in Protecting EU Values: An Introduction'.

[86] Kirst, N. (2021), 'Rule of Law Conditionality: The Long-awaited Step Towards a Solution of the Rule of Law Crisis in the European Union?'; see also the initial proposal for a Regulation of the European Parliament and of the Council on the protection of the Union's budget in case of generalised deficiencies as regards the rule of law in the Member States, COM(2018) 324 final.

[87] Regulation (EU, Euratom) 2020/2092 on a general regime of conditionality for the protection of the Union budget (henceforth Rule of Law Conditionality Regulation).

[88] CJEU C-156/21 (Hungary v Parliament and Council), ECLI:EU:C:2022:97 and C-157/21 (Poland v Parliament and Council), ECLI:EU:C:2022:98; see i.a. Pech, L. (2022), 'No More Excuses'.

[89] Kirst, N. (2021), 'Rule of Law Conditionality: The Long-awaited Step Towards a Solution of the Rule of Law Crisis in the European Union?'.

[90] Scheppele, K. L., Morijn, J. (2023), 'Frozen'.

keep on being introduced. It can be argued that such another, albeit somewhat unexpected, mode to motivate Member States to apply higher rule of law standards could be positive conditionality introduced through enhanced cooperation. In the following, I will examine the feasibility of such action.

To create such a positive conditionality incentive, Member States would first need to come up with an enhanced cooperation that would be beneficial for the Member States with rule of law-conflicts. Such action is not proposed at this time. Hence, the following scenario, which can illustrate how conditionality could be used as a political tool, is again hypothetical.

The incentive could consist, for example, of a new fund, which possibly would entail cuts to existing funds to the extent admissible under Art. 174 ff. TFEU. While this would be in conflict with the budgetary unity (Art. 310 TFEU), exemptions from this are not unheard of, and Art. 332 TFEU shows clearly that enhanced cooperations was always foreseen to have such effects.[91] Such a new support programme could be linked with broad rule of law criteria by design. The criteria would not stop at a mere protection of the funds, but could entail ensuring an overall success of the measure e.g. by including criteria on justice systems or media freedom. This would make it likely for such proposals to fail in the Council. In consequence, the way for enhanced cooperation would be paved, and the criteria could then reappear as 'conditions' in the sense of Art. 328.1 TFEU. Since the implementing law is only passed at a later stage, the final design could be such that it would be interesting for initially opposed Member States to join after all. Given that the overall aim in doing all this would be to sustain the rule of law in the Member States in a broad sense, and not only when it comes to the specific programme, the measure would qualify as a conditionality.

In such a context—and again, this is only a hypothetical scenario that can be replaced by others—it would be crucial to understand what types of conditionalities are legally feasible.

The first problem in this context is the notion 'rule of law' itself. The term is difficult to grasp; its precise content is contested.[92] Nonetheless, there are a notable number of previous experiences with rule of law conditionality. Usually, this tool is applied in the EU's foreign action, for example, in EU accession procedures or trade agreements (see Art. 21 TEU). In these cases of application, the

[91] Becker, P. (2017), *The next multiannual financial framework (MFF) and the unity of EU budget: In-depth analysis*, Brussels, European Parliament p. 14.

[92] See e.g. CJEU C-156/21 (Hungary v Parliament and Council), ECLI:EU:C:2022:97, para. 199, 205 ff., 227 ff. Note, however, the attempt to give a working definition to the term in Art. 2 (a) of the Rule of Law Conditionality Regulation. Other instruments.

EU never managed to do so with an agreed definition or one cohesive framework describing its content. To give an example, in the accession procedures for countries aspiring to become Member States, the EU either refers to the notion of rule of law as such, without further defining it, as in Art. 2, 49 TEU and the Copenhagen Criteria[93] or refers to single aspects of the rule of law in a somewhat "impressionistic manner",[94] different from case to case. In the Rule of Law Conditionality Regulation, a somewhat mixed approach is used: On the one hand, Art. 2 (a) of the Regulation tries to give a relatively broad definition of the rule of law for the purposes of the regulation: According to this,

> *"'the rule of law' refers to the Union value enshrined in Article 2 TEU. It includes the principles of legality implying a transparent, accountable, democratic and pluralistic law-making process; legal certainty; prohibition of arbitrariness of the executive powers; effective judicial protection, including access to justice, by independent and impartial courts, also as regards fundamental rights; separation of powers; and non-discrimination and equality before the law. The rule of law shall be understood having regard to the other Union values and principles enshrined in Article 2 TEU."*

At the same time, Art. 3 of the Regulation sets out three examples of statal behaviour that may be indicative of a breach of the rule of law, namely:

> (a) *endangering the independence of the judiciary;*
> (b) *failing to prevent, correct or sanction arbitrary or unlawful decisions by public authorities, including by law-enforcement authorities, withholding financial and human resources affecting their proper functioning or failing to ensure the absence of conflicts of interest;*
> (c) *limiting the availability and effectiveness of legal remedies, including through restrictive procedural rules and lack of implementation of judgments, or limiting the effective investigation, prosecution or sanctioning of breaches of law.*

Regarding enhanced cooperation conditionalities, it must be borne in mind that, as set out above, conditions must be *objective, unambiguous*, and possess a *genuine link* to the nature or functioning of the enhanced cooperation project. The ambiguity in the context of the concept, even taking into account the latest attempts of

---

[93] http://europa.eu/rapid/press-release_DOC-93-3_en.htm?locale=en (accessed 27.07.2018), see also.
https://ec.europa.eu/neighbourhood-enlargement/policy/conditions-membership/chapters-of-the-acquis_en (accessed 27.07.2018), chapters 23 and 24.

[94] Pech, L., 'The EU as a global rule of law promoter: the consistency and effectiveness challenges', *Asia Europe Journal*, Vol. 14, No. 1, pp. 7–24 for examples, see COM (2014) 700 final on the enlargement strategy regarding the countries of the Western Balkans and Turkey.

giving shape to it, would make it difficult to determine when exactly this threshold would objectively be met. Furthermore, the definition in the Rule of Law Conditionality Regulation has been elaborated within the context of the regulation's scope, namely the protection of the Union budget, which may not suffice for a broader attempt to protect the rule of law. Furthermore, it would be difficult to imagine an enhanced cooperation subject that is genuinely linked in a sufficiently close way to the rule of law in all its breadth to justify such a thorough interference with one of the founding principles of enhanced cooperation. Therefore, in the specific case of enhanced cooperation conditionality, the usage of the broad term 'rule of law' as a criterion would hardly be allowed by the Treaty framework as described above.

However, in the broad discussion and the instances of practical application of rule of law conditionality, single notions that are part of the broad rule of law term are pointed out in an exemplifying manner and could possibly be used instead. As pointed out above, the Rule of Law Conditionality Regulation used the examples of an endangered independence of the judiciary, a failure to prevent, correct or sanction arbitrary or unlawful decisions by public authorities, or a limited availability and effectiveness of legal remedies. While of course being very important to the rule of law, these notions are similarly wide, and would result in the same problems as described before. However, other aspects discussed in the meantime address more specific aspects. For example, the first proposal for a Rule of Law Conditionality Regulation[95] named examples such as a functioning recovery of funds unduly paid (proposed Art. 3.1.(e)). At least to the extent that it is established on a European level that funds were paid unduly, the question of whether or not they were recovered in a specific period can objectively be answered with a yes or no. It can be argued that for the allocation of funds, it is crucial that they are recovered in the case of undue payment, providing for a genuine link to the nature of such a hypothetical enhanced cooperation. Nevertheless, the policy objective of demanding the recovery of unduly paid funds goes beyond the primary purpose of ensuring the recovery of funds in this specific tool, namely a functioning recovery of unduly paid funds in general, making this hypothetical condition a true conditionality. Hence, while it would be a very narrow precondition, factors like this could be used as conditionalities under Art. 328.1 TFEU.

Finally, Art. 3.1(f) of that same proposal mentions effective and timely cooperation with the European Anti-Fraud Office (OLAF) and the European Public

[95] COM(2018) 324 final.

Prosecutor's Office (EPPO) as criteria. While the clarity of these terms, effectiveness and timeliness, again pose difficulties, there is an interesting aspect to the EPPO in this context. The EPPO was itself established through an enhanced cooperation.[96] Non-participating Member States include Hungary and Poland, which at the time of EPPO's creation were at the centre of the EU rule of law dispute[97]—from the point of view of most of the EU Member States and institutions, it would surely would have been desirable for them to participate in the project,[98] a policy objective that would go beyond the necessities of the hypothetical enhanced cooperation. At the same time, since the purpose of the EPPO is to prosecute crimes against the EU budget, there is a close link to EU action with the involvement of funds, and it can be argued that the existence and jurisdiction of the EPPO will be beneficial to the functioning of such action. Moreover, participation or non-participation is as objective as a factor can possibly be. What must be kept in mind, though, is that at least according to the Treaty drafters, the principle of openness does not only cover the right to join an enhanced cooperation but also the right to refrain from doing so.[99] Therefore, when making the participation in one enhanced cooperation a condition for participating in another one,[100] it is crucial not to give the impression of not actually giving the non-participants a choice by attaching a too significant incentive to it. Rather, the genuine link between measure and incentive, i.e. the necessity of participating in the EPPO for the functioning of the enhanced cooperation, would have to be well-balanced with the importance of the incentive: the more necessary for the functioning the participation in EPPO is, the greater the incentive can be. Another issue in this context would be the question of how to treat the Member States with an AFSJ opt-out, which do not participate in EPPO by definition.

However, if these issues were taken into account, the requirement to be part of EPPO could legally be established as a 'condition' under Art. 328.1 TFEU

[96] Though based on the specific legal base for facilitated enhanced cooperation in Art. 86 TFEU; see Council Regulation (EU) 2017/1939.

[97] http://www.consilium.europa.eu/en/press/press-releases/2017/10/12/eppo-20-ms-confirms/ (accessed 12.7.2018).

[98] See also proposals of EU Commissioner Jourová, https://www.politico.eu/article/eus-jourova-wants-funds-linked-to-new-prosecutors-office/ (accessed 11.09.2018).

[99] CONV 723/03, p. 21.

[100] In more detail on this question, Böttner, R. (2021), *The Constitutional Framework for Enhanced Cooperation in EU law*, Nijhoff studies in European Union law, Leiden The Netherlands, Koninklijke Brill NV.

and constitute a type of positive rule of law-conditionality under enhanced cooperation.[101]

#### 4.2.3.4 Conclusions on Conditions and Conditionality

In conclusion, the possibility to include conditions in enhanced cooperation projects (Art. 328.1 TFEU) enables enhanced cooperation Member States to try and incentivise other Member States to follow a certain conduct. Since the conditions can be driven by policy objectives that go beyond the mere functioning of the enhanced cooperation, these can constitute true (positive) conditionalities where participation is beneficial for Member States. However, the nature of enhanced cooperation and the principle of openness constrain Member States in introducing such conditionalities: The "conditions" must be limited to preconditions that have a sufficiently close link to the nature or the functioning of the enhanced cooperation. Moreover, it must be possible to clearly answer whether or not such a precondition is fulfilled, without major involvement (and especially discretion) of any institution. Finally, it must be stressed that the conditions and conditionalities must follow the general rules of the enhanced cooperation mechanism (respect of rights and obligations of non-participating Member States, obligation to promote participation), as well as the general principles of European law such as sincere cooperation, proportionality, and the fundamental rights of individuals as laid down in general principles and the Charter.[102] These are factors that need to be taken extremely seriously when trying to introduce enhanced cooperation conditionality. Provided this is the case, enhanced cooperation conditionality could be a novel instrument in the EU's toolbox when addressing internal problems and crises.

## 4.3 Conclusions on the Principle of Openness

In conclusion, the analysis of the principle of openness revealed that there is more to it than a changed Commission proposal before, and a Commission decision confirming participation after the enhanced cooperation is "in progress". With the Request Phase, the Preparation Phase, the Authorisation Phase, the Legislative

[101] On problems arising when a proposal for an EU legal act refers to an enhanced cooperation: Peers, S. (2010), 'Divorce, European Style: The First Authorization of Enhanced Cooperation', *Eur. Const. L. Rev*, pp. 339–358, p. 351 f.

[102] Viţă, V. (2017), 'Revisiting the Dominant Discourse on Conditionality in the EU: The Case of EU Spending Conditionality', *Camb. Yearb. Eur. Legal Stud.*, Vol. 19, pp. 116–143, p. 138.

Phase, and the Implementation Phase, there are five distinct phases which have different legal and political implications when states are interested in joining an enhanced cooperation.

Moreover, a valid argument can be made that enhanced cooperation is limited by the existence of an unwritten requirement of being sincerely willing to cooperate. Looking at the enhanced cooperation practice, one can see that the Commission is in agreement with this finding and conducts a benefit assessment before confirming the participation of interested Member States in an enhanced cooperation. The Commission could use the sincere willingness requirement to refrain from confirming the participation of a Member State or even declare the participation of a Member invalid *ex ante* (depending on the phase in which the Member State in question joined, this task might also be up to the Council).

And finally, the possibility to bind participation in an enhanced cooperation to the fulfilment of certain conditions according to Art. 328.1 TFEU could, in light of the challenges the EU is facing, be wakened from the deep sleep it has been in since the introduction of this possibility in 2007. If so, the conditions could not only be limited to mere criteria in the narrower sense but could, under some circumstances, amount to conditionalities. This would largely influence the nature of future enhanced cooperations and their usage. Yet it would not generally be excluded by the Treaties.

Despite these possibilities, the principle of openness stays above all a guarantor of the enhanced cooperation's nature as a tool for multi-speed integration, allowing for all Member States to join if interested. This can also be derived from the numbers presented above (Table 4.2): Member States joined ongoing enhanced cooperation projects on a total of 36 occasions, 15 of which happened significantly (>6 months) after the initiation of the procedure.

Hence, it can be said the principle of openness is successfully fulfilling its task as a one-way valve into enhanced cooperation.

# 5 Making Differentiated Integration Fit for the Future—"Incentivised Cooperation" as a Future Variant in the Treaties

Whenever EU Member States (MS) find themselves in difficulties to solve a controversial issue, and especially when unanimity among Member States is needed for decisions to be taken in the Council, it is almost inevitable that differentiation comes up as a proposed solution to the political logjam. This happens in the political sphere, but even more so in the public discourse. It is particularly the case in policy fields that have seen year-long blockades, such as climate and asylum policy, or the rule of law. Although mechanisms for introducing differentiated EU law exist, we have not seen such initiatives in the most controversial topics; rather, we have witnessed a tendency towards bare-minimum agreements or voluntary pledges which cannot be enforced (see Chap. 2). Why is this the case and what could be done about it?

In order to explore these questions, the first step in this chapter will be to recapitulate the findings on the factors that lead to the use of enhanced cooperation from earlier in this thesis. Having recalled them, a proposal for a concise Treaty amendment that could help solving the matter will be presented. This proposal is based on an alteration of political incentive structures. Finally, this proposal will be applied to one of the most controversial fields in EU policy making over the last years, namely asylum politics. This aims exemplify how the proposed 'incentivised cooperation' would fit into the picture of EU policy, notorious political problems, and differentiated solutions.


J. Graf von Luckner, *Enhanced Cooperation Revisited*,
https://doi.org/10.1007/978-3-658-51063-3_5

## 5.1 Concepts

### 5.1.1 Theoretical frameworks on the occurrence of differentiation

As was laid out in detail in Chap. 2, the occurrence of differentiation in general, and enhanced cooperation in particular, has been the subject of much scholarly attention[1] which produced different approaches to an explanation of when Member States resort to it and when they refrain. The following is aimed to recapitulate these findings made above, for all details consider Chap. 2.

A first approach studying why enhanced cooperation occurs focusses on the impact of *externalities* on the occurrence of enhanced cooperation.[2] Externalities are the effects that the enhanced cooperation would have on potential non-participants. According to this approach, neutral external effects of a project that Member States have fundamentally different opinions on make enhanced cooperation most likely, mirroring a spirit of live and let live among Member States. If, however, a project is set to have negative external effects, outsiders will try to prevent the project altogether. If that is not possible—which enhanced cooperation is precisely made for—outsiders will rather join a project than stay outside and face the costs, preventing enhanced cooperation from occurring, according to this theory. The European Positive external effects, equally, make it less likely that enhanced cooperation is resorted to. In this scenario, however, it is the participants who favour not to use enhanced cooperation, as they would have to bear the costs of the project whereas outsiders would get free benefits from it ("free-riding"). In this case, according to this theory, states will only resort to enhanced cooperation if their own benefits outweigh the costs of the freeriding outsiders.

A second approach assessed the occurrence of enhanced cooperation in the light of the "public goods theory".[3] According to this approach, states' policy decisions regarding differentiated integration (and specifically enhanced cooperation) depends largely on the character of the respective policy area. It is

---

[1] See Leruth, B., Gänzle, S., Trondal, J. (2019), 'Exploring Differentiated Disintegration in a Post-Brexit European Union', *JCMS: Journal of Common Market Studies*, Vol. 57, No. 5, pp. 1013–1030 for a "state of the art review of existing literature on differentiation".

[2] Kroll, D. A., Leuffen, D. (2015), 'Enhanced cooperation in practice. An analysis of differentiated integration in EU secondary law', *Journal of European Public Policy*, Vol. 22, No. 3, pp. 353–373.

[3] Milner, F., Kölliker, A. (1999), How to Make Use of Closer Cooperation?, Working Paper; further developed in Kölliker, A. (2001), 'Bringing together or driving apart the union? Towards a theory of differentiated integration'.

characterised by two sets of factors, namely the *excludability* of the good "produced" by a policy and its *rivalry in consumption.* The *excludability* measures whether non-participants can be excluded from the benefits of a specific good. To give examples, excludability is high for a highway bridge (non-participants can be forbidden to use it), but low for a radio broadcast (the signal can hardly be stopped from single recipients in its range). Accordingly, the *excludability* also measures the potential for free-riding by non-participants, i.e. the possibility to benefit from a good without participating in the sharing of its costs. *Rivalry in consumption* describes the effect that additional users of a good have on the good's benefits. Consumption can be *rival, neutral* or *complementary. Rival consumption* means that additional consumers lead to a decrease of the benefit; figuratively speaking, the benefit has to be shared. A classic example of this is a drink: an additional user (drinker) leads to lower benefit (less to drink) for the initial user *Neutral consumption* means that the benefit of the good stays the same even if further users benefit from it, such as a user of a radio broadcast is not affected by additional listeners of said programme. Finally, *complementary consumption* leads to an increase of the benefits, as for example a language becomes more useful the more people speak it.[4] This framework is used to determine the *centripetal effect* of a policy if introduced in a differentiated manner. The stronger the *centripetal effect*, the more likely it is that an initial non-participant joins the ongoing cooperation. This, according to the theory, can be used as an indicator to predict whether Member States are ready to start a project through enhanced cooperation. The *centripetal effect* is higher the higher the excludability (i.e. the harder it is for non-participants to free-ride) and the lower rivalry in consumption (as especially complementary consumption makes cooperating attractive per se).

In Chap. 2, in addition to externalities and public goods theory, *path dependency* is used to complete the framework. However, path dependency, as used there, helps to identify where enhanced cooperation could occur, not where it will not occur. Thus, it cannot serve as a basis for developing new models making differentiated integration more likely. For this reason, it is omitted in this chapter.

[4] Milner, F., Kölliker, A. (1999), How to Make Use of Closer Cooperation?, Working Paper; Kölliker, A. (2001), 'Bringing together or driving apart the union? Towards a theory of differentiated integration'.

### 5.1.2 Conclusion: A Theoretical Framework

Having laid out the theoretical considerations above, the following aspects of a framework for predicting the attractiveness for Member States of resorting to enhanced cooperations in controversial policy fields emerge:

If the public good that is supposed to be regulated by Member States is *complimentary in consumption* (more users lead to an increased benefit of a project) or at least *neutral* (more users leave the benefit unaffected), that makes cooperating even if not all Member States join more attractive, as does the possibility to exclude non-participants from the benefits of a project (*excludability*), preventing free-riding. This is the case if a project has neutral or negative external effects. That being said, negative external effects (*externalities*) can make an enhanced cooperation less likely, as non-participants in this case will try to prevent an enhanced cooperation. Where they cannot do so, they are more likely to participate in a project they are unhappy with, effectively preventing enhanced cooperation.

This is the framework that will be referred back to in the following.

## 5.2 Incentivised Cooperation

### 5.2.1 Introduction

The following argument is based on the assumption, as developed elsewhere in this thesis, that the enhanced cooperation mechanism is not as rigid as many may think. It is, in fact, a quite flexible flexibility instrument, allowing for action in a variety of fields and in a variety of ways. If it has not been the major disrupting instrument of European politics that some have envisioned it as, this is due to *political* rather than *legal* reasons. One the one hand, there is the political strive towards unity. Differentiation in general, but even more so differentiation within the EU legal framework is treated as a *very last resort*. This *very* last resort attitude goes far beyond the obstacles caused by the legal last resort principle (see Chap. 3). On the other hand—and this may just be the more relevant reservation—enhanced cooperation in the main fields of conflict, the real political battle fields, has been halted due to political incentive structures as described above.[5]

[5] Agreeing, though with a different proposal: Gerards, C., Wessels, W. (2019), Enhancing 'Enhanced Cooperation': constraints and opportunities of an inflexible flexibility clause, CEPOB, Bruges.

In many of these fields, prime examples are environment and migration/asylum policy, little can be 'gained' in the short-term by pursing action, be it joint or unilateral. Rather, Member State action is triggered largely by a shared sense of responsibility and a commitment to human rights etc. In this context, enhanced cooperation is an utterly unattractive tool because it would let unwilling states off the hook, and, even more importantly, allow them to free-ride on the cooperative states' efforts.

### 5.2.2 The Concept of the Proposed Incentivised Cooperation

Thus, if enhanced cooperation was envisioned to have a more relevant role in disputed areas, its incentive structure would have to be overhauled. This would only be possibly by way of a Treaty change, which, for the sake of the argument, shall be deemed politically feasible in the following.

This proposal explicitly does not entail that enhanced cooperation as it is should be abolished or altered altogether in future. As argued above, the enhanced cooperation mechanism does allow for flexibility just as envisioned. It did, in the past, allow for progress in single areas where unanimity and uniformity simply could not be attained—see in particular the examples in family law. Here especially, the results of enhanced cooperation help millions of international couples, albeit not all of the international couples in the EU. Moreover, the mere existence of the enhanced cooperation mechanism as it is has helped to reach important compromises by serving as "veto-buster"[6]—a prime example is the European Arrest Warrant, a true milestone in EU procedural criminal law. The procedural framework of the enhanced cooperation mechanism is there for a reason, and it has not failed altogether.

Instead, the proposal is to add to the Treaty framework single instances of 'incentivised enhanced cooperation' or in short: 'incentivised cooperation'. Just like the 'facilitated enhanced cooperation' framework, 'incentivised cooperation' should, according to this vision, be included in the Treaties in single policy areas and single articles conferring competences on the EU. Just like facilitated enhanced cooperation, incentivised cooperation should alter the enhanced cooperation legal framework of Art. 326 ff. TFEU. However, where facilitated

[6] Thym, D. (2005), 'United in Diversity: The Integration of Enhanced Cooperation into the European Constitutional Order', *GLJ*, pp. 1731–1747.

enhanced cooperation amends and simplifies the authorisation procedure for interested states, incentivised cooperation would change the incentive structure of the enhanced cooperation mechanism. In practice, this would probably—though not necessarily—mean that the costs for the implementation of certain policies would directly or indirectly be covered by the EU budget.

It may be argued that addressing the problems in areas such as the EU asylum policy with financial incentives is only a second-best alternative. In fact, the financial costs are a relevant factor, but probably not the main reason for the political blockades that have been seen in recent years. However, given that the argument in this chapter is based on an analysis of costs and benefits, a joint carrying of the *pecuniary* costs by all states jointly is quite simply a comparatively easy avenue to amend those incentive structures on the cost side. Beyond this, joint carrying of the financial costs of enhanced cooperation is—as will be shown below—not totally unknown to the enhanced cooperation framework. Moreover, particularly when it comes to the incentive structures as described above, the symbolic value of keeping other Member States from free-riding is immense. This, at least, would be avoided: One could argue that by compensating pecuniary costs, but not practical efforts and political costs, a financial compensation mechanism would turn *free-riding* of non-participants into *cheap-riding*, which is at least a notable difference in favour of the participants.

This is not to say, however, that problems in the EU are primarily to be solved with the help of money, or that another incentive could not be conceived.

Legally, the incentivised cooperation would alter the enhanced cooperation framework in particular by amending, in single instances, the rule foreseen in Art. 332 TFEU, which regulates the bearing of costs caused by an enhanced cooperation: According to this, expenditure arising from the implementation of an enhanced cooperation shall be borne by the participating Member States, with the exception of administrative costs arising for the institutions (these costs are covered by the EU as a whole). In the context of incentivised cooperation, this general rule would be replaced in single instances, and not the participating Member States, but the EU as a whole would cover costs arising from participating (whereas for the general enhanced cooperation mechanism, the rule would remain untouched). In consequence, the costs would be borne by the EU budget. As regards the detailed instrument, it is of course conceivable to combine elements of facilitated and incentivised cooperation to make the instrument even more likely to be used in practice. For this reason, there is not one but several different possibilities of what an incentivised cooperation could look like.

### 5.2.3 Legal Technique and Institutional Setup

#### 5.2.3.1 Modifying the Enhanced Cooperation Procedure

As explained above, the proposed incentivised cooperation mechanism builds on the example of the 'facilitated enhanced cooperation' as present in Art. 82–87 TFEU. Like the proposed incentivised cooperation mechanism, facilitated enhanced cooperation modifies the regular enhanced cooperation mechanism by replacing parts of its legal framework, as will be shown in the following. For this reason, Art. 82, 83, 86, 87 TFEU may serve as real-life models for the proposed incentivised cooperation mechanism. It should be noted that the existence of the present facilitated enhanced cooperation clauses can be explained mainly by the fact that the policy areas they can be found in one belonged to the "Third Pillar" in pre-Lisbon EU-law. This Third Pillar, which circled around questions of justice and home affairs, was characterised by being largely intergovernmental as opposed to the largely supranational first pillar, which entailed matters like customs and the internal market. It is this specific, intergovernmental background that paved the way for the inclusion of the facilitated enhanced cooperation mechanisms, which, in each case, gives Member States a particularly prominent role.[7] However, given the pillar structure seized to exist and the former third pillar was introduced into what has become the single body of EU law, there is no reason excluding the lessons learned from Articles 82–87 TFEU from being applied in other areas.

The facilitated enhanced cooperation mechanism exists in two varieties: One in the cases where the main legal basis foresees qualified majority decisions in the Council (Art. 82, 83 TFEU), and one in cases of unanimous decision-making in the Council (Art. 86, 87 TFEU). Although being quite similar, the two serve quite different purposes, which is also shown in the procedure that leads to their application. The two will therefore be discussed separately.

#### 5.2.3.2 Emergency Brake (Articles 82, 83 TFEU)

Art. 82 and 83 TFEU concern criminal law. Art. 82.2 TFEU, which is the only part of Art. 82 TFEU subject to facilitated enhanced cooperation, allows the EU to set minimum procedural rules, e.g. on the admissibility of evidence or the rights of victims and the accused in criminal procedures. Art. 83 TFEU

---

[7] I would like to particularly thank Prof. Dr. Hermann-Josef Blanke for pointing out this aspect. It was the last bit of feedback Prof. Blanke offered on this thesis before unexpectedly passing away in the beginning of 2022.

addresses substantive criminal law and enables the Union to set minimum standards with respect to the definition of criminal offences and sanctions of some serious crimes.

In the case of Art. 82.2, 83 TFEU, which require a qualified majority in the Council for legislation to pass, any Member State opposing a piece of legislation may refer it to the European Council if it "considers that a draft directive [...] would affect fundamental aspects of its criminal justice system", (Art. 82.3, 83.3 TFEU). Doing so effectively brings the procedure to a temporary halt, which is why it is also referred to as an "emergency brake" procedure.[8] Hence, the possibility of referring a file to the European Council and thus suspending the legislative procedure is primarily a mechanism for opposing states, which protects them from being outvoted. The mechanism is therefore most likely to be applied if the necessary qualified majority is present in the Council.

This power of opposing Member States is, however, counterbalanced: If it is not possible to find a solution on the Heads of State or Government-level within four months, a group of at least nine Member States may notify the European Parliament, the Council and the Commission of their interest to proceed using enhanced cooperation. In that case, the authorization "shall be deemed to be granted" (Art. 82.3 (2) TFEU, Art. 83.3 (2) TFEU). In providing this, the facilitated enhanced cooperation clause modifies the enhanced cooperation legal framework. For regular enhanced cooperation procedures, a *request* by at least nine Member States to launch an enhanced cooperation leads to the Commission evaluating the possibility of using enhanced cooperation. The Commission may or may not submit a proposal for a decision authorizing enhanced cooperation to the Council. If a proposal is submitted, it needs the consent of the European Parliament and qualified majority in the Council to pass (Art. 329.1 TFEU). Moreover, the Council may authorise enhanced cooperation only "as a last resort, when it has established that the objectives of such cooperation cannot be attained within a reasonable period by the Union as a whole" (Art. 20.2 TEU). All of these legal requirements, both procedural and substantive, are skipped by the facilitated enhanced cooperation. The procedure in Art. 82.3, 83.3 TFEU instead requires a mere *declaration* by nine interested Member States after the emergency brake has been pulled by an opposing Member State and the European Council has not been able to find a solution within four months. Without any further checks by the Commission or votes in the Parliament or Council, the enhanced cooperation is authorised and from then on blends into the regular procedure as foreseen in

[8] See e.g. Pasquale, P. de, Pesce, C. (2021), 'Art. 82 TFEU' in: Blanke, H.-J., Mangiameli, S. (eds.), *Treaty on the Functioning of the European Union—A Commentary.*

Art. 20 TEU, Art. 326 ff. TFEU. The facilitated enhanced cooperation clauses in Art. 82.3, 83.3 TFEU therefore take the place of the regular authorization mechanism in Art. 329.1 TFEU.

In sum, the facilitated enhanced cooperation clauses in Art. 82, 83 TFEU have a dual effect: On the one hand, they allow opposing Member States to suspend a procedure in which they could eventually be outvoted. Following this, even if the proposal is taken further and eventually adopted, they are no longer part of it. At the same time, it allows interested Member States to proceed swiftly with enhanced cooperation if there are fundamentally diverging opinions. This condition is, in the case of Art. 82, 83 TFEU, determined by the opposing Member States, which by triggering the emergency brake procedure effectively open a door out of the project for themselves.

#### 5.2.3.3 Brake and Accelerator (Articles 86, 87 TFEU)

Art. 86 TFEU allows the EU to establish a European Public Prosecutor's Office (EPPO), Art. 87 TFEU deals with establishing police cooperation between the Member States. The two articles are the only other norms in the Treaties containing a facilitated enhanced cooperation clause. Like Art. 82, 83 TFEU, they can only be triggered after a draft has been referred to the European Council, and the latter has not managed to find a compromise within four months. However, the process that leads to the reference to the European Council diverges from that in Art. 82, 83 TFEU.

Crucially, different from Art. 82, 83 TFEU, the Council may pass measures based on Art. 86, 87 TFEU only acting unanimously. For this reason, an emergency brake procedure protecting opposing Member States from the results of a majority vote is not required. Opposing Member States cannot be bound against their will by acts based on any of the two legal bases. For this reason, the process leading to a facilitated enhanced cooperation is not triggered by the opposing, but by the Member States interested in a measure. The only substantive condition for this is the "absence of unanimity in the Council" (Art. 86.1 (2) TFEU, Art. 87.3 (2) TFEU). In contrast to Art. 82, 83 TFEU, a group of at least nine Member States is required already at this stage. This can be interpreted as a sign showing that the procedure is in fact tailored for a swift action by way of enhanced cooperation, given that the same number of states is required to launch enhanced cooperation. This notwithstanding, the Council legal service, in a contribution drafted in the process leading to the adoption of the EPPO, took the view that interested Member States must take into account the general principles of enhanced cooperation. Therefore, a procedure "inclined in principle towards launching reinforced [sic] cooperation from the outset" would not be admissible if it assumed "without even opening negotiations, that unanimity was not possible". Consequently, the "Council must be able to demonstrate that it has worked actively to seek a generally, or at least broadly, acceptable solution" before proceeding with enhanced cooperation, according to the Council legal service.[9] Yet, even if one assumes that such an unwritten procedural hurdle exists, the inclination of the clauses in Art. 86.1 (2) TFEU, Art. 87.3 (2) TFEU towards launching enhanced cooperation is hardly disputable in light of the number of nine Member States needed to launch the procedure.

In the absence of unanimity, nine Member States may refer the draft to the European Council according to the so-called "brake/accelerator procedure".[10] If this avenue is chosen, the legislative procedure is halted for up to four months (the "brake" part). If, within this timeframe, no solution agreeable to all Member States can be found in the European Council, nine Member States may address the European Parliament, the Council and the Commission and notify their interest in launching an enhanced cooperation. From that point on, the procedure equals that laid down in Art. 82, 83 TFEU. After notifying the interest to launch enhanced cooperation, enhanced cooperation shall be "be deemed to be granted" without any further action or consent needed by the Commission, Council, or Parliament ("accelerator"). Thus, once again, the facilitated enhanced cooperation clause modifies the enhanced cooperation legal framework in that it replaces the regular authorization mechanism foreseen in Art. 329.1 TFEU by a quicker and more autonomous procedure.

In sum, the "brake/accelerator procedure" foreseen in Art. 87, 87 TFEU protects first and foremost the interests of Member States wanting a specific policy which is foreseen in one of the two legal bases. While their unanimity requirements *prima facie* gives veto powers to uninterested states, the facilitated enhanced cooperation clause gives interested states a possibility to deviate from an unpromising legislative procedure and facilitates their access to enhanced cooperation on their own terms.

### 5.2.3.4 Lessons for Incentivised Cooperation

Both types of facilitated enhanced cooperation clauses have in common that they replace parts of the enhanced cooperation legal framework in order to achieve the desired policy objective, namely a facilitated access to enhanced cooperation, and consequently an increased likelihood of the respective policy measures being implemented. However, they differ in design in so far as they are used in opposing

---

[9] Council, Legal Service Contribution, Doc. 6267/14, para 13, 14.

[10] Council, Legal Service Contribution, Doc. 6267/14, para 2.

scenarios, namely the protection of interested and uninterested states. Both are carefully designed to defuse problems in their respective legal context and provide counterweights to the voting arrangements in the Council, which showcases the importance of a contextualised design of modified enhanced cooperation clauses.

In both types of facilitated enhanced cooperation clauses, the European Council plays a leading role in the process leading up to enhanced cooperation. In the case of the proposed incentivised cooperation, both scenarios as well as a new mechanism without an involvement of the European Council are conceivable. The detour via the European Council could prove to be a way to put the enhanced cooperation on a sound political foundation as a prior consultation on all political levels is guaranteed. On the other hand, in fields with notorious difficulties in finding political compromises and accordingly a known need to create modified incentive structures, it can also be argued that the political consultation already takes place beforehand, in the context of a Treaty change introducing such a mechanism. Whether or not an involvement is desirable should, consequently, be carefully balanced in light of the political context of the policy field addressed.

As regards the institutional setup, the facilitated enhanced cooperation in Art. 82–87 TFEU is a matter of only the Council and the European Council. Both the Commission and the EP are merely notified of the decision to proceed with enhanced cooperation. From a democratic point of view, this is a questionable approach. However, for a (financially) incentivised enhanced cooperation, this approach would be even more problematic given the EP's shared responsibility for the EU budget. It would therefore be desirable to ensure a full EP involvement. Moreover, a Commission involvement could ensure that the interests of the EU as a whole are duly taken into account and is therefore also advisable for a newly formed incentivised cooperation. Consequently, the involvement of the other EU institutions should go beyond what is present in the facilitated enhanced cooperation clauses to put the politically sensitive procedure on the firm foundation of a sound political backing.

#### 5.2.3.5 Legal Technique for Financing Incentivised Cooperation

It was pointed out above that an incentivised cooperation procedure would build on the legal framework on expenditure caused by enhanced cooperation, laid down in Art. 332 TFEU. According to this provision, the costs caused by an enhanced cooperation are in principle borne by the participating Member States only. The general idea of the proposed incentivised cooperation mechanism is therefore to follow the example of the facilitated enhanced cooperation clauses and replace the general rule in Art. 332 TFEU for incentivised cooperations.

In order to explore how exactly this could be implemented, it is firstly relevant to note that Art. 332 TFEU is not an exception to Art. 310 TFEU, which lays down the principle of unity of the EU budget. According to this principle, all items of revenue and expenditure of the EU shall be shown in the budget.[11] Consequently, costs arising from an enhanced cooperation, which is by definition an EU project after all, are generally expected to appear in the common budget (though other constructions are not impossible).[12] The budget then requires a compensation mechanism to ensure that the costs are ultimately borne only the participating Member States.[13] This method was put to use in the only relevant case of an enhanced cooperation causing costs, the EPPO (Art. 91.3 (a), 91.7–8 Regulation 2017/1939 on the EPPO). However, the EU has further been using it for years in the case of the AFSJ opt-outs of Ireland and Denmark, marking it as a well-established method in differentiated policy fields.[14] Consequently, the main change caused by an incentivised cooperation in comparison with the regular enhanced cooperation mechanism would be that the costs are *not* adjusted in order to exclude the non-participants. In consequence, the regular procedure for the bearing of costs caused by EU policies would apply: The costs would remain in the EU budget, and without a compensation mechanism be borne by all Member States jointly, depending on their respective share of the budget.

[11] Martenczuk, B. (2013), 'Enhanced Cooperation: The Practice of Ad Hoc Differentiation in the EU since the Lisbon Treaty', *StudDipl*, pp. 83–100.

[12] It has to be noted, however, that this is not generally the case for costs arising for and within Member States. These costs are usually covered on 'costs lie where they fall' basis, meaning that each Member State covers the arising costs itself, assuming that they will even out. This would not, of course, work in the case of incentivized cooperation. Therefore, either the enhanced cooperation would have to entail sponsoring of efforts from the beginning, or actual costs would have to be charged to the EU by the participating Member States. The latter would not, however, be a total novelty: EPPO regulation foresees a possibility for the EPPO to cover particularly costly Member State operations (see recital 112 EPPO Regulation). Cf. Böttner, R. (2021), *The Constitutional Framework for Enhanced Cooperation in EU law*, Nijhoff studies in European Union law, Leiden The Netherlands, Koninklijke Brill NV.

[13] Böttner, R. (2021), *The Constitutional Framework for Enhanced Cooperation in EU law*, Nijhoff studies in European Union law, Leiden The Netherlands, Koninklijke Brill NV; diverging opinion: Becker, U. (2015), 'Artikel 332 AEUV' in: Groeben, H. v. d., Schwarze, J., Hatje, A. (eds.), *Europäisches Unionsrecht,* Baden-Baden, Nomos; see also Lasok, P. (2021), 'Article 299 TFEU' in: Blanke, H.-J., Mangiameli, S. (eds.), *Treaty on the Functioning of the European Union—A Commentary* [forthcoming].

[14] Böttner, R. (2021), *The Constitutional Framework for Enhanced Cooperation in EU law*, Nijhoff studies in European Union law, Leiden The Netherlands, Koninklijke Brill NV.

Crucially, even such a modification would not per se be a novelty in EU law. Art. 332 TFEU on the financing of enhanced cooperations does not only contain the basic rule described above, but also entails an exception to the rule: By a unanimous decision of all Council members, i.e. participants and non-participants, and after consulting the EP, the Council may decide to deviate from the regular financing rule. While not explicitly spelled out, this envisions that rather than only participants, all Member States would pay for the costs of an enhanced cooperation. Thus, although financing the costs of an enhanced cooperation by the Union as a whole as opposed to only by the participants may not be the rule, it is not unknown to the legal framework on enhanced cooperation either.[15] For this reason, the proposed incentivised cooperation framework would not replace the entirety of the rule foreseen in Art. 332 TFEU. In fact, incentivised cooperation clauses would merely alter the decision-making process for decisions to deviate from the regular Art. 332 TFEU procedure. A decision that currently requires unanimous voting in the Council with consultation of the EP would then, in the context of selected legal bases, be taken by a smaller Council majority,[16] such as a qualified majority, ideally with the consent of the Parliament and on a Commission proposal. As such, the proposed incentivised enhanced cooperation mechanism would, in fact, be much less intrusive on the regular enhanced cooperation framework than facilitated enhanced cooperation currently is.

#### 5.2.3.6 Treaty Revision

Introducing an incentivised enhanced cooperation clause to a single or several TFEU provisions containing legal bases for legislation would inevitably require a treaty revision, which is considered to be highly difficult in the current political environment. However, the Treaties provide an ordinary (Art. 48.3–5 TEU) and a simplified revision procedure (Art. 48.6 TEU). While still requiring consent and ratification by all Member States, the simplified procedure saves some complicated and time-consuming procedural steps such as convoking a Convention and/or a separate conference of representatives of the governments of the Member

[15] Böttner, R. (2021), *The Constitutional Framework for Enhanced Cooperation in EU law*, Nijhoff studies in European Union law, Leiden The Netherlands, Koninklijke Brill NV; slightly different reading: Becker, U. (2015), 'Artikel 332 AEUV' in: Groeben, H. v. d., Schwarze, J., Hatje, A. (eds.), *Europäisches Unionsrecht,* Baden-Baden, Nomos.

[16] It would even be conceivable that a unanimous or majority vote of the *participating* Member States sufficed to trigger the effect of the decision foreseen in Art. 332 TFEU, depending on how it is introduced in the Treaties.

States, whose consent is required.[17] The scope of the simplified revision procedure is limited to revisions of Part Three of the TFEU (Art. 48.6 (1) TEU). Simplified revision procedures may not lead to expanding the Union's competences (Art. 48.6 (3) TEU). Part Three entitled "Union Policies and Internal Actions", which the simplified procedure is limited to, contains a vast number of legal bases on the internal market, AFSJ, competition, social policy, etc. Given this, it is rather likely that a potentially desired incentivised cooperation would indeed fall within this part of the TFEU. Furthermore, an incentivised cooperation would merely amend a procedural rule usually foreseen in Art. 332 TFEU and therefore explicitly not expand any EU competences. It follows from this that introducing incentivised enhanced cooperation would be an optimal fit for the use of the simplified revision procedure.

Yet another way to introduce an incentivised enhanced cooperation clause might be the so-called *passerelle* clause in Art. 48.7 (1) TEU. This provision allows the European Council to authorise the Council to move from unanimous decision-making to qualified majority voting "in a given area or case". A decision to that effect must be taken unanimously by the European Council after obtaining the consent of the parliament and every national parliament has a right to veto it (Art. 48.7 (3–4) TEU).[18] As was described above, the legal technique to introduce an incentivised cooperation clause would be to amend the procedure foreseen in Art. 332 TFEU by which the Council may decide that the expenditure caused by an enhanced cooperation is not borne only by the participants. This decision is usually taken by a unanimous Council vote. It would, therefore, be conceivable to pass a decision based on Art. 48.7 (1) TEU to the effect that the Council may take the decision under Art. 332 TFEU by qualified majority in the area of enhanced cooperations based on the TFEU article in question.[19] This approach would have the benefit of an even simpler procedure than the simplified treaty

[17] Denza, E. (2013), 'Art. 48 TEU' in: Blanke, H.-J., Mangiameli, S. (eds.), *The Treaty on European Union (TEU): A commentary,* Berlin, Springer.

[18] Böttner, R. (2016), 'The Treaty Amendment Procedures and the Relationship between Article 31(3) TEU and the General Bridging Clause of Article 48(7) TEU', *European Constitutional Law Review,* Vol. 12, No. 03, pp. 499–519; Böttner, R. (2017), 'Brückenklauseln im europäischen Verfassungsrecht', *EuR,* Vol. 52, No. 3, pp. 381–400.

[19] Some areas are excluded from the use of the *passerelle* clause. These are named in Art. 48.7 (1) *in fine* TEU ("decisions with military implications or those in the area of defence") and Art. 353 TFEU.

revision.[20] The result would not be an incentivised cooperation *clause*, as the new voting mechanism would not be laid down directly in the TFEU, but have the same effect.

However, introducing incentivised cooperation by way of a *passarelle* clause would mean that the European Parliament would merely be consulted in the matter of introducing incentivised cooperation, which, as explained above, would be democratically problematic considering the budgetary responsibility of the Parliament. Furthermore, the Commission would not play a role in the procedure and could consequently not act as a guardian of the interests of the EU as a whole. In light of these arguments, as well as an increased level of transparency and democratic legitimation, a Treaty amendment by way of the simplified Treaty revision procedure might be a preferable approach.

### 5.2.4 Practical Example: Asylum Policy

#### 5.2.4.1 Asylum Policy and Enhanced Cooperation

In conclusion of the proposal on a new incentivised enhanced cooperation, the idea will in the following be placed in the context of a real-life policy field. Incentivised cooperation is proposed to break deadlocks in particularly disputed policy fields, in which enhanced cooperation has deliberately not been used (and thus a problematic incentive structure is likely to be part of the problem). For a long period, asylum policy seemed virtually irreformable and therefore appeared to be an obvious example of such a field. The following remarks, explaining the practical works of a proposed incentivised cooperation, were largely drafted under this hypothesis. This notwithstanding, in the end of 2023, the EU institutions agreed on a new Asylum Pact, in which a compromise was indeed found, and the institutions pledged to reform asylum policy promptly.[21] However, even though a political progress now seems certain, the year-long dispute continues to show the difficulties in governing this notoriously controversial policy field and it seems unlikely that the recent compromise will settle all disputed in the area once and for good. For this reason, asylum policy continues to be an interesting case study for a hypothetical incentivised cooperation mechanism.

---

[20] Note, however, that national constitutions may nevertheless require a full national ratification, which may entail amending the national constitutions; see e.g. BVerfG, 2 BvE 2/08 et al. (*Lissabon*), para. 315 ff., esp. 319.

[21] https://www.consilium.europa.eu/en/press/press-releases/2023/12/20/the-council-and-the-european-parliament-reach-breakthrough-in-reform-of-eu-asylum-and-migration-system/ (last access 26 January 2024).

The EU Common Asylum Policy was created in 2003 and a number of changes were introduced around 2013. However, especially the massive influx of asylum seeker in 2015 showed that the system was not fit for purpose. Among other issues, Member States with external borders easily got overburdened, relocation or other kinds of burden-sharing within the EU hardly worked. Prior to the recent compromise, which took years to find, it was proposed and demanded both in the European Parliament[22] and in academia[23] to make use of enhanced cooperation in order to overcome some of the salient issues at least with a couple of participating Member States. However, the incentive structures present in asylum policy predicted that it would not, in fact, be used under the current framework and it is therefore unsurprising that the compromise found eventually was one comprising the EU as whole and not using enhanced cooperation:

From an externalities point of view, enhanced cooperation—concerning virtually any kind of action—in asylum policy would have positive effects on outsiders—financial and potentially political costs arising from a stronger engagement with asylum seekers would be borne by the participants, the non-participants would benefit from fewer tasks to be fulfilled in that context. According to the theory laid out above, the positive externalities and thus the possibility for non-participants to free-ride keeps interested states from committing to action; this is exactly what he have seen in practice: if Member States act beyond their EU law obligations, they do so on a voluntary and informal basis.

Public goods theory confirms this finding: The benefits arising from cooperation in the area of asylum—be it that migrants are being helped, human rights are being respected or that states are faced with less pressure on their borders and asylum systems—are non-excludable between Member States. In the EU asylum system, the states benefit as a whole when progress is made, which again means that free-riding is possible if single states stay out. As regards the rivalry in consumption, additional users benefitting from the results of action in asylum policy do not affect the benefit for the participants, it is therefore neutral

---

[22] Motion for a Resolution to wind up the debate on the statements by the Council and the Commission pursuant to Rule 123(2) of the Rules of Procedure on migration and the situation of refugees (2015/2833(RSP)), B8–0835/2015, http://www.europarl.europa.eu/doceo/document/B-8-2015-0835_EN.html (accessed 12/12/2019).

[23] Kreilinger, V., Jacques Delors Institut Berlin (2015), *Proposal to use Enhanced Cooperation in the Refugee Crisis*, available at: www.delorsinstitut.de/en/publications/topics/institutions-and-democracy/proposal-to-use-enhanced-cooperation-in-the-refugee-crisis/; Jungfleisch, J. (2019), 'Verstärkte Zusammenarbeit im Rahmen der Flüchtlingspolitik: Ein Ausweg aus der Krise oder die endgültige Aufgabe eines einheitlichen Europas?' in: Kopetzki, M., Lanser, C., Leitner, P. (eds.), *Autoritäres vs liberales Europa: Tagung Junger Europarechtler*innen, Band 2, Wien 2019,* Wien, Jan Sramek Verlag.

in consumption. This is not as a strong an indicator against enhanced cooperation as rival consumption would be, but neither an indicator favouring enhanced cooperation. Hence, taking the two factors together, also the public goods theory confirms that enhanced cooperation in this field cannot be expected under the current framework.

Another significant argument against the use of enhanced cooperation—facilitated or not—in the field of asylum policy is that acts based on Art. 78 TFEU can be passed by qualified majority in the Council. This could mean, on the one hand, that there is simply a better, more appealing approach for Member States, namely to go ahead enforcing legislation that binds all Member States equally. Secondly, it could mean that where enhanced cooperation was sought, it would not be a *last resort*, and thus inadmissible under Article 20.2 TEU if the interested group is big enough to form a qualified majority.[24] However, it was also established above that enhanced cooperation in policy areas governed by QMV is not illegal or impossible.[25] In a fitting situation, Member States could use enhanced cooperation also to circumvent a qualified majority threshold in the Council. Secondly, the last resort criterion is largely substituted in the facilitated enhanced cooperation clauses, which serve as a role model to the proposed facilitated cooperation clause. Thus, just like in facilitated enhanced cooperation, checking whether a measure is a matter of last resort could be replaced e.g. by the European Council not finding a solution on a given matter, depending on the design of the clause. Furthermore, the modification towards a facilitated enhanced cooperation in the design of an emergency break (Art. 82, 83 TFEU) precisely takes place in areas where decisions are taken by QMV. Thus, a legal basis requiring QMV is not per se unfit to serve as an example for an incentivised cooperation, neither is one requiring unanimity. It should be kept in mind, though, that as pointed out above, whether a policy area is governed by unanimity or QMV in the Council has implications for an adequate design of the modified enhanced cooperation clause.

In light of these findings, in order for enhanced cooperation to play a relevant role in future asylum policy, the incentive structures would have to be amended. If (financial) costs arising from commitments in this field were covered by the EU as a whole, the externalities would be much less positive than they are right now. While the non-participants would still benefit from not having to engage in resolving the unsustainable situations at the EU's external borders, they would have to pay for any action pursued by the participants. This would at least stop

---

[24] See above, Sect. 2.3.1.10.2.

[25] See above, Sect. 2.2.1.

free-riding on a financial level. Such an approach is not guaranteed to shift the balance towards new, differentiated action by Member States, but it certainly would raise the chances.

#### 5.2.4.2 Draft Treaty Amendment

In the following, three variants for what an incentivised cooperation clause in a Treaty provision could look like will be presented. They are designed as an appendage to an existing Treaty clause, just like the facilitated enhanced cooperation clauses in Art. 82, 83, 86 and 87 TFEU. In this case, the proposal is to add them to Art. 78 TFEU on the common asylum policy. This norm entails a legal base for variety of arrangements concerning asylum procedures and standards (para 2), as well as a legal base for provisional measures passed by the Council in emergency situations (para 3).[26]

Three proposed variants (para 4A, 4B, and 4C) are laid out, differing in various aspects and building to different degrees on the existing examples in the Treaties.

Para 4A constitutes a basic mechanism for an incentivised cooperation. It presupposes a regular enhanced cooperation and then facilitates the path towards burden-sharing by making the decision as foreseen in Art. 332 TFEU dependant only on QMV vote in the Council. By further requiring a Commission proposal and EP consent, the interests of the EU as a whole are duly taken into account. This version would be apt for legal bases featuring QMV or unanimity alike, but would not make sense in cases of QMV if the group of interested states is large enough to form a qualified majority of its own, as in these cases, unwilling Member States could be forced to contribute to the costs of a policy measure by way of a uniform piece of legislation. Thus, given the Council majorities in the field of asylum policies in the past years, it would arguably not be a perfect fit for Article 78 TFEU.

Para 4B is based on the facilitated enhanced cooperation in Art. 82.3 and 83.3 TFEU, the so-called "emergency brake" mechanisms, and thus focus on the interests of Member States which do not want to participate in new policy measures. It would be particularly apt for legal bases that use QMV decision making in the Council, allowing the dissenting Member States to stay out and thus drop their resistance against a policy measure though paying their share of the arising costs.

Para 4C is based on the facilitated enhanced cooperation in Art. 86.1 (2, 3), 87.3 TFEU. They allow Member States that want a policy measure to go ahead

[26] Thym, D. (2021), 'Art. 78 TFEU' in: Blanke, H.-J., Mangiameli, S. (eds.), *Treaty on the Functioning of the European Union—A Commentary*.

in a facilitated way, even if the required majority cannot be found. It is therefore especially suitable for legal bases that require unanimity in the Council and consequently not a perfect fit for Article 78 TFEU.

*Article 78 TFEU*

*1. The Union shall develop a common policy on asylum, subsidiary protection and temporary protection with a view to offering appropriate status to any third-country national requiring international protection and ensuring compliance with the principle of non-refoulement. This policy must be in accordance with the Geneva Convention of 28 July 1951 and the Protocol of 31 January 1967 relating to the status of refugees, and other relevant treaties.*

*2. For the purposes of paragraph 1, the European Parliament and the Council, acting in accordance with the ordinary legislative procedure, shall adopt measures for a common European asylum system comprising:*

*(a) a uniform status of asylum for nationals of third countries, valid throughout the Union;*

*(b) a uniform status of subsidiary protection for nationals of third countries who, without obtaining European asylum, are in need of international protection;*

*(c) a common system of temporary protection for displaced persons in the event of a massive inflow;*

*(d) common procedures for the granting and withdrawing of uniform asylum or subsidiary protection status;*

*(e) criteria and mechanisms for determining which Member State is responsible for considering an application for asylum or subsidiary protection;*

*(f) standards concerning the conditions for the reception of applicants for asylum or subsidiary protection;*

*(g) partnership and cooperation with third countries for the purpose of managing inflows of people applying for asylum or subsidiary or temporary protection.*

*3. In the event of one or more Member States being confronted by an emergency situation characterised by a sudden inflow of nationals of third countries, the Council, on a proposal from the Commission, may adopt provisional measures for the benefit of the Member State(s) concerned. It shall act after consulting the European Parliament.*

4A

*If at least nine Member States establish an enhanced cooperation on the basis of a proposal as referred to in paragraphs 2 and 3, the Council, acting by a qualified majority on a proposal from the Commission and after obtaining the consent of the European Parliament, adopt a decision on the expenditures arising from that enhanced cooperation as referred to in Article 332. This may include that the expenditures arising for the EU or the Member States shall be borne by the EU as a whole.*

4B

*Where a member of the Council considers that a proposal as referred to in paragraphs 2 or 3 would affect fundamental interest of its society, it may request that the proposal be referred to the European Council. In that case, the ordinary legislative procedure shall be suspended. After discussion, and in case of a consensus, the European Council shall, within four months of this suspension, refer the draft back to the Council, which shall terminate the suspension of the ordinary legislative procedure.*

*Within the same timeframe, in case of disagreement, and if at least nine Member States wish to establish enhanced cooperation on the basis of the proposal concerned, they shall notify the European Parliament, the Council and the Commission accordingly. In such a case, the authorisation to proceed with enhanced cooperation referred to in Article 20(2) of the Treaty on European Union and Article 329(1) of this Treaty shall be deemed to be granted and the provisions on enhanced cooperation shall apply. The Council may, on a proposal from the Commission, after obtaining the consent of the European Parliament and acting by a qualified majority adopt a decision on the expenditures arising from that enhanced cooperation as referred to in Article 332. This may include that the expenditures arising for the EU or the Member States shall be borne by the EU as a whole.*

4C

*In the absence of unanimity in the Council, a group of at least nine Member States may request that the proposal be referred to the European Council. In that case, the procedure in the Council shall be suspended. After discussion, and in case of a consensus, the European Council shall, within four months of this suspension, refer the draft back to the Council for adoption.*

*Within the same timeframe, in case of disagreement, and if at least nine Member States wish to establish enhanced cooperation on the basis of the proposal concerned, they shall notify the European Parliament, the Council and the Commission accordingly. In such a case, the authorisation to proceed with enhanced cooperation referred to in Article 20(2) of the Treaty on European Union and Article 329(1) of this Treaty shall be deemed to be granted and the provisions on enhanced cooperation shall apply. The Council, acting by a qualified majority on a proposal from the Commission and after obtaining the consent of the European Parliament, may adopt a decision on the expenditures arising from that enhanced cooperation as referred to in Article 332. This may include that the expenditures arising for the EU or the Member States shall be borne by the EU as a whole.*

As can be seen from the formulations, variant A would have the smallest impact on the general structure of Art. 78 TFEU, and only add the proposed incentive mechanism. This has the advantage of requiring a very limited Treaty amendment (and, as shown above, the effect could also be reached by way of the *passarelle* clause in Art. 48.7 TEU). Yet, this also means that the amendment would have little to offer for states currently blocking reforms in the policy area except for future financial obligations. This could make the proposal hard to sell. Variant B, on the contrary, would offer states opposing asylum reforms a new emergency brake. For critical Member States, there is a constant risk that a qualified majority could pass asylum legislation binding them against their will.[27] Variant B would introduce a new emergency brake, which would avert this risk for good, though at the cost of having to financially participate in an enhanced cooperation concluded instead. For Member States pushing for reforms in the Asylum sector, this may not seem very attractive at first glance. However, it could be argued that despite the fact that reforms could be passed by QMV, this is not happening in practice and a communally financed enhanced cooperation might still be an improvement of the status quo. Variant C, finally, would be particularly interesting for these latter states. It would give them particularly easy access to enhanced cooperation and ensure its costs would be borne by the EU as a whole. However, this might be even harder to sell to diffident Member States.

As Art. 78 TFEU is placed within Part Three of the TFEU, the treaty revision necessary to introduce an incentivised cooperation clause to it could be taken by way of the simplified revision procedure (Art. 48.6 TEU). Furthermore, neither Art. 78 TFEU nor Art. 332 TFEU are excluded from the scope of application of the general *passerelle* clause in Art. 46.7 TEU, meaning that incentivised cooperation in variant 4A could also be introduced using this method.

## 5.3 Conclusions on Incentivised Cooperation

In policy areas with problematic incentive structures, research points towards an unlikeliness of enhanced cooperation being applied to create political progress. At the same time, such incentive structures are at the works in some of the areas that have seen the longest-standing blockades and the least momentum. For this reason, enhanced cooperation would be particularly helpful in these areas and is regularly called for. In order to break up these problematic incentive structures, "incentivised enhanced cooperation" or short: "incentivised cooperation" clauses could be introduced to the Treaties. Incentivised cooperation builds on the example of facilitated enhanced cooperation clauses as present in Art. 82–87 TFEU. Following their example, incentivised cooperation replaces a specific detail of

[27] See e.g. CJEU, C-715/17, C-718/17 and C-719/17 (European Commission v Republic of Poland and Others), ECLI:EU:C:2020:257.

the regular enhanced cooperation legal framework with effect for specific legal bases. Specifically, in order to change the incentive structures at place in legislation processes using these legal bases, they would make sure that costs caused by an enhanced cooperation are not borne only by the participating Member States, but by the EU as a whole. To ensure this, incentivised cooperation clauses would make use of Art. 332 TFEU, which foresees a possibility to take a decision to that effect by a unanimous Council vote. The incentivised cooperation clause would alter the decision-making process foreseen for this decision and lower its threshold in the Council. Ideally, a decision on the expenditure of enhanced cooperation could then be taken by a qualified majority in the Council, on a Commission proposal and with the consent of the European Parliament. Such clauses could even be combined with facilitated enhanced cooperation clauses to create even more momentum towards differentiated policy solutions. The Treaty changes required to introduce incentivised cooperation clauses could usually be taken by way of a simplified treaty amendment procedure (Art. 48.6 TEU) or even by using a *passerelle* clause (Art. 48.7 TEU), though this latter solution would limit the options in designing the clause. Incentivised cooperation could, in conclusion, be introduced in the Treaties in a comparatively simple process, but it could have a drastic impact on the appeal of enhanced cooperation occurring in disputed policy fields, characterised by political blockades.

# 6 Conclusions

EU integration, as policymaking in any multinational legal order, is inherently situated at the crossroads between the poles of unity and blockade. Given this, decision-makers have long since been turning to differentiation to move forwards in integration despite the reluctance of individual members. Over the decades, several approaches were pursued to adopt differentiated integration steps. In the recent history, enhanced cooperation has emerged as a low-key possibility to pass differentiated legal acts without the need of Treaty amendments or opt-outs, and without sacrificing the benefits of policymaking with the EU law framework.

After its introduction to the Treaties in 1997, enhanced cooperation laid dormant for a longer period. In the meantime, however, it has developed into what could be called a sparingly used normality, with a total of five cases of application.

Enhanced cooperation is a type of "supranational differentiation" as it enables Member States access to supranational EU law and procedures. At the same time, the strong role individual Member States have in its formation and the degree to which it respects individual Member States' concerns and preferences also places it firmly in the playing field of intergovernmentalism. Enhanced cooperation in itself is therefore an example of compromise and a carefully struck balance, as it balances the poles of supranationalism and intergovernmentalism within the EU legal order.

From the very beginning, enhanced cooperation has served as a screen for projecting both fears and hopes connected with differentiated integration—and this dispute was often led using images of integration as enabled by enhanced cooperation. One of the most frequently voiced criticisms includes the image that enhanced cooperation aims to a *core Europe*, an inner core of Member States



J. Graf von Luckner, *Enhanced Cooperation Revisited*,
https://doi.org/10.1007/978-3-658-51063-3_6

within the EU that only an elite may access. However, through its inherent openness, enhanced cooperation by design contradicts the idea of a core Europe, which can consequently not be seen in the practice of enhanced cooperation participation. The popular image is therefore not fit to describe enhanced cooperation—yet, the other popular images describing differentiated European integration are hardly apt to describe the realities brought about by enhanced cooperation either. The core image's best-known alternative, the image of a *multispeed* European integration, is contradicted by the fact that in practice, some of the enhanced cooperations build on a profound 'agreement to disagreement' meaning that in reality there is no significant change in the composition of membership of those enhanced cooperations, thus rendering the describing element of 'speed' inapt. At the same time, given that the membership in the single enhanced cooperation projects are varying and diverse, the idea of *concentric* circles equally fails to describe the reality brought about by enhanced cooperation, as this image presupposes a hierarchy among integration steps. If anything, therefore, one might describe European integration by enhanced cooperation as a *shaded* integration, allowing Member States to access a deeper shade of integration by accessing a given enhanced cooperation, or refrain from doing so.

When examining the scope of enhanced cooperation, it soon becomes clear that a distinction must be made between the *legal* and the *factual* scope. While the legal scope in the narrowest sense is defined extremely broad, namely all Union competences that are not exclusive to the EU, other legal hurdles enshrined in Art. 20 TEU, Art. 326 ff. TFEU diminish the field of potential applications of enhanced cooperation considerably. From what remains after this stage, it can be concluded that in practice in many areas, attempts to launch enhanced cooperation cannot be expected for political rather than legal considerations, which means that these areas are largely excluded from the *factual* scope of enhanced cooperation. Taking into account the theories developed by political scientists on when enhanced cooperation occurs and confronting them with the principal areas of shared competence of the EU, it becomes possible to draw a map of areas where enhanced cooperation could reasonably be expected to be attempted in the future.

According to this field map, enhanced cooperation is most likely where legal bases require unanimous decision making in the Council and could therefore occur in fields such as the harmonisation of taxes. In particular, company taxation (CCCTB/CCTB) or a digital tax seem fit for such differentiated approaches. Although the Eurocrisis, leading to major changes in the EMU legal framework, passed without the EMU members resorting to enhanced cooperation, EMU governance, too, could be a field to see enhanced cooperation in future, as well as social policy moving along the lines of the EMU, such as a European unemployment benefit scheme for EMU Member States. Furthermore, judicial cooperation in civil (especially family law) and criminal matters are prime candidates for future enhanced cooperations, the latter in the form of a facilitated enhanced cooperation, which could also be seen in police cooperation. Given that CFSP enhanced cooperation is explicitly mentioned in the Treaties with rules of its own, this, too, seems a reasonably likely candidate for future application. Finally, especially in times of crisis, it seems reasonable to expect that Member States could use the so-called flexibility clause in Art. 352 TFEU in an enhanced cooperation set-up.

When it comes to legal bases that do not feature unanimous Council voting but QMV, it can be concluded that enhanced cooperation in this context would require a novel approach by Council members, but is neither legally nor factually ruled out. What would be needed is a situation in which the necessary Council majority cannot be reached by states interested in a measure, yet one or several states are willing to lend their votes to the authorisation of enhanced cooperation as what I name "helper-states". Thus, QMV enhanced cooperation would require a change of the EU Member States' general approach to policy making in the Council, lowering the abstract value of unity as principle and being more open to agreeing to disagree. Among the policy areas governed by QMV, Art. 66 TFEU on measures protecting the EMU against capital from third states is a case that could see an enhanced cooperation if the necessity arose. Consumer protections might also be a field to see an enhanced cooperation under specific circumstances, for example to implement projects like a Common European Sales Law. As an interesting side note, going utterly against the logic of law-making in the EU, QMV arithmetics would enable Member States to pass an enhanced cooperation entirely without Commission involvement in the case of Art. 87 (2) TFEU on police cooperation, which could happen in future. Non-legislative measures like Environment Action Plans would be another totally new, yet possible application of the enhanced cooperation mechanism. What also became clear from analysing both the legal framework and the political surroundings, however, is that many other areas brought up for the use of enhanced cooperation in the past, such as legislation on environmental matters or migration, seem rather unlikely to see an application of enhanced cooperation in the future. This notwithstanding, the analysis of the scope of enhanced cooperation brought to light a large number of fields where enhanced cooperation could be used in the future to help Member States overcome blockades or solve crises with the help of European law even if not all Member States agree on a measure.

A main stumbling block keeping enhanced cooperation from having such a major impact on EU policy making is still being seen in the last resort criterion, according to which enhanced cooperation can only be resorted to when it has been established that the objectives of such cooperation cannot be attained within a reasonable period by the Union as a whole. However, my analysis of the last resort criterion results in a more nuanced picture.

The last resort criterion makes it perfectly clear that enhanced cooperation is not a normal mode of operation for law-making in the EU. Resorting to enhanced cooperation has to be preceded by a thorough search for compromise. What exactly such a thorough search comprises depends on the situation. Regularly, this will be a failed legislative procedure in which an agreement was sought on all levels of the Council, including the political level. Yet, a failed legislative procedure is not necessarily the only way to ensure a thorough pursuit of a solution comprising all Member States. Especially in cases of urgency, demanding a futile legislative procedure could unnecessarily slow down the process or even lead to Member States leaving the Treaty framework altogether and finding a solution in international law.

In such situations, Member States might have to, and can legally, shortcut the procedure if the positions of the Member States, in particular of those opposing a policy measure, are sufficiently clear. Moreover, enhanced cooperation does not necessarily have to be based on a discussion of a previous Commission proposal. Given that the Council has what is called an 'indirect right of initiative', i.e. a right to ask the Commission to bring forward a legislative proposal, substantive discussions on a given topic can equally take place in the process leading to the exercise of such an indirect initiative. If it becomes clear during the process leading up to such an indirect initiative that one or several Member States would only approve a measure "over their dead body", while others deem the measure indispensable, they can move on to enhanced cooperation directly from this stage. Thus, enhanced cooperation can be accelerated substantially if the need arises, and all positions are settled. In the light of these findings, it becomes evident that enhanced cooperation could indeed be used in times of urgency and crisis.

It should be noted, in this context, that the opposing scenario, namely that Member States agree on a necessity for a policy measure, but not on how to implement it, does not fall under the scope of these findings. While the CJEU clarified that also in this case, enhanced cooperation is possible, it becomes much more difficult. As, under such circumstances, Member States precisely do not agree to disagree, Member States need to thoroughly debate a proposal prior to turning to the conclusion that the necessary Council majority cannot be reached, and thus to enhanced cooperation. This encompasses Council discussions at all levels, including at least one discussion on the political level. However, this more traditional reading of the last resort criterion does not contradict the findings made above, according to which when need arises, enhanced cooperation can absolutely be implemented in a swift manner.

Once it has been concluded that unanimity cannot be reached and Member States turn to enhanced cooperation, different procedural hurdles apply. A most significant one is that enhanced cooperation has to be open to the non-participants at all times. The principle of openness serves the purpose of a one-way valve into enhanced cooperation. However, joining an enhanced cooperation is not always the same procedurally. Whether a non-participant applies to participate in the Request Phase, Preparation Phase, Authorisation Phase, Legislative Phase, or the Implementation Phase, has distinct legal consequences when it comes to what is necessary for Member States to join and political consequences when it comes to the influence that former non-participants can have on the outcome of the enhanced cooperation. Moreover, it can be argued that participating in an enhanced cooperation is limited by the existence of an unwritten requirement of being sincerely willing to cooperate, which the Commission checks through a benefit assessment prior to confirming participation.

A so far utterly unused yet politically relevant aspect of the principle of openness is the possibility to make participation depend on the fulfilment of conditions according to Art. 328.1 TFEU. In the light of the challenges the EU is facing, these conditions could not only entail basic requirements, but could, under certain circumstances, amount to *conditionalities*, following a policy goal going beyond the individual enhanced cooperation project. This would largely influence the nature of future enhanced cooperations and their usage. Yet it would not generally be excluded by the Treaties if the condition was objective, unambiguous, and possessed a genuine link to the nature or functioning of the enhanced cooperation.

While the innovative reading on being able to use enhanced cooperation also in QMV scenarios, the versatility of enhanced cooperation despite the existence of the last resort criterion and the additional tool of conditionality to be introduced by way of enhanced cooperation may raise the interest of political leaders in using enhanced cooperation, there are many issues in need of policy solutions that enhanced cooperation turns out to be unattractive for according to my analysis. This is first and foremost due to the incentive structures that are influencing decisions in these cases. Given that this affects some of the areas that have seen the longest-standing blockades and the least momentum, one might wonder if enhanced cooperation could, by way of an amendment of the Treaties, be changed in a way that makes it more likely to be used, and thus increases the likelihood of a political solution being found in some of the most delicate matters. Such a targeted Treaty amendment could see enhanced cooperation being upgraded towards an "incentivised enhanced cooperation" or short: "incentivised cooperation" in singular policy areas in order to break up the problematic incentive structures described.

Incentivised cooperation as proposed in this thesis would build on the example of the facilitated enhanced cooperation clauses already present in the Treaties. Accordingly, incentivised cooperation would replace a specific detail of the regular enhanced cooperation legal framework with effect for specific legal bases. In detail, incentivised cooperation clauses would ensure that costs caused by an enhanced cooperation that addresses a problem in the interest of the Union as whole are not borne only by the participating Member States, but by all Member States jointly. Thus, incentivised cooperation would be an attempt to change the negative incentive structures currently hindering Member States from applying enhanced cooperation in such cases. Incentivised cooperation clauses would be attached to existing articles containing the legal base for Union action in problematic areas. In order to have the desired effect, they would, for the specific legal base at hand, change the procedure foreseen in Art. 332 TFEU, according to which the Council can decide unanimously to carry the costs of an enhanced cooperation jointly, and replace it with qualified majority voting if proposed by the Commission and approved by the Parliament. Thus, incentivised cooperation would largely use a possibility that is already there, and merely change the decision-making process leading up to it. If, in a hypothetical Treaty revision process, the legislators wanted to raise the chances for enhanced cooperation further, the incentivised cooperation clause could be coupled with facilitated enhanced cooperation clauses as already present in the Treaties.

As the Treaty changes required to introduce incentivised cooperation clauses could usually be adopted by way of a simplified treaty amendment procedure or even by using a *passerelle* clause, incentivised cooperation could be introduced in the Treaties in a comparatively simple manner. It could, however, have a significant impact on the appeal of enhanced cooperation occurring, and thus on political solutions being found, in particularly disputed policy fields.

What emerges overall is the image of enhanced cooperation as a mechanism that is closely regulated by Treaty law, yet more flexible than many may think. It is usable in a wide array of policy fields, including those governed by QMV, some of which may not have been considered for policymaking by enhanced cooperation before. The last resort criterion, often seen as the highest hurdle in the application of enhanced cooperation, may not be as serious an obstacle as is often assumed, especially in situations of dire need. Thus, when need arises and the overall circumstances permit, solutions using enhanced cooperation could be applied swiftly to address the problem at hand. This finding is accompanied by the so far unexplored fact that enhanced cooperation could entail instances of conditionality. As such, it could serve for entirely different purposes than what it has been considered for until now. Finally, political will permitting, very targeted, surgical Treaty amendments could help to address problematic incentive structures that currently keep Member States from jointly addressing problems through enhanced cooperation, and thus further expend the number of situations in which enhanced cooperation could help Member States and the EU as a whole.

Adaptable and ready to use, enhanced cooperation offers a promising path towards efficient problem-solving for the EU when needed, paving the way for more European solutions where preferable in the light of subsidiarity.

# References


Alemanno, A., Stefan, O. (2014), 'Openness at the Court of Justice of the European Union: Toppling a taboo', *CMLRev*, pp. 97–140.

Allen, Franklin; Carletti, Elena; Gray, Joanna; Gulati, G. Mitu, eds. (2016), *Filling the gaps in governance: The case of Europe.*

Almeida, J., Costa, G. O. e. (2018), 'From the Unitary Patent Package to a Federal EU Patent Law', *Perspectives on Federalism*, Vol. 10, No. 1, pp. 126–146.

Amort, M. (2020), *Zur Ordnung des Verbraucherrechts. Mit europäischem Verbraucherschutz zu verfassungskonformer Typisierung.*

Avbelj, M. (2013), 'Differentiated Integration—Farewell to the EU-27?', *GLJ*, Vol. 14, No. 1, pp. 191–212.

Balladur, É. (1994), 'L'Union à trois cercles', *Le Figaro*, 31 August 1994.

Bär, S., Gehring, T., Homeyer, I. von, Kraemer, R. A., Mazurek, A.-G., Klasing, A., Tarasofky, R. G. (2002), 'Closer Co-operation, A New Instrument for European Environmental Policy?', *SSRN Electronic Journal.*

Beaumont, Paul; Danov, Mihail; Trimmings, Katharina; Yüksel, Burcu, eds. (2017), *Cross-Border Litigation in Europe.*

Beblavý, M., Lenaerts, K. (2017), 'Feasibility and Added Value of a European Unemployment Benefit Scheme: Main findings from a comprehensive research project'.

Becerill, B. (2009), 'The regulation of enhanced cooperation and its reform in Lisbon: Towards a model of differentiation that is closer to the community method' in: Beneyto Pérez, J. M., Baquero Cruz, J. (eds.), *Unity and flexibility in the future of the European Union: The challenge of enhanced cooperation,* Madrid, CEU Ediciones, pp. 9–20.

Becker, J., Kornwachs, L., Zembala-Börner, K. (2016), *Die gemeinsame Europäische Bankenaufsicht als Reformmodell für die verstärkte Zusammenarbeit?*, Heidelberger Beiträge zum Finanz- und Steuerrecht.

Becker, P. (2017), *The next multiannual financial framework (MFF) and the unity of EU budget: In-depth analysis*, Brussels, European Parliament.

Bender, T. (2001), 'Die Verstärkte Zusammenarbeit nach Nizza: Anwendungsfelder und Bewertung im Spiegel historischer Präzedenzfälle der differenzierten Integration', *ZaöRV*, Vol. 63, No. 3, pp. 729–770.

Beneyto Pérez, José María; Baquero Cruz, Julio, eds. (2009), *Unity and flexibility in the future of the European Union: The challenge of enhanced cooperation.*




J. Graf von Luckner, *Enhanced Cooperation Revisited*,
https://doi.org/10.1007/978-3-658-51063-3

Bettendorf, L., van der Horst, A., Mooij, R. A. D., Vrijburg, H., 'Corporate Tax Consolidation and Enhanced Cooperation in the European Union', *Fiscal Studies*, Vol. 31, No. 4, pp. 453–479.

Betts, A. (2003), 'Public Goods Theory and the Provision of Refugee Protection: The Role of the Joint-Product Model in Burden-Sharing Theory', *Journal of Refugee Studies*, Vol. 16, p. 274.

Biscop, S. (2017), European Defence: What's in the CARDs for PESCO?, EGMONT Security Policy Brief, Brussels.

Biscop, S. (2018), 'European Defence: Give PESCO a Chance', *Survival*, Vol. 60, No. 3, pp. 161–180.

Blanke, H.-J., Böttner, R. (2019), '§ 13 Binnenmarkt, Rechtsangleichung, Grundfreiheiten' in: Niedobitek, M. (ed.), *Europarecht: Grundlagen und Politiken der Union,* Berlin, De Gruyter, pp. 887–1114.

Blanke, H.-J., Bunse, S. R. (2019), 'Der Raum der Freiheit, der Sicherheit und des Rechts—ein Integrationswert?' in: Nitschke, P. (ed.), *Gemeinsame Werte in Europa?: Stärken und Schwächen im normativen Selbstverständnis der Europäischen Integration,* Baden-Baden, Bonn, Nomos; Konrad Adenauer Stiftung.

Blanke, H.-J., Johr, M. (2019), 'Rechtliche Vorkehrungen für die zivile Seenotrettung im Mittelmeer: „Sichere Häfen" und „verlässliche Ausschiffungsregelungen" in der EU zur Überwindung völkerrechtlicher Ungewissheit', *DÖV*, No. 23, pp. 929–939.

Blanke, H.-J., Pilz, S. (2020), 'Europa 2019 bis 2024—Wohin trägt uns der Stier?: Sieben Thesen zu den Herausforderungen der Europäischen Union', *EuR*, pp. 270–300.

Blanke, Hermann-Josef; Mangiameli, Stelio, eds. (2013), *The Treaty on European Union (TEU): A commentary.*

Blanke, Hermann-Josef; Mangiameli, Stelio, eds. (2021), *Treaty on the Functioning of the European Union—A Commentary.*

Blanke, Hermann-Josef; Pilz, Stefan, eds. (2014), *Die „Fiskalunion": Voraussetzungen einer Vertiefung der politischen Integration im Währungsraum der Europäischen Union,* Neue Staatswissenschaften.

Blocher, J., Gulati, G. M., Helfer, L. (2016), 'Can Greece Be Expelled from the Eurozone? Toward a Default Rule on Expulsion from International Organizations' in: Allen, F., Carletti, E., Gray, J., Gulati, G. M. (eds.), *Filling the gaps in governance: The case of Europe,* San Domenico di Fiesole, European University Institute, pp. 127–150.

Blockmans, Steven, ed. (2014), *Differentiated integration in the EU: From the inside looking out.*

Boele-Woelki, K. (2008), 'To Be, Or Not to Be: Enhanced Cooperation in International Divorce Law within the European Union', *Victoria U. Wellington L. Rev.*, Vol. 39, p. 779.

Bogdandy, A. von (1999), 'Die Europäische Union als supranationale Föderation', *integration,* Vol. 22, No. 2, pp. 95–112.

Bogdandy, A. von (2003), 'Europäische Prinzipienlehre' in: Bogdandy, A. von (ed.), *Europäisches Verfassungsrecht: Theoretische und dogmatische Grundzüge,* Berlin, New York, Springer, pp. 149–203.

Bogdandy, A. von (2010), 'Founding Principles of EU Law', *Revus*, No. 12, pp. 35–56.

Bogdandy, A. von, Ioannidis, M. (2014), 'Systemic deficiency in the rule of law: What it is, what has been done, what can be done', *CMLRev*, pp. 59–96.

Bogdandy, Armin von, ed. (2003), *Europäisches Verfassungsrecht: Theoretische und dogmatische Grundzüge*, Springer-Lehrbuch.
Bogdandy, Armin von, ed. (2003), *Europäisches Verfassungsrecht: Theoretische und dogmatische Grundzüge*, Springer-Lehrbuch.
Bonelli, M., Claes, M., Witte, B. de, Podstawa, K. (2022), 'Usual and Unusual Suspect in Protecting EU Values: An Introduction'.
Böttner, R. (2016), 'Ein scharfes Schwert der Kommission? Überlegungen zu Artikel 293 AEUV', *EuR*, Vol. 51, No. 1, pp. 105–122.
Böttner, R. (2016), 'Eine Idee lernt laufen—zur Praxis der Verstärkten Zusammenarbeit nach Lissabon', *ZEuS*, Vol. 19, No. 4, pp. 501–550.
Böttner, R. (2016), 'The Treaty Amendment Procedures and the Relationship between Article 31(3) TEU and the General Bridging Clause of Article 48(7) TEU', *European Constitutional Law Review*, Vol. 12, No. 03, pp. 499–519.
Böttner, R. (2017), 'Brückenklauseln im europäischen Verfassungsrecht', *EuR*, Vol. 52, No. 3, pp. 381–400.
Böttner, R. (2021), *The Constitutional Framework for Enhanced Cooperation in EU law*, Nijhoff studies in European Union law, Leiden, Koninklijke Brill.
Böttner, R. (2022), 'Book review: Enhanced Cooperation and European Tax Law by Caroline Heber', *CMLRev*, Vol. 59, Issue 4, pp. 1255–1257.
Böttner, R. (2023), 'The Instrument of Enhanced Cooperation: Pitfalls and Possibilities for Differentiated Integration'.
Brackhane, B. (2008), *Differenzierte Integration im Recht der Europäischen Union*, Ius Europaeum, Baden-Baden, Nomos.
Bribosia, H. (2007), *Les coopérations renforcées : quel modèle d'intégration différenciée pour l'Union européenne?: analyse comparative du mécanisme général de la coopération renforcée, du projet de coopération structurée permanente en matière de défense, et de la pratique d'autres coopérations renforcées „prédéterminées" en matière sociale, au sein de l'Espace de liberté, sécurité et justice, et dans l'Union économique et monétaire.*
Busse, C. (2000), 'Braucht Europa einen harten Kern?', *A PuZ*, B47.
Buttlar, C. von (2001), 'Rechtsprobleme der „verstärkten Zusammenarbeit" nach dem Vertrag von Nizza', *ZEuS*, pp. 649–688.
Cach, C. (2014), 'Die Verstärkte Zusammenarbeit und ihre Bedeutung für die Errichtung der Europäischen Staatsanwaltschaft', *EuR Europarecht*, Vol. 49, No. 6, pp. 716–729.
Cadet, F., Vascega, M. (2013), 'Fewer Woods for Robin Hood: Financial Transaction Tax under Enhanced Cooperation', *EuZW*, pp. 574–579.
Calliess, Christian; Ruffert, Matthias, eds. (2016), *EUV/AEUV: Das Verfassungsrecht der Europäischen Union mit Europäischer Grundrechtecharta: Kommentar*.
Cannone, A. (2005), *Le cooperazioni rafforzate: Contributo allo studio dell'integrazione differenziata*, Pubblicazioni della Facoltà giuridica dell'Università di Bari, Bari, Cacucci.
Cantore, C. (2011), 'We're One, but We're Not the Same: Enhanced Cooperation and the Tension between Unity and Asymmetry in the EU', *Perspectives on Federalism*, No. 3, E-1–E-21.
Capitani, E. de (2014), 'The Schengen system after Lisbon: from cooperation to integration', *ERA Forum*, Vol. 15, No. 1, pp. 101–118.
Cédelle, A. (2015), Enhanced cooperation: A way forward for tax harmonisation in the EU?, Working Paper Series.

Cerioni, L. (2006), 'The Possible Introduction of Common Consolidated Base Taxation via Enhanced Cooperation: Some Open Issues', *European Taxation*, pp. 187–196.

Chalmers, Damian; Arnull, Anthony, eds. (2015), *The Oxford Handbook of European Union Law.*

Chirac, J. (2000), *Notre Europe: Discours Prononce par Monsieur Jacques Chirac, President de la Republique Francaise, devant le Bundestag Allemand*, Berlin.

Clelia Lacchi (2017), 'How Much Flexibility Can European Integration Bear in Order to Face the Eurozone Crisis? Reflections on the EMU inter se International Agreements Between EU Member States' in: Giegerich, T., Schmitt, D. C., Zeitzmann, S. (eds.), *Flexibility in the EU and beyond: How much differentiation can European integration bear?*, Oxford, Hart Publishing, pp. 225–250.

Constantinesco, V. (1994), 'Les clauses de "coopération renforcée". Le protocole sur l'application des principes de subsidiarité et de proportionnalité', *Revue trimestrielle de droit europeen*, Vol. 33, No. 4, pp. 751–767.

Craig, P. (2004), 'Competence: Clarity, conferral, containment and consideration', *ELRev*, Vol. 29, No. 3, pp. 323–344.

Cramme, Olaf; Hobolt, Sara Binzer, eds. (2015), *Democratic politics in a European Union under stress.*

Cremona, M. (2009), 'Enhanced Cooperation and the Common Foreign and Security and Defence Policies of the EU', *EUI Working Papers*, No. 21.

Cremona, M., Scott, J. (2019), *EU law beyond EU borders: The extraterritorial reach of EU law / edited by Marise Cremona and Joanne Scott*, The collected courses of the Academy of European Law, Oxford, Oxford University Press.

Curtin, D. (1993), 'The Constitutional Structure of the Union: A Europe of Bits and Pieces', *CMLRev*, Vol. 30, pp. 17–69.

Curtin, D., Fasone, C. (2017), 'Differentiated representation: is a flexible European Parliament desirable?' in: Witte, B. de, Ott, A., Vos, E. (eds.), *Between Flexibility and Disintegration: The Trajectory of Differentiation in EU Law,* Edward Elgar Publishing Limited, pp. 118–145.

Davies, G. (2017), 'The Competence to Create an Internal Market: Conceptual Poverty and Unbalanced Interests' in: Garben, S., Govaere, I. (eds.), *The Division of Competences between the EU and the Member States : Reflections on the Past, the Present and the Future,* Hart Publishing.

Della Cananea, G. (2019), 'Differentiated Integration in Europe After Brexit: An Institutional Analysis' in: Pernice, I., Guerra Martins, A. M. (eds.), *Brexit and the Future of EU Politics: A Constitutional Law Perspective,* Baden-Baden, Nomos Verlagsgesellschaft mbH & Co. KG, pp. 45–89.

Derpa, U. (2003), *Die verstärkte Zusammenarbeit im Recht der Europäischen Union: Dogmatik, Interpretation und Praxis eines alternativen Integrationskonzeptes*, Schriften zum öffentlichen, europäischen und internationalen Recht, Stuttgart u.a., Boorberg.

Di Francesco Maesa, C. (2006), 'Repercussions of the Establishment of the EPPO via Enhanced Cooperation : EPPO's Added Value and the Possibility to Extend its Competence', *eucrim—The European Criminal Law Associations' Forum.*

Dougan, Michael; Currie, Samantha, -, eds. (2009), *50 Years of the European Treaties Looking Back and Thinking Forward.*

Duff, A. (2022), *Constitutional change in the European Union: Towards a federal Europe*, Basingstoke, Palgrave Macmillan.

Editorial Comments (2011), 'Enhanced cooperation: A Union à taille réduite or à porte tournante?', *CMLRev*, pp. 317–327.

Ehlermann, C. D. (1998), 'Differentiation, Flexibility, Closer Co-operation: The New Provisions of the Amsterdam Treaty', *European Law Journal*, Vol. 4, No. 3, pp. 246–270.

Ehlermann, C.-D. (1997), 'Engere Zusammenarbeit nach dem Amsterdamer Vertrag: ein neues Verfassungsprinzip?', *EuR*, pp. 362–397.

Ehmke, Horst; Scheuner, Ulrich, eds. (1973), *Festschrift für Ulrich Scheuner zum 70. Geburtstag*.

Erkelens, L. H.; Meij, A. W. H.; Pawlik, M., eds. (2015), *The European public prosecutor's office: An extended arm or a two-headed dragon? / L.H. Erkelens, A.W.H. Meij, M. Pawlik, editors*.

European Commission (2001), 'Towards an Internal Market without tax obstacles: A strategy for providing companies with a consolidated corporate tax base for their EU-wide activities', COM(2001) 582 final.

European Commission (2004), 'A Common Consolidated Corporate Tax Base: Commission Non-Paper to informal Ecofin Council, 10 and 11 September 2004'.

European Commission (2017), 'Establishing a European Pillar of Social Rights', COM(2017) 250 final.

European Parliament, 'White Paper on the 1996 Intergovernmental Conference: Volume II'.

European Parliament (2013), 'Challenges of multi-tier governance in the European Union: Effectiveness, efficiency and legitimacy', COMPENDIUM OF NOTES.

Fabbrini, F. (2013), 'Enhanced Cooperation under Scrutiny: Revisiting the Law and Practice of Multi-Speed Integration in Light of the First Involvement of the EU Judiciary', *LIEI*, pp. 197–224.

Fabbrini, F. (2014), 'Taxing and Spending in the Eurozone: Legal and Political Challenges Related to the Adoption of the Financial Transaction Tax', *ELRev*, Vol. 39, No. 2, Taxing and spending in the Eurozone: legal and political challenges related to the adoption of the financial transaction tax.

Fair Trials Europe, 'A Measure of Last Resort? The practice of pre-trial detention decision making in the EU'.

Falkner, G. (1994), *Supranationalität trotz Einstimmigkeit?: Entscheidungsmuster der EU am Beispiel Sozialpolitik*, Europäische Schriften des Instituts für Europäische Politik, Bonn, Europa Union Verlag.

Farahat, A. (2016), 'Solidarität und Inklusion', *DÖV*, pp. 45–55.

Feraci, O. (2013), 'L'attuazione della cooperazione rafforzata nell' Unione Europea: un primo bilancio critico', *Riv. dir. internaz.*, pp. 955–964.

Fiolka, J. (2015), 'Patent Enforcement in Poland' in: Heath, C., Stauder, D. (eds.), *Patent enforcement worldwide: Writings in honour of Dieter Stauder*, Oxford, Hart Publishing.

Fischer, J. (2000), *Vom Staatenverbund zur Föderation—Gedanken über die Finalität der europäischen Integration*, available at: www.cvce.eu/de/obj/rede_von_joschka_fischer_uber_die_finalitat_der_europaischen_integration_berlin_12_mai_2000-de-4cd02fa7-d9d0-4cd2-91c9-2746a3297773.html.

Fischer-Lescano, A., Kommer, S. (2011), 'EU in der Finanzkrise: Zur Leistungsfähigkeit des Verfahrens der verstärkten Zusammenarbeit für eine Intensivierung der Wirtschafts- und Sozialpolitik', *KJ*, 412–433.

Fisicaro, M. (2020), 'Rule of Law Conditionality in EU Funds: The Value of Money in the Crisis of European Values'.

Franssen, N. (2018), 'The future judicial cooperation between the EPPO and non-participating Member States', *New Journal of European Criminal Law*, Vol. 9, No. 3, pp. 291–299.

Gaja, G. (1998), 'How Flexible Is Flexibility Under the Amsterdam Treaty?', *Common Market Law Review*, Vol. 35, No. 4, pp. 855–870.

Garben, S., Govaere, I. (2017), 'The Division of Competences between the EU and the Member States: Reflections on the Past, the Present and the Future' in: Garben, S., Govaere, I. (eds.), *The Division of Competences between the EU and the Member States : Reflections on the Past, the Present and the Future,* Hart Publishing.

Garben, Sacha; Govaere, Inge, eds. (2017), *The Division of Competences between the EU and the Member States : Reflections on the Past, the Present and the Future.*

Geelhoed, Willem; Erkelens, Leendert H.; Meij, Arjen W.H, eds. (2018), *Shifting Perspectives on the European Public Prosecutor's Office.*

Geiger, Rudolf; Khan, Daniel-Erasmus; Kotzur, Markus, eds. (2015), *European Union Treaties: Treaty on European Union Treaty on the Functioning of the European Union.*

Gerards, C., Wessels, W. (2019), Enhancing 'Enhanced Cooperation': constraints and opportunities of an inflexible flexibility clause, CEPOB, Bruges.

Giegerich, Thomas; Schmitt, Desirée C.; Zeitzmann, Sebastian, eds. (2017), *Flexibility in the EU and beyond: How much differentiation can European integration bear?*, Schriften des Europa-lnstituts der Universität des Saarlandes—Rechtswissenschaft.

Giuffrida, F. (2023), 'The relations between the European Public Prosecutor's Office and the Member States that do not participate in the enhanced cooperation', *New Journal of European Criminal Law*, Vol. 14, No. 1, pp. 80–99.

Grabitz, E., Iliopoulos, C. (1984), 'Typologie der Differenzierungen und Ausnahmen im Gemeinschaftsrecht' in: Grabitz, E., Franzmeyer, F. (eds.), *Abgestufte Integration: Eine Alternative zum herkömmlichen Integrationskonzept?,* Kehl am Rhein, Engel, pp. 31–46.

Grabitz, Eberhard; Franzmeyer, Fritz, eds. (1984), *Abgestufte Integration: Eine Alternative zum herkömmlichen Integrationskonzept?*, Schriftenreihe Europa-Forschung.

Grabitz, Eberhard; Hilf, Meinhard; Nettesheim, Martin, eds. (2018), *Das Recht der Europäischen Union.*

Graf von Luckner, J. (2018), 'How to Bring It Home—The EU's Options for Incorporating the Fiscal Compact into EU Law', *European Law Blog.*

Graf von Luckner, J. (2020), *A Novel "Reinforced Cooperation" in the EU*, available at: verfassungsblog.de/a-novel-reinforced-cooperation-in-the-eu/.

Graf von Luckner, J. (2021), 'A Brexit last call: The strange practice of pre-Brexit opt-ins', *Maastricht Journal of European and Comparative Law*, Vol. 28, No. 4, pp. 556–572.

Graf von Luckner, J. (2021), 'Stay home, stay healthy: Das „Ergänzungs- oder besondere Näheverhältnis zum Unionsrecht" in der BVerfG-Rechtsprechung und die europäische Integration durch Völkerrecht', *Europarecht*, No. 2, pp. 209–224.

Graf von Luckner, J. (2022), 'The End of Satellite Treaty Law as We Know It? The German Federal Constitutional Court, European Integration by International Law and Treaties

"Supplementing or Being Otherwise Closely Tied to the EU"', *German Law Journal*, Vol. 23, No. 2, pp. 157–172.

Gray, J., Quinzá Redondo, P. (2013), 'Stress-Testing the EU Proposal on Matrimonial Property Regimes: Co-operation between EU private international law instruments on family matters and succession', *Familie & Recht*.

Groeben, Hans von der; Schwarze, Jürgen; Hatje, Armin, eds. (2015), *Europäisches Unionsrecht*, NomosKommentar.

Grosche, N., Wagner, E. E. (2016), 'Einführung in das Tagungsthema: Pfadabhängigkeit hoheitlicher Ordnungsmodelle' in: Wagner, E. E., Ganglbauer, N. M. (eds.), *Pfadabhängigkeit hoheitlicher Ordnungsmodelle,* Baden-Baden, Nomos, pp. 11–26.

Häberle, Peter; Mahrenholz, Ernst Gottfried, eds. (2011), *60 Jahre deutsches Grundgesetz: Beiträge aus dem Jahrbuch des öffentlichen Rechts der Jahre 2009–2011.*

Halmai, G. (2019), 'The Possibility and Desirability of Rule of Law Conditionality', *HJRL*, Vol. 11, 171–188.

Hanf, D. (2017), 'Balancing openness and coherence of enhanced cooperation: The principle of coherence affirmed by drawing its outer limits: *Spain v. Parliament and Council (Eurosur)*', *Common Market Law Review*, Vol. 54, No. 3, pp. 873–898.

Hatje, Armin; Terhechte, Jörg Philipp, eds. (2004), *Das Binnenmarktziel in der europäischen Verfassung.*

Hay, P. (1966), *Federalism and supranational organizations ; patterns for new legal structures*, University of Illinois Press.

Heath, Christopher; Stauder, Dieter, eds. (2015), *Patent enforcement worldwide: Writings in honour of Dieter Stauder.*

Heber, C. (2021), *Enhanced Cooperation and European Tax Law,* Oxford University Press.

Hein, J. von (2017), 'EU Competence to Legislate in the Area of Private International Law and Law Reforms at the EU Level' in: Beaumont, P., Danov, M., Trimmings, K., Yüksel, B. (eds.), *Cross-Border Litigation in Europe,* Bloomsbury Publishing.

Hendrickx, F. (2018), 'The European Social Pillar', *European Labour Law Journal*, Vol. 9, No. 1, pp. 3–6.

Hinarejos, A. (2015), 'An Asymmetric EMU' in: Hinarejos Parga, A. (ed.), *The Euro area crisis in constitutional perspective,* Oxford University Press, pp. 3–10.

Hinarejos, A. (2015), 'Institutional Responses to the Crisis' in: Hinarejos Parga, A. (ed.), *The Euro area crisis in constitutional perspective,* Oxford University Press, pp. 15–50.

Hinarejos Parga, Alicia, ed. (2015), *The Euro area crisis in constitutional perspective.*

Holzinger, K., Schimmelfennig, F. (2015), 'Eurokrise und differenzierte Integration', *Politische Vierteljahresschrift : PVS*, Vol. 56, No. 3, pp. 457–478.

Iara, A. (2015), *Revenue for EMU: A contribution to the debate on Fiscal Union,* Taxation papers. Working paper, Luxembourg, Publications Office.

Ipsen, H. P. (1972), *Europaisches Gemeinschaftsrecht*, Tubingen, J.C.B. Mohr.

Ipsen, H. P. (1973), 'Über Supranationalität' in: Ehmke, H., Scheuner, U. (eds.), *Festschrift für Ulrich Scheuner zum 70. Geburtstag,* Berlin, Duncker & Humblot, pp. 211–225.

Jaeger, T. (2013), 'Einheitspatent—Zulässigkeit der Verstärkten Zusammenarbeit ohne Spanien und Italien', *NJW*, pp. 1998–2001.

Jaeger, T. (2015), 'Nach l'Europe à la carte nun la loi européenne à la carte? Zur Erlaubnis der Umgehung der Unionsmethode nach dem Urteil in Rs. C-146/13 u.a', *EuR Europarecht*, Vol. 50, No. 4, pp. 461–476.

Jaeger, T. (2017), 'The End to a Never-Ending Story? The Unitary Patent Regime' in: Giegerich, T., Schmitt, D. C., Zeitzmann, S. (eds.), *Flexibility in the EU and beyond: How much differentiation can European integration bear?,* Oxford, Hart Publishing, pp. 269–281.

Jaeger, Thomas; Stöger, Karl, eds. (2019), *Kommentar zu EUV und AEUV: 85.–220. Lieferung. Kommentar in Faszikeln in Fortführung des Kommentars zu EU- und EG-Vertrag,* Manz Grosskommentare.

Joerges, C. (2002), "Deliberative Supranationalism'-Two Defences', *European Law Journal,* Vol. 8, No. 1, pp. 133–151.

Jungfleisch, J. (2019), 'Verstärkte Zusammenarbeit im Rahmen der Flüchtlingspolitik: Ein Ausweg aus der Krise oder die endgültige Aufgabe eines einheitlichen Europas?' in: Kopetzki, M., Lanser, C., Leitner, P. (eds.), *Autoritäres vs liberales Europa: Tagung Junger Europarechtler*innen, Band 2, Wien 2019,* Wien, Jan Sramek Verlag.

Kahl, W. (2018), 'Art. 192 AEUV' in: Streinz, R. (ed.), *EUV/AEUV: Vertrag über die Europäische Union, Vertrag über die Arbeitsweise der Europäischen Union, Charta der Grundrechte der Europäischen Union,* München, C.H.Beck.

Kamann, H.-G. (2018), 'Art. 113 AEUV' in: Streinz, R. (ed.), *EUV/AEUV: Vertrag über die Europäische Union, Vertrag über die Arbeitsweise der Europäischen Union, Charta der Grundrechte der Europäischen Union,* München, C.H.Beck.

Karakas, C. (2005), 'Für eine Abgestufte Integration: Zur Debatte um den EU-Beitritt der Türkei', *HFSK Standpunkte,* No. 4, pp. 1–16.

Kellerbauer, Manuel; Klamert, Marcus; Tomkin, Jonathan; Bogensberger, Wolfgang; Bouquet, Andre; Erlbacher, Friedrich, eds. (2019), *The EU treaties and the Charter of Fundamental Rights: A commentary.*

Kert, Robert; Lehner, Andrea, eds. (2018), *Vielfalt des Strafrechts im internationalen Kontext: Festschrift für Frank Höpfel zum 65. Geburtstag.*

Kingreen, T. (2017), Ein verbindlicher EU-Rechtsrahmen für soziale Grundsicherungssysteme in den Mitgliedstaaten, FORSCHUNGSBERICHT.

Kirst, N. (2021), 'Rule of Law Conditionality: The Long-awaited Step Towards a Solution of the Rule of Law Crisis in the European Union?'.

Kochenov, D., Amtenbrink, F. (2009), 'Towards a More Flexible Approach to Enhanced Cooperation' in: Ott, A. (ed.), *Fifty years of European integration: Foundations and perspectives,* The Hague, Asser Press, pp. 181–199.

Koenig, N. (2015), A Differentiated View of Differentiated Integration, Policy Brief, Berlin, Jacques Delors Institute.

Kölliker, A. (2001), 'Bringing together or driving apart the union? Towards a theory of differentiated integration'.

Kopetzki, Moriz; Lanser, Cornelia; Leitner, Philipp, eds. (2019), *Autoritäres vs liberales Europa: Tagung Junger Europarechtler*innen, Band 2, Wien 2019,* Europarecht.

Kotzur, M. (2004), *Grenznachbarschaftliche Zusammenarbeit in Europa: Der Beitrag von Art. 24 Abs. 1 a GG zu einer Lehre vom kooperativen Verfassungs- und Verwaltungsstaat,* Schriften zum öffentlichen Recht, Berlin, Duncker & Humblot.

Kramer, X. (2012), 'A European framework for private international law: current gaps and future perspectives', Bruxelles.

Kreilinger, V., Jacques Delors Institut Berlin (2015), *Proposal to use Enhanced Cooperation in the Refugee Crisis*, available at: www.delorsinstitut.de/en/publications/topics/institutions-and-democracy/proposal-to-use-enhanced-cooperation-in-the-refugee-crisis/.

Kroll, D. A. (2022), 'Promise unfulfiled?: Managing differentiated integration in EU secondary law through enhanced cooperation' in: Leruth, B., Gänzle, S., Trondal, J. (eds.), *The Routledge handbook of differentiation in the European Union,* New York, Routledge Taylor & Francis Group, pp. 170–183.

Kroll, D. A., Leuffen, D. (2015), 'Enhanced cooperation in practice. An analysis of differentiated integration in EU secondary law', *Journal of European Public Policy*, Vol. 22, No. 3, pp. 353–373.

Kuipers, J.-J. (2012), 'The Law Applicable to Divorce as Test Ground for Enhanced Cooperation', *ELJ*, Vol. 18, pp. 201–229.

Lamping, M., 'Enhanced Cooperation in the Area of Unitary Patent Protection: Testing the Boundaries of the Rule of Law', *Working Paper*.

Lamping, M. (2011), 'Enhanced Cooperation—A Proper Approach to Market Integration in the Field of Unitary Patent Protection?', *IIC*, No. 42, p. 879.

Lamping, M. (2013), 'Enhanced Cooperation in the Area of Unitary Patent Protection—Testing the Boundaries of the Rule of Law', *Maastricht J. Eur. Comp. L.*, pp. 589–600.

Lansdaal, A. (2002), 'Differentiation or Enhanced Cooperation: Formalizing Flexibility' in: Schrauwen, A. (ed.), *Flexibility in Constitutions: Forms of Closer Cooperation in Federal and Non-Federal Settings,* Groningen, European Law Publishing, pp. 47–57.

Lavenex, S. (2011), 'Concentric circles of flexible 'EUropean' integration: A typology of EU external governance relations', *Comparative European Politics*, Vol. 9, 4–5, pp. 372–393.

Leal-Arcas, R. (2007), 'Theories of Supranationalism in the EU'.

Lenaerts, K. (2020), 'No Member State is More Equal than Others'.

Leruth, B., Gänzle, S., Trondal, J. (2019), 'Exploring Differentiated Disintegration in a Post-Brexit European Union', *JCMS: Journal of Common Market Studies*, Vol. 57, No. 5, pp. 1013–1030.

Leruth, Benjamin; Gänzle, Stefan; Trondal, Jarle, eds. (2022), *The Routledge handbook of differentiation in the European Union*, Routledge International Handbooks.

Linke, G. (2006), *Das Instrument der verstärkten Zusammenarbeit im Vertrag von Nizza: Möglichkeiten eines Europas der differenzierten Integration*, Interdisziplinäre Europa Studien, Frankfurt am Main, Lang.

López-Ibor Mayor, V. (2009), 'Enhanced Cooperation and energy' in: Beneyto Pérez, J. M., Baquero Cruz, J. (eds.), *Unity and flexibility in the future of the European Union: The challenge of enhanced cooperation,* Madrid, CEU Ediciones, pp. 23–39.

Lurger, B. (2018), 'Art. 169 AEUV' in: Streinz, R. (ed.), *EUV/AEUV: Vertrag über die Europäische Union, Vertrag über die Arbeitsweise der Europäischen Union, Charta der Grundrechte der Europäischen Union,* München, C.H.Beck.

Malíř, J. (2019), 'Enhanced Cooperation in the EU: Its Evolution and Position of the Czech Republic', *Studia Europejskie*, No. 1, pp. 89–112.

Mangas Martín, A. (1998), 'Las cooperaciones reforzadas en el Tratado de Ámsterdam', *Comunidad Europea Aranzadi*, No. 10, pp. 27–38.

Martenczuk, B. (2013), 'Enhanced Cooperation: The Practice of Ad Hoc Differentiation in the EU since the Lisbon Treaty', *StudDipl*, pp. 83–100.

Martill, Benjamin; Staiger, Uta, eds. (2018), *Brexit and Beyond ? Rethinking the Futures of Europe.*

Messina, M. (2014), 'Strengthening economic governance of the European Union through enhanced cooperation: a still possible, but already missed, opportunity', *ELRev*, Vol. 39, pp. 404–417.

Meyer, F. C., Heidfeld, C. (2011), 'Europarechtliche Aspekte einer Finanztransaktionsteuer', *EuZW*, pp. 373–378.

Milner, F., Kölliker, A. (1999), How to Make Use of Closer Cooperation?, Working Paper.

Müller-Brandeck-Bocquet, G. (1997), 'Flexible Integration—eine Chance für die europäische Umweltpolitik?', *integration*, pp. 292–304.

Müller-Graff, P.-C. (2011), '60 Jahre Grundgesetz aus der Sicht des Europarechts' in: Häberle, P., Mahrenholz, E. G. (eds.), *60 Jahre deutsches Grundgesetz: Beiträge aus dem Jahrbuch des öffentlichen Rechts der Jahre 2009–2011,* Tübingen, Mohr Siebeck, pp. 174–201.

Nerudová, D., Dvořáková, V. (2014), *Financial Transaction Tax: Can it be Sufficient Resource of EU Budget when Introduced through Enhanced Cooperation?*

Niedobitek, M. (2019), '§ 1 Vertragliche Grundlagen, rechtliche Gestalt, Institutionen der Union' in: Niedobitek, M. (ed.), *Europarecht: Grundlagen und Politiken der Union,* Berlin, De Gruyter, pp. 3–204.

Niedobitek, Matthias, ed. (2019), *Europarecht*: *Grundlagen und Politiken der Union*, De Gruyter Handbuch.

Nitschke, Peter, ed. (2019), *Gemeinsame Werte in Europa?*: *Stärken und Schwächen im normativen Selbstverständnis der Europäischen Integration.*

Nováky, N. (2018), 'The EU's Permanent Structured Cooperation in defence: Keeping Sleeping Beauty from snoozing', *European View*, Vol. 17, No. 1, pp. 97–104.

O'Brien, M. (2005), 'Company Taxation, State Aid and Fundamental Freedoms: is the Next Step Enhanced Cooperation?', *ELRev*, 209–233.

Obwexer, W. (2004), 'Gesetzgebung im Binnenmarkt—die Kompetenzverteilung im Verfassungsentwurf' in: Hatje, A., Terhechte, J. P. (eds.), *Das Binnenmarktziel in der europäischen Verfassung,* Baden-Baden, Nomos.

O'Keeffe, David; Twomey, Patrick M., eds. (1999), *Legal issues of the Amsterdam Treaty.*

Ondarza, N. von (2014), 'Die vertragliche und außervertragliche verstärkte Zusammenarbeit als Katalysator einer engeren Integrationsgemeinschaft' in: Blanke, H.-J., Pilz, S. (eds.), *Die „Fiskalunion": Voraussetzungen einer Vertiefung der politischen Integration im Währungsraum der Europäischen Union,* Tübingen, Mohr Siebeck, 149–169.

Osieke, E. (1984), 'Majority Voting Systems in the International Labour Organisation and the International Monetary Fund', *ICLQ*, Vol. 33, No. 2, pp. 381–408.

Ott, Andrea, ed. (2009), *Fifty years of European integration*: *Foundations and perspectives.*

Paggi, E. (2017), *Acquis, integrazione differenziata, unità dell'ordinamento dell'unione: verso nuovi modelli di integrazione in Europa?*: *Spunti di una riflessione teorica a valle dell'introduzione del c.d. pacchetto sul brevetto europeo con effetto unitario.*, Padua.

Pawelec, S. (2015), 'Implications of Enhanced Cooperation for the EPPO Model and Its Functioning' in: Erkelens, L. H., Meij, A. W. H., Pawlik, M. (eds.), *The European public prosecutor's office: An extended arm or a two-headed dragon? / L.H. Erkelens, A.W.H. Meij, M. Pawlik, editors,* Hague, Asser Press, pp. 209–227.

Pech, L., 'The EU as a global rule of law promoter: the consistency and effectiveness challenges', *Asia Europe Journal*, Vol. 14, No. 1, pp. 7–24.

Pech, L. (2022), 'No More Excuses'.

Pechstein, Matthias; Nowak, Carsten; Häde, Ulrich, eds. (2017), *Frankfurter Kommentar zu EUV, GRC und AEUV*.

Peers, S. (2010), 'Divorce, European Style: The First Authorization of Enhanced Cooperation', *Eur. Const. L. Rev*, pp. 339–358.

Peers, S. (2011), 'The Constitutional Implications of the EU Patent', *European Constitutional Law Review*, Vol. 7, No. 2, pp. 229–266.

Peers, S. (2013), 'Towards a New Form of EU Law?: The Use of EU Institutions outside the EU Legal Framework', *European Constitutional Law Review*, Vol. 9, No. 01, pp. 37–72.

Peers, S. (2015), The law of Grexit: What does EU law say about leaving economic and monetary union?, EU Law Analysis.

Peers, S. (2017), 'Enhanced Cooperation: the Cinderella of differentiated integration' in: Witte, B. de, Ott, A., Vos, E. (eds.), *Between Flexibility and Disintegration: The Trajectory of Differentiation in EU Law,* Edward Elgar Publishing Limited, pp. 76–91.

Pernice, Ingolf; Guerra Martins, Ana Maria, eds. (2019), *Brexit and the Future of EU Politics: A Constitutional Law Perspective*, European Constitutional Law Network-Series (ECLN).

Philippart, E. (2003), *A new mechanism of enhanced co-operation for the enlarged European Union*, Notre Europe.

Philippart, E., Edwards, G. (1999), 'The Provisions on Closer Co-operation in the Treaty of Amsterdam: The Politics of Flexibility in the European Union', *JCMS: Journal of Common Market Studies*, Vol. 37, No. 1, pp. 87–108.

Pistoia, E. (2014), 'Enhanced Cooperation as a tool to…enhance integration?: Spain and Italy v. Council', *CMLRev*, pp. 247–260.

Pistoia, E. (2016), 'Outsourcing EU Law While Differentiating European Integration: The Unitary Patent's Identity in the Two "Spanish Rulings" of 5 May 2015.', *European Law Review*, No. 4, pp. 711–726.

Pop, V. (2017), 'Once Scorned, 'Multispeed Europe' Is Back', *WSJ*, 1 March 2017.

Posner, R. A. (2007), *Economic analysis of law*, New York, NY, Wolters Kluwer Law & Business : Aspen Publishers.

Proctor, C. (2006), 'The Future of the Euro—What Happens if a Member State Leaves?', *E.B.L.R.*, Vol. 17, No. 4, pp. 909–937.

Röttger-Wirtz, S., Eliantonio, M. (2019), 'From Integration to Exclusion: EU Composite Administration and Gaps in Judicial Accountability in the Authorisation of Pharmaceuticals', *European Journal of Risk Regulation*, Vol. 10, No. 2, pp. 393–411.

Savat-Gündüz, M. (2013), *Variable Geometrie: Subsidiarität und differenzierte Integration im Mehrebenensystem der Europäischen Union*, Europäische Hochschulschriften. Reihe II, Rechtswissenschaft, Frankfurt am Main, PL Academic Research.

Schäuble, W., Lamers, K. (1994), 'Überlegungen zur europäischen Politik'.

Schauer, M. (2000), *Schengen—Maastricht—Amsterdam: Auf dem Weg zu einer flexiblen Union*, Juristische Schriftenreihe, Wien, Verl. Österreich.

Scheppele, K. L., Morijn, J. (2023), 'Frozen'.

Schermers, Henry G.; Blokker, Niels, eds. (2011), *International institutional law: Unity within diversity*.

Schimmelfennig, F. (2015), 'Differentiated Integration Before and After the Crisis' in: Cramme, O., Hobolt, S. B. (eds.), *Democratic politics in a European Union under stress*, Oxford, Oxford University Press, pp. 120–134.
Schmidt, V. A. (2009), 'Re-Envisioning the European Union: Identity, Democracy, Economy*', *JCMS: Journal of Common Market Studies*, Vol. 47, No. 3, pp. 17–42.
Schmidt, V. A. (2019), 'The future of differentiated integration: a 'soft-core,' multi-clustered Europe of overlapping policy communities', *Comparative European Politics*, Vol. 17, No. 2, pp. 294–315.
Scholz, O. (2019), 'Germany will consider EU-wide bank deposit reinsurance', *Financial Times*, 11 June 2019.
Schrauwen, Annette, ed. (2002), *Flexibility in Constitutions: Forms of Closer Cooperation in Federal and Non-Federal Settings.*
Schröder, M. (2018), 'Art. 116 AEUV' in: Streinz, R. (ed.), *EUV/AEUV: Vertrag über die Europäische Union, Vertrag über die Arbeitsweise der Europäischen Union, Charta der Grundrechte der Europäischen Union,* München, C.H.Beck.
Schroeder, W. (2003), 'Verfassungsrechtliche Beziehungen zwischen Europäischer Union und Europäischen Gemeinschaften' in: Bogdandy, A. von (ed.), *Europäisches Verfassungsrecht: Theoretische und dogmatische Grundzüge,* Berlin, New York, Springer, pp. 373–414.
Schütze, R. (2009), 'The European Community's Federal Order of Competences—A Retrospective Analysis' in: Dougan, M., Currie, Samantha,—(eds.), *50 Years of the European Treaties Looking Back and Thinking Forward.,* Hart, pp. 63–92.
Schütze, R. (2015), 'EU Competences: Existence and Exercise' in: Chalmers, D., Arnull, A. (eds.), *The Oxford Handbook of European Union Law,* Oxford University Press, pp. 75–103.
Schütze, Robert; Tridimas, Takis, eds. (2018), *Oxford principles of European Union law.*
Schwarz, M. (2014), 'A Memorandum of Misunderstanding—The doomed road of the European Stability Mechanism and a possible way out: Enhanced cooperation', *CMLRev*, Vol. 51, pp. 389–423.
Schwarze, Jürgen; Bär-Bouyssière, Bertold, eds. (2000), *EU-Kommentar.*
Schwarze, Jürgen; Becker, Ulrich; Hatje, Armin; Schoo, Johann, eds. (2012), *EU-Kommentar.*
Scott, J. (2014), 'Extraterritoriality and Territorial Extension in EU Law', *American Journal of Comparative Law*, Vol. 62, No. 1, pp. 87–125.
Selmayr, M. (2013), 'Die "Euro- Rettung" und das Unionsprimärrecht: Von putativen, unnötigen und bisher versäumten Vertragsänderungen zur Stabilisierung der Wirtschafts- und Währungsunion' 2013, 68(2), Zeitschrift für Öffentliches Recht, 259', *ZÖR*, Vol. 68, No. 2, pp. 259–318.
Siems, K. (1999), *Das Kohärenzgebot in der Europäischen Union und seine Justitiabilität,* Nomos-Universitätsschriften, Baden-Baden.
Somek, A. (2002), 'On Supranationality', *EIoP*, Vol. 5, No. 3, pp. 1–15.
Stevenson, Angus, ed. (2010), *Oxford Dictionary of English.*
Stratenschulte, Eckart D., ed. (2015), *Der Anfang vom Ende? : Formen differenzierter Integration und ihre Konsequenzen.*

Streinz, R. (2018), 'Art. 2 AEUV' in: Streinz, R. (ed.), *EUV/AEUV: Vertrag über die Europäische Union, Vertrag über die Arbeitsweise der Europäischen Union, Charta der Grundrechte der Europäischen Union,* München, C.H.Beck.

Streinz, R. (2018), 'Art. 4 AEUV' in: Streinz, R. (ed.), *EUV/AEUV: Vertrag über die Europäische Union, Vertrag über die Arbeitsweise der Europäischen Union, Charta der Grundrechte der Europäischen Union,* München, C.H.Beck.

Streinz, Rudolf, ed. (2018), *EUV/AEUV: Vertrag über die Europäische Union, Vertrag über die Arbeitsweise der Europäischen Union, Charta der Grundrechte der Europäischen Union*, Beck'sche Kurz-Kommentare.

Stubb, A. C.-G. (1996), 'A Categorization of Differentiated Integration', *JCMS: Journal of Common Market Studies*, Vol. 34, No. 2, pp. 283–295.

Thym, D. (2004), *Ungleichzeitigkeit und europäisches Verfassungsrecht*, Schriftenreihe europäisches Verfassungsrecht, Baden-Baden, Nomos.

Thym, D. (2005), 'United in Diversity: The Integration of Enhanced Cooperation into the European Constitutional Order', *GLJ*, pp. 1731–1747.

Thym, D. (2009), The Evolution of Supranational Differentiation, WHI-Paper.

Thym, D. (2018), 'Legal Solution vs Discursive Othering: The (Dis)Integrative Effects of Supranational Differentiation', *SSRN Electronic Journal.*

Thym, D. (2018), 'Supranational Differentiation and Enhanced Cooperation' in: Schütze, R., Tridimas, T. (eds.), *Oxford principles of European Union law,* Oxford, Oxford University Press, pp. 849–883.

Tijmes-Lhl, J. (2009), 'Consensus and majority voting in the WTO', *World Trade Review*, Vol. 8, No. 3, pp. 417–437.

Tindemans, L., European Union, Bulletin of the European Communities.

Tosato, G. L. (2013), 'New institutional solutions for multi-tier governance?' in: *Challenges of multi-tier governance in the European Union: Effectiveness, efficiency and legitimacy,* pp. 152–160.

Trüten, D. (2015), *Die Entwicklungen des Internationalen Privatrechts in der Europäischen Union: Auf dem Weg zu einem europäischen IPR-Gesetz,* Europäisches Privatrecht (Bern, Switzerland), Bern, Baden-Baden, Stämpfli Verlag; Nomos.

Ullrich, H. (2013), 'Enhanced cooperation in the area of unitary patent protection and European integration', *ERA Forum*, pp. 589–610.

Valentová, L. (2016), 'Property Regimes of Spouses and Partners in New EU Regulations—Jurisdiction, Prorogation and Choice of Law', *ICLR*, Vol. 16, No. 2, pp. 221–240.

van Cleynenbreugel, P., Devroe, W. (2017), 'The Financial Transaction Tax Project' in: Witte, B. de, Ott, A., Vos, E. (eds.), *Between Flexibility and Disintegration: The Trajectory of Differentiation in EU Law,* Edward Elgar Publishing Limited, pp. 282–303.

van den Bogaert, S. (2008), 'Qualified Majority Voting in the Council: First Reflections on the New Rules', *MJ*, Vol. 15, No. 1, pp. 97–108.

van Kalmthout, Anton M.; Knapen, Marije M.; Morgenstern, Christine, eds. (2009), *Pre-trial detention in the European Union: An analysis of minimum standards in pre-trial detention and the grounds for regular review in the member states of the EU.*

Viarengo, Ilaria; Franzina, Pietro, eds. (2020), *The EU Regulations on the Property Regimes of International Couples: A Commentary.*

Vimont, P. (2018), *Flexibility is not the miracle solution,* available at: encompass-europe.com/comment/flexibility-is-not-the-miracle-solution.

Viţă, V. (2017), 'Revisiting the Dominant Discourse on Conditionality in the EU: The Case of EU Spending Conditionality', *Camb. Yearb. Eur. Legal Stud.*, Vol. 19, pp. 116–143.

Volkmann, U. (2016), 'Pfadabhängigkeiten im Recht' in: Wagner, E. E., Ganglbauer, N. M. (eds.), *Pfadabhängigkeit hoheitlicher Ordnungsmodelle,* Baden-Baden, Nomos, pp. 27–45.

Wagner, Eva Ellen; Ganglbauer, Nina Maria, eds. (2016), *Pfadabhängigkeit hoheitlicher Ordnungsmodelle.*

Walker, N. (1998), 'Sovreignty and Differentiation', *ELJ*, Vol. 4, pp. 355–388.

Weatherill, S. (1999), "If I'd Wanted You to Understand I Would have Explained it Better': What is the Purpose of the Provisions on Closer Co-operation Introduced by the Treaty of Amsterdam?' in: O'Keeffe, D., Twomey, P. M. (eds.), *Legal issues of the Amsterdam Treaty,* Oxford, Portland, Or., Hart Pub, pp. 21–40.

Weiler, J. H. H. (1981), 'The Community System: the Dual Character of Supranationalism', *Yearbook of European Law*, Vol. 1, No. 1, pp. 267–306.

Weiler, J. H. H. (2000), 'Federalism and Constitutionalism: Europe's Sonderweg'.

Wernsmann, R., Zirkl, C. (2014), 'Die Regelungskompetenz der EU für eine Finanztransaktionssteuer', *Europäische Zeitschrift für Wirtschaftsrecht*, No. 05, pp. 167–171.

Wessels, W., Gerards, C. (2018), *The implementation of enhanced cooperation in the EU: Study*, [Brussels], European Parliament.

Weyembergh, A. (2018), 'Enhanced cooperation in criminal matters: past, present and future' in: Kert, R., Lehner, A. (eds.), *Vielfalt des Strafrechts im internationalen Kontext: Festschrift für Frank Höpfel zum 65. Geburtstag,* Wien, Graz, NWV, pp. 605–624.

Wilderspin, M. (2011), 'Derechos fundamentales en materia de derecho de familia: en particular, la sustracción de menores', *Anuario español de derecho internacional privado,* No. 11, pp. 527–558.

Witte, B. de (2017), 'Exclusive Member State Competences—Is There Such a Thing?' in: Garben, S., Govaere, I. (eds.), *The Division of Competences between the EU and the Member States : Reflections on the Past, the Present and the Future,* Hart Publishing.

Witte, B. de (2017), 'The future of variable geometry in a post-Brexit European Union', *Maastricht Journal of European and Comparative Law*, Vol. 24, No. 2, pp. 153–157.

Witte, B. de (2018), 'An undivided Union? Differentiated integration in post-Brexit times', *Common Market Law Review*, Vol. 55, No. 2, pp. 227–249.

Witte, B. de (2019), *The Law as Tool and Constraint of Differentiated Integration,* EUI Working Papers RSCAS.

Witte, Bruno de; Ott, Andrea; Vos, Ellen, eds. (2017), *Between Flexibility and Disintegration: The Trajectory of Differentiation in EU Law.*

Wolfstädter, L. M., Kreilinger, V. (2017), European Integration via Flexibility Tools: The Cases of EPPO and PESCO, Policy Paper.

Zeitzmann, S. (2011), 'Das Verfahren der Verstärkten Zusammenarbeit und dessen erstmalige Anwendung: Ein Ehescheidungs- und Trennungsrecht für Europa', *ZEuS*, pp. 87–113.

Zeitzmann, S. (2013), 'Patentrecht: Ermächtigung zur Verstärkten Zusammenarbeit', *EuZW*, pp. 475–480.

Zeitzmann, S. (2015), 'Zuviel gewollt, zu wenig geregelt? Das komplizierte Verhältnis der Verstärkten Zusammenarbeit zum aquis communautaire' in: Stratenschulte, E. D. (ed.), *Der Anfang vom Ende? : Formen differenzierter Integration und ihre Konsequenzen,* Nomos, pp. 103–134.

Zeitzmann, S. (2017), 'A Rather Strange Animal, this "Enhanced Cooperation":—May it Serve as King of the Europen Zoonion? or: Is Enhanced Cooperation Anywhere Near a Constitutional Principle?' in: Giegerich, T., Schmitt, D. C., Zeitzmann, S. (eds.), *Flexibility in the EU and beyond: How much differentiation can European integration bear?,* Oxford, Hart Publishing, pp. 87–105.

MIX
Papier aus verantwortungsvollen Quellen
Paper from responsible sources
FSC® C105338

If you have any concerns about our products,
you can contact us on
**ProductSafety@springernature.com**

In case Publisher is established outside the EU,
the EU authorized representative is:
**Springer Nature Customer Service Center GmbH**
**Europaplatz 3, 69115 Heidelberg, Germany**

Printed by Libri Plureos GmbH
in Hamburg, Germany